SPIRITUAL RESILIENCY:

HARNESSING THE POWER OF THE SPIRITUAL LIFE TO OVERCOME ADVERSITY

BY DR. BRIAN BRANDON

"THOSE WHO WAIT ON THE LORD...WILL RISE ON WINGS LIKE EAGLES."

— ISAIAH THE PROPHET

Trilogy Christian Publishers | A Wholly Owned Subsidiary of Trinity Broadcasting Network

2442 Michelle Drive | Tustin, CA 92780

Copyright © 2024 by Dr. Brian Brandon | Scripture quotations marked NIV are taken from the Holy Bible, New International Version®, NIV®. Copyright © 1973, 1978, 1984, 2011 by Biblica, Inc.™ Used by permission of Zondervan. All rights reserved worldwide. www.zondervan.com. The "NIV" and "New International Version" are trademarks registered in the United States Patent and Trademark Office by Biblica, Inc.™ Scripture quotations marked MSG are taken from THE MESSAGE, copyright © 1993, 2002, 2018 by Eugene H. Peterson. Used by permission of NavPress. All rights reserved. Represented by Tyndale House Publishers, Inc. Scripture quotations marked ESV are taken from the ESV® Bible (The Holy Bible, English Standard Version®), copyright © 2001 by Crossway Bibles, a publishing ministry of Good News Publishers. Used by permission. All rights reserved. Scripture quotations marked CEV are taken from the Contemporary English Version®. Copyright © 1995 American Bible Society. All rights reserved. Scripture quotations marked NLT are taken from the Holy Bible, New Living Translation, copyright © 1996, 2004, 2015 by Tyndale House Foundation. Used by permission of Tyndale House Publishers, Inc., Carol Stream, Illinois 60188. All rights reserved. Scripture quotations marked NKJV are taken from the New King James Version®. Copyright © 1982 by Thomas Nelson. Used by permission. All rights reserved. No part of this book may be reproduced, stored in a retrieval system, or transmitted by any means without written permission from the author. All rights reserved. Printed in the USA.

All rights reserved, including the right to reproduce this book or portions thereof in any form whatsoever.

For information, address Trilogy Christian Publishing

Rights Department, 2442 Michelle Drive, Tustin, Ca 92780.

Trilogy Christian Publishing/ TBN and colophon are trademarks of Trinity Broadcasting Network.

For information about special discounts for bulk purchases, please contact Trilogy Christian Publishing.

Trilogy Disclaimer: The views and content expressed in this book are those of the author and may not necessarily reflect the views and doctrine of Trilogy Christian Publishing or the Trinity Broadcasting Network.

10 9 8 7 6 5 4 3 2 1 | Library of Congress Cataloging-in-Publication Data is available.

ISBN: 979-8-89041-045-0 | E-ISBN: 979-8-89041-046-7

Foreword

Throughout my youth, I heard of the power of the spiritual life. And while I have experienced glimpses, achieving growth has come more recently as I dedicated my life to the pursuit of God, faith, and spiritually empowered resilience. This ten-year journey was a result of decades of struggles with negative thinking and its accompanying stress. I wrote this book, in part to remind myself of the many lessons God taught me as he invited me deeper. I also believed these lessons would benefit my children to help each of them break through their struggles a little sooner than I experienced. But I realized in talking with many who struggle in their faith walk, these principles could serve the greater family of God. To this end I offer you a way forward in harnessing the power of the spiritual life to help you in and through your seasons of adversity. Welcome to my journey.

I started this book about four years ago. Since then, I have repeatedly heard religious leaders describe their sense of urgency for greater spiritual strength and resilience. One pastor expressed his prophetic burden that people of faith must develop spiritual resiliency now. These statements have served to reinforce my own sense that this topic is crucial. In this hour, I firmly believe God's message echoes that of King Ahaz recorded in Isaiah 7. Jerusalem was under attack by a coalition of kings from Israel's northern kingdom and Aram, intending to plunder the city and divide it amongst themselves. God gave Ahaz a clear word, "It will not take place, it will not happen."[1] However, like many people, Ahaz had doubts. He was so present to the enormity of the threat that God's encouragement did not produce the sense of confidence and peace it warranted. Aware of the king's doubts, Isaiah issued a stark warning, "If you do not stand firm in your faith, you will not stand at all."[2] In a spiritual sense, the hour is desperate. People of God must stand in faith and spiritual strength. Ahaz stood in his faith, and Jerusalem was delivered. Your faith is the key to your deliverance as well.

You may feel under attack right now. The spiritual battles in this world are very real. Our enemy has deceived humanity into embracing the darkness. He has unleashed a strategic offensive to limit the influence and impact of the Holy Spirit in the lives of people around the world. The ultimate goal: separating as many people as possible from the saving power of a good and loving God. The battles rage in the rejection of belief in God, persecution of people of faith, and in adverse circumstances that challenge the faith, hope, and love of God's people. Now is the time to hear the Word of the Lord. The enemy will not have the victory! He will attempt to undermine your trust in God's goodness and faithfulness. Resist the challenge with everything within you. Develop spiritual resilience and hold fast to your faith,

---

1 Isaiah 7:7
2 Isaiah 7:9

resisting the enemy with everything you have, standing at all costs.[3] Now is the time to lean into God, to focus your efforts on drawing near to Him. If you continue to get up when knocked down, to trust God through the good and the bad, you will experience the benefits in this life and the next.

---

[3] Ephesians 6:6–10

Table of Contents

Introduction 7
Part 1: Understanding Resilience 7
Part 2: The Case for Spiritual Efficacy 21

Section I: 12 Key Spiritual Disciplines

Introduction to the Spiritual Disciplines 33
Spiritual Discipline 1: Read Scripture Every Day 41
Spiritual Discipline 2: Pray, Fast, and Worship 59
Spiritual Discipline 3: Trust God! 75
Spiritual Discipline 4: Express Gratitude 87
Spiritual Discipline 5: Give Generously 91
Spiritual Discipline 6: Serve Others 95
Spiritual Discipline 7: Exercise Humility and Self-Awareness 99
Spiritual Discipline 8: Renew Energy, Stay Motivated, and Persevere 105
Spiritual Discipline 9: Develop Interpersonal Skills-Strengthen Relationships 109
Spiritual Discipline 10: Exercise Self-Control Always 113
Spiritual Discipline 11: Harness the Power of Your Tongue 117
Spiritual Discipline 12: Continually Learn and Grow 121

Section II: Spiritually Resilient Thinking Strategies ... 125

1. Guard Your Mind 129
2. Engage the Power of Faith 141
3. Exercise the Power of Interpretation 151
4. Include God's Purposes in Your Interpretation 159
5. Recognize and Contradict Thinking Traps 167
6. Iceberg Ahead: Identify the Real Issues 187
7. Welcome a Cleansing Stream 191
8. Fight off Fear 203

9. Drive Away Worry... 213
10. Get Prepared for the Fight................................ 223
11. Use Distractions to Change the Channel.................... 251
12. Leverage Your Strengths 255

Section III: Spiritually Resilient Actions . . . 263

1. Get the Quick Wins....................................... 269
2. Activate the Power of Your Words......................... 273
3. Use Your Speech to Encourage Others...................... 289
4. Refuse to Use Your Speech as a Negative Force............ 297
5. Train Your Body to Strengthen Your Being................. 307
6. Use Joy to Strengthen Your Being......................... 315
7. Build Connections with Others............................ 319
8. Set Goals, Make Plans, Solve Problems.................... 333
9. Resolve Conflicts Quickly................................ 343
10. Do the Right Thing—Moral Decision-Making 359
11. Get Back to the Basics—Love Others...................... 371
12. Navigate Change—Live in Victory 377

Conclusion.. 385
Epilogue: Persecution....................................... 387

Appendices.. 389
Appendix I: Scripture References............................ 389
Appendix II: Additional Scriptural References............... 413
Bibliography 423

Introduction

Part 1: Understanding Resilience

"I wish none of this had happened," said the small, huddled figure from the darkness.

"So do all who live to see such times," replied the ageless, robed figure as he grimly held his pipe.

"But that is not for them to decide. All we must decide is what to do with the time that is given to us. There are other forces at work in this world, besides the will of evil."[4]

The scene is from the blockbuster film, "Lord of the Rings." Frodo Baggins, a hobbit from the Shire, is trapped deep inside the Mines of Moria. He has just become aware that his enemy and previous bearer of the ring, Gollum, tracked the group into the mines to recover his prize. Unexpectedly ripped away from his peaceful life, Frodo began a dangerous journey to protect the ring of power. From the outset, evil Lord Sauron hunted Frodo and the ring. His dark servant stabbed Frodo, causing a grievous wound that continues to afflict him. When he finally reached the safety of the Elven Realm, he realized that the journey was far from over. Recognizing the threat to all Middle Earth, Frodo volunteered to continue the quest, to complete a mission that he does not have the strength for, while accompanied by several new companions he is not sure he can fully trust. Now, seated in the darkness of Moria, he is discussing their grave situation with Gandalf the Wizard. In his fearful circumstances, Frodo regrets that his Uncle Bilbo Baggins didn't kill Gollum when he had the chance and that the mission to destroy the long-lost ring of power had ultimately fallen to him. At his low point, fear, exhaustion, and the dark peril of Moria, Gandalf offers another word of hope. "Bilbo was meant to find the Ring, in which case you also were meant to have it. And that is an encouraging thought."[5]

Like the discouraging darkness of the Mines of Moria, disappointments and difficulties come to everyone. Life's ups and downs are part of the human condition. How do you cope when you're on the downside of your journey, or worse, when you face a series of setbacks that stretch your limits? The world is facing some tough challenges. The Coronavirus created a global panic, brought economic hardship, and heightened levels of fear and stress, making many people ask, what is next? Europe has seen its largest land war since World War II in the present Russia-Ukraine conflict, and nations that seem to have a diabolical agenda are developing nuclear weapons. Our nation is in turmoil with inflation, isolation, riots, and division. People are struggling with uncertainty, fear, and the practical challenges of life in the post-pandemic environment. This book is about how to find courage and faith despite reasons

---

[4] Peter Jackson, dir. *Lord of the Rings: Fellowship of the Ring* (USA: New Line Cinema / WingNut Films, 2001), DVD.
[5] Ibid.

for fear. You may be struggling to find peace and joy in your life or to have hopeful expectation for the future. Coping with and ultimately overcoming your darkness requires the perseverance and adaptability known as resilience.

Resilience is the inner strength and flexibility that enables you to adapt to hardship: to bend, not break.[6] Simply put, it is the ability to bounce back when life presents setbacks. Resilience gives you the ability to respond to traumatic or challenging life events by working through them, learning from them, and moving beyond them. You can overcome and grow through adversity in a healthy and constructive manner. Resilient people endure and rebound through severe hardships, maintain a healthy and positive perspective, and exude happiness, love, and generosity toward others despite personal loss.[7] In addition to revealing a loving God, Scripture reveals timeless wisdom for how to harness the power of the spiritual life for greater resilience.

In the middle of crisis, it's easy to embrace self-pity and regret. Do you continue to descend deeper into the darkness, or do you find a ray of light? The choice can mean the difference between a downward spiral of increasingly toxic thinking, negative feelings, and destructive behaviors or engaging positive, healthy thoughts that inspire hope and constructive action. The decision, for some, is literally life or death. Your resilience is the key. In the epic battle for Middle Earth, Frodo ultimately proved his resilience, overcoming hardships, setbacks, and fierce enemies to destroy the ring and free the world of the evil Lord Sauron. In the deep dark of Moria, it was his dear friend, Gandalf, whose encouraging words provided strength to continue the journey, appealing to the intent and workings of a higher power. This book will help you activate the potential of the spiritual life, strengthen your connection with the higher power known in Scripture as God, and give you strength through the difficulties of your life's journey. Spiritual fitness is the key to living the overcoming life, leveraging disciplines that develop a deeper relationship with God to transform your thought, life, and speech into positive, healthy, and constructive action.

Holistic Fitness

Several dimensions of fitness—social, family, physical, mental-emotional, and spiritual—related to the tripartite self—body, soul, and spirit—contribute to your being's overall resilience.[8] From a holistic point of view, we could use other sub-groups to describe total fitness, such as financial, nutritional, parental, or marital. For our purposes, we will use the first five listed above with an emphasis on the mind in the function of the emotional domain. Each dimension is a source of strength that underwrites your ability to bounce back from difficulties. When stressed, weakness in a particular dimension can produce damaging effects to your health and well-being. It is necessary to continuously evaluate how fit you are

---

[6] "Definition of Resiliency," accessed March 12, 2021, Resiliency | Definition of Resiliency by Merriam-Webster (merriam-webster.com).
[7] "Resilience: Build Skills to Endure Hardship," accessed March 12, 2021, Resilience: Build skills to endure hardship, Mayo Clinic.
[8] "Five Dimensions of Personal Readiness," accessed March 12, 2021, ARD: Five Dimensions of Personal Readiness (army.mil).

in each of these areas as you strive to improve your overall resilience. Fitness in the social dimension relates to the strength and support you derive from relationships with others, developing and maintaining trusted, valued, personally fulfilling relationships that foster good communication.[9] Fitness in the family dimension is partly social but separated here because of the critical role family relationships (parental, marital, culture, finances) play in well-being through factors such as love, support, identity, purpose, and teamwork. Fitness in the physical dimension relates to your body's ability to cope with stress, endure physical burdens, and to enhance its health and well-being. Fitness in the mental-emotional dimension relates to the strength and well-being of your inner world of thoughts and feelings, approaching life's challenges in a positive, optimistic way by demonstrating self-control, stamina, and good character with your choices and actions.[10] Your level of resilience fluctuates based upon your varying aptitude of a number of competencies related to these five dimensions, including social support and connections, optimism and confidence, internal locus of control, willingness to seek help, your self-identification as a survivor rather than a victim, self-awareness, empathy and compassion, effective problem-solving skills, ability to cope with stress in a healthy manner, and spirituality.[11]

Because the soul, body, and spirit are inseparable, the dimensions of fitness interrelate and overlap. If your physical health is poor, it is hard to draw on the energy to be patient and kind. Your physical health can strain your social relationships. The greater your mental-emotional health and well-being, the healthier your relationships tend to be. Mental stress and anxiety can significantly affect your physical health. Many sicknesses find their root cause in stress. Dependencies among the dimensions of fitness highlight the importance of the spiritual dimension. One advantage of the spiritual life is that it allows you to tap into a reservoir of strength outside yourself. The closer you connect with God, drawing strength from Him, the more energy is available to support other areas of fitness. The social dimension allows you to draw strength from others, but it has limits based on the depth of the relationship and the inner health/strength of the other person. What do you do when relationships are the source of your problem? If every other area of your life is under stress, you can still find hope, help, and strength in God. Your connections to God hold the potential to reinvigorate every area of fitness. But what do you do when you don't have a connection with God and several dimensions of fitness are stressed? That is the point where many people lose hope. You need the supportive power of the spiritual life centered in a relationship with God and reinforced by disciplines, thought patterns, and actions revealed in the wisdom of Scripture.

Spiritual Fitness

While each dimension of fitness is important, the focus of this book is spiritual fitness with its

---

9 Ibid.
10 Ibid.
11 Sivilli, Teresa I. and Thaddeus W. Pace, "The Human Dimensions of Resilience: A Theory of Contemplative Practices and Resilience," accessed April 15, 2021, The Human Dimensions of Resilience_9_9_14_14 (garrisoninstitute.org).

powerful and unique contribution to resilience. Some experts define fitness in the spiritual dimension as strengthening a set of beliefs, principles, or values that sustain a person beyond family, institutional, and societal sources of strength.[12] Other "experts" define it in emotional terms or ignore it altogether. Since many experts try to maximize inclusivity in their definitions, I propose my own: the ability to draw strength from your relationship with God, your core spiritual beliefs, values, and spiritual practices; to find identity, purpose, and meaning in your connection with God; and to spiritually reset your perspective for healthy action. This work will show that the spiritual domain has the potential to strengthen competencies in each of the resilience-building areas described above. Spiritual resilience informs all other dimensions and provides a supportive and protective footing for each. Like the muscular core of your body, the spiritual domain is the core and foundation of your being, supporting every other dimension. It provides the platform for strength: promoting stability and balance in life, supporting the good posture of a positive and healthy perspective, providing protective benefits for total health and well-being, enhancing your ability to meet life goals, and affecting progress in all other areas (mental-emotional, physical, social, family, etc.).

The Holistic Resilience Model below describes the relationship between dimensions of resilience and their levels of fitness. Imagine each dimension as an elevator that rises to higher floors through increased strength, adaptability, and fitness in that area. For example, the greater your physical health and strength, the greater the height and the number of above-ground floors your physical elevator can ascend to—representing greater resilience in that area and the physical dimension's increased contribution to your overall resilience. Your body's sickness or weakness can cause the elevator to descend below the ground floor to sub-levels, depleting your overall resilience, especially when stressed. Similarly, the greater the level of health in your inner world of thoughts and feelings, the greater your mental-emotional resilience, depicted by an elevator that can ascend to higher floors. Stressors can expose lack of health in your mental-emotional fitness. Your elevator may normally function in the subfloors of thinking traps and negative feelings and plummet rapidly when under pressure. A negative mental perspective can sap your strength and provide serious drag on your total resilience. One section of this book will deal almost exclusively with these issues. The same principles apply to the social and family dimensions. Fitness in one dimension not only lifts that area of resilience; it increases your overall strength and adaptability. Accordingly, fragility in one dimension can drain your total fitness. Relationship issues provide a crisis and elevator "free fall" for many people. Financial stressors can have a similar effect. These factors may quickly drain hope and energy, leaving your strength and resilience in the proverbial "basement."

---

12 Army Resilience Directorate, "Five Dimensions."

Introduction

Figure 1: Holistic Resilience Model

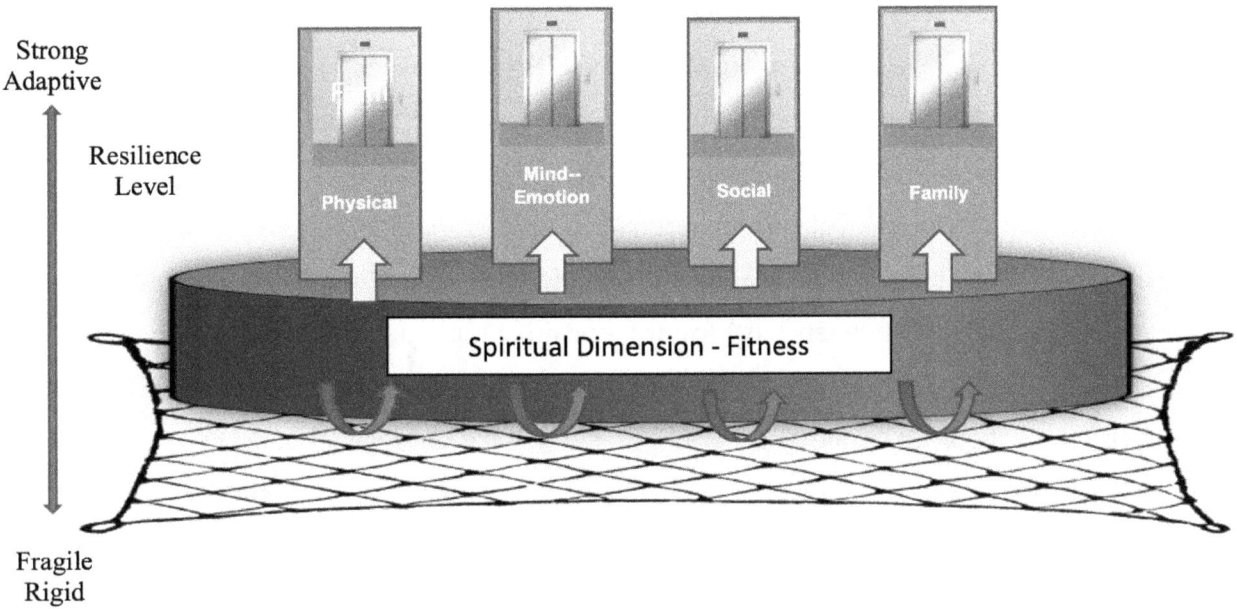

You could think of the spiritual dimension as an additional elevator, but the differences are significant enough to warrant a different role in the model above. The Holistic Resilience Model more aptly assigns the spiritual domain as the foundation for all others. Elevators represent the various domains of resilience, while spiritual resilience provides their ground floor foundation. The vertical arrows depict the potential elevating force of the spiritual life to all other domains, while the arrows above the net depict its potential ability to reverse or halt a catastrophic fall in an area (also pictured by the safety net in Figure 1 above). The spiritual dimension provides the stability of a ground floor for all elevators, delivering potential strength to lift each domain while offering a protective safety net for each if weakened. As the core foundation to total strength and well-being, the spiritual life can raise every one of your dimensional elevators while preventing them from crashing to the subfloors when you experience overwhelming pressures. As you expand your spiritual resilience with spiritual disciplines, scriptural thought processes, speech, and actions, you increase the lift provided to all other areas (elevators) of resilience by enhancing qualities such as strength, flexibility, optimism, toughness, and perseverance. Spiritual fitness can be a multiplication factor in your total resilience rather than simply adding to the cumulative effect of all other dimensions.

The spiritual life can provide support and lift to other dimensions by informing practices: providing information, guidance and direction, healthy beliefs, and action steps that maximize their strength and efficacy. For example, the dietary rules in the Old Testament Scripture provided instruction on healthy eating habits. While in the New Testament, God declared all foods clean from a spiritual standpoint, the dietary rules retain their wisdom in eating for physical health. These instructions can increase your physical fitness and resilience (related to the resilience-building competency of physically coping with stress). Ninety-four "One Another" verses from New Testament Scripture teach people how to relate socially to one another. They guide readers in healthy relational practices to maximize social and family resilience. The more you put these instructions into practice, the more you elevate your social fitness (related to the resilience-building competency of social support and connections). Several passages in Scripture provide key direction to promote mental-emotional health on topics such as gratitude, managing your thought life, forgiveness, and orienting your perspective toward a positive outlook (related to the competencies of optimism, internal locus of control, self-awareness, and empathy). Scripture informs the family dimension with wisdom for relationships, mutual care, and finances (related to social connections, empathy, compassion, self-control). You can find abundant guidance to strengthen every possible dimension through a thorough review of Scripture (along with every resilience-building competency).

The spiritual life provides another critical role in resilience, protection. Spiritual fitness provides a safety net to prevent a sudden free fall in another dimension. The deeper your spiritual life, the more cushion you provide to break the fall when you face great adversity in other areas (as depicted by the wider thickness of the spiritual life and the red "reverse direction" arrows shown in Figure 1 above). Your investment in spiritual fitness strengthens the safety net that will catch you when another dimension's elevator experiences a sudden, rapid, and destructive descent, such as a loss of relationship, financial crisis, or setback at work.

The average person can normally harness enough strength from their capacity in other dimensions to prevent a total breakdown when one area of life suffers adversity. In other words, if one elevator has a sudden drop, people normally recover. The risk of a catastrophic breakdown increases when difficulties deplete two or more dimensions of fitness at the same time. This is where the protective nature of the spiritual dimension shines. Your spiritual beliefs and practices can provide a safety net for all other dimensions at once, preventing your elevators from plummeting deep into the subfloors of despair, hopelessness, and inaction. This principle describes how faith and religion impact suicide. Spiritual beliefs and practices provide a powerful protective barrier against suicidal ideation. Persons with a shallow or nonexistent spiritual life succumb to hopelessness and despair more readily. Once the protective barrier is broken by a decision to harm oneself, the spiritual safety net has a limited impact on the outcome.

Introduction

You can draw resilience apart from the spiritual life, from your own resources such as your physical, mental-emotional strength, and coping skills such as humor. You can also draw strength from the support of family and close relationships. You probably know a person who doesn't prioritize the spiritual dimension yet exhibits relative health and resilience due to strength in other areas. However, the undeniable spiritual aspect of human existence makes it difficult, if not impossible, to demonstrate a lifetime of health and resilience. You will find it difficult to sustain loving relationships and the benefits of a healthy lifestyle over a lifetime, apart from spiritual guidance and strength. Life's struggles will eventually stretch you to the breaking point. Exercising the spiritual dimension allows you to maximize strength for all other dimensions and tap into the help and strength your relationship with God provides. You not only draw from your strength (physical, mental, and emotional) and the strength of others (social, family), you draw strength from God (spiritual). You can realize powerful lift from your spiritual fitness when all other dimensions fail. These benefits are not automatic. You may know someone who claims to be spiritual/religious but experiences dramatic swings in their resilience. The benefits of spiritual fitness come as you validate your values and beliefs with action.[13]

Those with a superficial or nonexistent spiritual life lack the depth necessary for its supportive and protective effects. Failure to prioritize the importance of your inner life will leave you spiritually malnourished, lacking the lift to support other areas (depicted in Figure 2 by a thin foundational spiritual fitness layer, fewer and smaller supportive vertical arrows, and fewer arrows to help you rebound). A shallow spiritual life also limits its protective potential. Without the spiritual safety net of consistent spiritual disciplines, your dimensional elevators can crash through the thin layer of spirituality to the sublevels of hopelessness, despair, and self-destructive behaviors when adversity comes.

---

13 Matthew 7:24–25

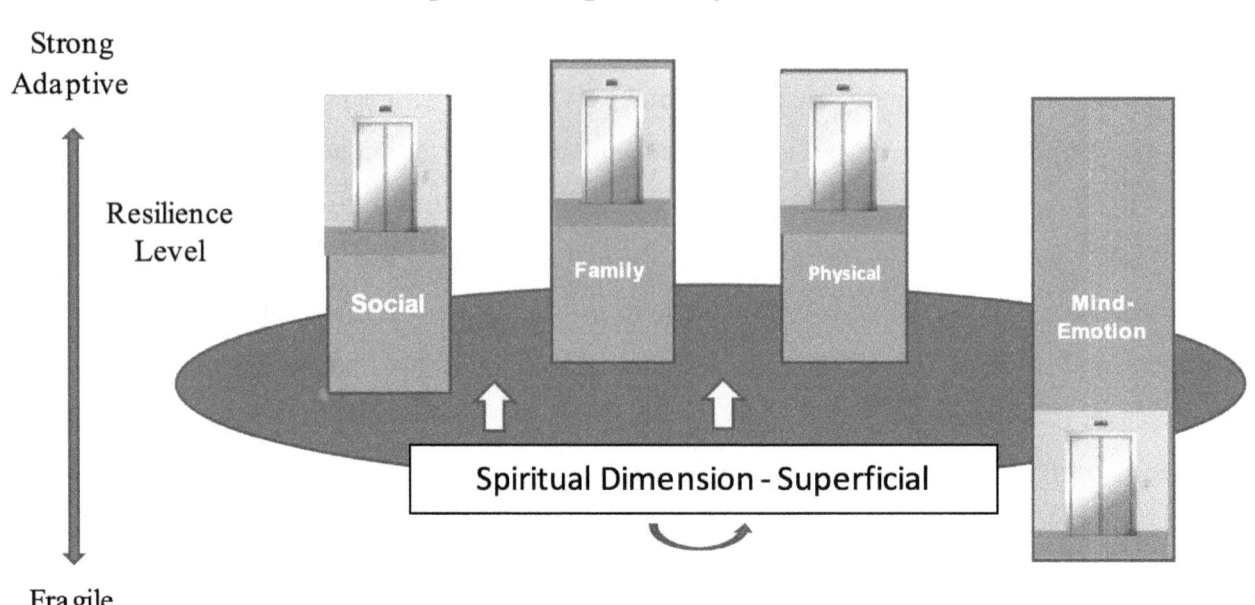

Figure 2
Superficial Spirituality in Holistic Fitness

Circumstances can test your total fitness: relationship troubles, financial hardships, work stressors, emotional trauma, physical illness, etc., affecting you so deeply you get stuck. People get stuck when problems are deeply traumatic or they affect multiple areas of life, such as relationships with a significant other, work issues, or finances, becoming stacked on one another. The aggregation of problems can make the next struggle the proverbial "straw that broke the camel's back." The effects of trouble on your life can be physical, emotional, and mental. Sometimes, the invisible mental-emotional wounds present the greatest challenge. Your mind naturally tries to protect itself by forgetting painful memories, but those experiences can continue to shape your thinking and future when not dealt with in a healthy manner. When painful events continue to negatively affect your present, it's a sign you are stuck and you need a change. Have you faced anything that has you trapped in a destructive pattern? Have past experiences helped you "learn" unhealthy coping strategies? Many people have.

Harness the power of the spiritual life by leveraging the positive effects of consistent spiritual disciplines, spiritually resilient thinking strategies, and spiritually resilient actions to overcome difficulties. These three themes provide the organization for this book, each a major section with twelve supporting chapters. The chapters present processes: decisions, micro-steps, and activities that combine in spiritual synergy. The benefits of spiritually resilient activities increase as you consistently exercise your spiritual muscles. While the essence of the spiritual life centers in relationship with God, it also gives you the inspiration, direction, and power to think and act in healthy and constructive ways. These behaviors

Introduction

have the potential to enhance your resilience-building competencies and increase your fitness level in every other dimension. You will reap the benefits of the spiritual life as you direct scriptural counsel toward practical applications such as decision-making, conflict resolution, exercise, adequate rest, healthy eating habits, relationship-building, mental disciplines, problem-solving, etc. The sacred text of Scripture—God-breathed words inspired by the Holy Spirit—provides a handbook for maximizing your health and wellness. The ancient wisdom of Scripture provides direction for every other dimension of fitness. Let it guide your spiritual life. By following its wisdom and priorities, you will deepen your connection with God and others, enhance your physical health, and strengthen your inner being.

Normal life can drain you. Sooner or later, everyone faces difficulties; life just happens. The physical, mental, and emotional strains of life can cause you to get stressed, fatigued, or burned out. Sometimes, you face difficulties that challenge the very core of your being. One of the great prophets of old endured great hardship. He questioned God's justice as he struggled with why godless, wicked people around him prospered when those who tried to serve God suffered. God's answer spoke directly to the prophet's resilience. "If you have raced with men on foot and they have worn you out, how can you compete with horses? If you stumble in safe country, how will you manage in the thickets by the Jordan?"[14]

In essence, God said, "If the lesser challenges of life test the limits of your strength and flexibility, how will you ever endure the larger ones?" The comparison game ensnared the prophet Jeremiah like it does many people today. There's only one direction to look when you're facing great hardship—up. You cannot look around, comparing yourself with others to find constructive answers. You must look to God. Similarly, you cannot run in circles trying to determine "Why?" when the most relevant question is "Who?" you will rely upon for help. Where is your focus?

In another story related to spiritual resilience, the Apostle Paul faced a demonic affliction, perhaps related to his eyes. He prayed earnestly for God to remove this "thorn in the flesh." God answered his prayer, "My grace is sufficient for you, for My power is perfected in your weakness."[15] That is not the kind of answer you want to hear. Like me, you probably prefer deliverance, but God's way is always better, even when you do not like it. God's answer meant victory was going to be a journey they made together. Paul received help as he pressed through the affliction. God gave him the strength and sustaining power—resilience, to endure his hardship. Your weakness creates opportunities for God's goodness and power to shine brightly in your life.

The writings of the major prophet, Isaiah, provide assurance for circumstances that challenge your resilience. Consider the wisdom of these words before you get caught in the comparison game, exhaust your patience and persistence, or become ensnared in the labyrinth of "Why?" These words hold the key to expanding your strength.

---

14 Jeremiah 12:5
15 2 Corinthians 12:8

> The Lord is the Everlasting God, the Creator…his understanding no one can fathom. He gives strength to the weary and increases the power of the weak. Even youths grow tired and weary and young men stumble and fall; but those who hope in the Lord will renew their strength. They will soar on wings like eagles; they will run and not grow weary, they will walk and not be faint.[16]

Soaring on wings like an eagle; what a thought. I grew up on a small farm with lots of chickens. They're always scratching around in the dirt, heads down, looking for something to eat or curious about something shiny. Scratching and pecking, scratching, and pecking—that's the life of a chicken. But on the nearby hillside, hawks often perched in the tall trees. They soared high in the sky, observing the farm and pasture from a very different perspective. Chickens see the ground right around them. Hawks see the whole countryside. You can live like a chicken with your head down in the dirt, or you can see the big picture, soaring with the eagles as you're carried on the winds of the Holy Spirit. You can focus on the scope of the problem, or you can focus on God's goodness and promises. It truly is a choice. Looking back, I confess I often focused on the problem with my head down in the dirt. I saw mountains when many of my problems were molehills. I regret that I did not trust God enough to enjoy His peace while He led me through hard circumstances. He has proven Himself faithful in my life, time and time again. I should trust Him because He has earned my trust. You can focus on and magnify your problem or choose to trust God and magnify His love and faithfulness. Your mind will not magnify both at the same time. Forget the "Why God, why?" Forget the comparison game. Stop complaining about God's timing. Choose to trust God, focus on His goodness, and let His presence lift you above your struggles. By developing spiritual fitness, you will run and not wear out; you will endure trouble and not quit.

Spiritual fitness is the key to resilience, health, and wholeness. But how do you build it? In addition to establishing the primacy of spiritual fitness in total fitness, we will walk through a process for strengthening your spiritual fitness and resilience. The foundation of spiritual fitness is a close relationship with God based in spiritual disciplines. The closer you grow to God, the greater the consistency in turning your inner world of thoughts and feelings into a sound mind. As your thinking becomes more spiritually resilient, the words you speak will become more constructive and faith-filled as well. As you think and speak with greater trust in God, your decision-making process and behaviors will reflect greater health, strength, and resilience. This process forms the organization for the book: Section I describes spiritual disciplines that will help you draw closer to God. Everything else in life proceeds from your inner health. Section II discusses the spiritual principles you can leverage to transform your thinking and mind. You are how you think. I heard someone quote H.G. Wells recently, "By age fifty, every person has the face they deserve." Your countenance reflects your inner life. Over time, your face will

---
16 Isaiah 40:28–31 (New International Version)

reveal its quality. Section III addresses your speech and practical action steps you can apply to help you bounce back from adversity. A healthy relationship with God (built upon healthy spiritual disciplines) will produce a healthier thought life (which, in turn, will produce healthier emotional responses) and will produce greater health in your speech and healthier decisions and behaviors. Another way to appreciate the connection between these steps is to replace health with the descriptors faith-filled or spiritually resilient. A deep relationship with God leads to a spiritually resilient thought life, which leads to spiritually resilient speech and actions. A faith-filled relationship with God leads to faith-filled thinking, which leads to faith-filled speech and actions. This process produces greater strength and resilience. It multiplies as each cycle produces more fruit.

Just as actions have consequences, you can leverage a powerful dynamic of cause and effect to improve your life and overcome adversity, as illustrated in Figure 3 below. The importance you place on your spiritual life and the consistent, disciplined efforts you make to draw closer to God are the foundation upon which every strategy builds. The investment in spiritual disciplines will help you draw closer and feel closer to God; superficial or no investment will leave you feeling distant and disconnected. As you apply Scripture and your sense of God's leading to your thought life, you will find that God is replacing fear, confusion, and doubt with a sound mind. Your inner world of thoughts and feelings will move toward greater love, peace, and joy. As you replace harmful thoughts with scriptural, Spirit-led thinking, you will transform your speech into a positive, constructive, and profitable force that reinforces your thought life and empowers you to healthy and resilient action. Finally, your closeness to God and beneficial thoughts and speech will help you make better decisions and move from self-destructive, relationship-breaking behaviors toward healthy, profitable ones that strengthen your relationships.

Figure 3
Spiritual Resilience Process Model: Effects on the Inner Life

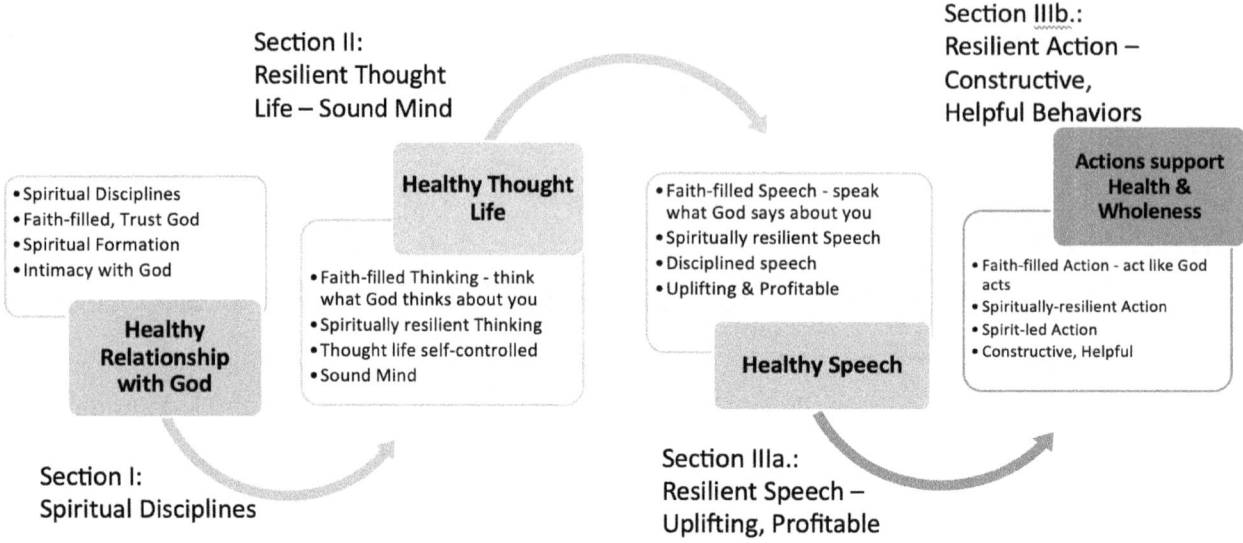

The model below shows how your actions, for good or bad, proceed from the foundational layers of your inner life: your relationship with God, secret spiritual disciplines, your thought life, and self-talk. Your thoughts proceed from your real faith, trust, and reliance upon God (your relationship). Your speech comes from your thoughts. "Out of the overflow of the heart, the mouth speaks."[17] And your actions derive from what you think and speak.[18] You must clean up the inner life so the outer life can follow. The contrasting pyramids reveal how a weak and shallow spiritual life propagates negativity and harmful tendencies in your life while prioritizing spiritual fitness with consistent adherence to scriptural beliefs and practices produces fruit in your inner and outer worlds of thoughts, emotions, speech, and actions.

---

17 Luke 6:45
18 Matthew 23:25–28

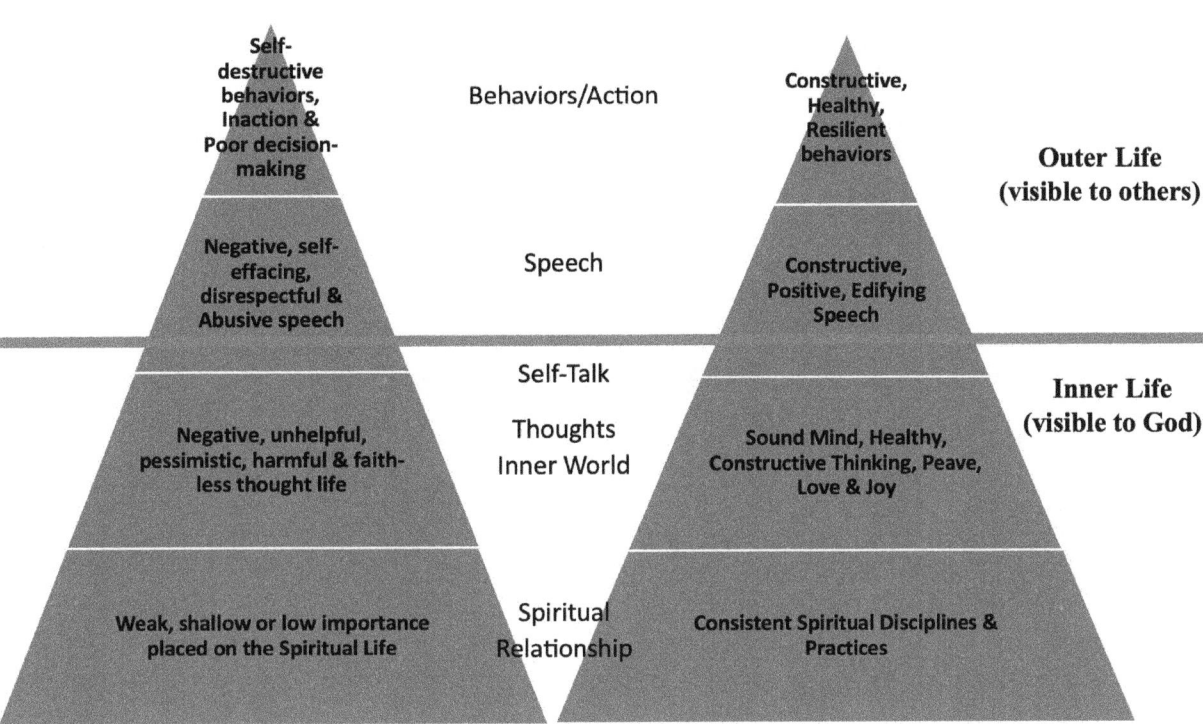

Figure 4
Superficial Spiritual Fitness vs. Spiritual Fitness Prioritized

Spiritual resilience is the foundation and key to your total strength and ability to bounce back from adversity in a healthy manner. The purpose of this book is to elevate your spiritual fitness and resilience. This chapter described and illustrated an important process for revitalizing your spiritual life. Before we delve into the specific strategies to accomplish these objectives, we will examine the scientific evidence and other support establishing the critical nature of the spiritual life to health, wholeness, and your ability to overcome adversity.

Introduction, Part 2:

The Case for Spiritual Efficacy

Contemporary culture staunchly opposes the idea that spirituality and religion should play an important role in society. You will have to resist the many influences of society and culture to prioritize the spiritual life. This opposition is advanced through multiple efforts. First, modern culture uses all manner of education and media outlets to cast doubt on the relevance of the spiritual dimension. Those efforts have effectively diverted the mainstream of public thought. However, culturally correct thinking doesn't have to shake your faith. You don't need a majority to agree for Scripture and faith to be true. The wisest man who ever lived, Israel's King Solomon, stated, "God has set eternity in the hearts of men, but they cannot fathom it."[19] Connection with God is mysterious, inspiring you to reach out to Him while humbly looking inward to search your soul. The eyes of your heart must be open in the quest. These requirements create a stumbling block for many who look at spiritual things with suspicion and unbelief. In her scientific research, Dr. Lisa Miller concluded, "Biologically, we are hardwired for spiritual connection."[20] God placed the need for spiritual expression in your DNA. Spirituality is innate, engraved in your genetic code. This fact is also confirmed by a UCLA study that concluded human spirituality, the inner life of the mysterious, sacred, and mystical, "is a universal impulse and reality."[21] Scientific research confirms Solomon's observation. Kings and queens came from all over the world to listen to Solomon's wisdom. He was a great scientist with knowledge of nature and the animal kingdom unheard of in his time. He had an insightful medical mind with deep knowledge of the workings of both the body and soul. Solomon understood the spiritual aspect of human existence—that God hardwired humanity with eternal spiritual components. Some people are oblivious to its existence, some ignore its quiet whispers amidst the din of modern life, and some embrace and pursue it. Regardless of the importance you place on the spiritual life, it retains an element of uncertainty. No one has it all figured out, and no one controls it (or controls God). Even those who strive to integrate God into every aspect of life have periods of doubt, questions, and struggles.

As Jacob wrestled with God for his blessing, humanity wrestles to understand God's will, ways, and heart.[22] The spiritual life holds tensions such as God's imminence (God with us) and eminence (God's awesome majesty); His mercy and His justice; the kingdom that has come now and the kingdom that

---
19 Ecclesiastes 3:11
20 Lisa Miller, *The Spiritual Child: The New Science on Parenting for Health and Lifelong Thriving* (New York: Picador, 2015), 3.
21 Higher Education Research Institute, "*The Spiritual Life of College Students: A National Study of College Students' Search for Meaning and Purpose,*" accessed May 22, 2019, https://spirituality.ucla.edu/docs/reports/Spiritual_Life_College_Students_ Exec Summary.pdf.
22 Genesis 32:22–32

is yet to come; and the injustices of the world and the justness of its Creator. These tensions reflect the mysteries of God's interactions with humanity. Your journey to personally reconcile them has the potential to draw you closer to God and deepen your faith. Adversity can complicate or impede your journey, but you must overcome. You don't have to have the spiritual life all figured out to know that God is with you, that He loves you, and that He is working to bring about good in your life. Your pursuit of spiritual fitness involves continuous change and personal transformation anchored upon the solid foundation of God's unchanging nature. Growth occurs as you apply the teachings of Scripture and the leading of the Spirit to your present life circumstances, however challenging. The more you allow God's authority to direct your life in healthy, positive, and constructive change, the more you will see your capacity for resilience grow.

In another effort to diminish the value of the spiritual life, modern culture has used inclusivity to water down definitions of spiritual resilience to the point they hardly seem spiritual or religious, including belief in no God at all. This reflects the current ambivalence towards spirituality, especially organized religion. If you make its definition meaningless, it will eventually become meaningless. You must prioritize what society has minimized. In today's secularized society, the loudest voices in the culture marginalize scriptural beliefs and practices. The campaign to suppress the social influence of spiritual-religious beliefs and practices and to silence open debate on the issues is proof that opponents have a narrow, close-minded agenda that does not sincerely seek truth. Do not be intimidated by such tactics. The voice that interrupts and shouts down its opponent just may not have sufficient evidence to win the argument on its own merits. Antagonists have used pseudo-science to "prove" the insignificance of God and religion, falsely promoting their theories as scientific facts. The crusade to discredit the sacred text of Scripture and prove the irrelevance of the spiritual-religious life has culminated in today's environment, where it is faux pas to publicly express scriptural religious beliefs and practices. But does the science of human spirituality reinforce the progressive, culturally correct movement? In her search for tangible evidence to explain the human relationship with an intangible realm, Dr. Miller concludes, "An inner spiritual compass is an innate concrete faculty whose evidence for biological endowment is hard, indisputable, and rigorously scientific."[23] In other words, the scientific verdict is in—human spirituality is a fact.

The idea that God placed an eternal spiritual component inside mankind is scientifically indisputable despite many appeals to deny it. Dr. Miller's conclusion is a bold rejection of those who want to strip spirituality and religion from the human experience. She offers a message of hope for further study into the many facets of human health, "Spirituality is an untapped resource in our understanding of human development, resilience, illness, health and healing."[24] The spiritual life impacts every aspect of

---
23 Miller, *The Spiritual Child*, 6.
24 Idem, 3.

Introduction, Part 2:

human existence. I am confident further study will continue to reinforce the assertion that the spiritual dimension is foundational for all other dimensions of fitness and resilience. I personally heard Dr. Miller state, "If the level of efficacy supporting spirituality was present in a pill, it would be a multi-billion-dollar money maker for the pharmaceutical industry." Most recent studies show the efficacy of spirituality is far higher than the average "miracle drug" peddled by drug manufacturers and without the side effects that typically accompany them! We know you cannot bottle spirituality or press it into tablet form, but this observation reveals that the best medicine for health and wholeness is to pursue spiritual-religious beliefs and practices.

Another effort to minimize the impact of spirituality and religion has come through the courts and legal system with the mantra of "separation of church and state." The strategy to separate spiritual-religious belief and practice from the public square is not harmless. It is unconstitutional in the U.S.; there is no constitutional "separation of church and state." The First Amendment to the U.S. Constitution reads, "Congress shall make no law respecting the establishment of a religion or prohibiting the free exercise thereof."[25] The Constitution lists the prohibition of government restriction on free exercise of religion—aka religious freedom—before freedom of speech or the press. Recognize that your quest for the spiritual life is legally protected in the Constitution and First Amendment.

It is dangerous to human health and well-being to deprive children of spiritual-religious development. Dr. Miller's research among youth clearly shows through clinical and genetic evidence the adolescent journey of spiritual search and growth is essential for physical and emotional maturity. Further, the neglect of spirituality is "a crisis in the making."[26] She continues, "People cannot live a healthy, fulfilled life with the toxicity of culture's dominant values and amputation of spirituality and religion from human existence."[27] Dr. Miller's research reveals that spiritual development in the early years prepares young people to more successfully wrestle with difficult issues that typically challenge teens. It also provides a protective health benefit, reducing the risk of depression, substance abuse, aggression, and high-risk behaviors, including casual sexuality.[28] Since humans develop resilience in their youth, hostility toward spirituality and religion in our educational institutions hinders growth and maturity and serves to produce an adult population with reduced resilience. When spiritual interest surges in youth, developing a collaborative relationship with God is more protective against depression than anything known to medical or social sciences.[29] If you experienced limited spiritual expression in your childhood, it is not too late to make it a key part of your life. The spiritual disciplines in Section 1 will help you develop your spiritual life and identity.

---

25 National Archives, "The United States Bill of Rights," accessed March 12, 2021, The Bill of Rights: A Transcription | National Archives.
26 Miller, *Spiritual Child*, 4.
27 Ibid.
28 Idem, 3.
29 Idem, 277.

As research shows, spiritual beliefs and practices are essential to the health and well-being of humans. The difference in conclusions between those who promote the importance of religion and those who dispute it is apparent in the assumptions and worldview of the parties, not the evidence itself. Simply put, it's a heart problem, not a head problem. The evidence is present but will not convince the person who refuses to believe. Such a person refuses to accept the logical presentation of the evidence because, in their heart, they refuse to accept its possibility. A study of the Universe provides countless examples of design requiring a designer or Creator. Yet some refuse to acknowledge the possibility of a Designer, instead eschewing a natural scientific law for randomness and chance (The 2nd Law of Thermodynamics: natural systems degenerate when left to themselves).[30] Numerous studies show that spiritual-religious beliefs and practices produce positive, tangible results in people's lives, yet our culture and media outlets, whose narrative runs counter to this evidence, ignore or cover up these benefits. Do not make the same mistake.

In order to prioritize your spiritual life, you must lovingly push back on social correctness, religious bigotry, and other forces that seek to sever spiritual-religious belief and practice from its place of personal and social primacy. Not only are the postulations on religion by figures such as Karl Marx ("Religion is the opiate of the masses."), Friedrich Nietzsche ("God is dead."), and Sigmund Freud ("Religion is a delusion or neuroses.") so romanticized by our intellectuals, wrong, they are destructive to the health and well-being of humanity.[31] Marx had an agenda of advancing socialism. He recognized human acceptance of any authority, such as God, above the state was a threat to revolution and the resulting state. Under socialism, he expected the need for religion to dissolve. Historically, however, socialist and totalitarian states have never been content to just let religion dissolve. They suppressed (and continue to suppress) religion and adherents to the point of genocide. Marx was wrong about the source of spirituality/religion as we now know it (it is genetic), but he was also wrong about what socialism could deliver, hence the need to brutally compel acceptance. Marx used opiates as an analogy, but in pursuit of his revolution, he deflected the fact that opiates (drugs: illegal and legal, such as alcohol) are and have always been the opiate of the masses. Unfortunately, today, Marx is often errantly referenced to discount the importance of religion/spirituality. While other great minds pushed back against the historical corruption of authoritarian church leadership with its gross abuses, they lost their way when they asserted all religious belief and practice was destructive. Proverbially, they threw the baby out with the bathwater. Don't let their bitter cynicism toward religion influence your pursuit of the spiritual life. The modern campaign to suppress the value of the spiritual-religious life has only served to accentuate its importance. The decrease of religious practice has ushered in untold social harm, including the destruction of the family unit, increase in mental health issues, increase in suicide, and many other destructive consequences. In

---

30 Lord Kelvin, as quoted in A.W. Smith and J.N. Cooper, *Elements of Physics*, 8th edition (New York: McGraw-Hill Publishing, 1972), p. 241.
31 Karl Marx, *Introduction: A Contribution to the Critique of Hegel's Philosophy of Right*, trans. A. Jolin and J. O'Malley, ed. J. O'Malley (Cambridge: Cambridge University Press, 1970).

fact, scientific study reveals that depression correlates with a narrowing of the brain's perceptual field, its ability to see the big picture in relationship with others and the larger world. In comparison, MRIs of people with strong spiritual awareness had a healthier brain structure able to protect itself from neural structures of depression.[32] Scriptural religious belief and practice is the key to future health, wholeness, and well-being for individuals and society.

Those opposed to religion and spirituality today use science as a bully pulpit to disprove the credibility of religious beliefs and sacred texts. But are these efforts honest? The Scientific Method, the approach used in natural sciences for over 400 years, begins with basic assumptions but inherently involves the auxiliary assumptions of those involved. Auxiliary assumptions affect how you interpret the information you observe. What are your biases? Confirmation bias is the common tendency of individuals to interpret new information in a manner that reinforces their existing beliefs. People with opposing beliefs will tend to interpret the same information in a way that reinforces their existing worldview. A case supported by incontrovertible evidence, let alone sufficient evidence, may fail to convince the person who holds an opposing belief. In religious terms, this condition is hardness of heart or spiritual blindness. Jesus called the condition "eyes that cannot perceive and ears that cannot hear."[33] Do not be influenced by those who fall into this trap. Some people will refuse to believe regardless of the evidence. Modern science proves the importance of spiritual-religious belief and practice. Consider and accept the evidence, but don't be discouraged by those who refuse.

Scientific Evidence for the Power of Religion and Spirituality

The spiritual life powerfully impacts the physical world that we live in—it can produce miraculous changes. The Scripture affirms this idea in many places in addition to Solomon's observations.[34] Medically speaking, the positive effects of the spiritual life are evident in scans of the brain.[35] Other scientific inquiries reveal the foundational contributions of spiritual-religious expression to human life. Numerous studies conducted over decades of research demonstrate religious beliefs and practices are associated with better health, reducing stress and its effects, lowering the use of health services and leading to greater wholeness and true health.[36] Generally, most personal manifestations of religious behavior—indicative of deeply held spiritual worldviews—were more strongly related to psychological well-being.[37] Religious behaviors have been shown to provide great benefit during chronic illness such as cancer.[38]

32 Lisa Miller, *The Awakened Brain: The New Science on Spirituality and Our Quest for and Inspired Life* (New York, Random House, 2021), 147–151.
33 Matthew 13:13–15
34 John 16:33, Matthew 7:7, Romans 12:2, Philippians 4:13, Hebrews 4:12
35 Miller, *The Awakened Brain*, 7.
36 Harold G. Koenig, Michael E. McCollough, and David B. Larson, *Handbook of Religion and Health* (New York: Oxford University Press, 2001), 394, 433–434,591–592.
37 U.S. Department of the Army, "*Comprehensive Soldier and Family Fitness (AR 350–3),*" (Washington DC: U.S. Department of the Army, 2014), 7–8.
38 Sarah O. Meadows, Megan K. Beckett, Kirby Bowling, Daniela Golinelli, et al, *Family Resilience in the Military: Definitions, Models and Policies* (Santa Monica, CA: Rand Corporation, 2015), 4.

The first spiritual fitness metric, possessing a spiritual worldview, is associated with well-being and general psychological health. Spiritual beliefs serve as "an integrating and stabilizing force that provides a framework for interpreting life's challenges," acting as a set of adaptive skills that one researcher refers to as spiritual intelligence.[39] Spirituality may indirectly protect against suicide by preventing "the psychological, social, behavioral, and physical factors that drive people to commit suicide" or by influencing "genetic risk factors for suicide."[40]

Regarding the second metric, personal religious and spiritual practices, studies have shown links to improved health and functioning. In particular, they found highly significant correlations for "personal devotion" to religious practices with mental health.[41] Repeated research has found that prayer had therapeutic value for anxiety and depression and led to improved recovery following surgery.[42] Attendance in religious observances in various forms also appears to be associated with decreased substance use. A survey of undergraduates found that family church attendance and parental religiosity acted as protective factors against adolescent substance use.[43] Spiritual meditation had a stronger effect than did secular meditation on pain tolerance and mood, anxiety, and spiritual health.[44] Individual spiritual meditation, performed daily for one month, decreased migraine headaches, which are often associated with depression and anxiety, in addition to increasing pain tolerance, well-being, and daily spiritual experiences.[45]

Regarding the third metric, support from a spiritual community, strongly positive relationships between "institutional religion" or the "social and behavioral aspects of religion," such as attending religious services or participating in church activities, have been related to mental health.[46] Evidence suggests that support from a spiritual community is generally beneficial to health and well-being, more so than secular support. Spiritual community support improves health status, has a protective or buffering nature, has an inverse relationship with depression, and helps support coping with financial difficulties.[47]

Regarding the final metric, religious coping, a positive relationship was found between religious coping and an individual's psychological adjustment to stress. It included several other positive outcomes related to well-being.[48] Pargament and colleagues (1998) found that positive religious coping was associated with better psychological and spiritual outcomes.[49] For church members who had experienced a variety of traumas, including natural disasters, motor vehicle accidents, violent or sexual

---

39 Idem, 5–6.
40 Idem, 7–8.
41 Idem, 8.
42 Idem, 7–8.
43 Froma Walsh as cited in Meadows, *Family Resilience*, 8.
44 Douglas Yeung and Margaret Martin, *Spiritual Fitness and Resilience: A Review of Relevant Constructs, Measures, and Links to Well-Being* (Santa Monica, CA: Rand Corporation, 2013), 5.
45 Wayne Jonas et al., as cited in Douglas Yeung, *Spiritual Fitness*, 5. David Hufford, Matthew Fritts, and Jeffrey Rhodes, as cited in Douglas Yeung, *Spiritual Fitness*, 5.
46 Yeung, *Spiritual Fitness*, 6.
47 Ibid.
48 Charles Hackney and Glenn Sanders, "Religiosity and Mental Health: A Meta-Analysis of Recent Studies," *Journal for the Scientific Study of Religion* (Vol. 42, No.1, March 2003), 43–56.
49 Yeung and Martin, *Spiritual Fitness*, 19–20.

assault, and war/combat, positive religious coping was related to post-traumatic growth.[50] Spiritual coping may influence psychological states that buffer stress, such as helping people cope with an uncertain and dynamic world. Religious beliefs may help preserve people's sense of personal control in changing circumstances.[51]

Summary of Spiritual-Religious Efficacy

Numerous studies reveal that religious practice/spirituality contributes to health, wholeness, and well-being. Harold G. Koenig, a psychiatrist and researcher on the faculty of Duke University, reviewed 102 studies in 2000, 81 of which found positive associations between spirituality and well-being. Since that review, they found an additional 224 studies, 175 of which found positive associations between spirituality and well-being.[52] A Rand study's findings regarding four key metrics of spiritual fitness—spiritual worldview, personal religious or spiritual practices and rituals, support from spiritual and religious communities, and spiritual coping—echo these overall findings. Researchers identified research linking each of these spiritual fitness metrics to improved resilience and better outcomes for overall well-being.[53] The positive influence of religion in reducing suicidal ideations is also significant.[54] On the other hand, lacking a spiritual worldview or violating one's spiritual beliefs may have serious negative consequences. Nonspiritual well-being—not feeling peace or purpose and meaning in life, or not deriving comfort from a relationship with God—has been associated with lower quality of life and life satisfaction.[55] In her research on the awakened spiritual brain, Dr. Miller concludes, "When we make full use of how we're built, our brains become structurally healthier and better connected, and we access unsurpassed psychological benefits: less depression, anxiety, and substance abuse; and more positive traits such as grit, resilience, optimism, tenacity, and creativity."[56] This research-based evidence reveals a very important truth echoed throughout Scripture, your spiritual life matters. It can profoundly change your future.

The science behind the positive health benefits of religious belief and practice is becoming more recognized. I recently watched a documentary on factors contributing to the longevity of groups of people who live to 100 years of age. These "blue zones" have common factors that account for why people tend to live so much longer than those living in other areas. Religious practice was one of the factors identified in the research. What caught my attention in the discussion was the statement that attending and participating in religious activities more than once per week adds an average of seven years to a

50 Idem, 20.
51 Ibid.
52 Hackney and Sanders, "Religiosity and Mental Health," 43–56.
53 David Moberg, "Research in Spirituality, Religion, and Aging," *Journal of Gerontological Social Work* (Vol. 45, No.1, 2005), 11–40.
54 Ray Merrill, Jeffrey Folsom, and Susan Christopherson, "The Influence of Family Religiosity on Adolescent Substance Use According to Religious Preference," *Social Behavior and Personality* (Vol. 33, No.8, 2005), 821–836.
55 Amy Wachholtz, and Kenneth Pargament, "Is Spirituality a Critical Ingredient of Meditation? Comparing the Effects of Spiritual Meditation, Secular Meditation, and Relaxation on Spiritual, Psychological, Cardiac, and Pain Outcomes," *Journal of Behavioral Medicine* (Vol. 28, No.4, 2005), 369–384.
56 Miller, *The Awakened Brain*, 9.

person's lifespan. This research-based observation is more evidence of the efficacy of the spiritual life, one more confirmation of the holistic benefits of religious belief and practice and the power of spiritual resilience. Diet, activity, and strong relationships are other important factors in longevity, but apart from these, how many decisions can you make that add seven years to your life? How many decisions can significantly improve not just the quantity but the quality of your life? The evidence is real.[57]

Thoughts of Great Leaders from the Past

This evidence is one reason the U.S. military includes spiritual fitness in its list of dimensions for total soldier fitness. Military leaders from various cultures throughout history understood that the spirit of the soldier or warrior is far more important than physical strength alone. As General Dwight D. Eisenhower once said, "It's not the size of the dog in the fight, it's the size of the fight in the dog."[58] I once watched a tiny Yorkshire terrier mount such a ferocious charge at a German shepherd, the larger dog turned tail and ran from the yard. Armies are composed of ordinary people prepared for battle through training designed to strengthen morale, inner confidence, courage, cohesion, and esprit de corps, as well as physical conditioning. With strength of spirit, disciplined soldiers form a potent weapon on the battlefield. Without these qualities, they are potentially less reliable. To combat potential weakness from their conscripts, ancient leaders burned the ships after they landed on foreign shores. The lack of options for retreat in battle served to motivate the army to a "win or die" mindset, especially effective for undisciplined troops.

Emperor of France and military genius Napoleon Bonaparte said, "There are only two forces in the world: the sword and the spirit. In the long run, the sword will always be conquered by the spirit."[59] He went on to remark, "The first virtue in a soldier is endurance of fatigue; courage is only the second." Notice the inferences to the power of spiritual resilience. A military leader, among many other strategic and tactical proficiencies, is a dealer in hope. General George C. Marshall, U.S. Army Chief of Staff during World War II, echoed Napoleon's view. "It is not enough to fight. It is the spirit which we bring to the fight that decides the issue. It is morale that wins the victory."[60] The great Chinese warrior-philosopher Sun Tzu stated, "To fight and conquer in all our battles is not supreme excellence; supreme excellence consists in breaking the enemy's resistance without fighting."[61] Grand Chancellor of China's Easter Han Dynasty wrote, "He who can prevail in battle by taking advantage of his enemy's doubts is invincible." Although examples of the importance of the warrior's spirit abound in the writings of great historical

---

57 Dan Buettner, *Live to 100: Secrets of the Blue Zones, An Unexpected Discovery*, S1, E2, Netflix, 2023.
58 Dwight D. Eisenhower, "Eisenhower Spurs G.O.P. Vote Drive to Win Congress by William S. White," *New York Times*, January 31, 1958, 1, ProQuest.
59 J. Christopher Herold, in "*The Mind of Napoleon*," (New York: Columbia University, 1961), p 76 (and note on p.300), indicates it's from a "Conversation with Fontanes, cited in Martel, III, 7" Tancred Martel, Napoleon Bonaparte:Oeuvres Littéraries, 1888.
60 George C. Marshall. *Speech at Trinity College*, (John Hopkins University, 1941), accessed April 16, 2021, 2–484 Speech at Trinity College, June 15, 1941, Library (marshallfoundation.org.
61 Sun Tzu, *The Art of War*, Trans. Samuel B Griffith, (Oxford: Oxford University, 1988), Verse 3.02.

military leaders, we will close with a final thought attributed to arguably the greatest military leader of all time, Alexander the Great. He remarked, "I am not afraid of an Army of lions lead by a sheep; I am afraid of sheep lead by a lion."[62] If military leaders throughout history recognized the importance of spiritual resilience to victory, how much more should we recognize its importance in the battles we face?

Typology of Spiritual Resilience in Scripture

Scripture repeatedly addresses the idea of resilience in both the Old and New Testaments. The first example or type of spiritual resilience is a New Testament parable. Jesus highlighted the centrality of the spiritual life with His parable of the wise person who builds his house on the rock.[63] In the parable, there are two types of builders: those who build their house on a foundation of rock and those who build on a foundation of sand. The contrast is whether the builders obey His teachings. Those who obeyed built on a solid foundation of rock. Those who did not obey built on sand. Both houses look fine until the storms come. In the parable, it is the storms of life that expose the wisdom of the builder. By obeying Christ's teachings, you can endure the storms of life. Your life may look great until the storms come, then they expose the foundation. Build on the rock with obedient action. Jesus reduced Scripture to two commands: love God and love other people. As you deepen your connection with God, you can generously treat others with God's love. Build your life on an unshakeable foundation capable of enduring the erosive forces of adversity. Leverage spiritual fitness principles to overcome troubles in your life.

A second example of resilience comes from the prophet Jeremiah, the tree with deep roots planted by streams of water. It does not fear the heat or drought. It continues to flourish, bearing green leaves and fruit through the harshest of climates.[64] The deep roots refer to the deep connection you establish when you trust God. The heat and drought represent the difficulties and struggles of life. The deep roots of your spiritual life continue to nourish your whole being regardless of harsh conditions. The strength that flows through your spiritual roots, nourishes your body, mind, and spirit as well as your relationships. They are the key to overcoming adversity.

In another example, the Book of Hebrews presents the analogy of the runner who must persevere to finish his race.[65] The runner must endure opposition, hardship, and the stressors of running a physically exhausting race. Like the runner, you have resources to help you finish: the friendship and power of Jesus, who won the ultimate victory; the inspiration of a great cloud of witnesses who have not only completed the race but are spiritually cheering for your success; and God's counsel to throw off everything that slows you down as you run. As learned by those who have gone before, adversity can help

---

62 Attributed to Alexander the Great, as quoted in *The British Battle Fleet: Its Inception and Growth Throughout the Centuries to the Present Day*, 1915, by Frederick Thomas Jane, accessed April 16, 2021, Lions, Wikiquote.
63 Matthew 7:24–27
64 Jeremiah 17:7–8
65 Hebrews 12:1–3

motivate you to prioritize your spiritual life. Difficulties can also lead you into self-destructive behaviors (aka sin). You cannot finish well carrying the burdens of bad decisions along with the accompanying mental-emotional baggage. Reject wrongdoing and cast off the weights of the past so you can run your spiritual race well.

Wisdom is another scriptural contributor to resilience. Personified as the woman who cries out in the public square, wisdom is available to those who choose to listen.[66] She will keep the hearer safe and at ease with no fear of harm in time of trouble. However, to the one who will not heed God's wisdom, calamity may overwhelm. Human stubbornness often resists instruction and correction. People enjoy the easy path, doing what they want to do. The folly of this short-sighted life approach (the pleasurable and easy way) is evident when difficulties happen. Wisdom lays the foundation for obedient trust in the Lord, providing direction when storms make it difficult to find your path. Your investment in the spiritual disciplines helps you hear wisdom's voice more clearly as they strengthen you each day. In contrast, trials expose the inner weakness resulting from patterns of self-destructive, sinful behavior when ignored. The more you follow the voice of wisdom, the more you strengthen resilience.

The Extraordinary Resilience of Israel's King David

This book spotlights one example of extraordinary resilience. It is the story of defeat in the life of the renowned military leader who would eventually be known as Israel's King David.[67] David was highly honored by the people and very successful as a military leader in his service to the previous ruler, King Saul. Saul became jealous of David and, in desperate need of his followers' approval, disobeyed God in key decisions. He became increasingly unstable to the point of relying upon David's talent on the harp for psychological relief. On one occasion, in a fit of jealous rage, Saul attempted to murder David. He and his army spent years chasing David through the countryside, even into foreign territory. During those years, David gathered six hundred disaffected but very capable warriors with him. Together, they achieved remarkable success and enjoyed the favor of the local people. Eventually, Ziklag became the home base for his warriors' families and possessions. One day, while David and his men were away on a campaign, Amalekites, nomadic raiders of the desert, attacked and plundered the city. David and his men returned home to find the city looted and burned, their possessions and families gone. It was the low point of David's life. His men, heartsick and bitter, talked of stoning him. They were so overwhelmed by grief, they wept. Six hundred tough, seasoned warriors cried themselves to physical exhaustion and then proposed stoning their beloved leader to ease the pain. David, once the son-in-law of the king and his top general, for years an exile facing near-death on numerous occasions, hit a wall. He was physically and emotionally exhausted, stressed out, and fearing for his life, this time at the hands of his own men.

---
66 Proverbs 1:20–33
67 1 Samuel 30

Introduction, Part 2:

This moment was the low point of David's life.

Put yourself in David's shoes for a minute. You've lived on the run for years trying to hold your followers together, and now everything you have is gone, your home burned, and your family an unknown—at best enslaved, worst-case, dead in the desert. To make matters worse, the people who stood by you through it all want to kill you. It's hard to imagine a more stressful, hopeless situation. Yet the Scripture records, "but David encouraged himself in the Lord his God."[68]

This is a striking statement. Somehow, David rose above his sorrow, fear, stress, and physical exhaustion to connect with God in a manner that brought encouragement, renewed motivation, and energy to move forward in his circumstances. How did he bounce back when six hundred seasoned warriors were self-destructing in their grief? I believe David was resilient because he had a deep relationship with God reinforced by critical spiritual disciplines and biblical wisdom. The great lesson of David's example is you can tap into that same spiritual power to overcome your difficulties. This book presents many of the spiritual disciplines, strategies, and skills that can help you find strength, as David did. Section One of this book presents spiritual disciplines that can help you deepen your spiritual connection with God, Section Two presents spiritually resilient thinking strategies, and Section Three presents spiritually resilient action strategies.

David stands out in the Bible as a seminal example of a person connected with God. He grew up composing, playing, and singing songs to God in the fields, tending sheep. He faced the elements and wild animals alone as a young boy, yet he was never alone. All that time, he was talking to God. He wrote prayers, songs, and poems to God we know today as the Book of Psalms. He learned spiritual disciplines and connected deeply with God from a young age. He faced bears, lions, giants, armies, criticism, betrayal, envy, and numerous false accusations. And through it all up to his lowest point, David trusted in his personal God. When David had to bounce back from this difficulty, he called on spiritual momentum built upon years of prayer, worship, and trust in God's faithfulness. That's a lot of force!

The first thing David did after he "spiritually refreshed" himself in God was to seek God's direction. This is great counsel for all of us—to go to prayer and Scripture first. As soon as he received the word "Go!" from the Lord, he led his warriors in pursuit of the Amalekite raiders who plundered Ziklag. Not only did they recover their possessions and family members unharmed, but they also seized a treasure trove of additional spoils the raiders had stolen from other towns. Soon after this victory, David became King of Judah. What a turnaround! David's example teaches us key lessons for overcoming hardships. I want that kind of resilience! I'm sure you want it too.

In the following chapters, we will discuss the keys to spiritual resilience using David's life as a model. You develop resilience through consistent spiritual disciplines, stretching and strengthening your

---
[68] 1 Samuel 30:6b

capacity for resilience as you think, speak, and act in healthy, constructive ways. We will explore each of these vital areas in detail.

Summary

Spiritual fitness is the key to resilience, health, and wholeness through the ups and downs of life. You can enhance your fitness level by developing spiritual disciplines, renewing your thought processes, and regulating your actions. These steps provide the outline for this book. Section I centers on twelve spiritual disciplines that help you draw closer to God and develop a healthy spiritual life. Your spiritual life provides a strong foundation for all other actions. Section II spotlights the importance of a healthy, spiritually resilient thought life, describing twelve key principles to promote health in the inner life of your thoughts and emotions. Adversity has a way of getting on the inside of you. Keep it from invading your mind, and you will set yourself up for the next key to overcoming. Section III emphasizes the importance of healthy, spiritually resilient speech and actions, describing twelve constructive action steps that can enable you to thrive through adversity. The process for overcoming adversity requires sincere spiritual disciplines, which promote a healthy thought life that produces positive, faith-filled speech and empowers constructive, resilient responses and actions. There is a powerful aggregate effect to the spiritual strategies discussed in this book. The more you practice these principles, the more you will experience their benefits and the more you will see their impact multiply in your life. We begin with the building blocks.

Section I

12 Key Spiritual Disciplines for a Faith-Filled (Spiritually Resilient) Life
Introduction

"My heart and my flesh may fail, but God is the strength of my heart."[69]

You can live a resilient life by following twelve key spiritual disciplines from Scripture. This list is not exhaustive but covers the primary spiritual practices that enable you to live an abundant, victorious life. The person who knows God will live by faith.[70] The spiritual disciplines enable you to build a deep and abiding relationship with God, your Creator. They form the building blocks of a vibrant spiritual life, providing a foundation for all other dimensions of fitness, elevating your thoughts, emotions, attitude, relationships, and physical well-being. The spiritually resilient life is a faith-filled life—meaning you direct your life by faith in God and your relationship with Him. In practice, the disciplines become pillars of strength that can act as both a safety net and a trampoline that propel you upward when you face adversity. David is a perfect example of this principle. His close relationship with God proved to be the critical factor in his ability to overcome the devastating losses of Ziklag. David's consistent spiritual practices strengthened his relationship with God and anchored his faith. They enabled him to trust God for a good outcome when everything collapsed around him. In the same way, your practices of prayer, reading Scripture, trusting God, fasting, serving, giving, etc., can help you draw closer to God and find strength in Him to overcome. The convictions of your heart matter. The confidence that God cares about you, is with you, and is working to strengthen and help you is a powerful force through the ups and downs of life.

The twenty-third Psalm provides a powerful picture of David's reliance on God and the spiritual resilience it provided him. He made this confession of the certainties in his relationship with God.

> The LORD is my shepherd, I lack nothing. He makes me lie down in green pastures, he leads me beside quiet waters, he restores my soul.
> He guides me in paths of righteousness for his name's sake.
> Even though I walk through the valley of the shadow of death, I will fear no evil, for you are with me; your rod and your staff, they comfort me.

---
[69] Psalm 73:26
[70] Romans 1:17

> You prepare a table before me in the presence of my enemies.
>
> You anoint my head with oil, my cup overflows. Surely goodness and love will follow me
>
> all the days of my life, and I will dwell in the house of the LORD forever.[71]

David began with an intimate description of God's role in his life—shepherd. He found everything he needed in God. God sustained his physical body and strengthened his inner being. God provided guidance and direction to keep him on a healthy, wise, and God-honoring path. God provided protection, peace, and security even in great trouble. Because of God's work in his life, David felt no fear. He gave David victory over his enemies even when circumstances appeared the darkest. God empowered David, gave him peace, encouragement and filled him with joy. David was confident of God's favor and desire to endow abundant blessings. He was confident that God's goodness, mercy, and grace would be with him every day of his life until he went home to be with God forever. His steadfast trust in God's love and faithfulness gave him supernatural strength and exceptional resilience.

God is no respecter of persons.[72] You can share the same kind of connection as David's relationship with God. Like David, your practice of the spiritual disciplines will enable you to draw close to God and strengthen your inner being. This is a deliberate and ongoing process that takes time. They have an aggregate effect—meaning, their influence in your life compounds as you exercise them over time. Just as interest compounds on an investment, the influence of spiritual disciplines accrues with each use. If you deposited a dollar in your account every time you trusted God, you can imagine how much you could gain with interest over a year. You invest the dollar in your account by your thoughts and actions; God compounds the interest. Imagine how much you could have in a year. Five years? Ten years? People give up on God in their struggle, saying, "I tried faith," or "I tried prayer, and it didn't work." If you try one spiritual discipline for one week, you have just started the car; you haven't even put it in gear yet. You cannot expect to make much progress this way. You will experience spiritual synergy as you exercise more of the spiritual disciplines. Together, they will enable you to build speed and spiritual momentum that carries you through greater challenges. They make you stronger and more resilient. Together, they increase motivation, help you feel closer to God, empower you to trust God more, and equip you to appropriate by faith the power and authority God has already provided for you. You will be spiritually resilient.

To illustrate the effects of spiritual disciplines another way, if the pathway through your struggle is a door, banging on it with desperation won't accomplish much. Throwing up a half-hearted, superstitious prayer for it to open probably won't do much, either. If you continue to knock on that door through prayer, fasting, and a faith-filled expectation for God to open it, you release God to work on your behalf.

---

71 Psalm 23
72 Acts 10:34

God may intend to sovereignly deliver you. Many miracles of Scripture reveal God's intent to take care of the problem Himself. Sometimes, God's plan is for you to overcome that obstacle with His help. He gives you the wisdom and power to open that door. It may be a quick answer, or it may be God's intent to sustain, strengthen, and mature you through the longer journey. Your ability to move through these doors is dependent on your trust in God at that time. The key to your perseverance is the depth of relationship you have built with Him in the regular and consistent practice of spiritual disciplines. You never know when the next struggle will come. It is vitally important to strengthen yourself in advance. Make a serious commitment to the spiritual disciplines now, deepen your relationship with God, and strengthen your spiritual being. You will lessen the impact of adversity on your life and profoundly impact your ability to respond to it.

God Wants to Bless You!

Believe it; God wants to bless you! Do you know that every good thing that has ever happened in your life has come from Him?[73] He bestows favor and honor on His people and withholds no good thing.[74] Try thinking about God as if everything He does is good and that every intention of His heart toward you is only for your benefit.[75] He loves you that much. He is your heavenly Father, and He is storing up good things for you.[76] He has a spectacular plan for your life that will bless you, honor Him, and lead you home to heaven with great reward and the words, "Well done!"[77] He will exceed your expectations if you truly trust Him.[78] When things go wrong in your life, He will turn what was meant for your harm into something that profits you.[79] God does all these things because He loves you and wants to bless you.

It may be hard for you to believe God truly wants to bless you. Many people suffer with "God-and-the-world-are-against-me" thinking. They have learned cynicism because of difficult life experiences. They cannot believe that God could possibly care about their problems. He seems too far away and too unconcerned. Some people live so present to past hurts, their pain has tainted their whole perspective on life. For them, God's blessings appear too good to be true. The leper came to Jesus, barely hoping God cared about his suffering, "Lord, if You are willing, You can heal me." Jesus replied, "I am willing; be healed."[80] The leper wasn't convinced God was a good God. Jesus settled the issue. Don't let life's troubles permanently rob you of hope. The enemy wants to make you feel self-pity, despair, and hopelessness, that God is distant, unconcerned, or has forsaken you. This is all part of the enemy's plan to

---
[73] James 1:16–17
[74] Psalm 84:11
[75] Psalm 34:8, Psalm 139:17, Psalm 145:9
[76] Psalm 31:19
[77] Jeremiah 29:11, Matthew 25:23
[78] Ephesians 3:20
[79] Romans 8:28
[80] Matthew 8:2–3

make the dark seem darker and the light of a better day seem farther away, if not impossible. The intent is to keep you stuck and constrained. But a careful reading of Scripture communicates a very different message from God.

God wants you to ask Him for help all the time, but especially in hard times. The disciple Peter, one of Jesus' inner circle, exhorted struggling believers, "Humble yourselves under God's mighty hand, that he may lift you up in due time."[81] Everyone suffers through times of difficulty. You can respond in self-pity, blaming God for the problem, or you can humble yourself, trust God, and receive His mercy and grace to endure. Peter continued his encouragement, "Cast your anxiety (cares) on him [God], for he cares for you."[82] God wants you to share your life with Him, the ups and the downs. The Apostle Paul urged believers to ask God for everything, "Do not be anxious about anything, but in everything, by prayer and petition, with thanksgiving, present your requests to God."[83] Your refusal to ask Him for help hurts. Several times in the Old Testament, we hear these words, "Is there no God in Israel that you (God's people) seek another god (source) for help?"[84] The doubts of His people grieve Him. He asked Moses, "Is the arm of the Lord too short?"[85] He was angry with Israel for seeking military help from Egypt but not looking to Him.[86] In the New Testament, James reiterated the same thought, God's people tend to look to other places for help first. He wrote, "You do not have because you do not ask God."[87] God's help should be your first course of action, not the last resort when all else fails.

My aunt was told she had terminal cancer. Over two years ago, when praying for God to relieve the horrific pain of melanoma throughout her body, she had a vision. She saw Jesus turn and smile at her. Instantly the pain vanished. Since then, her hospice care team has continually tried to get her to take pain medicine. She tells them she does not need it. She doesn't have any pain, so there is no point. She believes God healed her of the cancer. She should not be here. She prepared her finances and adult children for her death, but after God's touch, she is still hanging around. Hospice caregivers have reduced her care and are about ready to discontinue services. To this day, my aunt has no pain and feels no cancer symptoms. Visible lumps in her body have disappeared. God can change your experience of adversity and outcomes. Ask my aunt. She has a clear explanation: God healed her.

Seeking God's help for your situation is an act of faith. Praying, asking God to intervene in your circumstances, is an act of faith. Prayer is not idleness. It truly is the best first response. Believers have a whole lot of reasons why they don't ask. They boil down to a simple lack of faith. The father of a possessed boy asked Jesus, "If you can do anything, take pity on us and help us." Jesus answered, "If you can?

---

[81] 1 Peter 5:6
[82] 1 Peter 5:7
[83] Philippians 4:6
[84] 2 Kings 1:3, Isaiah 30:2
[85] Numbers 11:23
[86] Isaiah 31:1
[87] James 4:2

Everything is possible for him who believes."[88] The man had low expectations appealing to Jesus' pity to move Him to help. He wasn't even sure if Jesus could. I heard a pastor share a profound truth in church one day, "God is not so moved by your need as He is moved by your faith in Him to help you through it." God wants to be so central in your life that you ask for help with an expectation that good things will follow.[89] However, you must believe He will reward your efforts. Jesus taught the asking principle,

> "Ask and it will be given to you; seek and you will find; knock and the door will be opened to you. Which of you, if his son asks for bread, will give him a stone? Or if he asks for a fish, will give him a snake? If you, then, though you are evil, know how to give good gifts to your children, how much more will your Father in heaven give good gifts to those who ask him."[90]

The tense in the original language of this passage communicates you should keep asking, keep seeking, and keep knocking. Expectation for receiving is based upon the nature of God. Faith says, "My good God will reward the trust I put in Him." My kids never worried they would have rocks or snakes on the dinner table. They always knew they had a bed to sleep in. I didn't interrogate them about their behavior while away and refuse to let them in the house if they had done wrong. Yet you may doubt God's care and provision. Maybe your father wasn't good. Then, Jesus' words become a contrast rather than a comparison. God is so much better than earthly fathers. He is always good and always wanting your best. He is also working in your life to draw out your confident trust in Him. Greater faith comes by internalizing the Word of God. Transform your faith by renewing your mind with Scripture. Knowing Scripture is a key factor in growing more spiritually fit. Consider these passages that discuss a wide range of ways in which God wants to bless you.

> **2 Chronicles 16:9 (NIV)**
> For the eyes of the LORD range throughout the earth to strengthen those whose hearts are fully committed to him.

> **Psalm 33:18 (NIV)**
> But the eyes of the LORD are on those who fear him, on those whose hope is in his unfailing love.

---

88 Mark 9:22–23
89 Hebrews 11:6
90 Matthew 7:7, 9–11

Proverbs 3:3–10 (NIV):

Trust in the LORD with all your heart and lean not on your own understanding; in all your ways acknowledge him, and he will make your paths straight. Honor the LORD with your wealth, with the first fruits of all your crops; then your barns will be filled to overflowing, and your vats will brim over with new wine.

Jeremiah 29:11–13 (NIV)

"For I know the plans I have for you," declares the LORD, "plans to prosper you and not to harm you, plans to give you hope and a future. Then you will call upon me and come and pray to me, and I will listen to you. You will seek me and find me when you seek me with all your heart."

Malachi 3:10 (NIV)

"Bring the whole tithe into the storehouse…Test me in this," says the LORD Almighty, "and see if I will not throw open the floodgates of heaven and pour out so much blessing that you will not have room enough for it."

Matthew 6:26–27, 30–33 (NIV):

So do not worry, saying, "What shall we eat?" or "What shall we drink?" or "What shall we wear?" For the pagans run after all these things, and your heavenly Father knows that you need them. But seek first his kingdom and his righteousness, and all these things will be given to you as well.

John 10:10 (NIV)

The thief comes only to steal and kill and destroy; I have come that they may have life, and have it to the full.

Romans 8:28 (NIV)

And we know that in all things God works for the good of those who love him, who have been called according to his purpose.

Romans 8:31 (NIV)

If God is for us, who can be against us?

2 Corinthians 1:20 (NIV)

For no matter how many promises God has made, they are "Yes" in Christ. And so through him the "Amen" is spoken by us to the glory of God.

Ephesians 1:3 (NIV)

Praise be to the God and Father of our Lord Jesus Christ, who has blessed us in the heavenly realms with every spiritual blessing in Christ.

Ephesians 3:20 (NIV).

[God] is able to do immeasurably more than all we ask or imagine, according to his power that is at work within us.

Philippians 4:19 (NIV)

And my God will meet all your needs according to his glorious riches in Christ Jesus.

Hebrews 11:6 (NIV)

And without faith it is impossible to please God, because anyone who comes to him must believe that he exists and that he rewards those who earnestly seek him.

James 1:17 (MSG)

So, my very dear friends, don't get thrown off course. Every desirable and beneficial gift comes out of heaven. The gifts are rivers of light cascading down from the Father of Light. There is nothing deceitful in God, nothing two-faced, nothing fickle.

3 John 1:2 (NIV)

Dear friend, I pray that you may enjoy good health and that all may go well with you, just as you are progressing spiritually.

These are just some of the Scripture passages that clearly demonstrate God's intent and earnest desire to bless your life. Write these verses down, post them in conspicuous places for encouragement, and highlight them in your Bible for easy reference. You must hold fast to these truths during hard times. The enemy will try to strip them from you. God guarantees His promises.[91] His answer is "yes" in Christ. The reference list at the end of this book provides a more complete Scripture Index of the passages for every spiritual discipline you can use in spiritual battles.

---
91 2 Corinthians 1:20

A final note before we dive into these twelve key spiritual disciplines. Spiritual disciplines are very personal because our divine Creator reached out to humanity in the most personal way possible. He became one of us and walked among us. Over three years, Jesus Christ lived the struggles, sorrows, and difficulties of the human experience. And when He completed this identification, He gave up His life as a spiritual offering for humanity's rejection of God. You see, He is the gate to God's friendship, presence, and, ultimately, heaven.[92] You will live for eternity; that is a certainty, according to the Bible. The question is where you will spend that existence. Compared to eternity, your time here on Earth hardly measures. And yet it is everything! Because your time here on Earth is your one opportunity to connect with God. Every human, regardless of race, sex, religion, age, or any other possible distinction, is a physical child of God. We are all genetic brothers and sisters because we are all descended from God's first children, Adam and Eve. But there is a deeper connection with God than merely the physical. We must also become spiritual children of God and brothers and sisters in His spiritual family. This only happens as you personally connect with Jesus. You must personally recognize Christ's divine nature, His sacrifice for your rejection of God's authority in your life, and your subsequent need for His forgiveness. It is only through your sincere, repentant, and personal commitment that you can know Him as your spiritual Father and Friend. It is a simple prayer to start down the road. "Father, I thank You for sending Your Son to rescue me. Thank You for paying the price for my life. Forgive my rebellion and rejection of Your authority. I commit my life to Jesus as my Savior and Lord. Come live in my heart and walk with me as a Friend. In Jesus' name, amen." It's a little harder, but well worth it, to continue down that path, living your life committed to Him. I pray you find joy and peace in your personal relationship with God!

So now we begin. It is time to take the next step toward greater spiritual resilience. Develop your spiritual fitness. Learn the disciplines. Practice the disciplines. But most importantly, deepen your relationship with God!

92 John 14:6

Spiritual Discipline 1

Read Scripture Every Day

Your Word is a lamp unto my feet and a light unto my path.[93] —David

Read Scripture every day! Scripture is God's primary way to speak to you. Faith is a relationship, and relationships need communication to grow. God wants to talk to you. The more consistently you read Scripture, the more you will hear God speak. Read three chapters a day and five on Sunday, and you can read through the Bible in a year. Yes, it works. I have repeatedly used this plan to read through the Bible. Most importantly, choose a reading plan that works for you. A consistent reading discipline is the single most important step you can make to strengthen yourself spiritually. Knowing Scripture will bring you encouragement and will equip you to make faith-filled declarations over your life and future. The more you know, the more equipped you will be to face decisions, struggles, and attacks from the enemy. Additionally, your knowledge of Scripture will support other resilience-building strategies. As you read, the Holy Spirit will impress passages on your heart that bring direction and encouragement for your current circumstances. Reading and studying will help you to understand the heart of God as you strengthen your personal relationship with Him. You will increase your faith and learn to trust Him more through adversity.

David's Reliance on God's Word

David overcame his tribulation at Ziklag with a rich knowledge of Scripture. He penned in the Psalms, "Thy word is a lamp unto my feet and a light unto my path."[94] He used God's Word like a spiritual flashlight in his life. He went on to write, "I will hide your Word in my heart that I might not sin against God."[95] He recognized his most valuable possession was his relationship with God, and he wanted to protect it at all costs (mostly from himself). David wrote some of these passages as a young man watching his family's sheep out in the fields. The Scripture he learned as a child encouraged him as he faced the dangers of shepherding and later served as the raw material for the future Scripture he would write under the inspiration of the Holy Spirit. David was a model for humility and transparency. He talked to God openly about his feelings of sadness and discouragement in Psalm 42–44, sometimes feeling

---

93 Psalm 119:105
94 Ibid.
95 Psalm 119:11

alone as enemies pursued him and friends ridiculed him. Despite his feelings, he encouraged himself to remember God's faithfulness to His Word, to place his hope in God, and to look forward to the day he would praise God again with joy. Perhaps this is the same self-talk David used to find strength in the tragedy at Ziklag. God knows circumstances can make you feel like you are all alone, but He authored Scripture to remind you He is always with you.[96] Your struggles can push you toward Him or push you away, depending on your thoughts and reactions. Follow David's example. Openly share your thoughts and feelings with God. He can handle it. He knows your thoughts anyway. When you choose to share your joys and sorrows, you deepen your relationship and release the therapeutic power of faith.[97] David's knowledge of Scripture was a key contributor to his ability to find spiritual strength at Ziklag. He knew God's Word was completely reliable, what God said He would do. Even when all seemed lost, David wasn't lost. He knew where his help came from, and he stood on that faith. Dig into God's Word, seek Him, and stand on His promises as David did.

God's Word Is Spiritual Food

God's Word is spiritual food, just as important to your spiritual health and well-being as food is to your physical well-being. This illustration highlights the importance of a Scripture-reading discipline. As your diet affects your physical health, so a healthy diet of Scripture reading will affect your spiritual health. If you neglect reading Scripture, you will become spiritually anemic in the same way you would from starving yourself physically. Jesus, the living Word of God, called Himself the Bread of Life.[98] He faced His struggles with Scripture stating, "Man does not live on bread alone, but on every word that proceeds from the mouth of God.[99] Bread doesn't sound like the best meal among today's options, but in Bible times, bread was essential. My great-uncle Harold was a German prisoner of war for several years in World War II. He suffered immensely, including near starvation, as the German soldiers refused to feed the prisoners. Thankfully, local German farmers living near the camp tossed bread over the fences every day. Their compassion enabled him to return home after the war. He was thin, but their bread kept him alive. In the same way, the bread of God's Word is spiritual nourishment, a life-giving force in your day-to-day life. A consistent diet of Scripture grows and refines your faith, the critical component to the spiritual life. Without it, your growth will be stunted, you will be vulnerable to the work of the enemy, and struggle to find clear direction. You can only build spiritual resilience through consistent reading and study of the Word of God.

---

96 Hebrews 13:5
97 Philippians 4:6–7
98 John 6:25
99 Matthew 4:4

Spiritual Discipline 1

God's Word Is True

God's Word is without error, historically accurate, and factually true. It is not a collection of myths or fables. It is not a series of allegorical stories that teach moral lessons. It is not a good luck charm or a book of chants for the superstitious. It is as it claims to be, a work of the Holy Spirit, recording factual history, prophetic messages, and divine encouragement, produced through human authors to help all people draw close to God and strengthen their spiritual being while benefiting every other aspect of their lives: physical, emotional-mental, social, and relational. God moved, with prophetic inspiration, upon nearly forty of his personally chosen messengers to write these words, binding the various writings together over a period of approximately 1600 years to become what we know today as the Holy Bible. It is nothing short of miraculous that sixty-six separate books written over such a long period of time contain such a powerfully unified message. Peter, one of Jesus' closest disciples, wrote this about Scripture.

> For we did not follow cleverly devised fables when we made known to you the power and coming of our Lord Jesus Christ, but we were eyewitnesses of His majesty. Above all, you must understand that no prophecy of Scripture comes from the prophet's own interpretation. For prophecy never had its origin in the human will, but prophets, though human, spoke from God as they were carried along by the Holy Spirit.[100]

Peter testified, as did others, that Scripture contains eyewitness accounts of Jesus' life, such as those recorded in the Gospels. Most of the human authors of Scripture were eyewitnesses of the events they recorded. Additionally, they received by revelation from the Holy Spirit the principles, wisdom, and spiritual truths they wrote. God breathed it into them. Faith recognizes Scripture as fact. The more you read and study God's Word, the more you accept it as truth for your life. Faith grows in the reading, and with it comes more trust in God to see you through hard times. Trust enables you to persevere, mature spiritually, and overcome.[101] Your testimony through adversity reinforces your faith in God and His Word for the next struggle. This cycle of faith was evident in David's life, and it will work for you as well. David's battles with lions and bears in the shepherd's fields prepared him to defeat Goliath and ultimately overcome the loss of Ziklag. Without his knowledge of and trust in the truth of God's Word, these victories would never have happened.

---

[100] 2 Timothy 3:16
[101] James 1:3

How Did We Come to Embrace the Lie?

The vast amount of written historical testimony (thousands of ancient and painstakingly copied manuscripts) recorded by these authors is more than sufficient to convince an unbiased court of law of its truthfulness. However, nearly every human institution tries to discredit God's Word. This all-encompassing campaign to discredit Scripture and faith derives from the strategic intent of the enemy. His attack on the truth and authority of God's Word is an effort to neutralize the one force that truly threatens his power and influence over humanity. But this tactic is not new. In the Garden of Eden, the devil convinced Eve that God's instructions were false. He began with a question, twisting God's words and attempting to sow doubt in her mind.[102] When she shared God's command and warning, he denied its truth and accused God of holding back His best from her. Nothing was further from the truth. She could eat the delicious fruit from thousands of trees in the garden, but she fell for the lie they were not enough.[103] What she and Adam received from the Tree of Knowledge was loss of innocence and overwhelming guilt they had betrayed the one who truly loved them. They embraced the lie; God's Word was inconsequential. The enemy continues the same strategy to this day, using every possible tactic to undermine trust in the Word of God.[104] He is called a liar and the father of lies for a reason.[105] He wields deception as a weapon of mass destruction to neutralize the power of Scripture, undermine human trust and reliance on God and lead humanity further down the path toward self-destruction. Jesus warned His followers, "There is no truth in him (the devil). When he lies, he speaks his native language."[106] That warning is just as necessary in today's deceptive media environment; you must hold to the truth of God's Word at all costs. I will spend the rest of this chapter trying to convince you to doubt all those who try to spread doubt in Scripture. God's Word is not inconsequential. It is the most relevant message in the universe, and one day, whether it be death or Christ's return, everyone will know that to be true.

Humanity has made astounding technological advances in the last century, yet the verdict is still out whether we are healthier and more whole in our inner being. Unfortunately, scientific study has developed with antagonism toward spiritual life. Be prepared to hear people publicly mock Scripture. Throughout history, under the broad influence of the enemy, so-called experts have tried to cast doubts on its historical accuracy and veracity. In the modern era, Charles Lyell and his more famous pupil Charles Darwin, through the mechanistic explanations of science, appeared to have irrefutably determined how everything came into being apart from God. Nietzsche, Russell, Freud, Marx, and many others propelled humanity into the twentieth century with the idea that their scientifically based vision of the cosmos was the last and final word. There is no God in the personal sense, no afterlife, no soul,

---
102 Genesis 3:1
103 Genesis 3:9,16-17
104 Genesis 3:4
105 John 8:44
106 Ibid.

no inherent justice in the world. Humanity is on its own. Patrick Glynn, a former atheist, described his journey from this "enlightened state of acceptance of the random universe" to a spiritual life in God through the recognition of intelligent purpose and organization in a thousand details vast and small in the universe but without which life would not exist.[107] This anthropic principle, recognized by many physicists, astronomers, and other scientists, interprets the many "mysterious coincidences" essential for life as necessary "in advance of" its appearing. Coincidences such as the constant of gravity in relation to electromagnetism, the relative mass of protons, neutrons, and electrons in an atom, the force of the nuclear weak and strong forces, the properties of water so essential for life, the synthesis of carbon, and many other critical phenomenon.[108] In other words, the universe needed to know in advance what it was going to be in order to start itself.[109] That doesn't sound very random. Frankly, there is enough we know and too much we don't know to rule God out of the picture. It can only be described as the worst of hubris to think we should.

The archaeologist is more important than archaeology in the search for truth. When I was young, people claimed Scripture was in error because there was no historical evidence to support the Hittite Empire described in the Old Testament. A decade later, archeologists discovered proof of the Hittites' existence. I never heard a retraction on that point. The agenda is most important in modern science, honesty and transparency less so. The evidence for the truth of Scripture is in the earth and the skies. Frankly, it's all around.[110] Some is undiscovered, some has been misinterpreted. Dinosaur skeletons have been effectively used to discredit the Bible, yet the Book of Job provides two clear descriptions, one probably a brontosaurus or other sauropod; the other unique description perhaps a Parasaurolophus, Kronosaur, or a relative of the Plesiosaurus.[111] The "leviathan" of Job and Psalms is also like a creature Pliny the Elder, an ancient Roman historian, described. It was a carcass found in 58 BC along the coast and displayed at Rome's largest theater; forty feet long with ribs taller than an elephant and an eighteen-inch-thick spine.[112]

I learned in grade school that the spark of life began in the primordial waters of ancient Earth. Years later, as a teenager, I read an article in the newspaper with the headline, "Scientists Believe Spark of Life Happened in Absence of Water." I cut the article out of my local paper and kept it for many years. Since then, the experts have been back and forth on how life started in the universe, many times theorizing grandiose explanations of far-distant stars, black holes, and antimatter presented as conclusive evidence. Despite lacking definitive proof to support their claims, they have no problem pandering their theories as fact, largely without critical scrutiny. Do not expect to find open-minded discussion of evi-

---

107 Patrick Glynn, *God the Evidence: The Reconciliation of Faith and Reason in a Postsecular World*, (Rocklin, CA: Prima Publishing, 1997), 9.
108 Idem, 29–30.
109 Fred Hoyle, *The Origin of the Universe, and the Origin of Religion*, (Wakefield, RI: Moyer Bell, 1993), 19.
110 Romans 1:20
111 Job 40:15–24, Job 41:1–34
112 Pliny, *Natural History, Book IV*, trans. by H. Rackham, 1949.

dence supporting biblical history in most modern forms of media. They cater to contributors who carry a philosophical hostility to Scripture and faith. You will regularly encounter criticisms of both. Don't let the raucous voices discourage you. They are just one more proof of the material-spiritual war. You will need to stand on Scripture for everyday life and especially for encouragement during times of adversity. The verdict is still out on details of the creation of the cosmos. The short version is found in Scripture.[113]

The science behind most of these theories is not scientific at all. The scientific method starts with a theory based upon assumptions that must then be verified and/or modified through observation and experimentation. The Bible is not hostile to science. You don't have to choose science or Scripture. Given time, non-biased assumptions, and open-minded study, I am confident scientific discovery would complement and support the Biblical account of creation. According to Scripture, creation reveals the existence of a Creator.[114] Natural science, the study of the natural world, reveals evidence of design, hence the existence of a Designer. We who believe in the truth of the Bible know Him as God, the Creator. However, if, in your bias, you theoretically assume that God is not real and cannot exist, then no amount of scientific evidence will convince you to affirm Scripture.

A clear example is the debate on a global flood. Many scientists reject a global flood as found in the Bible, conjecturing instead that the Earth was shaped by regional and local floods over hundreds of millions of years. This message continues to be promoted despite significant evidence to the contrary, revealing quickly settled, non-eroded layers in the Earth's crust like those found at the Grand Canyon. These layers tell the story of sediment deposits that were suddenly and catastrophically distributed in the Grand Canyon and all over the world. The fact that each has clear lines of separation with no evidence of erosion makes their formation over millions of years an impossibility. Seams of coal reveal the same conclusions. Another proof of a global flood is the fact that marine fossils can be found all over the world, even in the mountains. Even dinosaur fossils are often distributed together in formations that were created by the movement of powerful water currents. These were not local floods but a global flood that caused giant herds of animals to cluster as the rising waters pushed them to higher and higher elevations until they were overcome. This means dinosaurs were present in the pre-flood world. Although debates like this one rage every day, the scientific method is not antagonistic to Scripture or your faith. It is only hostile in the bias of those who use the method, those whose assumptions and presuppositions reject God and the scriptural account before observation and study ever happen.

As described earlier, many scientists, without a bias against a Designer, find abundant evidence in the layers of rock in the Earth, the fossil record, ocean salinization, physics, astronomy, and many other complex fields that support the possibility of a Creator and the biblical account of creation. Many scientists with noteworthy expertise in their fields can describe the clear scientific evidence for the scriptural

---

113 Genesis 1
114 Romans 1:20

account of creation. If you have never heard these presentations, they are worth considering.[115] Darwin's theory of origins is still nearly universally accepted as evolution-minded opponents of creation continue to push their agenda. One of the rally points has been using human-like skull discoveries as evidence of a missing link between man and ape. If humanity evolved from nothingness, then Scripture is untrue. There is nothing special about us; we are a cosmic accident with no accountability and no reason for moral restraint. These unusual skull discoveries have been effective, convincing evidence. However, the supposed evidence severely lacks consensus. Experts disagree over every fossil candidate.[116] Creation scientists cite DNA analysis that shows these skulls are either human or ape; they are not a link between the two.[117] They are either one or the other, or in some cases, something else altogether, like in one early discovery, the skull of a pig. Regardless of the facts, these discoveries are still promoted as proof of the missing link. While the focus has always been to find an evolutionary link between apes and mankind (supposing if you have that link, nothing else matters), the theory of evolution requires a multitude of transitional creatures in the tree of species before that of the ape-man. It is not that evolutionists are merely missing a link between ape and man. They do not have a true evolutionary fossil link between any species of creatures.[118]

Evolution theory is compulsory in our educational institutions with no tolerance for open scholarly debate, yet it continues to lack clear evidence in the fossil record. This scientific travesty exists because it is the best possible theory to discredit the Scriptural account of creation and advance the premise there is no God. The vehement social reaction to debate about evolution is itself evidence of an enemy. There is sufficient evidence in the Bible to convince someone who is open-minded, but it lacks incontrovertible evidence. You cannot compel someone to believe, nor can you convince the one who refuses to believe, no matter how much evidence you have. Belief and faith must be a free choice. Faith is not blind belief: the universe alone offers numerous proofs, as discussed above, the near-universal human belief in an afterlife and something (or someone) bigger than us, the witness of hundreds who have died and come back to life with accounts of a heavenly encounter, the millions of testimonies of lives changed by the power of God, and the written testimony of eyewitnesses recorded in Scripture. However, faith is not tied entirely to the evidence or scientific theories. It is fundamentally a belief in God and commitment that transforms the heart.

The stakes in the war for truth are very high. Billions of people are taught through public institutions and media forums that the Bible is mythical, irrelevant, or, at best, a collection of good moral lessons. Most of them never hear the simple Scriptural message of Jesus, known as the Gospel. Our young people are brainwashed with the self-centric religion of humanism. In her research, Dr. Miller described

---

[115] Answers in Genesis, www.answersinGenesis.org; Institute for Creation Research, www.icr.org; Is Genesis History, www.isgenesishistory.com.
[116] Brian Thomas, *Two Excuses for Human Evolution Confusion*, www.icr.org/article/two-excuses-for-human-evolution-confusion.
[117] Joel Tay and Robert Carter, *Do These Skulls Prove Common Ancestry Between Apes and Humans?* www.creation.com/ape-human-transitional-skull.
[118] Todd Wood, "Life & Design: Humans & Apes," *Beyond is Genesis History*, Vol. 2, DVD, 2018.

the devastating effects of depriving children of spiritual-religious engagement; the life-long stunting of maturity and growth, with its ultimate constraint of inner strength and resilience.[119] Put bluntly, depriving someone of the opportunity to pursue the spiritual life is a death sentence. Ultimately, Scripture is true whether you and I believe it. Most people do not believe. When I wanted to do something that my parents had forbidden, I would say, "Everyone else is allowed to do it." Invariably, Mom would reply. "If everybody jumped off a cliff, would you do it?" How do you answer that as a kid? I never had a good reply. The popular path is not always the best path. Jesus echoed this thought as well, "Broad is the path to destruction and many travel on it."[120] You must decide to believe Scripture is God's Word; you cannot follow the crowd. It is between you and God. The stakes are high. As you pursue the truths of the spiritual life, you must be prepared to stand alone at times. You will have to resist the powerful currents of culture. Take God at His Word. He is the one who loves you the most.

God's Word is Power

Scripture is powerful because it is the very Word of our omnipotent God. Like a seed, it inherently contains life. It presents transformative spiritual principles and life-giving words from God's heart to yours. Scripture is true, and it contains eternal, unchanging truth. As such, it can change your reality. Addition 2+2=4 is factually true, but it's not going to transform your life. The truths of God's Word can literally change your life, your present circumstances, and your future trajectory. As you put your faith in God and the truth of his Word, his life-changing power will be released.[121] Scripture reveals a personal relationship with God providing forgiveness, redemption, deliverance, and blessing for all humanity.[122] Its dynamic words promote health, wholeness, and strength. It offers profound guidance on living your best possible life; it is your handbook. When released to work for you, it will accomplish its intended purposes.[123] Scripture pierces the heart shaping motives and character.[124] As a boy, I watched my parents commit their lives to God, leaving behind a family legacy of alcoholism and tobacco addiction. The power of God's Word made this radical change possible. Many of my relatives continue in the destructive cycle of alcohol and drug addiction to this day. I am certain that I would have followed the family legacy had not the power of God touched my parents and then personally touched my life as a child. God's Word has power to set captives free, whatever the prison looks like.

Reading the Bible is different from every other book. You can read it through ten times and still discover something new, relevant, and impactful. God is holding out numerous gifts for you in His Word. You must take them out of his hand by reading, studying, and believing them. All the promises of Scrip-

---
119 Miller, Spiritual Child, 71–72.
120 Matthew 7:13
121 John 8:32
122 Romans 1:16
123 Isaiah 55:10–11
124 Hebrews 4:12

ture are "Yes" for you in Jesus. However, they won't do you any good until you appropriate them with "Amen," literally, "I agree. Let them come to pass."[125] Amen adds your "Yes" to God's "Yes." The power of God's Word is released as you speak the words of Scripture over yourself and your circumstances. Sometimes, like seeds, the Word takes time to produce growth that is visible. It may take longer for that growth to produce fruit. Make no mistake: from the moment of your faith, the roots of change begin to form. As kids, my brother and I used to plant seeds in paper cups. We would impatiently watch them every day for the sprout to break through the ground. One year, we were away from home for a week. When we returned, we were amazed at how much the little plants had grown from those sprouts. In the same way, your use of Scripture may seem to have little effect at first. Be patient. Roots that will support growth and later fruit are forming. You will look back after several months or a year and recognize the dramatic effects of change.

God's Word a Sword for Spiritual Battle

Scripture is a powerful weapon for battle against every attempt of the enemy to destroy your life.[126] Jesus used Scripture to refute the enemy's temptations in the wilderness.[127] This example is a clear model for you to follow in your difficult times. Paul taught the Ephesian believers that the Word of God is the sword of the Spirit, an offensive weapon against the spiritual forces of evil in this world.[128] The writer of Hebrews described it as a two-edged sword capable of discerning thoughts and motives of the heart.[129] Scripture will empower you to confront your unhealthy thoughts and develop wise, constructive solutions to problems. It will equip you to face the ideas, philosophies, assumptions, and logic in the deception-rich media environment of this world. You need a spiritual weapon to face the discouraging thoughts the enemy will throw at you when you face adversity. There is no way to live the overcoming life without the principles and wisdom of the Bible. Your battles come through circumstances, people, or even your own mind. Whatever the vehicle, it is critical for you to build a familiarity and practical knowledge of the Scriptures you can quickly draw from to face trouble. This consistency enables you to use your sword when needed. You rarely have the opportunity in the heat of a difficult moment to say, "Time out, let me sharpen my sword." You must always be ready with some well-known passages that will help you face your battles. The more you know, the more you can face. You will likely face longer, enduring struggles that allow you time to get into your Bible and find help. In these moments, you want it to be familiar enough to locate highlighted verses or other relevant passages quickly. The time to ready your sword, increasing your knowledge and understanding of God's Word is now.

---

125 2 Corinthians 1:20
126 Ephesians 6:16–17
127 Matthew 4
128 Ephesians 6:10
129 Hebrews 4:12

God's Word, A Resilience Builder

Scripture reading serves three critical roles in strengthening your resilience. First, it provides encouragement and hope. Difficulties can drain hope. Hopeless people get stuck in life, in feelings of discouragement and despair. Paul reminded the Corinthian believers that hope, along with faith and love, is an eternal, universal force enduring forever.[130] Scriptural hope is not wishful thinking. It is spiritual optimism inspiring you to take positive action with expectation. It meets a temporary problem with an eternal perspective. Peter related God's work to a living hope, offering assurance that God remembers His people, encourages them in their struggles, and helps them move forward toward their future.[131] Hope is motivational. It energizes you to trust God, expect good things from him, and take positive action. Consider these encouraging verses:

God is watching over you for good. For the eyes of the LORD range throughout the earth to strengthen those whose hearts are fully committed to him.[132] God has good plans for your life. I'll show up and take care of you as I promised and bring you back home. I know what I'm doing. I have it all planned out—plans to take care of you, not abandon you, plans to give you the future you hope for. "When you call on me, when you come and pray to me, I'll listen. "When you come looking for me, you'll find me.[133] God can turn what was meant for evil to your good. And we know that in all things God works for the good of those who love him.[134] God wants you to have a blessed life. I have come that [you] may have life and have it to the full.[135] God is not the source of evil in your life, he only brings good things. Every good and perfect gift is from above, coming down from the Father of the heavenly lights.[136]

Reflect a moment on these statements. Let them fill your heart, trusting God to help you rise above your struggles. Meditation on Scripture can be powerful. Take one verse and focus on it. Repeat it, personalize it, and break it down by each word as you reflect on God's message to you. Does God really care? Yes! Does God want good things for you? More than you know! Will God help you overcome your difficulty? Absolutely! Scripture gives you the ammunition to fight off discouragement and despair.

God's Word, Light in the Dark

Scripture serves a second role in strengthening your resilience, direction. Difficulties can make you feel as if surrounded by darkness, causing discouragement, confusion, sapping your confidence, and stifling constructive action. When you face a decision, it is wise to seek the counsel of Scripture. It is a lamp post illuminating your path to healthy, wise choices. The more you read and familiarize yourself

---

130 1 Corinthians 13:13
131 1 Peter 1:3
132 2 Chronicles 16:9
133 Jeremiah 29:11–14 (MSG)
134 Romans 8:28
135 John 10:10b
136 James 1:17

with it, the more you will sense the guidance of the Holy Spirit in that critical moment of decision. The first challenge is committing yourself to grow in the knowledge of His Word. The second is seeking Him in the moment of need, listening for the still, small voice of the Spirit, and third, following His lead when you sense His direction. Hiding God's Word in your heart—internalizing it—will help you guard against the confusion and misdirection of false reasoning. It will help you obey God and avoid sin. Sin is the technical term for wrongdoing, selfish, destructive behaviors motivated outside true faith that run contrary to God's Word. There are no harmless sins. Like a wrecking ball, they always destroy something: health, relationships, emotional well-being. The enemy uses sin to his strategic advantage, shrouding the truth in the darkness of ignorance, confusion, and deception. He shapes conditions to ensnare you in your selfish desires. Once you accept, he will accuse and condemn you, so you want to hide your sin and shame with more darkness. He will fight to hold you captive in this deep, dark, destructive cycle. The antidote is truth, to shine the light of Scripture into your heart, allowing God to restore you in humility and obedience.

Scripture provides a cautionary road sign to sin the way parents warn their children of the dangers of crossing a street. Parents instruct children to look both ways because they want to keep their children from being hurt by oncoming traffic. God loves you so much that He provided healthy boundaries to keep you from harm. I cannot overstate the protective benefits of Scripture. All the suffering in the world derives from the sin of those who ignored, rejected, or directly opposed God's Word. Individuals, families, communities, societies, and nations suffer from the neglect or rejection of Scriptural counsel. Its light will enable you to navigate the darkness of temptation and to avoid the negative second, third, and fourth order consequences that always follow sinful choices. When you're facing hard times, make sure you keep the lights on by reading and studying God's Word.

In my twenties, I had the responsibility of spiritual leadership for the first time. After about a year, a person from the community asked to meet with me, saying she had a message from God. I went to that meeting with openness and expectation but was shocked when she shared that God told her he had written "Ichabod" over the church. Ichabod means, "the glory has departed," and meant in her mind that God's favor was not on my ministry. I frantically searched my memory to identify what I had done that so offended God. She could offer no details. I left that meeting thinking I should probably step down from leadership to prevent the church from losing God's blessing. Immediately, I began to sense God speaking to my heart. I was reminded of a Scripture verse, "It is not the one who commends himself who is approved by God, but the one the Lord commends." I searched my Bible and quickly found and read 2 Corinthians 10:18. The words were a bright light, replacing confusion and doubt with a burst of hope in my spirit. I sensed the Lord's approval replace my fear and desire for approval from others. The conversation was an attack of the enemy through a well-meaning albeit misguided person. God used the Scripture to shine light on a situation that could have ended God's calling in my life before it barely got started.

God's Word, Compass for Mid-Course Corrections

Scripture serves a third role in strengthening your resilience, personal growth. It can, like a compass, point toward important corrections in your life. Experiencing hardships can make you resistant to growth and change. But these qualities are often the key takeaway. Everyone needs mid-course corrections. Sometimes, your actions worsen the struggles you face. The Word acts as a mirror, revealing where you need to change. It functions as a refiner's fire. Ancient silversmiths heated the raw silver ore in a crucible, skimming the impurities from the surface of the molten metal as it liquefied. The more clearly the silversmith could see his reflection in the molten ore, the greater the silver's purity. In the same way, Scripture exposes the impurities of your heart and allows you to identify and correct them. It is an interesting fact that manufacturers use silver to coat the back of mirrors. In the same way, you can see clearly to make changes in your life by looking into the reflection of God's Word. I had a high school friend who unknowingly returned from the lunchroom with food on his face. Those sitting next to him laughed at him, but nobody told him why. Sensing he had a problem, he demanded someone tell him what was wrong. Finally, one of the girls in class took a small mirror from her purse to show him the truth. God loves you too much to allow you to walk around like my friend. He provided Scripture as a mirror, helping you see the truth and make constructive changes.

Scripture reveals what is important to God, informing your value system and developing character. Values are the core beliefs that reveal who you are, what is important to you, and how you make decisions. They are the motivations of your heart. Your decisions and actions reveal your core values. Jesus emphasized the importance of the heart to God in His Sermon on the Mount. Sin is not just evident in outward behaviors but in the motivations of the heart.[137] Your inner life is the source of your well-being.[138] Your character and spiritual identity determine many of your future choices and outcomes. Experiences will shape your character, but for the believer, they also reveal it. The fires of adversity expose the qualities of your heart. This is an important reason why you cannot wait to deepen your walk with God. You must build spiritual disciplines now. They help shape and refine your character so you can stand in the time of trouble. You must submit the clay of your heart to God's potter's wheel, allowing Scripture to shape your beliefs, values, and character. Character ultimately determines outcomes, so obedience to Scripture will shape your life for long-term success. Without it, even the most successful person will eventually suffer loss. My grandfather had several businesses handed down from his father. By all standards, he was set up for success. Unfortunately, he let his pain and alcohol rule his life. He never conquered the addiction. Alcoholism robbed him of his wealth, respect in the community, family's well-being, and, ultimately, his health. He died in poverty on welfare, his internal organs destroyed. God had a better plan. You must read and follow the Word to see the change.

[137] Matthew 5–7
[138] Proverbs 4:23

Human nature finds God's commands burdensome, but disobedience (sin) is wrong because, inherently, it harms you and/or others. If sin didn't cause harm, the Bible (God) wouldn't call it wrongdoing. Some people have the notion that God is trying to keep them from fun. Truthfully, there is a fun/pleasure factor to much of sin. Pleasure is the bait that lures people into destructive behaviors, exploiting their natural desires. But the definition of sin is not fun. Sin is a destructive force; spiritually, physically, mentally, emotionally, and relationally. You can enjoy fun in life without committing sin. You do not have to get drunk or high to relax, laugh, and enjoy life. The problem with sin is it appears fun and pleasurable at first, but ultimately, it is destructive and harmful. As I shared, my grandfather loved to drink. Unfortunately for my family, he was a mean alcoholic who left a wide destructive path—he lost the family business, left his wife and children emotionally scarred, and ultimately died in poverty. I had a front-row seat to the consequences of alcoholism. As a child, I feared getting too close to my grandfather's rocking chair because he would try to swat me with his yardstick. What a nice Hallmark memory. Lots of people find getting drunk fun. They forget their cares and enjoy the party. Family members of alcoholics have a different view. There is a dark, destructive underbelly to every form of sin. God's work in your life is always meant to bring about your long-term good. Sin does not bring about good or freedom. It is devastating to people's health and relationships. Many sins the world calls fun, lead to addiction or some other form of slavery. What started out with the mantra, "It's not hurting anyone," shows its true self-centered nature in alienating others and eventually exposing the damage caused by the second, third, and fourth order effects. Scripture lists behaviors that promote health and freedom.[139] They have constructive long-term effects that promote only good for others. Sin always hurts someone. Sin (wickedness), in contrast, often exploits others for selfish benefits and alienates them from God and others.

Cain's life is a tragic example of the many after-effects of sin. God warned Cain before he killed his brother, "Sin is crouching at your door. It desires to have you, but you must master it."[140] Cain ignored God's loving counsel and gave in to the crouching beast. After murdering Abel, God sent Cain into exile, away from his home and family. However, in mercy, He marked Cain so that no one would kill him for his murderous act. One choice caused Cain to spend the rest of his life in exile, fearing for his life. One way to truly know if something is sin is the "slavery test." Sin will always try to expand its control of your life; it wants to master you. God's commands may require discipline and self-control, but they ultimately promote freedom. You can submit to the one who loves you, or you can submit to the harsh rule of sin. You will never have the option to be your own master. The enemy will ensure your self-focused pursuits ultimately enslave you.

Scripture will help you recognize the difference between where you are and where God wants you to be. It will help you move toward His best for your life. It is the handbook or User's Manual for hu-

---
[139] Galatians 5:22–23
[140] Genesis 4:7

manity. Paul penned the following words to Timothy. "All Scripture is God-breathed and is useful for teaching, convicting, correcting, and training in righteousness."[141] Every story is a moral lesson, every precept a source of wise counsel. Scripture teaches principles that optimize the well-being of men, women, and children in their relationships with God and others. Following the user's manual is the prescription for your best possible life. You cannot prevent all difficulties from happening (though many are preventable through following Scripture), but you can choose how you handle them. Bad situations can be made worse by wrongdoing or improved by obedience to the Word. Things may seem to get worse at first, such as when you admit you have lied, but over time, you will find yourself in a better place, stronger, and planted on a firmer foundation. You must be humble and open to following God's direction in adversity. Often, people accept Christ as Savior because their personal difficulties create an openness in their heart to spiritual truth. Personal and spiritual growth is more likely when you face challenges. Following the handbook can help you turn adversity into greater strength, maturity, and selflessness. The growth cycle (struggle—humility/openness—obedience—growth—repeat) can transform your experience of life's difficulties. The more you embrace Scripture for teaching, conviction, correction, and training (the opportunity for growth) during times of adversity, the more you will develop strength to face future struggles. Let adversity be the catalyst that drives you to God's Word with its potential for transformation.

Make Reading God's Word a Habit

Many people like to start their day reading the Bible. Since I am a night person, I find it easier to read right before I go to bed. It does not matter when you do it. The key is doing it consistently. Find a time that works for you. If you miss a day, just pick back up the next day. Several times, I fell behind on my reading plan. I just increased my readings until I caught up. You do not have to read through the whole Bible at first, get started somewhere (the Gospels or New Testament) and work up to a larger reading plan. Try one chapter a day. Get a highlighter, a pen, and a journal, and make your Bible your own. Part of sharpening your sword is knowledge, and part is familiarity with your Bible so you can readily find passages that speak powerfully to you. Your Bible will not have the exact same highlights and notes as someone else because God speaks to each personally. Some people are afraid to write or highlight their Bibles because of reverence to God's Word. I respect that. However, the sacredness of God's Word is not the ink and paper; it is the principles, values, and message. Use whatever means you can to make that message more accessible and impactful for your life. There is no rule against things that strengthen your faith.[142] However, if your conscience forbids you from highlighting or writing in your Bible, get a notebook and write in it as you read and study.

---
141 2 Timothy 3:16
142 Galatians 5:22–23

Spiritual Discipline 1

God Wants to Speak to You

God's heart and earnest desire is to speak to you, helping you to know Him better. In fact, He is always trying to speak to you in many ways. Understand, this is a spiritual fact and is never in question. Protect this truth from the enemy. You don't have to be sinless to hear God's voice.[143] God speaks from a "no judgment" zone. The difficulty hearing God's voice lies with you and me. We must make time, quiet our minds, and listen with an open heart. The easiest way to hear God's voice is in His Word. God will encourage and direct you as you read it. You may feel verses "leap off the page," speaking specifically to your circumstances. A verse may stand out in your mind or have an emotional impact upon you. This effect is likely God speaking personally to your situation. It is not the only way God will speak to you, but it is a very important one. Your knowledge and familiarity with Scripture provide the raw material God uses to speak to you in other ways. As you go about life, you may have impressions based in Scripture God uses to guide and encourage you. The Holy Spirit will bring relevant verses to your conscious thought and apply them to your time of need. Many spiritual battles happen in the mind. You don't always have time to research a Scripture. The more you know, the more the Spirit can draw His Word from you at the point of need. Jesus chided culturally influenced Jewish teachers for their disbelief because they did not know the Word of God or its power. Your knowledge of Scripture will provide the power to increase your inner strength.

The Holy Spirit may speak a word into your heart or give you a sense or impression. Jesus promised the Spirit would be a Counselor teaching and reminding His followers of His Word.[144] Expect God to speak to you. Listen quietly for the still, small voice of the Spirit within. In addition to the Scripture and the leading of the Holy Spirit, God will normally use several other means to speak to you. An obvious but rare means is God's audible voice. I have never experienced it, but a mentor relayed how God spoke audibly, calling him to ministry as he drove his truck down the road. The prophet Samuel heard an audible voice.[145] God's peace is another way to sense God's direction and hear His voice. Scripture admonishes you to let Christ's peace be the controlling factor in deciding and settling questions that arise.[146] God will give you inner peace about a decision, or He may trouble your heart to check your proposed course of action. This is an important and common means of hearing God that many believers find helpful. Another way God speaks is through dreams and visions. Joseph had several dreams that helped him escape Herod's plot to kill baby Jesus.[147] As a young minister, I had a powerful dream that I was seated around a large campfire with a Shaman. I understood we were supposed to conduct a spiritual

---
143 James 1:5
144 John 14:25–27
145 1 Samuel 3:3–15
146 Colossians 3:15–17 (AMP)
147 Matthew 2:13, 19–20

duel, but at the last minute, two arms grabbed me from behind and pulled me very quickly away from the fire and out of sight. I wasn't sure who it was, so I repeatedly asked the arms, "Is that You, Lord?" I wrestled with its meaning for several months until I told my dream to a friend. He shared that it was the Lord who had pulled me away and that God did not want me to start a new outreach I was considering. Later I had a dream that led me to a new place of ministry. I have also had visions. Paul had a vision that led him to travel to Macedonia to start a new work there.[148]

God will use other people to speak to you. He has given believers gifts of prophecy, teaching, and wisdom to encourage and strengthen you. God used Peter to share His message to the leaders of the early church that He had accepted the Gentiles.[149] As I was seeking God's will for my next step of ministry, I only considered potential applications in a neighboring state. A mentor shared a message of counsel from the Lord, encouraging me to place applications in the state where I lived at the time. I desired to go back to my home state, but I prayed and decided to follow his counsel. Very quickly, a door of opportunity opened, and I took a ministry position in a nearby town. God will use others to speak to you, but it is important to remember two conditions: their counsel must align with Scripture, and it should normally confirm something God has spoken to you or be confirmed by something God later speaks to you. Other people are often used by God as a primer to help us look at a situation in a new way or consider new options. Circumstances may also be a means for God to speak or direct you. While adversity can be used by God to direct you, it must be noted that opposition does not necessarily mean a course of action is outside God's will. Sometimes, the struggle is part of the spiritual battle requiring perseverance. Neither does it mean it must be God's leading because a course of action is very easy. Many people look at circumstances as a way of communicating an open or closed door for action. Circumstances are best understood with the leading of the Spirit or a sense of peace with your interpretation of them. They should not be the sole determination of God's will or message. A final way I find God's direction is by being able to see the possible course of action come to pass in my mind. If I cannot picture it coming to pass, if it seems impossible or unlikely, I place that possibility on hold. This is one of the ways I often use as a final test to determine God's leading. I look for the confirmation that God is bringing the course of action to fruition.

God's Word is a multi-layered message. The Bible has a context, written in a specific period of time to specific groups of people. This is as true of historical and prophetic books in the Old Testament as it is for Paul's letters to the churches in the New Testament. God wrote the Scripture *to* specific groups at a specific time for a specific purpose, but He wrote it *for* all of us today. In His omniscient wisdom, God inspired the writers of Scripture to pen their words in a way that gave them eternal relevance and application. When you read Scripture, you are reading words God spoke to instruct and encourage peo-

---
148 Acts 16:6–10
149 Acts 10:17–18

ple's faith in their circumstances but that He also intended to encourage and apply in yours. Studying Scripture to understand the message in the original context enhances its relevance and application for you. But you don't need to be a Bible scholar to use the power of the Scripture here and now. The Holy Spirit will lead you to understand what God has to say to you today.[150]

Through the Holy Spirit, God personalizes His Word for you. You never know what will happen in life. Some people face tragic struggles. Some seem to live in relative ease. All face hardships on some level. Perhaps you face struggles with your health, relationships, family, career, or other basic needs. Following the teachings of Scripture will lead you to the best possible life, given the specific struggles you will experience. I don't know why some people have it easier than others or why seemingly "good" people endure great suffering. However, I do know it is not God's fault. After thirty-plus years of ministry, I have found everyone has personal burdens to bear. Some people seem outwardly very blessed but endure great inner struggles. Struggle is part of the human condition in a world controlled by the evil one and profoundly marred by the consequences of humanity's rebellion against God. One day, Jesus will return to Earth to end every injustice, every sorrow, every tear, and every pain once and for all. Until then, take comfort in the knowledge God provided the Scripture to help you know you are never alone. He is helping you find and develop a deep, meaningful relationship with Him. Your struggles can have positive effects as well: to strengthen your faith, refine your character, and help you deepen your walk with him. Although God cares deeply for your suffering, understand that He is most concerned with you finding help and hope in a growing relationship with Him. He created you with a unique set of strengths, abilities, and characteristics tailored specifically for your divinely appointed purpose while taking into consideration the specific twists and turns of your life's journey. It's mind-blowing to think that God had a plan for your life while you were still in the womb, his thoughts intent on bringing about good for you.[151] He inspired Scripture to be relevant to your context, regardless of who you are or what you will face in life. You can leverage every promise to overcome anything you face through your faith and trust in God. Scripture will sustain you, helping you navigate your life with the compass of divine wisdom and counsel; every story, lesson, and revelation designed to help you live your best possible life in relationship with God and others.

I began with this discipline because it is foundational for all others. Scripture provides guidance that informs every other discipline in some way. Scripture can be used for prayer and meditation, for guiding your thoughts and speech, informing your actions, and ultimately for everything necessary to live the overcoming life. The more you read Scripture, incorporating it into your values, thought life, speech, and behaviors, the more you will see your resilience grow.

---

150 1 Corinthians 2:10–16
151 Psalm 139:13–18

Spiritual Discipline 2

Pray, Fast, and Worship

"Cast your cares on the LORD and he will sustain you."[152]

Pray daily! Prayer is your primary way to talk to God. Faith requires participation. It is a relationship with God, strengthened like any other, by regular mutual communication. Jesus emphasized the importance of abiding and growing in this relationship.[153] God talks to you primarily through Scripture, His Word. Prayer is your primary way to talk to God. It allows you to share your heart, and commune with Him. Faith is a friendship with God based on interaction and trust. As you share your life with God, you strengthen your health, wholeness, and well-being. When you go through hard times, it is important to have a good listener in a judgment-free zone. Your adversary will use difficulties to say you are all alone. It is not true. God wants to hear your concerns and worries. He says in Scripture, "Cast your cares on me for I care for you."[154] He wants to hear what's going on in your life. Remember the words God spoke to the Prophet Jeremiah during his time of great loss, "A bruised reed he will not break and a smoldering wick he will not snuff out."[155] He does not add extra burdens when you are weak and discouraged. Just the opposite. He is trying to lighten your load. Paul encouraged the believers in Philippi with these words:

> The Lord is near to you. Do not be anxious about anything, but in every situation, by prayer and petition, with thanksgiving, present your requests to God. And the peace of God, which transcends all understanding, will guard your hearts and your minds in Christ Jesus.[156]

Prayer is a catharsis, the means to exchange your stress, anxiety, and worry for God's peace. As you pour out your heart to God, the Holy Spirit will lift the emotional weights and comfort you in His presence. God is close to you in your struggles. The peace is not logical because your circumstances haven't changed, but something spiritually has. You leave your prayer time feeling more at peace because you have more confidence God is with you, cares for you, and is working on your behalf. You have passed

---
152 Psalm 55:22
153 John 15:5
154 Psalm 55:22
155 Isaiah 42:3
156 Philippians 4:5–7

the weight of those cares to God and enlisted His help and support to resolve them.

David excelled at the conversation of prayer. Many of the Psalms read just like a prayer. They convey the agonizing of the psalmist's heart to God. They are honest and vulnerable. Sometimes, adults try to mask their feelings and condition, but children are very open and free to share the truth of their joys and pains. Jesus used a little child to illustrate the heart condition of the person who approaches God with innocence and trust.[157] Many of the Psalms demonstrate David's childlike vulnerability as he openly poured out his joys and sadness to God. He talked to God and talked to himself, encouraging himself to be more hopeful in trusting the Lord.[158] David's prayers and meditations translated into action. As king, David brought the Ark of the Covenant to Jerusalem. In the procession, he danced joyfully before the Lord. He danced so hard he stripped to his undergarment and danced unashamedly before the people.[159] His wife saw his undignified, childlike exuberance and despised him. That didn't stop David. He declared he would become even more undignified for the Lord if necessary.[160] When dating, a person may go to great lengths to convince the other person of his/her love. Impassioned demonstrations of love, not respectability, are what make the impact. In the same way, God is not interested in your sense of respectability and pride. He is very interested in a loving, humble, and obedient heart. Value what God thinks more than what people think. Carry that spirit into your prayer and worship life, and it will equip you with the strength that gave David the encouragement he needed when he faced the tragedy of Ziklag. David's proclamation to his wife, Michal, was a repetition of the proclamation he made when everyone was against him in Ziklag. He was willing to stand alone in his utter reliance on God if need be. That is true passion.

Pray to Ask God for What You Need

Jesus came to offer you a more abundant life.[161] He is not trying to fill your life with additional burdens. He gave you a way to unload stress by pouring out your heart to Him. God wants you to share your requests with Him. Do you realize that sharing your needs with God is an act of faith? The author of Hebrews wrote, "And without faith it is impossible to please God, because anyone who comes to him must believe that he exists and that he rewards those who earnestly seek him."[162]

God is pleased when you trust Him enough to ask for His help. Believe God will help you throughout your life and that He absolutely wants to help you in the situation you face right now. You're not the first person to doubt God wants to help. A leper came to Jesus, unsure whether God cared enough about

---

157 Matthew 18:3–4
158 Psalm 42:4
159 2 Samuel 6:14
160 2 Samuel 6:21–22
161 John 10:10
162 Hebrews 11:6

his life to heal him.[163] After all, he was unclean. His leprosy prevented him from participating in Jewish society and offering sacrifices at the temple. He was an outcast, forced to live outside the city walls, avoided by others at all costs. An inadvertent touch from a leper could make a worshipper unclean. I can hear the leper ask Jesus, steeling himself for the inevitable rejection. "Lord, if You are willing, You can heal me." But this leper had faith. Many in the leper colony were unwilling to face the possible rejection. They were certain that God had no concern for their misery. How does this attitude compare to scriptural counsel on faith? The writer of Hebrews states, "You must believe God exists *and* you must believe that he rewards those who earnestly seek him."[164] If God's Word is true, you already know Jesus' answer. But when you have faced a lengthy or severe struggle, what you know in your mind may not reach to your heart. Jesus settled the issue with the leper. He reached out and touched him, "I am willing, be healed."[165] Jesus cared so much for that leper he took his uncleanness upon himself with the touch of identification, care, and compassion. God wanted to help the leper, and He wants to help you. The leper left Jesus with clean skin and a heart full of God's love, peace, and joy. God sent Jesus to heal all of humanity, including you. Salvation is translated from the Greek word *sozo*, which means spiritual salvation, healing (mental/emotional and physical), deliverance, and blessing. Your complete healing is inevitable. You will spend eternity with God in heaven, no more pain, sorrow, or suffering. But Jesus paid the price for you to have *sozo* in this life here and now. In the 23rd Psalm, David wrote, "Surely goodness and mercy will follow me all the days of my life and I will dwell in the house of the Lord forever."[166] Like David, the leper found God's goodness and mercy. Eventually, he died, but he found healing in this life and the next. Ask God for help, expecting Him to reward you as He did David and the leper. Jesus taught the same principle in His Sermon on the Mount.

> Ask and it will be given to you; seek and you will find; knock and the door will be opened to you. For everyone who asks receives; he who seeks finds; and to him who knocks, the door will be opened. "Which of you, if his son asks for bread, will give him a stone? Or if he asks for a fish, will give him a snake? If you, then, though you are evil, know how to give good gifts to your children, how much more will your Father in heaven give good gifts to those who ask him!"[167]

Jesus didn't suggest you ask God for help. He commanded it. Ask, seek, and knock; literally, keep asking, keep seeking, keep knocking are three ways of asking God for assistance. God is a Good Father. He doesn't play games. He doesn't try to trip you up. He is for you, but you must bring faith and trust.

---
163 Matthew 8:24
164 Hebrews 11:6
165 Matthew 8:2–3
166 Psalm 23:6
167 Matthew 7:7–11

Jesus used a loving earthly father as an example of how accessible he is during your hardships. Some people stumble over the word "father" because they have had bad experiences with their earthly fathers. This passage provides encouragement to trust Him as your good, good heavenly Father. It may be a stark contrast to your not-so-good earthly father, but trust God the way your earthly father should have been. Trust God as He has always been and is, your supportive, loving, heavenly Father. Believe God wants to help you. Believe He will answer you. And believe that, in Christ, the answer is yes to all of God's promises.[168]

Let Prayer Do the Grunt-Work

Sometimes, you feel so powerless and uncertain what to do, you need prayer to be your main effort. "Grunt-work" is a military expression for the hard work done by junior soldiers in combat. They usually face the fiercest fighting on the battlefield. In your battles, you may initially need to rely solely on prayer to enable you to move forward. Extreme difficulties can make you re-evaluate everything. They can move you to realign your goals and priorities. Don't let that process push you away from God. In hard times, recommit yourself to the Lord and seek Him in prayer. The Prophet Habakkuk faced a crisis of faith. He saw the wickedness of his people punished by a godless nation that was far worse. He asked God, "Why do you watch silently as the wicked swallow up those more righteous than themselves?"[169] God answered his doubts with the assurance that He would eventually punish the evil conquerors, and He did. Life can appear unjust, and God may seem slow to address the problems. In truth, life is often unjust. It is a world controlled by the excesses of people's basest desires and the strategic deception and manipulation of the enemy. However, God is always "just," always desiring the best for you and all people. He is not at fault for the evils of our world. Scripture is one way God tries to guide people into justness. Humanity's obedience to just one command, "Treat others as you want to be treated," would change the world. Truly, God is the only one who is good and just. Many people clamor for justice today, but love is the only solution without a catch. Social outrage and action are ineffective without Jesus, the Righteous Judge. God could fast-forward His clock on this world of evil, but He is patient, trying to reach more and more people with the message of salvation. Part of God's slowness is a test for humanity to recognize its evil and turn toward Him. He is merciful and willing to give humans a chance to do right.[170] Part of that slowness is a desire to save as many lives as possible before the time us up. Another part of the equation is the work He accomplishes in all of us, in you, through hardship. God's pruning brings you back to the root to prepare you for new growth. He wants you to seek Him in prayer.

Military soldiers call artillery the King of Battle because of its ability to degrade the enemy's pow-

---
168 2 Corinthians 1:20
169 Habakkuk 1:13
170 Genesis 4:6–7

er from a distance. Prayer works just like artillery. It can shape your battlefield as you speak to God, releasing divine power and loosening the enemy's hold on your life. If you're not sure what to do, pray. Prayer will encourage you. Prayer will give you a sense of God's direction for the situation. Prayer will prepare your situation for future action. And prayer can bring about the change in God's timing. A mentor once told me, "Pray like it's all God, work like it's all you." This describes one of the tensions of faith, "Does God expect you to make the change happen, or will He make it happen?" It depends. In one story of Scripture, God told His people to stand back and watch Him work.[171] Other times, God blessed the obedience of His people.[172] Many times, it was a combination of both, such as at Jericho when the people marched, shouted, and God performed a miracle.[173] One thing you know for certain: God always wants you to seek Him first in faith. Expect any solution to be a partnership with you and God. God rewards those who put their faith in Him. Your faith is always a part of your solution. Some quote the saying, "God helps those who help themselves." This has partial truth, but it is not in the Scripture. The problem with this thought is that it can lead you to act on your own, expecting God to bless your solution. God can and will help you, but He wants you to follow His lead. Don't presume He will bless your mess when you act independently. Prayer and Scripture help you understand God's will for your next step more clearly.

Pray to Get Closer to God

But prayer is not just about asking God for things. It's about growing closer to God and allowing Him to change you in the process. Fundamentally, prayer is an expression of your desire to grow closer to God and to know Him better. Try this spiritual exercise; pretend that Jesus is right beside you everywhere you go. Talk to Him throughout the day as if He is right there, and when you pray, picture Him listening as a friend. In reality, Jesus is with you wherever you go through His Spirit, who lives within you. Envision His presence with you everywhere and always. Pray conversationally, like you would talk to someone very close. The Scripture states, "There is a friend that sticks closer than a brother."[174] Jesus is that friend. He is Emmanuel, "God with us," as well as the Eternal, Almighty God who is King of Kings and Lord of Lords.[175] Although God is preeminent, He is also with you.

Resist the temptation to make prayer formal, ritualistic, repetitive, or formulaic. Jesus taught His followers how to pray.[176] This model of prayer is often simplified with the acronym ACTS: adoration, confession, thanksgiving, and supplication. It begins, "Our Father in heaven, hallowed be your name, your kingdom come, your will be done, on earth as it is in heaven." It is important to begin prayer with

---
171 Exodus 7:12,14
172 Joshua 8:3–23
173 Joshua 6:1–27
174 Proverbs 18:24
175 Matthew 1:23, Revelations 19:16
176 Matthew 6:9–13

the right focus on God rather than the struggles. Adoration, or praise, places your focus on God as the source of everything you need. Hallowed means holy, noting the worthiness of God for worship. Proclaiming His will (Your will be done) helps align your desires and expectations with His intent, which is always best. Confession, the second piece of the prayer model, emphasizes the importance of asking forgiveness, releasing wrongdoing the enemy could use to keep you stuck or manipulate you with guilt and shame. "Forgive us our debts (trespasses) as we also have forgiven our debtors (those who trespassed against us)." It is worthy to note releasing others of their wrongs against you is necessary to overcome. Thanksgiving, the third part, is a very important part of regular prayer. Although not specifically mentioned in this prayer, it is discussed repeatedly in Scripture and will be addressed more fully in the chapter on gratitude. Thanksgiving is an essential part of worship (adoration) that begins and ends the model prayer. Supplication, the final piece meaning making requests, is listed early in the prayer. "Give me this day my daily bread." As mentioned earlier in this chapter, asking God for what you need is an act of faith that God rewards.

Several times in my life, I have used the Lord's Prayer as a template for my daily prayer discipline. Most days, I prayed each line of the prayer and then expounded on it, asking for God's work in the world and help with issues in my life. It is a great way to develop your prayer habit. The Lord's prayer is simple and straightforward. You may feel you have to pray a certain amount of time, using old English language or following a ritual like a magical incantation. Prayer is not a manipulation of God; it is a conversation. Your only formula is the one given above from Scripture. Prayer is for an audience of *one*; it is meant to help you connect with God. Some feel that they must use many words or flowery language. Avoid babbling, numerous and repetitive words, as well as praying to impress others. Use the Lord's Prayer as your guide. Keep it simple and personal.

Spend enough time with God so He is bigger than your problems. Your mind tends to magnify problems. Humans are good at making mountains out of molehills, assuming and planning for the worst. You can allow yourself to dwell on the problem, filling your mind with anxiety and draining your strength. This is not only counter-productive but emotionally and physically damaging. Your prayers can and should help break this destructive cycle as you focus on God. Your recognition of His presence and power can eclipse the problems. Sometimes, you must wrestle in your mind to stay focused. A friend of mine called this exercise the "crucible of prayer," where you force the unspiritual and distracting thoughts that come to your mind out as you focus on God and your communion with Him. Praying and reading Scripture out loud can help with the distraction. Prayer and meditation (on God and His Word) help keep you reaching upward for His presence and the divine potential of His power. This is where the real possibilities lie. Prayer helps reveal the stumbling blocks in your relationship with God and helps you feel closer to Him. Your sense of God's presence will empower healthy action. Hanging out with the wrong crowd can get you in trouble. Hanging out with the right people can make you better. Hanging out with God can make you whole and strong. Feelings motivate action. The more you pray, the closer you feel to God. The closer you feel to God, the easier it is to make constructive, God-honoring decisions, model the fruit of the Spirit, and resist temptation. Use prayer to draw closer to God and leverage those positive feelings as much as possible to strengthen your resilience in hard times.

Like Scripture reading, many people like to start their day in prayer. I have always found it easier to spend my longest time in prayer at the end of the day. However, I recommend you start your day in prayer. You wouldn't get ready, eat breakfast, clean up, and leave for work without ever saying a word to the family you love, right? Similarly, greet God when you wake up. Start your day in communion with Him. Regardless of when, find a time and make it work. If you miss a day, don't get discouraged. Keep at it. Paul encouraged believers to pray continually.[177] That means you continue a conversation with God all through the day. When you get yourself in the mindset that God is always with you, it becomes easier to speak out to Him with your joys, sorrows, needs, thanks, etc. Make time each day for dedicated time to talk to God. Continue the conversation all through the day and close with a thank you prayer. David wrote, "It is good to praise the Lord…proclaiming your love in the morning and your faithfulness at night."[178] Your relationship with God will deepen and change your life.

More Prayer, More Possibilities

The spiritual disciplines open the aperture of your life to God, His work, and the possibility of His help in your difficulties. Prayer, as with any communication, strengthens the relationship. Some people talk vaguely about the power of prayer as if it has some inherent benefit apart from God. Apart from God, there is no power in prayer. Prayer is powerful because you are talking to your Divine Creator, who listens and responds. Prayer is not manipulation. It doesn't make God help you. You can't use your prayers like a magic spell attempting to force God's hand. You don't have to say the right words or pray a certain amount of time to ensure you are heard. In fact, Jesus pointed out that prayer is not about lengthy displays.[179] Prayer is communicating with God and then allowing Him to decide *how* and *when* to help. I confess I consciously remember very few times God responded on my timetable. But I guess that's the point, right? It's a dialogue, not a set of commands. In the military, Privates don't give Generals orders. Part of the dialogue is giving God permission to use His perfect judgment when and how He answers your prayers. Honestly, I wish it weren't the case. I want God to answer my prayers when I want Him to do it. But a key aspect of the spiritual life is submission. You must accept that God's in charge and that He knows better than you. He is God and the Master of not only the Universe but of your life. Trust

---
177 1 Thessalonians 5:16–17
178 Psalm 92:1–2
179 Matthew 6:7

Him to take care of you. Expect good things. Faith is key. You must believe in God, His goodness, His faithfulness to the promises He has made you in Scripture, and you must act on those beliefs.[180] That is true faith. Much of the time, our lack is a failure to ask in faith. Faith is a recognition of the ability and willingness of God to help you in the here and now. As a man with military authority, the Centurion recognized Jesus' divine authority. He asked Jesus to heal a servant who was near death. Jesus offered to travel home with him to touch his servant, but the Centurion declined. "Just say the word, and he will be healed." He understood Jesus had the power to work miracles with a word. Jesus marveled at the Centurion's great faith. When He returned home, the Centurion found the servant healed.[181] With Centurion-like faith, you will see miraculous change in your life. With faith, you will persevere through hardship as you trust God's timing.

God wants to hear from you. He wants you to get to know Him so well, you are certain of His help. He wants to spend enough time with you to become best friends. And He wants to be your "go-to" option when you're in trouble, not your last resort. Your prayer life can help you realize God's dreams for your relationship with Him. You're never alone so don't let anyone convince you otherwise.[182] The more committed you are to the spiritual disciplines, the more you will feel close to God. Remember, everyone goes through seasons where they don't feel God is present. That's a normal part of the spiritual life. Difficulties affect you emotionally, making you feel sad, discouraged, and alone. But feelings don't lead your life. If you committed your life to Christ, you are a temple of the Holy Spirit. Jesus, by the Spirit, lives in your heart. He is with you everywhere you go, always, no matter what you feel. He will never leave you nor forsake you.[183] Nothing can separate you from His love and presence in your life.[184] Feelings are not the indicator of spiritual realities. Faith in God and His Word is the key. Let your faith, your spiritual senses, be your guide. Like the caboose on a train, feelings follow behind the engine. Keep asking, seeking, and knocking, believing that God is with you, cares about you, and is working on your behalf. Eventually, the positive feelings will catch up again. Prayer is a key in this process and in building your expectation for a multitude of possibilities in God.

Persevere in Prayer

Jesus taught a very important parable on prayer. He used the illustration of a woman bringing her case to an unjust judge. Because of her perseverance, she eventually got justice.[185] The lesson is to always pray and never give up.[186] The comparison between God and the unjust judge is in fact a con-

---
180 Hebrews 11:6, James 2:26, 2 Corinthians 1:20
181 Luke 7:2–10
182 Romans 8:38–39
183 Hebrews 13:5
184 Romans 8:38–39
185 Luke 18:1–8
186 Luke 18:1

trast—how much more will the just God who loves you answer requests over a judge who cares neither for you nor justice? If an unjust judge will respond to persistence, how much more will the just God who loves you respond? The point is, keep praying. Don't let anything stop you even when life seems unfair."

Sometimes, answers to prayer take time. The Word of God is like a seed. There is a natural process of planting, watering, growing, and bearing of fruit. That process begins the moment you pray in faith, sowing that seed. I want that seed to bear fruit immediately, and at times, God's miracle is instantaneous. Sometimes, however, God's answer is a process that works through stages of growth until it appears. God has told you the promises of Scripture are "Yes" in Christ, so you can say, "Amen."[187] So why the delay? Sometimes, people struggle to believe Him. God uses struggles in life to help you develop greater faith.[188] Jesus often challenged people to greater faith when they came with their needs. He told the lame man to pick up his mat and walk. He told the lepers to go wash in the river. If they had responded with, "No, I can't do that—I'm sick. I don't believe you can heal me," they would not have been healed. They obeyed, and they were healed. God is not the author of your suffering, but He will use it to grow your faith. He is working for you with the intent of turning the test into your testimony. As you pray, challenge yourself to believe with more certainty that God is the giver of every good and perfect gift, He is the rewarder of those who seek Him, and that He purposes to bring you a more blessed and abundant life.[189] Your faith can shorten the wait. Sometimes, the reason for the delay is unknowable. Trust God for the timing as you wait for additional direction. Trust that he loves you beyond comprehension and has your best interest in mind. Do not let the enemy assign meaning to the delay. Delays do not mean God is against you. They can have important benefits even when you cannot understand the reasons.

Sometimes, answers to prayer get delayed through the work of the enemy. Daniel waited three weeks for an answer to prayer because the enemy tried to prevent it from coming.[190] Maybe your answer is delayed for a similar reason—heavenly battles. Maybe your answer is caught up in the battles someone else endures as a human messenger. Fear or doubt can keep someone from sharing a message from God for you. Maybe it is held hostage in the spiritual battles within your own mind. The loud voices of stress and worry can keep you from hearing the still, small voice of the Holy Spirit. Sometimes, you must battle in prayer through the delays without fully knowing what is happening or why. In these situations, patience is key. Scripture is clear: If you continue to stand—not giving up—you will overcome.[191] You may receive your answer and victory only to have the same problem or issue happen again. The enemy will try to get you to quit. He will try to make you think that your problem has come back for good, that your victory was only temporary. Do not believe this lie. Remember, you are in a spiritual battle. It's not natural warfare. It involves arguments (thoughts, lines of reasoning, and conclusions) that

---
187 2 Corinthians 1:20
188 1 Peter 1:7
189 James 1:17
190 Daniel 10:12–14
191 Ephesians 6:6–10

set themselves against God and His work in your life. You must take captive these negative thoughts and replace them with Scripture and faith.[192] If you keep pushing back in prayer against what you see and feel in your circumstances, you will secure the victory for good. You walk by faith (spiritual sight), not by natural sight. Let your spiritual sight be your guide. You must persevere in prayer, regardless of how many times you revisit the same problem or circumstance, no matter how long it takes. Stand on Scripture and your faith in God, and you will win the victory.

Fasting

"Return to me with all your heart, with fasting."[193]

Fast regularly! The Pharisees fasted twice a week. Tradition holds the early disciples also fasted twice a week after Jesus ascended. Fasting helps you draw closer to God. It amplifies your prayer volume. It thins the wall between heaven and Earth, making you feel closer to God. You will likely hear the leading of the Spirit more clearly and will feel greater conviction that your prayers are heard. Fasting is an essential spiritual discipline and can be very helpful when you face adversity.[194] You can make shorter fasts a regular part of your schedule but be open to the leading of the Spirit to longer periods of time (three to ten days). I have fasted longer than ten days, but I recommend it only with a high level of conviction that God is leading you. Jesus taught the disciples, saying, "When you fast…" indicating it was as important a discipline as prayer and helping those in need.[195]

Fasting strengthens your resilience by helping you draw closer to God and helping you recognize that He is with you and will bring change to your situation. It amplifies your requests, demonstrating that you not only believe God can help but that your best hope is His help. God is spirit. Fasting helps your spirit connect to the Spirit of God in a mysterious yet meaningful way. It increases your sensitivity to the leading of the Holy Spirit and the use of your spiritual gifts. It helps you disconnect from the focus on your normal physical needs and wants to prioritize God and strengthening your faith in Him.

On a physical level, it provides a positive distraction from the feelings of suffering and stress by shifting your focus to hunger. This phenomenon is reminiscent of the adage, "Let me help take away the pain in your hand by stomping on your foot." It sounds minor, but this distraction is significant. Fasting redirects your inner emphasis to the spiritual without conscious effort. You don't have to feel spiritual to reap the benefits. It is also a powerful way to stretch self-control. Fasting will promote self-discipline in every other area of your life.

---
192 2 Corinthians 10:3–5
193 Joel 2:12
194 Matthew 6:16–18
195 Ibid.

David knew the importance of fasting. When he faced the deathly sickness of his young son, he fasted and prayed.[196] He did not relent until God answered him. Unfortunately, the answer was not what David wanted to hear. But he fervently sought God, knowing that God's power could bring about his son's healing. Because of their intimate relationship, David knew God was his Divine Healer. He understood that if he fervently sought God through fasting, He might change his mind. God's character never changes, His prevailing quality is love and mercy, but He does change His mind.[197] You can appeal to His mercy by demonstrating your humble surrender to His will for your life.[198] David's faith underscores a key point. You must fundamentally believe that God desires to bless you with good things.[199]

Biblical fasting normally means abstaining from eating and drinking water only for a specified length of time. However, throughout the centuries, the Christian community has exercised many types of fasting. Some deny themselves certain types of food like sweets or a favorite food. Some eat only fruits and vegetables, as Daniel did in captivity.[200] You decide the details as you feel led by the Lord. Breakthroughs in your struggles can happen. Every time I've fasted, I've sensed God's presence and power at a higher level. Usually, this realization comes later in the fast, during prayer or ministering to others. God's power seems more readily available. Fasting has several purposes, such as deepening your spiritual growth. Other purposes are seeking God for His will, a specific answer to prayer, or for power to serve. Fasting can transform your character. Be cautious about asking God for a breakthrough but mistreating others in the process. God is moved by your faith but also by your obedience to His Word. If you're looking for your circumstances to radically change, you must ensure you treat others with love and honor God in your actions.[201] What good is it for God to do miracles in your life if you use His blessings to take advantage of others? God cares about your struggles, but He is more concerned about your relationship with Him and the long-term character of your life more so than the short-term relief from a difficult circumstance. Difficulties come and go, but your spiritual life is eternal.

Sometimes, people face roadblocks that prevent progress. They get stuck. These obstacles can be normal life occurrences or have a spiritual origin. Jesus healed a sick boy who was bound by an evil spirit. The spirit caused such shocking symptoms (convulsions rolling on the ground, foaming at the mouth), the disciples, overwhelmed by what they saw, lost confidence (faith) in their ability to cast out the spirit. After healing the boy, Jesus used the moment as a teaching point to state, "This kind (circumstances that shock the senses such as this evil spirit caused) can only come out through prayer and fasting."[202] Some obstacles appear so large, so intimidating, you need an extra source of leverage to turn them around. Fasting can help you revitalize your faith and provide the edge you need. If you sense a persistent road-

---
196 2 Samuel 12:16
197 Jonah 3:10
198 Jonah 3:10
199 Hebrews 11:6
200 Daniel 1:12, 16, 10:3
201 Isaiah 58:5–8
202 Mark 9:29

block is hindering your progress, it could be an indicator you need to fast. Ask God to lead you in the details of the fast, and then step out in His timing. Whether your roadblock has a demonic influence is often unknown. In one sense, it doesn't matter. An obstacle is an obstacle, and God's power is easily enough for either.

Fasting is difficult, especially if you are led to a multiday fast. The first day, you become aware of your desire for food. The body screams out for it with aches and hunger pains. You also become keenly aware of the positive emotions associated with eating. During the fast, you may feel sad. Drink lots of water to stay hydrated. If you fast for more than a day or two, you will reach a point beyond the hunger pains. You are less focused on food cravings but still may feel weak, tired, or uncomfortable. If you are stressed out by your struggles, fasting can eclipse those emotions and help your mind find greater peace. In your spiritual focus, progress may be occurring, but you're not sensing much of anything. That dynamic can convince you to quit your fast early. I've been tempted to quit the fast sooner than originally intended almost every time. The key is obedience. Follow God's leading in your timing and method. Fasting is difficult, but you will be glad you persevered. You are building your relationship with God and moving mountains in the spiritual realm, even if you are only vaguely aware of your progress.

Worship

"I remember how I used to go up with the procession to worship God with joy."[203]

—David

Worship every day! Worship describes the acts you do that communicate the value and worth of God in your life. Prayer and singing are the normal mediums of worship, but it may also include any actions with the intent to honor God. Paul encouraged believers to present themselves as a living sacrifice of worship to God.[204] The idea here is that your whole life, everything you do, can be an expression of worship. Your faith is a relationship with God. Like reading the Scripture and prayer, worship is a way of communicating with God. People in love say, "I love you," often. Sometimes, they write a poem or sing a love song to their loved one. They reignite their own passion as they seek to increase the esteem of another. Worship works the same way. As you let God know how you feel, you not only invoke His favor, but you also increase your own attachment. Worship helps you feel closer to God. In times of struggle, people feel distant. Where is God right now? Does He really care? Will He help? Worship is an important remedy for doubts. It's empowering. It helps you feel closer and changes your focus from your struggles to God's goodness and power. The more God fills your view, the more your problems diminish. To overcome, God must become bigger than your struggle. You increase resilience by orienting your mind in a positive direction and by pursuing communion and intimacy. The resulting feelings of

---
203 Psalm 42:4
204 Romans 12:1

hope, peace, and meaningfulness empower you for constructive action. The simple act of worship helps spiritually reset your perspective.

It's not difficult to find time to worship each day. The hard part is making the change of habit. Look for alone time where you can play some praise music you like and sing along; the shower, the drive in the car to work, the bus with a set of headphones, a walk or run outside. Even when you're not alone, a set of headphones with worship music playing can be a great background when you're busy. The important thing is that you focus your thoughts on God at some point in your day. It is in the communion with God that worship finds its true power in your life.

Music is powerful. The enemy knows the power of worship; Scripture indicates he was anointed to serve in worship on the holy mountain of God before he fell.[205] Music fills people with joy and has many other positive effects. Music is based on a mathematical scale, and some music, such as classical, can literally help your mind recalibrate. You can think more clearly and be more productive. The power of music also has a dark side the enemy uses to sow discouragement, regrets, and deception. He effectively uses music to promote the worst in human character and behavior. Some types of music intentionally distort mathematical scale and disrupt your thinking. The point is music is intrinsically powerful. Music touches the emotions, releasing endorphins that make you feel happy and encouraged, sad, unsettled, or depressed.[206] Avoid music that will trouble, discourage, or depress you. Sad or nostalgic music can seem gratifying, but it can also make you feel helplessness and self-pity. Harness the power of music in worship to uplift and encourage yourself in hard times. Make time each morning to worship God in prayer or music. Commute time can be a great time to worship. You will strengthen your inner being and increase your motivation for action when you start your day worshipping.

The Book of Revelation describes a spectacular scene around the throne of God that exceeds any earthly concert.

> And the one [God] who sat there had the appearance of jasper and ruby. A rainbow that shone like an emerald encircled the throne. From the throne came flashes of lightning, rumblings, and peals of thunder. In front of the throne, seven lamps were blazing. These are the seven spirits of God. Also, in front of the throne there was what looked like a sea of glass, clear as crystal.[207] Then I looked and heard the voice of many angels, numbering thousands upon thousands, and ten thousand times ten thousand. They encircled the throne and the living creatures and the elders. In a loud voice they were saying: "Worthy is the Lamb, who was slain, to receive power and wealth and wisdom and strength and honor and glory and praise!" Then I heard every creature in heaven

---
205 Ezekiel 28:12–14
206 Vanessa Van Edwards, *"The Benefits of Music: How the Science of Music Can Help You,"* accessed November 12, 2022, https://www.scienceofpeople.com/benefits-music/#music-improves-workouts.
207 Revelation 4:3–6

and on earth and under the earth and on the sea, and all that is in them, saying: "To him who sits on the throne and to the Lamb be praise and honor and glory and power, for ever and ever!"[208]

Today's large concerts feature numerous instruments, groups of singers, dancers, and fantastic light shows in modern auditoriums. All pale in comparison to the flashes of lightning, thunder, brilliant colors, vast sea of glass, and the singing of hundreds of millions of angels and every creature on earth in this heavenly scene. What a day that will be! When I was young, I thought of heaven as beautiful but boring. This passage describes a divinely orchestrated rock concert, with live shows every day, complete with lighting, special effects, an awesome sound system, and pyrotechnics. Best of all, we will be with God and know the joy of His presence. There is no feeling on earth that compares to how it will feel to worship God in heaven. Today, you can feel encouraged and strengthened by joining the heavenly assembly in worship. Paul spoke of the supremacy of Christ and the day when every knee would bow, and every tongue confess, in heaven and on earth and under the earth, that Jesus Christ is Lord.[209] Believers have the privilege to worship God here and now and to join the worship assembly of Revelation 4–5. If you worship Christ now, you will be ready and willing to do it on that day when every human, angel, and demonic spirit will have to acknowledge Christ. God will sadly remand billions of people and every fallen angel to the lake of fire (what we commonly call *hell*) for failing to acknowledge Christ while on earth. From that moment on, those billions will beg for the opportunity to join the assembly of worshippers around God's throne. But their cry will never be heard because they rejected His free offer of mercy and grace. What a privilege to be able to worship God here and now! And what an awesome expectation to eventually join billions of angels and all creation in worship in the fullness of God's presence.

Consider that every time you worship, you spiritually connect with God's throne room and thousands upon thousands of angels, cherubim, and seraphim. These are not chubby little babies with cute wings. These are powerful supernatural beings that reflect the glory of God. They stand in His presence. Gabriel rebuked Zechariah, the father of John the Baptist, for doubting his words. He said, "I am Gabriel. I stand in the presence of God, and I have been sent to speak to you and to tell you this good news. And now you will be silent and not able to speak until the day this happens because you did not believe my words, which will come true at their appointed time."[210] Gabriel knew God's power and authority were without question because he experienced them firsthand. When you stand in God's presence, your perspective radically changes. Seek God in worship and pursue His presence. You will strengthen your faith and equip yourself to withstand adversity.

David was a worshipper! Countless Psalms express his love of God.

---

208 Revelation 5:11–13
209 Ephesians 2:5–11
210 Luke 1:19–20

I will exalt you, my God the King; I will praise your name for ever and ever. Every day I will praise you and extol your name for ever and ever. Great is the Lord and most worthy of praise; his greatness no one can fathom. One generation commends your works to another; they tell of your mighty acts. They speak of the glorious splendor of your majesty—and I will meditate on your wonderful works. They tell of the power of your awesome works—and I will proclaim your great deeds. They celebrate your abundant goodness and joyfully sing of your righteousness. The Lord is gracious and compassionate, slow to anger and rich in love. The Lord is good to all; he has compassion on all he has made. All your works praise you, Lord; your faithful people extol you.[211]

David praised God, describing the greatness of God's character and works, calling people everywhere to honor Him. The excitement expressed through his choice of words communicates the sincerity of his heart. The Psalms reveal the intimate relationship David had with God and the openness with which he shared his feelings through good and bad times. This is one reason they stand as a model for believers today. The Holy Spirit used David's gift for transcribing timeless poems to encourage you to sing or speak your love for God today. The essence of worship is found in expressing your heart of love to God. David's consistent worship practice is one reason why he was able to find strength in God at his low point. From a young age, he was crying out to God, seeking Him, sharing his heart, celebrating with songs of praise, and finding comfort when troubled. It was second nature for David to reach out to God, so it was automatic when he faced loss at Ziklag. You want to get to the place where praise, worship, and seeking God in prayer and fasting become second nature. That is where you commune with the one person who knows you better than your best friend, loves you more than your closest family members, and has the means to help you through the best and worst that life may bring.

---

[211] Psalm 145

Spiritual Discipline 3

Trust God!

"Blessed is the man who makes the Lord his Trust."[212]

—**David**

Those who trust the Lord lack no good thing.[213]

Trust God no matter what happens! Trust is the action part of faith. Faith is a belief in God, His Word, and His promises that inspires you to trust Him in God-honoring or obedient action. Simply put, faith equals belief plus trust. It is the confidence to trust in God and His promises. The challenge of faith is to trust Him despite what you may feel emotionally, reason out in your mind, or see with your natural sight or senses. Life happens—both good and bad circumstances. Hard times may challenge your confidence in God to see you through to the other side. You must live by spiritual sight—what God has promised in His Word or spoken to your heart, above your physical sight.[214] Faith is what you need in the middle of your struggle when the problem is all you see with natural sight. Faith is needed before you see the manifestation of God's promise. In fact, your faith appropriates God's promise to make it your present reality. You can strengthen your faith by envisioning God's promise to you, making the picture of answered prayers more important to you than what you see right now. David faced Goliath, proclaiming a vision of what would happen, "This day I will strike you down and cut off your head."[215] David saw with natural sight what Israel's army saw, a giant, nine feet nine inches tall with intimidating weapons and armor. Israel's army could not see past their natural sight, so they hid in fear. To the army, David was no match for Goliath. David saw with spiritual sight. A nine-foot-tall giant was no match for the God David trusted. In fact, with spiritual sight, it was clear that Goliath was no match for David. David's spiritual sight was far more relevant to His future outcome than His natural senses. You can be like David. Your faith and trust in God can change the odds and shape your outcomes. We will discuss faith in greater detail in a future chapter, but trust means you face your struggles with spiritual sight.

Remember "Doubting Thomas?" After the resurrection, he had to see Jesus' scars with his own eyes. When Jesus finally revealed Himself to Thomas, He told him plainly, "Stop doubting and believe."[216] After stubbornly promising His fellow disciples he would not believe Jesus was alive until he saw and

---
212 Psalm 40:4
213 Psalm 34:10
214 2 Corinthians 5:7
215 1 Samuel 17: 46
216 John 20:24–29

touched Him, Thomas knelt and worshipped. Jesus continued the teachable moment, "You believe because you have seen. Blessed are those who have not seen and yet believe."[217] In Christ, spiritual sight is a better guide for your life. Trust is all about acting on what's inside of you (belief, faith) when what's happening around you (natural sight) is not going your way. Trust is one of the big challenges you face during adversity. Paul assured believers that all God's promises are "Yes!" in Christ Jesus, and so we can speak the "Amen."[218] Amen literally means, "Let it be," you agree with God, it will come to pass. It is challenging to stand on a promise from a God you cannot see when things get tough. The key is to speak the amen by faith to His promises when you cannot see with natural sight. You must agree with God's promise when others doubt. God responds to the person who believes, who stands in agreement with Him in the middle of the struggle. Without faith, it is impossible to please God.[219] God is no respecter of persons.[220] You don't have to be David to see a breakthrough; simply be like him. God is searching for those who will stand when they do not see, who believe He exists, and rewards those who trust Him.[221] Demonstrate better sight than Thomas. Your eyes are only a snapshot in time. Trust spiritual sight to lead you through to God's promise.

During Job's great struggle, his wife told him to curse God and die. Job's reply, "Can we accept good from God and not adversity?"[222] He recognized bad things happen along with the good. Life is not always fair. But he also trusted the God who is always fair and good. The world functions by natural laws of cause and effect. Everyone experiences days of sun and days of rain. The label, good or bad, is relative. If you are a farmer, the rain may be great. If you are a baseball player at game time, the rain is terrible. If you're living through a drought, rain is great. If you're in flood, rain is deadly. What is bad in the moment may turn out to be good.[223] While bad things may be happening to you, God is also working to bring about good in your life. In Christ, "bad things" may be happening *for* you. The promise from Scripture is to make all things work for good in your life as you follow Him.[224] Part of that good is God's work to resolve your problem. Another part of that good is the personal and spiritual growth that will strengthen you for the future. Still, another part is the silver lining when some unexpected blessing comes from the effects of the problem. The storm that knocked over your house provided an opportunity for something better.

When I was in middle school, a fire burned our house to the ground. Our house was an old tavern from the 1800s. We had to heat it with a wood furnace. It meant a lot of my weekends in the summer were spent cutting firewood in the mountains, and it meant very cold mornings in the winter waiting for

---
217 Ibid.
218 2 Corinthians 1:20
219 Hebrews 11:6
220 Acts 10:34
221 2 Chronicles 16:9, Hebrews 11:6
222 Job 2:10 (NAS)
223 Ecclesiastes 3:1
224 Romans 8:28

the house to heat up. It was so cold, we tried everything to stay in bed as long as possible. After the fire, the community gave us clothes, household items, and toys to help. I will never forget the generosity of those in our town. Six months later, we had a new house with a real furnace; no more cold mornings and no more wasted summers. God didn't burn our house down, but He sure did bless us through the love and concern of our community, plus we got a brand-new house. Do you trust God to confirm faithfulness to His Word, or will you take matters into your own hands? Will you allow worry, anxiety, fear, and stress to drive you toward selfish reactions, or will you patiently, peacefully wait on God's timing? David wrote, "The righteous person may have many troubles, but the Lord delivers him from them all."[225] Don't let the experience of trouble keep you from experiencing God's deliverance. Trusting God calls in God's blessings, strengthens your inner being, and makes you more resilient for the next challenge.

Every day, you face numerous decision points. Do you trust God to handle the situation, or do you take matters into your own hands, reacting from a self-centered perspective? The Ten Commandments are a God-centric way of interacting with your world. Do you put God first or something else in your life? Do you ensure your speech is God-focused? Do you commit time to worship God each week? Do you submit to earthly authorities in your life as unto the Lord? Do you trust God to provide what you need, or do you focus on what you don't have (covet) and try to take it for yourself (steal, manipulate/deceive, commit adultery)? Do you trust God to punish those who wrong you, or do you try to take matters into your own hands (revenge, murder)? Your level of trust is evident through your actions and reactions. Scripture highlights the benefits of trust, "Do not be anxious about anything, but in every situation, by prayer and petition, present your requests to God. And the peace that surpasses all understanding will guard your heart and mind."[226] When you trust God to help, your prayers produce a protective layer of peace. Fight for God's peace. Reject doing it your way, and you will prevent worry and stress from controlling your mind.

**Figure 3a.
The Faith Spectrum**

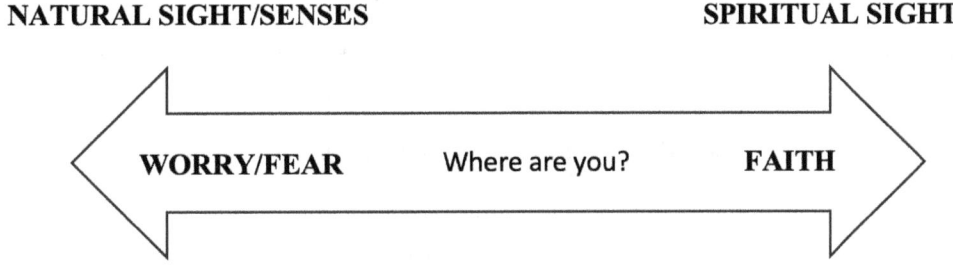

---

225 Psalm 34:19
226 Philippians 4:6–7

Trust is the opposite of worry and fear. Trust and worry are at opposite ends of the same spectrum (faith). To the degree you trust God, you will not worry. To the degree you are worrying, or in fear, you are not trusting God. You can rely on God or rely on your own strength. Jesus said simply, "Do not worry."[227] That's easy to say but much harder to live. The command requires trust in God to take care of you. In the same way He sustains His creation, God knows what you need and will provide it for you. Practically, Jesus appeals to the logic that worry is neither a constructive approach nor a solution to a problem. Jesus asked, "Can anyone by worrying add a single hour to your life?"[228] Worry is worse than just not being helpful; it is destructive. Studies have shown that stress shortens your life. Some speculate by as much as ten years. Like smoking, worry is toxic. Each cigarette takes seven to eleven minutes off your life.[229] Habitual smokers can shorten their lives by eight years. In the same way, your worry and anxiety have long-term effects. Excessive amounts of the stress hormone cortisol, regulating the fight-or-flight response, can lower your immune system and reduce heart health. Today's worrisome reactions can predict your chronic health conditions ten years from now.[230] Reduce stress by trusting God. Jesus offered an alternative, "Seek first God's kingdom and his righteousness and let God take care of everything else."[231] This promise is the reason we began the section with the disciplines of Scripture reading and prayer. They provide the key "seeking" disciplines to deepen your relationship with God, strengthen your inner being, and make you more resilient.

At Ziklag, David faced a level of adversity he had never faced before. Everything precious to him was gone. His "mighty men," renowned for their great feats and loyalty, wanted to kill him. He had only one person he could lean on—God. No matter what your situation, God is enough. I've heard it said, "You and God are a majority." God told King Amaziah, David's descendant, "God can give you much more than [you lost]."[232] Job found this promise to be true as well.[233] If David had known the outcome, how much he was going to gain, the struggle wouldn't have mattered much. But in the moment when he didn't know, his loss was devastating. Despite the magnitude of his pain, David trusted God. Your ability to trust God is one of the decisive challenges you face during suffering. It is a discipline because you must make the choice to walk by faith (spiritual sight), not trusting your natural senses.

I don't know about you, but there is an uneasy question that always rises to the surface when I hear about or face great trouble. That question is, "Why?" How could God allow His servant David, a man after God's heart, to suffer such loss? Couldn't He have prevented Ziklag's fall? How can God allow the innocent to suffer? How can God allow you to suffer? After years of considering "Why?" I'm convinced

---

227 Matthew 6:25
228 Matthew 6:27
229 Mary, Shaw, Richard Mitchell, and Danny Dorling, "*Time for a Smoke,*" accessed December 7, 2022, https://www.ncbi.nlm.nih.gov/pmc/articles/PMC1117323/.
230 Mark Stibich, "How Anxiety Affects Health and Longevity," accessed May 28, 2022, https://www.verywellmind.com/worry-and-anxiety-impact-longevity-2223983.
231 Matthew 6:33
232 2 Chronicles 25:9
233 Job 42:11–12,16–17

it's irrelevant. "Why?" is not a constructive question in struggles because it is usually unknowable. What really caused your problem? Was it your sin, someone else's sin, or, like Job, part of the enemy's greater strategy to drive a wedge between you and God? It is a given the enemy will use any situation to cast doubts on your trust in God. If he can get you questioning God's fairness or faithfulness to His Word, he's nearly won the battle. Consider Job. He didn't know the answer to "Why?" at the time of his struggle, but his story shows us he didn't need to know. Most of the Book of Job is vain speculation about the "Why," yet it was more of a hindrance than a help. Job's friends said a lot but very little that helped him. Job ultimately had to pray for them as they offered sacrifices for their sin. God was angry they had not spoken truth about him.[234] Do not make your situation worse by vocalizing your unbelief. Where words are many, sin is not absent.[235] Job said his piece, but at the end, when God spoke to him, he acknowledged that he should have kept his mouth shut.[236] He repented of his words and the knowledge gap between the God he thought he knew and the God he came to know.[237] You have a mental picture of God; we all do. Your struggles will force you to re-evaluate who God is and what you believe. Use the situation to refine your faith and character. Stand firm in your faith and Scripture through this process so that you don't repeat the mistakes of Job and his friends.

God is not responsible for troubles that come into your life. Only good and perfect gifts come from Him.[238] Many people look at the harshness of life on this earth and cannot see the work of a good God who created it all. The truth is the earth is not like it was at the time of creation. When God created the earth and called it good, there were no predators. No meat-eating creatures of any kind were initially created by God because He gave all creatures, along with mankind, only plants and fruit to eat.[239] God did not create carnivores because the "survival of the fittest" principle did not exist in the Garden of Eden. Mankind lived in perfect harmony with nature as vegetarians. Animals had no fear of man (they were not food), and Adam and Eve took care of the Garden and its creatures. No hurricanes, floods, tornadoes, earthquakes, or any such storms occurred in this harmonious natural environment. In the pre-flood world, based upon the creation narrative, the earth was likely a high-pressure, high-oxygenated environment like a hyperbaric chamber where everything grew larger and stronger in the fertile conditions.[240] Adam and Eve were created as immortal beings free to eat from the Tree of Life. There was no sickness, sorrow, or pain.[241] This beautiful, idyllic world, a literal paradise, was shattered because of the disobedience of Adam and Eve. They chose to do the only thing they were forbidden to do in the Garden—eat from the one tree they were instructed to avoid, of thousands (or millions), the Tree of the

---
234 Job 42:1–9
235 Proverbs 10:19
236 Job 40:5
237 Job 42:5–6
238 James 1:17
239 Genesis 1:29–31
240 Genesis 6:1–10
241 Genesis 2:9, 16–17

Knowledge of Good and Evil.[242] It is unbelievable they chose to break the only limitation they had in a world of limitless beauty, peace, and joy where God came down to the Garden and met with them.[243] This one act of sin fractured their relationship with God and all of creation with it. The natural order was fundamentally changed into one of antagonism toward man and hostility between the creatures as the present "survival of the fittest" principle became reality.[244] Death came into the world for the very first time as God killed animals to create garments of skin to cover Adam and Eve. The now mortal couple was banished from the Garden to eventually die as warned.[245] Paul confirmed these truths in Scripture that natural creation was subjected to frustration by sin and is now in bondage and decay.[246] Creation cannot wait to be restored to its original state when Christ returns. This brings us to one reason all people suffer so much trouble in life, sin. The original sin of Adam and Eve transformed God's perfect world of harmony into a dangerous, predatorial, kill-or-be-killed environment where you must live on high alert all the time. Stress, fear, and worry dominate the human psyche in a dangerous world of strife. The curse that Adam brought on creation continues to affect you, producing troubles even when you have not done anything to directly cause them. Original sin, not God, has become a primary source of problems and human affliction to this day.

God rewards those who seek and follow Him, but personal sin, like original sin, produces negative consequences and harsh second, third, and fourth order effects. The harmful results of personal sin are illustrated in the life of David. David slept with Bathsheba in an adulterous liaison that produced a child. To cover his sin, David sent her husband, Uriah, one of David's elite mighty men, to perish in the front lines of battle. David's sin of adultery and murder brought about the death of his child.[247] God sent the prophet Nathan to point out his sin, producing one of the most beautiful Psalms in the Bible, Psalm 51, the Psalm of Repentance. One of the powerful messages in this story is God's mercy. You might think God would curse David's marriage to Bathsheba because of its foundation in sin. On the contrary, Scripture records how God loved their next child, Solomon. He eventually became King of Israel and led the kingdom through the glory days of Israel's powerful, prosperous era of global influence. Even in difficulties caused by your own sin, God is merciful. You cannot allow the enemy to lure you into condemnation even when you may be at fault.[248] Paul encouraged believers in Rome, "There is now no condemnation for those who are in Christ Jesus."[249] God has already accounted for all the sin you will ever commit, and still, His mercy abounds to you. God is the ultimate recycler. He even uses the trash in life, the debris of your sin, to bring about good for you.

---

242 Genesis 1:17
243 Genesis 3:8
244 Genesis 3:17–19
245 Genesis 3:21–23
246 Romans 8:19–22
247 2 Samuel 11:1–12:25
248 Romans 8:1
249 Romans 8:1

Spiritual Discipline 3

The Bible is very clear that the big answer to "Why do you have troubles?" is Satan, the accuser, your adversary. Jesus said, "The enemy comes to steal, kill, and destroy."[250] He is a liar and the father of lies."[251] He is a manipulative, destructive spiritual force greater than anything except God and the most powerful angels. He is not the funny cartoon character with the cute horns, red suit, and trident. He is a powerful, superior intellect with a malevolence only surpassed by the depth of God's love. There is no negotiation or truce. His aim is the total destruction of humanity, the object of God's love and mercy. The reason you don't have to live in fear is because of Jesus. The Holy Spirit is at work in the world restraining evil, and in Christ, you walk in the protection not only of God's angels but in the power of Christ's blood and the protective intercession of Christ Himself.[252] The Holy Spirit lives in you, and you are spiritually seated with Christ in heavenly places with authority over your enemy.[253] One day, God will crush Satan underneath your feet.[254] While the devil is working, Christ also is working. Jesus said, "I have come that you may enjoy life and have it in abundance.[255] Scripture is clear that the growth of evil in this world originates in the destructive work of Satan and demonic powers.[256] At the same time, they are defeated foes; destruction is their destiny.[257] It is critically important to practice spiritual disciplines at all times, especially in trials, to protect yourself with the armor of God. God's truth, salvation, prayer, faith, obedience, and knowledge of the Word of God all function as protective armor and spiritual weapons in your battles against the enemy.[258] Put on your spiritual armor, stand in the battle, and trust God for the outcomes. You will overcome.

The "Why?" question is ultimately irrelevant in the battle, but we have examined the reasons for it to encourage you to trust God and not get stuck on "Why?" I'm always amazed that people ask, "Why do bad things happen to good people?" and then blame God. God is an easy target when things get tough. After all, He is omnipotent. He could have prevented your trouble, right? Unfortunately, I do not agree. Lots of things happening on this Earth are outside God's will. God did not plan to have the Israelites wander for an extra thirty-nine years in the wilderness. The delay came from their refusal to fight for the land.[259] It was flat-out disobedience. God wants every person to know Him personally.[260] He desires no one be lost. This truth is expressed in both the Old and New Testaments of Scripture.[261] Yet, many refuse to accept His love through Christ. Every lie, theft, and act of murder is outside God's will. These are just a few of countless examples of events outside the will of God. Scripture is given to help people follow God's will, thereby preventing a lot of trouble in this life.

---

250 John 10:10
251 John 8:44
252 Romans 8:26
253 Ephesians 2:6
254 Romans 16:20
255 John 10:10b (AMP)
256 Ephesians 6:12
257 John 12:31, Matthew 25:41
258 Ephesians 6:10–18
259 Numbers 14
260 John 5:34
261 Isaiah 45:22, Ezekiel 33:11, 1 Timothy 2:4, 2 Peter 3:9

Understand—God does not bring evil to your life.[262] His intentions are only good for you. Second, God doesn't promise your life will only be good all the time.[263] This world is at war. God doesn't insulate you from every trial because you are a participant in God's story. You're not on the bench; you are on the field of battle.[264] One day, the battle will end when Christ returns. Until then, you must run the race and fight the good fight of faith.[265] The good thing is the battle will not destroy you. In fact, you can grow through the struggles. David moved from shepherd to warrior to General through the battle with Goliath. Lifting weights is a physical example of a spiritual process. Lifting weights tears the muscle fibers so they can rebuild stronger than before. Struggles may break you down, but ultimately the process helps strengthen your spiritual muscles and resilience. Although God allows you to experience trials, He promises you victory from all of them.[266] He will also protect you from reaching your breaking point. "God is faithful; He will not let you be tempted beyond what you can bear. But when you are tempted [tested], He will also provide a way of escape so that you can endure it."[267] God will not allow you to break. He has His hand on the "emergency stop" switch. He promises to be with you always.[268] Jesus' best friend during His earthly ministry, John the beloved disciple, encouraged believers to walk in peace with this thought, "In this world you will have trouble, but take heart I [Jesus] have overcome the world [with all of its distress and suffering]."[269] Some people say, "Everything happens for a reason." That statement is self-evident. That's like saying 2+2=4. However, it doesn't explain anything. There is a cause for everything, but cause does not imply meaning. It does not mean God brought trouble on you to bring about some good. God does not bring trouble on you, but He will use the troubles of life for your good when you trust in Him. Some cynically say, "Nothing happens for a reason." The "why" ultimately doesn't matter. The truth of Scripture is, when you give your situation to God, He can make it profitable for you, no matter how bad it is.[270] Trust God regardless of the "why."

You can also blame God, thinking that if He did not keep you from trouble, He should have at least delivered you from it already. This speaks to the timeliness of God's help. I question God's timing sometimes as well. To be honest, the timeline for most of my prayer requests was yesterday. You may not appreciate God's timing but understand—you don't see everything God sees. Like a tapestry, God is weaving the lives of billions of people together in a plan to draw all of them closer to Him. God may tie answers to your struggles into His plan for others. Your story may just be the encouragement someone else needs. Paul encouraged believers with that same thought, "Praise be to the God of all comfort, who comforts us in all our troubles so that we can comfort those in any trouble with the comfort we have

---

262 James 1:17
263 John 16:33
264 Ephesians 6:10–13
265 1 Timothy 6:12
266 Psalm 34:19
267 1 Corinthians 10:13
268 Matthew 28:20
269 John 16:33 (AMP)
270 Romans 8:28

received."[271] I don't know exactly why God's timing is late for you but consider the possibility that God is right on time. Do not let the unknowns of your situation keep you from doing what you know you should do. The timing may remain a mystery, but I know that God loves you more than you realize. Life isn't always fair, people aren't always fair, but God is always fair. He is good, just, and perfectly righteous. Perhaps God is waiting on you. Have you told God how important the situation is to you? Have you asked Him specifically for His help? Prayer is an act of faith.[272] Faith asks God with a belief that God will reward you.[273] Are you expecting God to answer? You must stand on the promises of God. They must go from your head, what you know about, to your heart, your believer, where faith resides. Your knowledge must become the confidence that the Scripture you know in your head is going to be the promise God will fulfill in your life. Your faith will move God more than your need. Faith is the force that will sustain you throughout your spiritual life. You will always have needs, but your faith is the substance that will see you through them all. Perhaps God's timing is truly your best timing. I know that as much as you and I need God as Savior in our lives, we need Him as Lord and Master. We need to submit to His Lordship to thrive in this life. Spiritual rebels do not thrive in the spiritual life. It feels good, it is popular, but it is not constructive for the abundant life. God can be trusted to lead your life. Perhaps your answer will come when you get the truth of God's word deep in your heart. Place your complete trust in Him and see what happens.

James, the half-brother of Jesus, who, along with his brothers, didn't think much of Jesus during His earthly ministry, found his faith after the resurrection. He spoke some important counsel to early believers who faced persecution, displacement, and intense suffering. "When tempted [tested], no one should say, 'God is tempting me.' For God cannot be tempted by evil nor does he tempt anyone."[274] God doesn't play games with you or try to set you up for failure. Jesus, above all, as the sacrifice, once and for all, for all wrongdoing, knows the consequences of sin. He will not throw you off balance, so you stumble into evil. God is on your side, pulling for your success, leading you to overcome, and empowering you to defeat the enemy while growing closer to Him. James continued, "Don't be deceived… Every good and perfect gift is from above coming down from the Father of the heavenly lights who does not change."[275] God's work in your life brings good results, outcomes that bring blessings, health in your whole being, and strengthens your relationships with God and others. God wants you free from worry, fear, and depression.[276] God wants you healthy and whole.[277] God wants you free from the oppression of the enemy.[278] God wants you blessed in every way.[279] God wants your life to be a light in a

---
271 2 Corinthians 1:3–5
272 Matthew 7:7
273 Hebrews 11:6, James 4:2
274 James 1:13
275 James 1:16–17
276 Matthew 6:25–34, 2 Timothy 1:7, 2 Corinthians 4:8–9
277 Matthew 8:3
278 1 John 3:8
279 Ephesians 1:3

dark world.[280] Understand—God will use your struggles to bring about good in your life.[281] Constructive questions might be, "How can I get closer to God? How can I honor Him in my situation? How can I be an example/help to others? How can I grow in my faith and my relationships? What does God's best look like for me when He delivers me from this adversity?" Believe that no matter why this happened, God is working to produce something very good for your life. The fruit could be personal and spiritual growth, and it could be some material blessing. David found both through his test at Ziklag. Trust God. He deserves your trust.

Ultimately, trust is about deepening your relationship with God to the point where you are confident in His character, His attitude toward you, and that He is working for your best good. This empowers you to act on your beliefs in God. When you experience salvation, you accept Christ as your Savior and commit to making Him Lord of your life.[282] The process of maturing in your faith normally involves the growing understanding that Jesus is more than just the one who paid the penalty for your wrongdoing (Savior). He deserves to be your Lord—to have charge over your life. Lordship means you live your life for Christ.[283] As you deepen your relationship with God, you trust Him with more control. Some areas are harder to give to Him. You may feel safer if you have control over them. As you grow in your practice of the spiritual disciplines, you will deepen your relationship with God and expand His control of your life, such as in your time, your character, your relationships, your finances, and other important areas. You will feel safer and more secure entrusting these to Him. Salvation is vitally important. You begin your relationship with God by trusting Him to forgive you, place His Holy Spirit inside of you, and ensure your place with Him forever in heaven. But making Jesus Lord of your life is also very important. It means seeking His counsel, subordinating yourself to the principles of His Word, and pursuing His will for the direction of your life. You need His Lordship almost as much as you need His salvation. You are safer with God than going it on your own. As you trust Him enough to follow His Word and the leading of His Spirit, your faith releases His power to work for you. You are better off with Him in charge. The figure below illustrates as you grow closer to God, you give God more Lordship in your life, trusting Him to take care of your needs in the same way you trust Him for salvation. This a process of growing in faith and maturity as you get to know God better, trust Him more, and increase your reliance on Him for your everyday life.

---

280 Matthew 5:14–16
281 Romans 8:28
282 Romans 10:9–10
283 Romans 14:7–9

Figure 3b.
Development of Trust

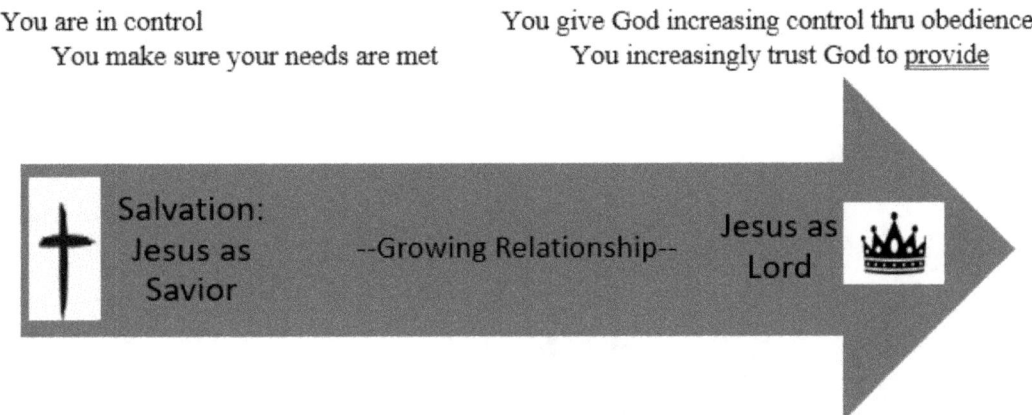

Relationships require trust to grow, but at the same time, trust grows as you get to know the other person, in this case, God, better. When you trust Him enough to rely on Him, you bring action to your beliefs about God and His Word. You release the power of your faith. We countered several issues that hinder trust to help you step out in greater confidence. We examined several accounts from Scripture where people trusted God when it was very difficult to do so. Get to know God better through reading the Word, prayer, fasting, and worship. These will help strengthen your trust and build courage to practice the remaining disciplines.

Spiritual Discipline 4

Express Gratitude

Praise the LORD, O my soul and forget not all his benefits.[284]

—**David**

Thank God for at least three good things each day. If you want to over-emphasize gratitude as a discipline, list seven each day (seven blessings, seven days a week—7x7). Roll your list into a short prayer and thank God for His blessings. As a pastor, I encouraged church members to go on a daily God hunt, recording the good things that happened each day along with their reflections on the events. It is a good practice for anyone. You can easily come up with three to seven reasons to be thankful each day. Do you have a job, a home, a family, people who love you, coworkers who support you, a good boss, food on the table, clothing, or a vehicle? Are you thankful for Jesus, God's love, salvation, healing, or other spiritual blessings? You probably have many things to be thankful for, but are you truly aware of how blessed you are? According to a 2018 newspaper article, if you are American, you probably profoundly underestimate how rich you are compared to the rest of the world. As the global median income then was about $2100 per year, most Americans ranked comfortably in the top 10 percent of the world's population.[285] That means, if you live in America, you are rich compared to the rest of the world. The article noted that most Americans do not appreciate how well they live compared to the rest of the world. Do not be one of those people. It is easy to focus on what you do not have. Some people will never be happy. They will always want more. More is a monster that devours the soul. Thank God for His blessings and be content with what you have. Give generously and ask for God's increase, but never forget—you are blessed.

The Scripture reminds believers to follow God's will by giving thanks in every situation."[286] Regardless of the struggle, it is God's will for you to give thanks. The reason is clear. Gratitude starts you down the path to victory. You may not have any other direction to conquer the problem at this point, but you can make a lot of progress by simply expressing thanks to God for all His blessings. The passage begins with, "Rejoice always." There is a strong connection between joy and gratitude. God created you. He knows it's not healthy for you to ruminate on the negatives in life, especially when you are facing serious struggles. Making a daily list of the good helps you remember that even in difficult circumstanc-

---
284 Psalm 103:1–2
285 Gautam Nair, "Most Americans Vastly Underestimate How Rich They Are Compared To The Rest Of The World. Does It Matter?" *Washington Post*, August 23, 2018, accessed December 07, 2022, https://www.washingtonpost.com/news/monkey-cage/wp/2018/08/23/most-americans-vastly-underestimate-how-rich-they-are-compared-with-the-rest-of-the-world-does-it-matter/.
286 1 Thessalonians 5:18

es, God is working. Life isn't perfect. When you focus on the negatives, even on a good day, the result is predictable: frustration, anger, and other destructive negative emotions. At the same time, the person with a grateful heart who thanks God for the daily blessings can rise above the frustrations of a bad day with an optimistic, joyful heart.

How does giving thanks help your resilience? Studies show that gratitude is associated with better psychological health, increased happiness, and life satisfaction.[287] Gratitude is a positive emotion generator. Positive emotions are not only important for your long-term mental health, but they are also critical in helping you overcome difficulties. When you reflect on good things, you inspire hope (spiritual optimism) and brighten your situation. Hope encourages positive action helping you to step out in faith to better your situation. God can choose to help at any time. He loves you and wants the best for you. But your faith leverages His power and promises. Picture your circumstances as quicksand. The resulting feelings of worry, fear, and stress only make you sink deeper. They are not only ineffective, but they also drain your energy. The way of escape lies outside the quicksand. You need to be still and search for a way of escape: a vine, tree root, or something else that can help. When you recognize and thank God for the good things in life, you look outside your situation. You reach out with optimism to the hope of God's help. After all, He has done it before, He can do it again. You feel empowered to act, trusting God to help. Can gratitude really strengthen your expectation for God to act? Scripture states believing God rewards those who seek Him pleases Him.[288] So, the answer is yes—gratitude is a powerful act of faith.

David frequently worshipped with gratitude. Worship and thanksgiving were part of David's spiritual DNA. He wrote, "It is good to praise [thank] the Lord and make music to your name, O Most High, proclaiming your love in the morning and your faithfulness at night."[289] Other translations of this verse state it plainly: It is wonderful, beautiful, and beneficial to give thanks each day. David thanked God for His love every morning and His faithfulness every night. David had a daily ritual. He thought back on how God had been faithful throughout his day and specifically thanked Him for all the ways He had blessed him. Is it no wonder God called David a man after his own heart?[290] David's gratitude not only drew him closer to God, but it also strengthened his optimism and inner being. He believed no matter what he faced on a given day, God would be faithful to see him through. This level of spiritual confidence is essential when you face difficulties. Thankfulness paves the way.

I encourage you to record your answered prayers, successes, and victories in a journal. Journaling will give you the strength to confront your current challenges as you look back and remember God's past faithfulness. In one sense, the Bible is a record of God's faithfulness. Use the Bible and your journal to encourage you in your present difficulties. The journal entries you write today will help you remember

---

287 Summer Allen, *The Science of Gratitude*," May 2018, accessed November 13, 2022, https://Ggsc.berkeley.edu/images/uploads/GGSC-JTF_White_Paper-Gratitude-FINAL.pdf.
288 Hebrews 11:5
289 Psalm 92:1–2
290 Acts 13:22

God's faithfulness in the future fight. Collect your thoughts and feelings. Your record will encourage you to trust God and grow through your present circumstances. I keep a top-ten prayer list. As prayers are answered, I cross the need off the list and note how it was answered. Then, I add a new request to the list. It has been very encouraging to look at that list and remember how God has been faithful to answering prayer. Each of these challenges presents another opportunity to recognize God's faithfulness and to give Him thanks. He deserves praise for His active engagement in your life. You will generate greater optimism and hope, strengthen your inner well-being, and deepen your relationship with God.

Spiritual Discipline 5

Give Generously

"Blessed is he who cares for the poor; the Lord will deliver him in trouble."[291]
"A generous man will prosper; he who refreshes others will himself be refreshed."[292]

Give generously! Scripture states, "God loves a cheerful giver."[293] Why is that true? Because God is generous in all the ways He relates to you. He wants to see you [and all people] look out for others with the same heart. Giving is an important way to maintain perspective, to see the big picture. The Bible is clear: you are a temporary steward in this life.[294] Steward means that you are a manager, not the owner. While success usually requires your hard work and focus, remember much of what you have is a result of God's gifts and grace. God gave you the health, abilities, and opportunity to earn it. He sustains every creature in the Universe. The temporary in "temporary steward" means that your life on Earth is a short season of opportunity to use your worldly wealth to make an eternal impact.[295] Ancient cultures tried to ensure wealth passed beyond this life in the burial of the deceased, but it has never worked. The treasures did not travel with the owner to the afterlife. They remained behind to fill the pockets of grave robbers and treasure seekers or to display in museums. Scripture is very clear the only way to take worldly wealth beyond this life is to exchange it for the currency of love.[296] You must give it to help others in need [in acts of love] for it to become heavenly reward.[297]

Giving is a way of serving. Like so many of the spiritual disciplines, the more you give of yourself, your time, and resources, the more you receive both in this life and the life to come. During my first job, a friend approached me several times, needing money for his family. I always helped him, assuring him he didn't need to pay me back. However, when he relocated, he insisted on repaying me several times what I gave him. I tried to resist, but he insisted. My initial investment saw 250 percent returns. That is an exceptional return on investment by any standards. You will receive rewards in this life for your generosity, but what return holds more value? The intangibles—peace, joy, contentment, goodwill, confidence—are more valuable than the material. God promises He will increase your income if you give cheerfully and generously.[298] Thank God for His financial blessings. We all need them. But cherish the

---
291 Psalm 41:1
292 Proverbs 11:25
293 2 Corinthians 9:7
294 Matthew 25:14–30
295 Luke 16:1–13
296 Luke 16:9
297 Matthew 6:1–4
298 2 Corinthians 9:10–11

rewards of health, wholeness, and inner strength. Don't forget the greatest returns on investment are the treasures you store up for eternity through love and good deeds. I intended to sow my initial investment, so I sowed the 250 percent increase in an offering to the Lord. You cannot outgive God. Give generously. God will send the returns in many forms when you need them most.

Giving can help you think eternally. It is also a constructive way to deflect focus away from your struggles. I've heard it said the surest way to stay in misery is to keep looking in the mirror. To generate a positive perspective, you must find a way to change the channel. Looking outward is just the prescription. It is better to give than to receive.[299] My great-grandfather was wealthy enough to buy a new car every other year. At the same time, he stingily refused to order the optional back seat. My grandfather and great-uncles had to sit on wooden turkey crates in the back. His miserly attitude and unhealthy love of money produced a dysfunctional family dynamic. Do not be like him. Generosity is good for you. Jesus made it clear that giving is a positive force in your life. It meets the needs of others, so they have a reason to thank God, opens the door for miracles to happen, and leads to many positive spiritual outcomes. The Scripture is clear, "Give and it will be given to you."[300] The measure you use will be measured back to you. Since generosity is the heart of God, giving helps you align closer to His heart and deepens your personal relationship with Him. Generosity can elevate positive feelings, enhance your personal sense of meaning, and increase hope. Your obedience will strengthen your confidence that God will faithfully provide as you have provided for others.

David lived a spirit of generosity. While in exile under the constant threat of capture by King Saul's army, David and his men protected the fields and flocks of Jews who lived on Israel's borders. David could have easily used this protection as a means of support, but he refused to extort money from the Israelites. After his victory against the Amalekite raiders who burned Ziklag, David made two decisions of extraordinary generosity. First, he commanded his 400 victorious warriors to share the spoils of war with the 200 who were too exhausted to keep up the pursuit—despite the unwillingness of the 400 to share. He established this policy of generosity for all future military campaigns. Second, he shared the plunder with elders from the tribe of Judah, who supported him while in exile, and with residents of the cities in the region who protected him while evading King Saul's army. David's generosity didn't originate from great wealth. He had very little during the most formative years of his life. It is no different today. Generosity does not magically appear because you have extra. Surveys show that the wealthiest people give the least to charity. The most generous givers are people of average means. According to Jesus, "He who is faithful with little will be faithful with much."[301] Generosity is a character trait you develop despite lack of income and wealth. It is a spiritual practice that requires consistent personal discipline.

---

299 Acts 20:35
300 Luke 6:38
301 Luke 16:10

Another remarkable event exemplifies David's material priorities. During his reign, a plague came upon Israel. God sent David to offer sacrifices on behalf of the land at the threshing floor of Araunah the Jebusite.[302] Araunah offered to give David the wood and oxen for the sacrifice. David refused, "No, I insist on paying you for it. I will not sacrifice to the LORD my God burnt offerings that cost me nothing."[303] As David recognized, giving to the Lord has a cost. That cost is a test of your heart. Offerings that cost nothing mean nothing. The time, energy, and other resources you commit to make God a priority prove the value of your relationship with Him. God wants to be first in your heart. Jesus was clear: God and love of material wealth cannot share first place in your heart.[304] They are mutually exclusive. You can subordinate the love of worldly wealth/money by offering it on the altar as a sacrifice to God. Your choices determine who sits on the throne of your life. Love of money and worldly pleasures will weaken you and your family. It is the root of all kinds of evil, self-destructive behaviors.[305] My aunt once told me a sad story from her childhood. My great-grandfather was a kind, generous man. He gave all the grandchildren a dime whenever they came to visit. Unfortunately, my great-grandmother was not. She would stand at the door and collect each dime as they left. Greed is a destroyer of love in families. My grandmother was very generous. Although living on social security, she faithfully mailed me twenty dollars and a box of homemade cookies every month for my whole four years of college. My Gram's giving spirit made such an impression upon me as a child, I prayed she would accept Christ into her heart so she could reap the heavenly rewards of her kindness. She was a true blessing to all her grandchildren. I thank God she is with Him today. Love of God, first and foremost, will produce strength, health, and wholeness in this life and fortify you in its struggles. If you seek God first, He will take care of all your needs.[306]

What should you give? Teachers debate what generosity looks like. Many believe the tithe, the giving of 10 percent of one's income, is just as important today as it was in Old Testament times. While the New Testament is clear that we do not live under the Old Testament Law, giving the tithe is spiritually significant. The tithe is an acknowledgment you are a steward and that growing your personal wealth is subordinate to building God's kingdom. In Scripture, God challenged His people to test Him with their tithing, to see if He would not throw open the floodgates of heaven.[307] God blesses those who honor Him with the tithe. Jesus rebuked the Pharisees for giving the tithe but neglecting mercy with the words, "You should have practiced the latter (mercy) without neglecting the former (tithing)."[308] That recognition forms the foundation for all other giving. Much discussion centers around where that tithe should go, from supporting your local church to all other reasons for giving (missionaries, helping those

---

302 2 Samuel 24:16–25
303 2 Samuel 16:24
304 Matthew 6:24
305 2 Timothy 6:10
306 Matthew 6:33.
307 Malachi 3:10–11
308 Matthew 23:23

in need, Christian charities, the poor, prisoners, etc.). More important is the attitude you bring to giving. Consider the tithe the minimum standard.[309] If you view it begrudgingly as if you have done your duty for the month and that's it, you are not giving from a heart of generosity. Scripture is very clear that God gives you resources for your own needs (seed to eat) and a portion specifically for building His kingdom (seed to sow).[310] The passage does not delineate the amount, only that God loves a cheerful giver. You must approach giving with a cheerful, generous spirit, not a "get by with the bare minimum" attitude. Determine in your heart to be generous as God is generous. Give your regular tithe or whatever amount God lays on your heart, but also be ready and quick to help those in need. God will see what you give and reward you. Make each act of giving an expression of faith and worship. Your generosity will deepen your walk with God, build expectation for God's provision, and shape your future for God's blessing.

---

309 Luke 11:42
310 2 Corinthians 9:10–12

Spiritual Discipline 6

Serve Others

[The Lord] chose David his servant and took him…from tending the sheep he brought him to be the shepherd of his people Israel his inheritance. And David shepherded them with integrity of heart; with skillful hands he led them.[311]
"He who refreshes others will himself be refreshed."[312]

Look for opportunities to serve others every day! Simple acts of kindness can powerfully impact others and strengthen you in several ways. Serving takes the focus off your situation and helps you see the needs of others. Problems try to dominate your view, but serving helps you see divine possibilities. Focus on something else, preferably God's power and blessings, and you increase your potential to overcome. Serving can mend relationships. As you serve, you communicate value to others. They will esteem you for your kindness, and you will feel a greater connection with them as well. Over time, consistent service can restore trust. One of the superpowers of service is the win-win it normally creates. Others are blessed, and it helps you feel a greater connection and meaning in life. You don't have to make a large commitment to serve others. While it is important to use your talents, abilities, and spiritual gifts to serve your family, church, and community, you can live the life of service by simple acts of kindness. Start with the goal of encouraging those in your workplace. Look for opportunities to communicate God's love through simple acts like smiling, a warm greeting, or asking others how they are doing.

Serving draws you closer in your relationship with God because serving is close to His heart. Jesus came to earth to serve, to seek after, and rescue those who were lost.[313] Jesus modeled servanthood for His disciples. In an interesting story from the Bible, the mother of James and John asked Jesus to grant seats at His right and left in heaven. The other disciples were so angry when they heard of the request, Jesus had to call them together. "You know worldly rulers love power and lord it over others. Not so with you. If you want to be great, you must be a servant. Just as I did not come to be served but to serve."[314] Jesus clearly articulated a key value of God's kingdom: servanthood. The principles of the kingdom of God are often opposite to the way people think and operate. People love power and its many benefits, including the attention it brings. Jesus was 100 percent God, yet He showed us a very different way. He was born in a stable, worked among common people as a carpenter, traveled among the crowds healing

---
311 Psalm 78:70–72
312 Proverbs 11:25
313 Luke 19:10
314 Matthew 20:25–28

and teaching them, and then offered His own life as a final sacrifice for all of humanity. He had the ability and power to claim divinity, yet He chose to serve rather than be served. Being in very nature God, He took the nature of a servant.[315] Jesus' example is not just exceptional; it is unmatched by any other life in history. We think of life-changing heroes like Gandhi and Mother Teresa, who lived unforgettable lives of human compassion—what powerful examples. Yet they do not compare to the extent of Christ's sacrifice. He was the King of all kings throughout history, God Himself, yet He emptied Himself of those entitlements to serve humanity. Servanthood is the heart of God because its spirit is the spirit of love, and God is love. If you want to get closer to God, serve others without expectation of reward.[316]

The spirit of serving is contrary to the spirit of our present culture. People love to serve a good cause today, but they are so intent on publishing their latest acts of compassion on social media, they do not recognize their service is primarily aimed at serving themselves. Servanthood doesn't need to be advertised. You can receive all the benefits of serving others without ever telling another person what you have done. Good deeds tell the story themselves, and God doesn't need to look on social media to keep track of what you are doing for others. You are not in a competition for the most likes of how you serve. True servanthood chooses to serve rather than be great. Greatness comes later with God. This is not the way the world thinks, but it is the way that maximizes the spiritual benefits of serving. Most people want the VIP (very important person) treatment. They want all the perks. Last year, my boss's boss came into the office with a six-person entourage and a photographer. Yes, he is a powerful person. I was tempted to covet his position and power, but the voice of reason spoke up. I don't need all the attention to be valuable to God. The benefits of power can be alluring, addictive even, but they do not promote wholeness and health. The quest for position reduced Jesus' disciples to a squabbling rabble. Jesus nailed it, "If you want to be great, be the servant of all."[317] You can make power, fame, and influence your life pursuits, but you will end up more self-centered and stressed. As you serve God and others, pursuing the nature of Christ, you welcome His friendship, His peace, love, and joy into your heart.

God rebuked Israel for not fulfilling their purpose in the world. Isaiah prophesied, "We were with child, we writhed in labor, but we gave birth to wind. We have not brought salvation to the earth, and the people of the world have not come to life."[318] God intended His people be a blessing to the world, that they reveal the reality of God's love to all nations. As rulers came from around the world to hear King Solomon's wisdom in his day, Israel was meant to draw the people of the world to Jerusalem to seek God. Israel had God, but they continually cast him aside for idolatry and worldly pleasures. Rather than being a light, they became a stumbling block to the nations. Because they dishonored God, they were sent into captivity. In the same way, God has placed His love and light inside of you. His purpose is for

---

315 Philippians 2:6–
316 Matthew 5:41
317 Matthew 20:26
318 Isaiah 26:18

your life to bring salvation to the world through love and good deeds.[319] The greatest impact of your witness comes in a lifestyle of loving service. Your actions communicate the reality of God's presence and set the stage for your message to be received. The stakes have never been higher for the world than they are today. The spirit of the antichrist, selfishness, pride, and lawlessness openly flaunt their cultural influence to a degree I have never seen before in my life.[320] This spirit can only be countered by the example of loving sacrifice as God's ambassador.

Like many of the disciplines, serving is another way to create an outward focus. Scripture describes the importance of seeing everything you do, regardless of who you are serving, as service to God.[321] Jesus stated the same principle in the Parable of the Sheep and Goats,

> Come, inherit my Kingdom for I was hungry, and you gave me something to eat. I was thirsty, and you gave me something to drink. I was a stranger, and you took me into your home. I needed clothes, and you gave me something to wear. I was sick, and you took care of me. I was in prison, and you visited me. Then the people who have God's approval will reply to him, 'Lord, when did we see you hungry and feed you or see you thirsty and give you something to drink? When did we see you as a stranger and take you into our homes or see you in need of clothes and give you something to wear? When did we see you sick or in prison and visit you?' "The king will answer them, 'I can guarantee this truth: Whatever you did for one of my brothers or sisters, no matter how unimportant they seemed, you did for me.[322]

Serving the neediest and most rejected members of our society is serving God. When no one else cares, God's people should, without expectation of applause from the world.

As a fugitive, David found a way to serve others. While in the wilderness, he and his 600 warriors guarded the borders of Israel, protecting the Israelites from raiding parties. He found meaning and purpose in those years of exile, protecting God's people. It was common for armed bands of warriors to attack vulnerable farms, towns, and settlements without provocation. David voluntarily guarded the flocks and herds of the townspeople who allowed his men to camp nearby. This was not always an easy task. Raiding parties of Philistines, Amalekites, and other nomadic warriors regularly attacked Israel. Wherever he sought refuge, David put himself at risk to protect others. His service was a means of serving God. Scripture notes that people who produce a spiritual crop by serving others, like land that receives rain and produces a fruitful harvest, will be especially blessed by God.[323] You can deepen your walk with

---
319 Hebrews 10:2
320 1 John 4:3
321 Colossians 3:23–24
322 Matthew 25:31–46
323 Hebrews 6:7

God as you live the ministry of serving others every day. You can strengthen your sense of meaning and purpose by serving others in hard times, just as David did.

Spiritual Discipline 7

Exercise Humility and Self-Awareness

All of you, clothe yourselves with humility toward one another, because "God opposes the proud but shows favor to the humble."[324]

Continually develop humility and cultivate self-awareness in every aspect of your life. The first group of disciplines focused on doing things to deepen your relationship with God. We now turn to the inner qualities of being that enable you to grow in that relationship. Humility is being humble, not thinking more highly of yourself than you ought to, while having a scriptural view of your importance.[325] The temptation is to view yourself through the lens the culture uses to define value and importance. This is an earthly (carnal-fleshly) and arrogant standard. People value themselves in relation to others by characteristics such as beauty, wealth, position, possessions, education (knowledge), intelligence, talents, race, sex, etc. Those who have more or have the right talents, qualities, and characteristics are elevated in the culture and among peers. Pride makes people value themselves above others using these criteria. A friend once shared how her brother laughed at her, stating the cars in his driveway were worth more than everything she owned. This is not the standard God uses—His ways are not our ways, and His thoughts are not our thoughts.[326] God clarified what was important to Him when David was anointed king. Samuel traveled to Jesse's (David's father's) house to anoint the next king. When Samuel saw Eliab, the oldest brother, he thought, "Surely, this is the next king." However, God spoke to him and said, "Do not consider his appearance or his height, for I have rejected him. The Lord does not look at the things people look at. People look at the outward appearance, but the Lord looks at the heart."[327] Jesse did not think David was worthy enough to bring him in from the fields to stand before Samuel. After he passed by each of David's seven brothers, Samuel asked Jesse if he had more sons. It was then that David was brought from the fields to the banquet.

Humility is loving; you don't have to put others down to establish your personal value. Neither does it mean you have to think low of yourself or that others are better than you. Do not put yourself down to make others feel valued. You must see yourself the way God sees you while recognizing the value God places on every other person. Everyone has been endowed by God with specific talents, abilities,

---
324 1 Peter 5:5
325 Romans 12:3
326 Isaiah 55:8–9
327 1 Samuel 16:6–7

meaning, and purpose—each is fearfully and wonderfully made.[328]

Jesus instructed people to love others as they love themselves.[329] Humility is having a balanced perspective of your importance. The Scripture states that people are like dust on a scale, yet God values each person beyond comprehension.[330] The dust on the surface of the scale is insignificant when weighing yourself. Yet Scripture declares the extent of God's love is beyond earthly measurement.[331] He loved you so much, He devised a costly rescue plan to restore you to His spiritual family—sending Jesus to earth to bear the penalty for your and all humanity's sin and rejection of God. That is the level of your significance to God. Humility is the recognition of your smallness and your value (and the value of all people) to God.

Jesus summarized all of Scripture in two commands: love God with all your being and love your neighbor as yourself.[332] Loving others means prioritizing the needs of others in the same way you prioritize your own. People have a need for love, value, appreciation, and acceptance. Paul encouraged believers to "prefer" one another the same way Jesus humbled Himself, took the nature of a servant, and laid down His life as a sacrifice for sin.[333] Prefer and prioritize mean putting others first. Humility does not mean you have no love for yourself, fail to provide for your own needs, or put yourself down. It doesn't help you or anyone to disrespect yourself to make them feel better. You are no better than anyone else, but you are no less than anyone, either. You cannot love others in a healthy way if you do not love yourself. You must receive God's love to fill your own love tank, so you have love to share with others. The more you give God's love away, the greater your supply to give. You can communicate the importance of others by serving and sacrificing.

Self-awareness is the ability to recognize areas where you lack humility and love. It enables you to identify your strengths and weaknesses, areas for growth, greater obedience, and development of character. And it allows you to evaluate how you place value on others in relation to yourself, your interactions, and your thoughts about them. It is an essential ingredient in personal and spiritual growth because it promotes progress through the stages of healthy transformation without negatively comparing yourself to others or measuring yourself against an impossible standard. Some live under condemnation, viewing God and other authority figures as the harsh enforcers of rules and regulations demanding perfection. Do not fall into that trap. God has promised you His leading in a healthy growth process free from all condemnation and false guilt.[334] Self-awareness is your friend, nudging you in the right direction. It is not your critic pointing out all your faults and failures. Discern between the counsel and correction of the Holy Spirit and the condemnation of the enemy and your perfectionistic fleshly impulses. The enemy

---
328 Psalm 139:13–15
329 Mark 12:31
330 Isaiah 40:15
331 Ephesians 3:18
332 Matthew 22:37–40
333 Philippians 2:5–10
334 Philippians 1:6, Romans 8:1

isn't called "the accuser" for nothing. He loves to find fault.

It's not just what you do but the attitude with which you do it that demonstrates true humility. Attitude reveals the importance of humility to self-awareness. IQ is your human intelligence quotient. EQ is your emotional intelligence. AQ, your awareness quotient, describes awareness intelligence. How well do you see yourself? Do you see how your way of being affects you, others, and your relationship with God? It takes humility to look critically at yourself. By critical, I don't mean you criticize and put yourself down. I mean, you honestly evaluate your motives, your manners, and your behaviors to recognize how you better can love others in a healthy, constructive manner. Paul encouraged believers with these words, "But if we judged ourselves rightly, we would not be judged."[335] If you evaluate (judge) your actions against Scripture and seek self-improvement, God won't judge you. As you take the initiative to grow more like Christ, God doesn't have to persuade you to do it. Judging doesn't mean you belittle, criticize, or condemn yourself. We are not under condemnation in Christ.[336] Self-awareness allows you to look at your actions and say, "I wasn't entirely truthful in that conversation; I told a lie." It allows you to look at your motives and say, "I really didn't do that to help the other person; I was primarily focused on the benefit I was getting back." This kind of introspection helps you to sift out attitudes and behaviors that hinder your relationships and refine your character. It requires self-awareness to see yourself with the clarity of God's sight and humility to allow God to sift your motives, character, and actions. God gave me a humility check as a young pastor. I was visiting a friend at Bible college, and we began to talk about faith and ministry. It was late, and he turned out the light, but we continued the conversation in his dorm as we lay on our bunks. Excited about starting a new church, I began to pour out all the lessons and wisdom I learned in my new position. I proudly talked continuously for some time when I was interrupted by the sound of a loud snore. I was embarrassed at first by the fact that I had rambled on in such a way, but then I had a good laugh at myself, thinking he was mesmerized by my new-found knowledge. It was a humbling experience.

When you face difficulties, you need self-awareness to show you self-destructive thoughts and patterns that contribute to your struggles. You do not need negative and unhealthy views of self, unrealistic expectations of others, flawed views of God's thoughts about you, condemnation, shame, false guilt, and the like blocking your path toward positive progress and growth. Humility enables you to place yourself on God's potter's wheel, allowing Him to use difficulties to strengthen your character. Self-awareness enables you to discriminate between the voice of the Holy Spirit calling you higher amid the background noise of other competing voices. When Martha complained that Mary was not busy helping with the chores necessary to host Jesus and His disciples, Jesus replied, "Martha, Martha, you are worried and upset about many things, but only one thing is needed. Mary has chosen what is better, and it will not

---
335 1 Corinthians 11:31
336 Romans 8:1

be taken away from her."[337] Some of the background noise in your life may be good. Martha was busy trying to take care of Jesus; she had good intentions. However, Mary knew what was most important: she needed to spend time with Jesus. At times, the choice you face is between the good and the "better." Listen for the still, small voice of the Holy Spirit. This normally requires you to get alone, turn off the electronics, and get quiet. Seek the leading of the Spirit and God's peace as a confirmation. Developing a sensitivity to God's leading will draw you closer to Him and bring you more fully into His will.

Self-awareness is a critical quality for enhancing resilience. Many of the resilience-building strategies require you to honestly and openly evaluate your thought processes and behaviors to identify and refute unhealthy patterns. Defensiveness is a spiritual stronghold that the enemy uses to protect self-destructive patterns and inhibit your growth. Some of these patterns have roots so deep in your past that they require significant strength and discipline to tackle them. Building healthy thought processes and engaging constructive behaviors is not for the faint of heart; however, the rewards are great. Difficult times expose weaknesses and provide a key opportunity for personal change and growth. Forest fires are a painful, destructive event, but the removal of excess overgrowth presents a necessary opportunity for new healthy growth in the forest. Look at your life in the same way. Trials are difficult and stressful, but they also expose areas of your life that are limiting your potential and provide both motivation and opportunity for positive change. It is wise to appreciate the benefits and seek to maximize personal and spiritual growth.

Many people walk through life ignoring the warning signs that accompany self-inflicted problems. Scripture calls this blindness self-deception, a total lack of self-awareness. A big problem with self-deception is that you don't realize that you are deceived. You are convinced that the real problem lies elsewhere. You assume you would recognize you have a problem after the same issues keep repeating themselves, but the blindness of self-deception prevents any change. Jesus' fiercest critics were the educated religious leaders who had the knowledge to recognize the coming of the Messiah. Unfortunately, they lacked the self-awareness and humility to truly see. They deceived themselves into believing they were doing God's will without the humble evaluation and personal introspection necessary to reveal the truth. A few religious leaders secretly did believe, and some openly followed Christ after His resurrection. The difference between those who ultimately believed and those who whipped the crowd into a frenzied call for Jesus' death was their heart condition. They were hard-hearted. They had no room for humble self-evaluation. Their example is a dire warning of the need for humility and self-awareness.

---

337 Luke 10:41–42

Spiritual Discipline 7

The Problem of Pride

Pride, the opposite of humility, is grievous to God because it identifies with the nature of the enemy rather than the nature of Christ. Jesus humbled Himself to the point of death on a cross to redeem your life.[338] In His earthly ministry, He was meek and lowly in spirit, not haughty and proud. On the other hand, Satan's fall came about due to pride.[339] God cast the great worship leader of heaven, the morning star and son of the dawn, out of heaven for arrogant rebellion. Satan said, "I will ascend to the heavens. I will raise my throne above the stars of God. I will sit enthroned on the mount of assembly. I will ascend above the clouds. I will make myself like the Most High."[340] In his attempt to seat himself above God, the devil deceived one-third of the most powerful angels (hundreds of millions of them) and led them in a revolt that continues to rage on to this day. Although Christ's resurrection established his ultimate defeat, Satan's great strategy in the war against God and humanity is not to worship him (the devil)—although, in his great pride, I am certain that he craves that end. It is to deceive you into worshipping yourself, to say in your heart as he said, "I am in charge. I will raise myself above God on the throne of my life." This rejection of the authority of God in your life is the ultimate form of arrogance and the great inhibitor of God's favor, help, and blessing.

This brings up another reason why humility is so important to building resilience and overcoming difficulties. God generously helps those who humble themselves.[341] He opposes arrogance.[342] Pride makes it harder for you to gain traction in solving your problems because it prevents you from making wise choices, following through with constructive action, and deprives you of God's blessing. Scripture states, "Pride cometh before a fall and a haughty spirit before destruction."[343] Simply put, pride makes you do stupid stuff. Humility promotes wisdom. Difficulties help you to recognize you may not have included God in your life as much as you needed. It may be time to apologetically ask God to take His rightful place on the throne of your life. In hard times, you need the pilot and navigator, not the passenger at the controls. Humility and self-awareness help you draw closer to God, set you up for success, and serve as building-block qualities that support other resilience-building strategies.

---

338 Philippians 2:5–8
339 Isaiah 14:12–15
340 Isaiah 14:13–14
341 James 4:10
342 James 4:6
343 Proverbs 16:18

Spiritual Discipline 8

Renew Energy, Stay Motivated, and Persevere

I can do everything through him who gives me strength.[344]

Stir up motivation and energy to persevere through adversity. Passion is powerful. Loving relationships produce energy and motivation. The world uses this fact to make billions of dollars in romantic music, movies, and other entertainment. You feel good around those you love and those who love you. In the same way, your relationship with God should energize you. When you truly understand how much God loves you, how much He has done for you through Christ, and how active He is in your life, your passion will grow. Use that energy to move you to faith-filled action. Adversity does not change God's heart toward you. Troubles come to the righteous in life, but God can deliver you from each one.[345] Do not let adversity change your heart toward God while you wait for His deliverance. Continue to invest in your relationship, draw closer to God, and use the struggle to motivate you to go further than you have before. Do not let the temporary discouragement that often comes with struggles derail your passion for God and expectations of good from Him. Use that zeal to propel you over the hump of the struggle. Perseverance is a key ingredient for overcoming adversity and any attack of the enemy. You have already won your battle. The only way to lose is to quit. You must harness every positive aspect of your relationship with God: faith, love, joy, the Word, God's past faithfulness to you and to others in the Scripture, and support of spiritually minded friends to stand your ground.

Beware of the negatives of emotionalism—living by emotions rather than faith. Most people make decisions based on their emotions, how they feel. Salesmen make their living by this principle. They get you all excited about how great a product is, then push you to close the deal on the spot. The power of emotion is used to sell all kinds of unnecessary products in infomercials, online banners, and relentless sellers of timeshares. You probably have experienced the "pushy" salesperson trying to make a quick sale. Emotions cause people to experience buyer's remorse and cause people to say things they later regret. Emotional decisions are rarely the wisest decisions, but they are common. On the other hand, apathy and resignation can be just as dangerous when you face difficulties. As teenagers, my friends and I used to take hours to figure out what we were going to do during the summer break. One would suggest an idea, then another would say, "I don't feel like it." On and on that routine would go. It was like spending hours channel surfing. It's amazing we did anything because someone always vetoed the ideas

---

344 Philippians 4:13
345 Psalm 34:19

mentioned with, "I don't feel like it." Spiritual apathy is an enemy that will keep you stuck.

To be spiritually resilient, you must prioritize faith over feelings. Your compass is Scripture, not how you feel. Many people use their feelings to determine if God is present or helping them. You must walk by faith (the Word of God and the leading of the Holy Spirit), not sight (reliance on your natural senses and feelings).[346] Feelings are important, but spiritually, they are irrelevant. If you use your natural senses or feelings as your spiritual guide, you will be tossed like a wave of the sea.[347] You must rely completely on Scripture and the leading of the Spirit regardless of how you feel about it or your situation. Reliance on Scripture will create a spiritual fire of tenacity within you. People who face adversity tend to feel drained of energy and optimism. You may not feel motivated to pursue spiritual disciplines during struggles. That is why Scripture encourages believers to maintain their zeal and spiritual fervor when they face afflictions.[348] Life has a way of draining people. You must rest and recharge to go the long haul. Many of the disciplines mentioned can help you recharge. These are important, but our focus is the necessity to maintain your spiritual energy and motivation. When every other source of energy fails, you must be able to find your strength in the Lord as David did. You must persevere.

David reached his breaking point at Ziklag. He and his men were physically and emotionally exhausted. They were drained by grief from the loss of their families. In the stages of grief, David's men had reached the anger stage, blaming David for the loss and demanding revenge. At his low point, grief-stricken, exhausted, feeling isolated, David reached out to his one remaining lifeline—God. Scripture records, "David encouraged himself in the Lord his God."[349] The next sentence in the story records David in action. He developed a constructive plan of action and sought God for His direction and confirmation. Plans, hope, action require energy. You must find your strength in the Lord to move forward when the future looks grim. David did it; you can do it too.

Like David, you must cultivate your relationship with God to the point that when all else fails, God remains. When you know as you know as you know God is with you and wants to help you, you can grab hold of that spiritual ladder and start climbing. I love praying Psalm 23. "The Lord is my Shepherd I shall not want…he restores my soul. He prepares a table in the presence of my enemies, he anoints my head with oil, my cup runs over."[350] These portions describe how God touches the emotions as we walk with Him. They encourage me to trust God to be recharged. When you need your soul restored, when you need an empty cup to run over, God is there for you. He will provide everything you need so you lack nothing. Your faith and prayers are powerful.

When you face a season of adversity, you must engage your spirit and will to make yourself take constructive action. During a season of trouble in his life, David had a conversation with himself, "Why,

---
346 2 Corinthians 5:7
347 James 1:6
348 Romans 12:11–12
349 1 Samuel 30:6
350 Psalm 23:1, 3, 5

my soul, are you downcast? Why so disturbed within me? Put your hope in God, for I will yet praise him, my Savior, and my God."[351] Sometimes, in faith, you need to tell yourself to keep moving forward. You must do it, even if you do not want to. Paul encouraged his protégé, Timothy, "Stir up the gift of God that is in you from the laying on of my hands."[352] Timothy was going through a hard time, but Paul reminded him that he had everything he needed. He had to reach inside and awaken the faith and hope necessary to move him forward. If you ask Jesus into your heart, you are a temple of the Holy Spirit—God lives inside you.[353] The Spirit inside you can handle anything you will ever face in your life. Your part is to stir up your faith, your mental energy we call optimism, your spiritual gifts, your abilities, and your expectation that God will take your simple offering and multiply it to meet your needs. It only takes faith the size of a mustard seed, but it requires a faith that engages your trust in God to see it through.[354]

Faith is forceful. You will face struggles in this world because the enemy tries to steal, kill, and destroy.[355] God's work in the world is forceful to combat these attacks. Faith requires people to forcefully push back against the enemy's lies and oppression.[356] The enemy uses deception and bullying as tactics to keep you from exercising your authority over him.[357] God has given you the resurrection power of Christ that lives in you and has seated you in heavenly places in authority over the enemy. As Paul instructed believers, you must stir up your spiritual fervor and the power within you to combat the works of the enemy in your life.[358] As you press into the Lord, you can keep the fire of that relationship burning in your heart and use it to move forward. Paul warned believers of the need to stand against the tactics of the enemy and not allow him to move them backward.[359] You cannot get discouraged by your struggles. The enemy is trying to wear you out, so you give up. If you keep motivated, keep standing, and don't quit, you cannot lose. That is a secret the enemy desperately tries to hide. If you keep standing in the fight, you cannot lose.[360] Keep motivated, maintain that energy, and never quit. You will be victorious.

As a teenager, I was introverted and timid. Throughout my elementary school years, I had been bullied on the playground by a couple of kids, but none worse than David. In middle school, I saw him less at school events, but somehow in first semester of eighth grade, he ended up in my gym class. Gym class for the guys was wrestling, and the teacher allowed the students to choose the person they wanted to wrestle. Of course, the teacher chose David in class one day, and he called me out to be his partner. I think he expected it would be easy to beat me up on the wrestling mat, since he had bullied me throughout elementary school, but things had changed. I was heavily involved in sports, and he had been

---

351 Psalm 42:11
352 2 Timothy 1:6
353 1 Corinthians 6:19
354 Luke 17:6
355 John 10:10
356 Matthew 11:12
357 Ephesians 1:18–23, 2:6
358 Romans 12:11–12
359 1 Corinthians 15:58
360 Ephesians 6:13

involved in unhealthy behaviors. Although lacking confidence, I quickly found out he was no match for me on the wrestling mat. I beat him handily. David talked big talk, but when the battle came, he couldn't hold up to the older me. That is how it is with the enemy. When you accept Christ, something changes inside you that dramatically alters the battle. Don't let past failures and bullying keep you from victory. You are a new creation with more power than you know. You have the resurrection power of Christ living inside of you.

It is spiritual energy that empowers initiative to solve your problems along with an optimistic belief in God's help that produces confident action. It is not that you are in denial about the gravity of your circumstances. It is optimism based on the potential available in your omnipotent God. The doctors may have given you a bad diagnosis, but you confess your faith in the power of God. You can say, "The doctor told me I will never walk again, but I serve a God who is able to make the lame walk, the blind see, and the deaf hear. I choose to believe in the power of God." You can be hopeful about life and the future because the resurrection power of God lives in you.[361] You can give your troubles to God and receive the power of His illogical peace.[362] Your circumstances have not changed yet, so others question why you are at peace in the storm. But you know the God of peace is also the God of the storm. He can handle whatever you face so you can live at peace and rest. Do not lose heart; God is renewing you each day.[363] Use your spiritual sight to see the future God promised. Stir up the energy to act with optimism, with a clear recognition of your obstacles, an expectation of God's miraculous deliverance, a restful peace in the grace of God that allows you to focus, and a perseverance that trusts God to work it out for your good in His timing. You will need motivation and energy to exercise spiritually resilient thoughts, speech, and actions. You can do this. You can do all things through God, who gives you strength.

---

361 Romans 6:10–11
362 Philippians 4:6
363 2 Corinthians 4:16–18

Spiritual Discipline 9

Develop Interpersonal Skills—Strengthen Relationships

"In all things, treat others as you want them to treat you."[364]

—Jesus

Strengthen your relationships and learn how to become a better friend! Studies show that people with a greater number of supportive relationships are more effective in overcoming difficulties.[365] You not only need more friends—you need a small number of very close friends. Jesus is a great example of this principle. He had a group of twelve disciples who walked closely with Him throughout His ministry. Three of those twelve composed His inner circle. Scripture also reveals He had close relationships outside His twelve disciples with others such as Lazarus and his sisters, Mary and Martha. Scripture describes the various benefits of having friends share your life journey.

> Two are better than one, because they have a good return for their labor: If either of them falls down, one can help the other up. But pity anyone who falls and has no one to help them up. Also, if two lie down together, they will keep warm. But how can one keep warm alone? Though one may be overpowered, two can defend themselves. A cord of three strands is not quickly broken.[366]

Scripture makes it clear that you are more effective across a broad spectrum of activities and challenges when you have a close friend: productivity, adversity, warmth, defense, and, ultimately, strength. The synergy produced by mutual support has the potential to affect every domain of your total fitness. A friend can encourage you, give you counsel as a "word from God," help carry the load of your burdens, provide aid or resources to help you in a time of need, or point out a blind spot in your perspective that limited you from moving forward.[367] Sooner or later, you will need someone else to help you stay the course or move forward in your relationship with God. You need wise, godly friends to speak into your life. They will be a resource in the season of adversity. The time to build healthy relationships is now

---

[364] Matthew 7:12
[365] Marisa T. Cohen, "Resilience and Relationships," Psychology Today, January 30, 2020, accessed December 10, 2022, https://www.psychologytoday.com/us/blog/finding-the-love-the-scientific-take/202001/resilience-and-relationships?amp.
[366] Ecclesiastes 4:9–11
[367] Proverbs 17:17, 20:6, 27:6

before the struggles come. If you are in a season of difficulty, it's not too late to start. You will grow by helping others in their time of need as well.

Scripture uses sheep as a metaphor for people.[368] Humans, as social beings, often exhibit herd-like behaviors. Jesus encouraged His followers to think of themselves as family, brothers, and sisters with spiritual mothers and fathers. He intended the bonds to be intimate so they could share the joys and sorrows of life together. God never intended you to navigate life alone. You need friends to strengthen your resilience, and they need you to strengthen theirs. Scripture offers numerous pearls of wisdom that help you strengthen your relational skills. Foremost, to love one another.[369] This command is so important it occurs at least sixteen times. Ensure you communicate the value and worth of others in everything you do. Honor one another above yourselves.[370] Everyone deserves to be treated with dignity and respect regardless of whether you agree with them. Be kind and compassionate towards one another.[371] Scripture states, "Everyone should be quick to listen, slow to speak and slow to become angry."[372] Listen to what others have to say. Allow them to express themselves and actively listen to understand their thoughts and heart's intentions. Do not criticize others but speak the truth of a concern in love with the same approach you would want someone to share it with you.[373] Be patient with one another and similarly bear with one another (be tolerant of them) in your dealings.[374] Live in harmony with one another.[375] Make every effort to keep unity in the Spirit through the bond of peace.[376] Peace in relationships takes intentionality and hard work. Accept others even when they do not act according to your standards.[377] Forgive one another.[378] People will let you down, but you cannot get cynical or stuck in a past wrong. Forgiveness lets you move forward in your relationships as you do what God does. Buildup, encourage, and pray for one another.[379] As you invest in others, you will strengthen healthy relationships with them. Following the simple principles above will enhance your relational skills and help you dramatically improve your relationships, even during times of adversity.

In one of the low points of his life, while hunted by King Saul, David experienced the power of a best friend. David became very close to Jonathon, the king's oldest son, when he served in Saul's household. Jonathon repeatedly advocated for David when his father expressed anger toward him. In one incident, Jonathon warned David of Saul's intent to kill him, enabling him to escape from the palace.[380] Knowing his life was in jeopardy, David came close to despair as Saul and his army pressed their pursuit

---
368 Mark 6:34
369 John 13:34
370 Romans 12:10
371 Ephesians 4:32
372 James 1:19
373 Ephesians 4:15,25
374 Ephesians 4:2, Colossians 3:13
375 Romans 12:16
376 Ephesians 4:3
377 Romans 15:7
378 Ephesians 4:2,32
379 Romans 14:19, 1 Thessalonians 5:11, James 5:16
380 1 Samuel 20

at Horesh in the Desert of Ziph. Jonathan secretly traveled to encourage David. The Scripture states, "[Jonathon] helped him find strength in God."[381] It is interesting how closely this language resembles the words used to describe David's response at Ziklag, where he encouraged himself in the Lord. Before David stood alone, God provided strength and encouragement through his friend Jonathon. Jonathon made three very important statements: "Don't be afraid, Saul will not lay a hand on you," and "You will be king over Israel."[382] He encouraged David to embrace faith rather than fear and prophesied over his future. Jonathan's words addressed David's worst fears and his biggest dreams. Encouragement is just one of the benefits friends can bring to your struggles. I believe David remembered Jonathon's words at Horesh as he faced his angry warriors at Ziklag, making it easier to stand in faith.

After pastoring a church for several years without seeing much fruit, I confided in a pastor-friend of my doubts about whether I should continue to serve there. I had been seriously contemplating applying to a new church. Dan was a wise person, a pray-er, and a person I was confident would tell me the truth, not just what I wanted to hear. He was a true friend. I will never forget his comment that day. He looked straight into my eyes and said, "Brian, God has called you to this church, and if you cannot lead it through these struggles, no one else can!" It may not sound impressive, but when I heard those words, I cried. They resounded in my spirit. Within a short time, many of the problems disappeared. Eventually, the church came into its season of blessing, we finally had our own building, and we experienced amazing growth. A large part of my ability to press through was a few simple words from a wise friend.

Difficulties may cause you to withdraw from friendships. You may be ashamed of your struggles, fearing that friends will think less of you. You may feel afraid to trust, having been let down before. However, this is when you need friends the most. Fears of betrayal or rejection are not your friend, especially now. Resist the impulse to distance yourself from others. You may not have many friends, or you may find it difficult to make friends. Now is a great time to widen your relational circle. Connect with people of strong faith, a church, a small group, or a Christian community. At a minimum, find a Christian counselor to help you. Loneliness magnifies problems, drains energy, and hinders positive action. Make the decision to walk with someone on your journey by intentionally building and strengthening relationships. Relationships provide strength and allow you numerous opportunities to practice your faith. Future chapters will delve deeper into the importance of relational skills.

---

381 1 Samuel 23:16
382 1 Samuel 23:17

Spiritual Discipline 10

Exercise Self-Control Always

Like a city whose walls are broken through is a person who lacks self-control.[383]

Exercise self-control always. Self-control is the ability to govern your impulses, submitting your emotions, desires, and inclinations to reason, critical thinking, the discipline of your will, and the leading of the Holy Spirit. That person at work makes you so mad, you want to give them a piece of your mind. Instead, you take a deep breath and say nothing, with the intent of resolving the conflict that's brewing between you at a better time. A rude driver cuts you off in traffic, making you slam on your brakes to avoid an accident. You want to pull up next to him and let him know what you think of his driving. Instead, you slow down, avoid eye contact, and keep a safe following distance. Both are examples of self-control. Do you act on what feels good? After all, you need to let off some steam. Or do you take the high road? Difficulties increase your internal pressure, stress, and frustration. They can make it harder to act with wisdom and discipline. If you harbor unresolved anger from past experiences, stress can weaken the dam that holds it back. Harsh words, disrespect, or conflict are just some of the catalysts that can cause a wave of anger to breach that dam. Your limits are put to the test when you face adversity. Stress normally causes people to relate differently to others. You may normally be calm and collected, but under extreme stress, you may be tempted to lose control, to relate in an aloof, defensive, rebellious, or authoritarian manner.

Self-control can keep you from making your situation worse. Impulsive decisions, speech, or actions can complicate your situation and add an additional burden to your struggles. Scripture compares the person who lacks self-control to a city with broken-down walls.[384] That person is vulnerable to the enemy. In counseling, I have never heard a person sincerely regret things they didn't say during conflict. However, I have often heard people express profound regret at things they did say during a tense interaction. I have heard people repeatedly express their desire for a "do-over," wishing they could go back to a situation and act differently (almost always desiring to act with self-control). The wounds you create in others by your impulsive behaviors will require your care and effort to heal them. You will have to humble yourself, make amends, work hard to rebuild trust and heal the damaged relationship. Many people who end up in jail can look back to a decisive moment, a foolish and impulsive choice they made that changed the trajectory of their lives. Your difficulties will tempt you to act in a rash manner. Don't

---
[383] Proverbs 25:28
[384] Proverbs 25:28

give in. Exercise self-control and make your thoughts, your tongue, and your behaviors submit to you.

David exercised self-control at Ziklag. He could easily have digressed into the same paralyzing grief and self-pity that his warriors embraced. He could have ranted against his men or God, describing their betrayal and venting his rage toward them. We can imagine how some of these impulses might have turned out. Would David's men have responded in violence? Would God have continued to actively help and support him? Would grief have kept David from following the band of Amalekites? The Scripture excludes any mention of these types of destructive behaviors. Instead, it reveals the picture of a man of faith who believed God would help him find and defeat his enemy. He took deliberate, positive, and constructive action, leaning on God for help, and won a great victory that set him up for Israel's throne.

In the Genesis story of Cain and Abel, God talked to Cain, encouraging him to do the right thing. He warned Cain against impulsive anger, stating, "Sin is crouching at your door, it desires to have you, but you must master it."[385] This story is a tragedy. Cain unreasonably felt God played favorites, yet God came down and specifically met with him to restore their relationship. In doing so, God showed him mercy when he was unmerciful. He showed him the constructive path forward, yet Cain rejected every word. He allowed his anger toward God, the anger he projected onto Abel, to dictate his actions. Cain ignored the warning, attacking and killing Abel in the very next verse. The story screams lack of self-control, a complete failure of Cain to manage his jealousy and anger. Was Cain's anger so close to the surface that Abel's mere presence set him off? We don't know, but it sounds like Cain didn't need another catalyst. He already made Abel the scapegoat for all his frustrations. Cain felt cheated out of God's blessings—really a result of his own bad behavior, but his impulsivity made the situation far worse. In the end, he became a wanderer under the shame of his guilt, exiled from his family and outside of God's blessing. He deprived his parents of two sons. Don't let impulsive actions, hasty words, or negative emotions control you. Use self-control to protect yourself from making a bad situation worse.

Self-control can help resolve your problems, giving you the space to develop and execute a solution. Scripture offers this counsel, "If a ruler's anger rises against you, calmness can lay great errors to rest."[386] The first impulse you may have when you make a big mistake is to immediately try to fix it. The emotions cry out to relieve the stress and anxiety. The phrase "courage under fire" applies here. When you're facing a big problem, stop, take a deep breath, and prayerfully think it through, seeking God's direction. When you have figured out the best and healthiest way forward, execute your plan, carefully gauging your timing. Self-control, like the other disciplines, is a source of strength that increases your resilience. But it is also an effective tool that can be used to manage tough situations.

Self-control is a fruit of the Holy Spirit.[387] That means God is working through His Spirit to develop that quality as a core part of your character. There is no dark side to self-control. Like all the fruit

---

385 Genesis 4:7
386 Ecclesiastes 10:4
387 Galatians 5:22–23

mentioned, they work only for good in your character and behavior. Make it a goal to develop greater self-control in your life. You can exercise that "muscle group" by stretching your denial of self. Fasting is an effective method of developing this discipline in addition to its many other spiritual benefits. Training your tongue to speak only positive words is another powerful exercise. Self-control in speech is difficult and presents both a challenge and an opportunity to take your spiritual practice to the next level. Setting goals for helping others, giving, and serving can also effectively stretch your self-governance and help your resolve to follow through when temptations come. Paul used athletes as an example of those who discipline themselves to win the prize. In the same way, he made his body a slave to his spiritual life.[388] Difficulties present an opportunity to train and grow yourself.

Finally, self-control reveals maturity. Maturity is a tricky concept having nothing to do with your age or how long you have believed or practiced your faith. Maturity is proven by your behavior. Forest Gump's mother told him, "Stupid is as stupid does."[389] Similarly, maturity is as maturity does. Selfless, patient, peace-loving, God-honoring, obedient action demonstrates maturity. If you're selfish, jealous, and divisive, you are not mature, no matter how long you've been involved in your faith or what you have done to serve. Some people like to measure their spirituality by age, years saved, or service to the church. Maturity is measured in obedience alone. Jesus was clear that many will say to Him, "'Lord, didn't we do [great deeds] in your name?' and I will tell them plainly, 'Away from me, I never knew you.'"[390] God does not measure the way people measure. Self-control is critical for constructive action. The Scripture promotes a high standard of morals to guide your behaviors. Moral decision-making has eternal consequences, as Jesus taught, but it also has a huge payoff in this life, promoting wholeness and health. Moral decision-making requires self-control as you sometimes "have to do the thing you (human nature) don't want to do" to do the right thing. Scripture often teaches principles you don't want to hear so you can become the person you want to be. The road to a moral and mature lifestyle requires self-control in your thoughts and speech. Adversity makes self-control more challenging, but you can use it to your advantage.

On a mission trip to South America one year, I met a local evangelist who told me an interesting story. I don't know if it's true or allegory, but he made it sound true. A famous church leader in that country went up on a mountain to battle the devil. He called out to the devil to meet him as he had met Jesus in the wilderness. He fasted and prayed, but the devil never appeared on the mountain to battle him. At the end of forty days, he left the mountain confident that his spiritual power was so great the devil feared to face him. When he reached his city, he sat down on a park bench next to a beautiful young woman. They struck up a conversation, and he told the story of his battle with the devil. She was enamored of the account and his spiritual power, and before long, the pair began passionately kissing, pledging their love

---
388 1 Corinthians 9:24–27
389 Robert Zemeckis, *Forest Gump*, United States: Paramount Pictures, 1994.
390 Matthew 7:22–23

to one another. At that moment, the devil appeared and claimed his victory, for the man was married. In the moment of greatest strength, his vulnerability was exposed. A similar lack of self-control by many Christian leaders has caused a credibility crisis for the faith worldwide. Self-discipline will protect you. It will never hurt you.

Self-control in the use of Scripture is essential for many of the action steps that follow. Scripture calls the self-controlled person stronger than a warrior who conquers a city.[391] It empowers you for constructive action. You cannot exercise spiritually resilient thinking, speech, or action without this discipline. It empowers you to make progress. Don't be the person who refuses to take up your cross (Jesus' phrase for denying your wants and desires).[392] To follow Jesus and to overcome adversity, you must do the things that most people will not do. They don't do them because they lack the discipline and refuse to pay the price (in denying themselves) with the actions that will make the difference. If it was easy to follow Jesus, live by faith, or be resilient, everyone would be doing it—no one would be struggling with their problems. In fact, many people struggle with their problems, use unhealthy coping strategies such as alcohol abuse or other addictions, or become so emotionally crippled by them that they cannot love or live selflessly as God intended. Self-control will empower wise, patient, and healthy action.[393] Your self-discipline will limit the negative fallout of your problems and help you work through and overcome them. In the process, God will refine your character and help you grow into a person who carries His love and light in the world.

---

[391] Proverbs 16:23
[392] Matthew 16:24–26
[393] Titus 2:12, 2 Peter 1:6

Spiritual Discipline 11

Harness the Power Your Tongue

...the tongue of the wise brings healing.[394]

Harness the power of your tongue to work for you, not against you. Your speech has power and influence disproportionate to its size.[395] Scripture states an important principle, "By the fruit of his mouth a man enjoys good things."[396] You will suffer gain or loss by the way you use your tongue. Using your speech to your advantage requires self-control, as we discussed in the last chapter. Scripture warns harnessing the power of your tongue requires a special degree of discipline.[397] It is so easy for your words to get away from you. Your tongue can play a powerful role in drawing near to God, prayer, worship, proclamation, etc. God's heart is to bless. He speaks blessings over humanity. The accuser, the enemy, uses his tongue to spew criticism, curses, and accusations. You get to choose the side you pick. Ally yourself with the heart of God and choose to be a blesser with your speech. The way you use your tongue will draw you closer to God or will distance you from Him. Use your speech to deepen your walk.

Scripture warns of the grievous harm you can do with your tongue.[398] I found over a hundred verses that warn against the destructive power of speech. One proverb compares telling lies about someone to shooting them with an arrow or hitting them with an axe.[399] One writer describes speech as a flame that can set your whole life on fire.[400] You need a place of security from which to counter your difficulties. Failure to manage your speech can quickly negate hard-fought progress. One of the most self-destructive behaviors is to let your tongue control you. Harnessing the power of your tongue starts with protecting yourself and others from its destructive potential. A wise person builds the house of his life with wise, disciplined, and constructive action. The foolish person tears down his house with his own hands by immoral and unrestrained impulses.[401] Restrain the impulse of your tongue, and you will prevent a lot of harm to yourself, others, and God's kingdom.

Your words have a disproportionate influence for your benefit as well. Scripture affirms the benefits of wise words, "From the fruit of his mouth a person's stomach is filled, with the harvest of his lips they

---
394 Proverbs 12:18b
395 James 3:5
396 Proverbs 13:2
397 James 3:8
398 James 3:5–6
399 Proverbs 25:18
400 James 3:3–6
401 Proverbs 14:1

are satisfied.402 A gentle tongue is a tree of life."[403] Over fifty verses encourage positive speech, some in beautiful, poetic terms. "An apt reply is like apples of gold in settings of silver.[404] Kind words are like honey—sweet to the soul and healthy for the body."[405] Wise speech can be a great asset in improving your circumstances and resolving problems. Conflict can be an added burden when you're facing difficulties. An appropriate response can prevent conflict or moderate the tension when tempers flare.[406] Words can encourage and heal. As you use your tongue to help others, you will feel better. Positive feelings are important, providing motivation to take constructive action when you face the discouragement of adversity. Using positive speech can provide greater joy in your life as you occupy your mind with good things.[407] It also provides protection from the mental angst associated with using your tongue in negative ways. You engender the goodwill of God and others by using your tongue to bless.[408] People will want to help you as you have encouraged them with your words. Their help will make a valuable contribution to bettering your circumstances in times of trouble. Scripture states that those who refresh others will themselves be refreshed.[409]

Much will be said about the critical importance of speech in section three, positive action steps, because speech is so important and a difficult spiritual discipline to master. According to Scripture, if you can control your speech, you are perfect, capable of doing anything.[410] The challenge is on; one of the most helpful quick wins you can achieve is to keep your tongue from making your circumstances worse. Set a guard over your mouth. When Moses led God's people through the wilderness, they repeatedly transformed mountains into molehills. Their incessant grumbling and complaining led them into outright rebellion. Despite experiencing powerful miracles of provision, they focused on the negative reports. None of their generation finished the journey. On the other hand, positive speech can transform your life and help you overcome. Joshua and Caleb used their words to proclaim God's faithfulness as they prepared to enter the Promised Land. Even though the rest of their generation refused to go, God brought them into the land with the next generation thirty-nine years later. Your speech matters.

David repeatedly demonstrated self-discipline in his speech. At Ziklag, he could easily have vented his frustration and anger at those around him, especially concerning the betrayal of his men. In another instance, when he prepared to face Goliath, his oldest brother Eliab accused him of wickedness and conceit. David shrugged off the slander. He could easily have argued with his brother about the unfair attack, but he refused to get distracted by battles that did not matter. Later in his life as king, David had to endure the ranting curses of Shimei as he fled for his life. Instead of allowing his men to kill Shimei,

---
402 Proverbs 18:20–21
403 Proverbs 15:4
404 Proverbs 25:11
405 Proverbs 16:24
406 Proverbs 15:1
407 1 Peter 3:10
408 Proverbs 18:4
409 Proverbs 11:25
410 James 3:2

David accepted the rebuke and trusted God for His ultimate vindication. Each of these incidents reveals David's remarkable ability to hold his tongue, trusting God to be his advocate. As with the life of David, all spiritual disciplines prove your ability to trust God. Your faithfulness to study, pray, fast, give, serve, etc., ultimately relies on your willingness to trust God. As you count on God to bless your efforts, you can restrain your mouth to speak only what is constructive and loving. This discipline will help you draw closer to the heart of God and take large strides toward overcoming your present difficulties.

Spiritual Discipline 12

Continually Learn and Grow

Until we all...become mature, attaining to the whole measure of the fullness of Christ.[411]

Continually learn and grow, pursuing a lifelong process of personal and spiritual development. Living things grow. Jesus described a growth process that depends on your connection with God.[412] No one has God all figured out or has attained everything He has to offer in relationship with Him. There is always more to learn and room to grow. It is arrogant for someone to think they have finished the race before it's over. God uses many tools to help you grow in the faith, His Word, prayer, experiences, other people, etc. God's school helps you draw closer to Him, develop greater Christlike character in the fruit of the Spirit, develop more compassion in the way you treat others, and strengthen your trust in God. The most impactful opportunities for growth come through difficulties. When things go well, you are less introspective, but trials cause you to challenge your beliefs and behaviors. Recognize one of the silver linings of adversity is growth. As the ultimate recycler of life's experiences, God will use every circumstance to produce good.[413] Jesus continued His teaching on growth to emphasize that growing things need pruned.[414] The ultimate purpose of pruning is fruitfulness.

Many years ago, I bought a small farm with fruit trees. One tree was so full of dead branches, I couldn't tell what type it was. I thought about cutting it down to plant a new tree, but I pruned it instead. I cut that tree back so far, it looked like Charlie Brown's Christmas tree. I wasn't sure if it would survive. The next year, it grew new branches with a few plums—a type I had never seen before. At least I knew it was alive, and I knew it was a plum tree. I pruned it one more time, preserving the main branches. The second year, that small tree exploded with growth. It had so much fruit, it seemed impossible for the tree to carry it. God spoke to me that summer about the importance of pruning to my life. It is painful, it makes you uncomfortable, but it is very profitable.

God is not the source of evil in your life. Life in this fallen world brings enough troubles of its own, and sometimes, your sin will produce troubles for you as well as others. God does not insulate you from all difficulties, especially those you bring on yourself. He allows some trials to come to your life so He can challenge, refine, and improve your character. You were not meant to live your life thinking only about your own best good. God created you with the purpose of making a positive difference in this

---
411 Ephesians 4:13
412 John 15:5
413 Romans 8:28
414 John 15:1–2

world. Your service to God and others bears fruit. A special benefit of adversity is the sensitivity it affords toward others' pain and suffering. God will use your difficult experiences to prove His faithfulness to you so you, in turn, can encourage others as they journey through similar experiences.[415]

Growth begins with the recognition that everything that happens in life is formative, an opportunity to grow closer to God, strengthen your faith, and refine your character. To maximize the benefits of God's pruning process, you must be open to change. If God's school is always in session, then some measure of learning is always happening. Scripture states two important principles: first—that God is not setting you up for failure or evil, and second—that God will not break you in the process.[416] He knows your limits, and while He will allow you to be stretched and challenged, He will not allow you to endure what you cannot bear. At some point, you may disagree with God on your limits. It is worth stating again, while God may use tragedy to bring about good in your life, He does not cause it. The enemy, life in this fallen world, and your own mistakes produce enough grief. God does not need to create it. No matter what happens in your life, remember—God loves you and is always working to bring good to you, no matter how much you suffer.[417] The enemy's strategy is to drive a wedge between you and God. If you get angry with God, you remove yourself from the "potter's wheel," the classroom where the Divine Potter shapes the clay of your life and character to create a vessel for noble purposes.[418] Trust God enough to stay in class.

David was continually open to God's growth process. That is one reason he was called a man after God's own heart. He continually allowed God's Word to speak to his life and shape both his character and actions.[419] Even after grievous sin, David was open to the rebuke of the Lord's prophet. He maintained that soft heart, crafting the great Psalm of repentance during God's correction.[420] The discipline of continual growth allows you to persevere through trials even when you have failed miserably—perhaps even caused the hardship by your own sin. God is your Living Hope, always extending fresh grace and hope to you as you continue the journey with Him.[421]

I recently visited one of California's historic missions, where priests established religious communities among the native people that lived there in the seventeen and early eighteen hundreds. In the mission's museum hung a wineskin from the early winery that financed the community. It was a pigskin, shriveled and hard to the touch, useful only as a museum showpiece. It reminded me of Jesus' teaching of the wineskins.[422] Jesus pointed out that people get hard-hearted, stuck in their ways, and resistant to the new things God wants to do in their lives. You must cultivate an open heart like a fresh new wineskin

---

415 2 Corinthians 1:4
416 James 1:13, 1 Corinthians 10:13
417 James 1:16–18
418 2 Timothy 2:21
419 Psalm 119:9–16
420 Psalm 51
421 1 Peter 1:3
422 Luke 5:37–39

to pursue spiritual growth. The religious leaders of Jesus' day could not let go of their misplaced priorities to embrace His message and ministry. They were as unyielding to God's new work as that wineskin hanging in the museum. Do not let your heart become like that. God is always working to do a new thing in your life.[423] If you are open to growth, He will shape you—regardless of your past—into something that is beautiful and useful.

The growth process offers numerous benefits as you allow the Lord freedom to work. Your openness to change can create opportunities for fresh insights. God wants to help you navigate every challenge and difficulty. Scripture charts growth steps in faith, character, self-control, perseverance, and hope, to name a few.[424] Growth opens the aperture for creativity. God is creative, but more than that, He is the source of all creativity and innovation. Creation reveals the awesome wonder of God.[425] God can birth new thoughts and ideas to shape your situation and, more importantly, your life. As you submit yourself to God, the growth process opens your heart to formation of character, maturity, and fresh vision. Expect growth as you face adversity. Search for it, asking God to shape you according to His will. Your submission will help you realize the Father's purposes for your life.

Growth is your final discipline in this section. It looks forward, opening the door to everything else God wants to do in your life. It offers the opportunity for every blessing, every promise, every work of God to be fulfilled so you can honor Him and serve others. He recycles the pain, suffering, and tragedy you endure in this life. God is faithful to keep working toward completion, so you reach heaven without regrets.[426] Remember, the end is already written; you win! This life endures only for a season. One day, you will enter the eternal house of the Lord, where there will be no more tears, no more sorrow, no more suffering, no more pain. Every evil will be wiped away.[427] All that will remain is the love, hope, peace, joy, warmth, and beauty of your perfect life with God. Christ is the light, and in Him is life.[428] He is the Resurrection and the Life.[429] Even though you die, you shall live with Him in heaven forever, along with all those who believe. Keep running your race with the confidence that God is making your life more impactful as you run home.

You have completed Section I with its discussion of twelve spiritual disciplines that help you deepen your relationship with God and establish a firm foundation for the resilience strategies that follow. As you draw closer to and strengthen your trust in God, you can recognize and confront the unhealthy thought patterns in your mind. You can replace them with God's truth, transforming your life through the renewing power of Scripture. Every strategy to strengthen your spiritual resilience discussed in Sections II and III builds upon a personal relationship with God and faith in Him and His Word.

---

[423] saiah 43:18–19
[424] James 1:2–5
[425] Romans 1:20
[426] Philippians 1:6
[427] Revelation 21:4
[428] John 1:4
[429] John 11:25

Section II

Spiritually Resilient Thinking Strategies (Faith-Filled Thinking)

"Be transformed by the renewing of your mind."[430]

Section I addressed the many disciplines that develop faith and deepen your relationship with God. In Section II, we build on the foundation of spiritual disciplines to develop spiritually resilient thinking. Your relationship with God will produce more cognizant awareness and promote healthy thought processes if you allow the truth of Scripture to shape your mind. Scripture counsels you not to conform to the pattern of this world, which relies solely upon your natural senses, humanist arguments, and unscriptural conclusions of life experiences.[431] Human patterns of thinking tend to focus on gratification of selfish desires and, when unmet, the accompanying negative reactions. God does not think the way people think; the wisest of human thoughts are foolishness to God.[432] To think with spiritual resilience, you must see as God sees, accept God's truth as truth, and interpret life experiences through the lens of Scripture. Your life will be transformed as you renew your mind in it.[433] You can change your experience of difficult life events—reduce stress, fear, worry, and angst as you spiritually renew your mind in faith. Faith develops by hearing (reading and studying) the Word of God.[434] You can change your outcomes and future by belief in God's nature and Word. Jesus said, "You shall know the truth and the truth shall set you free."[435] God's truth can set you free, but you must know that truth with conviction in your mind and heart. It is not enough to be familiar with truth; you must be confident that God's truth is truer than any belief, argument, or temporary situation. You must agree with God.

How healthy is your thinking? Do your thoughts regularly lead you to a stressful, worrisome, fearful, or negative mindset? You will learn to recognize negative thought processes and replace them with healthy, constructive ones. Section II covers twelve critical thinking strategies for nourishing your mind while demolishing harmful strongholds the enemy uses to hold you captive. The primary spiritual field of battle for most people is in their minds. I was driving on an interstate highway a few months ago and saw a billboard with the words, "Battles are won within." Underneath the slogan, it read, "U.S. Marines." I think we can agree the Marines know something about winning battles. The inner world of

---
430 Romans 12:2
431 Romans 12:2a
432 1 Corinthians 3:18–20
433 Romans 12:2b
434 Romans 10:17
435 John 8:32

your thoughts and feelings is the key battleground. The enemy uses lies, false assumptions, flawed logic, and incorrect conclusions to limit people's fullness of life. You must reprogram your mind with childlike faith and a scriptural worldview to defeat this foe. Accept your identity as a child of God, embrace forgiveness, reject numerous subtle but powerful thinking traps, including fear and worry, and root out heart issues such as unbelief, false guilt/shame, and anger. Scripture encourages you to protect your head with the helmet of salvation.[436] Salvation involves your future eternal destination but also includes your healing (health, wholeness, well-being) and deliverance (freedom) in the present. Jesus focused on the will of the Father. He viewed every experience, the accolades and the opposition, sicknesses and healings, spiritual blindness, and the teachings of the parables through the perspective of his mission and relationship to the Father. He did not respond defensively with pride or selfishness because He had already subordinated His perspective, His personal needs, goals, and wants to the will of God. When you unequivocally make God your top priority, the battle in the mind becomes simpler. Healthy, faith-filled thinking will prepare you for the final step in maximizing your spiritual resilience, faith-filled action.

David at Ziklag

Spiritually resilient thinking was evident in David's life. Consider the incredible mental and emotional challenge David faced in the grievous loss at Ziklag.[437] To make matters worse, his loyal warriors blamed him. He had to feel alone. Scripture records some of the extraordinary feats of his mighty men. On one occasion, three warriors fought through enemy lines just to bring David a drink of water.[438] One man, Eleazar, was so brave he continued to fight alone when the rest of the army retreated.[439] Another fought two heroes of Moab, went into a pit to kill a lion, wrestled the spear out of the hand of a giant Egyptian warrior, and killed him with it in battle.[440] This was the character of David's warriors. Yet when faced with the loss of their homes and families, David's six hundred men cried themselves to exhaustion. Their unhealthy thinking led them to blame David for the loss. In this intense atmosphere of loss and grief, David could have blamed himself. If modern investigative reporters had existed back then, the grief of David's men would have repeatedly been spotlighted by the media with the banner of David's failed leadership. After all, he could have been in Ziklag rather than supporting the Philistine army. They should have been protecting their homes. If only David had done things differently. "Could have. Should have. Would have!" These are natural human thought patterns, yet they are toxic. You can second-guess yourself all day long, especially when everyone else is blaming you. David was additionally distressed

---
436 Ephesians 6:17
437 1 Samuel 30
438 2 Samuel 23:15–17
439 2 Samuel 23:9–10
440 2 Samuel 23:20–23

because the men talked of stoning him. Despite the pressures, he refused to allow his mind to descend into self-pity and despair. I have not found a single instance in David's life where he allowed himself to succumb to the blame and shame mode of thinking. The friends who risked their lives to bring him water now plotted against him in their self-pity. However, David did not join them in their despair. Instead of embracing a victim mentality, he trusted God. Scripture states, "But David found strength in the Lord his God."[441] David protected his mind. He refused to internalize the accusations. He refused to play the blame game. He let faith guide his thoughts, and it prepared him for the next step—resilient action. Your challenge is to critically examine your attitude, outlook, and thoughts to identify the negative patterns, stop their destructive cycle, and replace them with healthy, constructive, and spiritually resilient (faith-filled) thinking.

---

[441] 1 Samuel 30:6

Chapter 1

Guard Your Mind

"Guard your heart, for it is the wellspring of life."[442]

The Importance of Healthy Thought Processes

Guard your mind; it is the key to wholeness and inner health. It is the well that sustains your life and gives you strength to overcome. Your mind provides the critical linkage, allowing the Holy Spirit within you to be the Spirit who guides you. You must protect your well from the enemy and every source of negative influence. Everyone needs computer virus protection. Protect your mind's computer from viruses, worms, and every form of malware. Your thoughts run your life (and determine much of its outcomes) the way software programs run processes on a computer. You must have healthy thinking patterns to truly be spiritually resilient. Scripture offers profound guidance to develop a healthy thought life. Life happens. Past experiences from childhood, as well as other formative life experiences, shape your thought processes, attitudes, and perspectives for good or ill. For many people, painful experiences have produced a mental software program that runs negative, unhealthy, and damaging thoughts. You previously read how humans are hard-wired for spirituality through the human spirit. Humans begin life with the innocence of a child. Jesus used childlikeness as an example of the attitude you must use to relate to God.[443] Think about the qualities of a young child: they trust with naïve innocence, not cynical or jaded; they take people at their word; they are ever hopeful with a fun-loving and joyful spirit; and they have flexible minds, curious, asking questions, wanting to learn. However, many children learn very quickly the world is unsafe for their innocent, trusting spirits. Painful experiences caused by the selfishness, pride, and wrongdoing of others overwrite the initial version of their inner software. These life lessons, intended for their protection, often have numerous negative second and third-order effects. The resultant patterns of thinking with all their malware become a basic operating system for adulthood.

Another way to think of this dynamic is an emotional backpack. Every person has one. Painful experiences in life go into that backpack. Some people forgive or let go of the hurts, eventually lightening the load by discarding them along the road of life. Some hold onto those painful experiences, allowing them to grow into anger and bitterness. A simple way to assess your thought life is to ask yourself how you feel. If you carry a significant number of negative emotions, you likely have harmful thought pro-

---
442 Proverbs 4:23
443 Matthew 18:3

cesses at work in your mind. Everyone has a backpack, but for many people, that pack carries heavy mental-emotional weights that wear them down. While the pack in our illustration is on your back, the real load is carried inside, in your thoughts and emotions. The weights damage your attitude and perspective. Scripture advises you to "throw off everything that hinders and the sin that so easily entangles. And let us run with perseverance the race marked out for us, fixing our eyes on Jesus."[444] You are not designed to run the race of life with big rocks in your backpack.

God gave His Word to protect you. Pain is an important reason why Scripture provides numerous commands to avoid wrongdoing (sin is the technical, spiritual term). Scripture states plainly: Sin is always destructive; it is never victimless.[445] It inherently damages human health and well-being, relationships, and thought processes (your mental-emotional software). Your thoughts determine your emotions, reactions, and, ultimately, your outcomes.[446] The enemy knows the mind is your critical vulnerability determining your health, success, and impact in this world. In strategic terms, the mind is your "center of gravity," the hub of your strength. This term derives from the writings of infamous military theorist General Carl von Clausewitz, who used the term to describe military sources of strength.[447] Your mind is the strategic field upon which battles rage to determine whether you find strength in God through adversity or you trust yourself. Scripture uses the analogy of warfare to make a similar point in the spiritual life.[448] Many people do not recognize that the negative, hurtful, and self-destructive thoughts they entertain every day find a catalyst in the unseen world of dark spiritual forces that war not only against the kingdom of God but also against every human being as representations of God's image.[449] The enemy of your well-being knows how important your thoughts are to your outcomes and quality of life. He wars unceasingly in the primary field of battle, your mind, to contaminate your thinking.[450] His minions work tirelessly to ensnare you in wrongdoing, exploiting not only the spiritual vulnerabilities created by it but also the resultant damaged thought processes, attitudes, and perspectives (known, in severe cases, as moral injury). You must win your freedom on the battlefield of the mind before you can ever realize the abundant fullness of life God planned for you.[451]

God designed you to endure storms in life. I love to relax in a boat out on the water. I have owned motorboats, canoes, kayaks, and even a pedal boat. Boat builders design them to displace water as they travel through it or ride on top of it, called planing.[452] A boat has no problem on the largest and deepest bodies of water until water gets inside the boat. Too much water inside and the boat will capsize or sink.

---
444 Hebrews 12:1–2
445 Romans 6:23a
446 Robin Nicholas, "*How Do My Thoughts Impact My Life?*" accessed December 12. 2022, Https://www.chariscounselingcenter.com/blog/how-do-my-thoughts-impact-my-life/.
447 Carl von Clausewitz, *On War*, pages 485–486, 595–596, trans. J.J. Graham (Ware, England: Wordsworth Classics of World Literature, Wordsworth Editions, 1997).
448 Ephesians 6:10
449 Ephesians 6:12–13
450 2 Corinthians 7:1
451 John 10:10
452 Boater Exam, "*Boat Hull Types & Designs*," accessed October 2, 2021, https://www.boaterexam.com/boating-resources/boat-hull-types-designs/.

In the same way a boat easily navigates deep waters, God designed you to cope with and overcome adversity. The problem comes when you allow difficulties to consume your heart and mind like water filling your boat. Bail the water out by refusing to let negative thoughts (regrets, self-pity, recrimination, despair, etc.) dominate your mind. You cannot stop thoughts from coming to your mind, but you don't have to let them hijack your thinking. David refused to let the accusations of six hundred seasoned warriors replace his faith. He refused to allow his grief and their blame game to push him down into the depths of despair. He let those messages go in one ear and out the other as he focused on the love and faithfulness of God. Don't let adversity get inside of you.

Protect your mind by feeding it spiritually healthy inputs and insulating it from the numerous pollutants that will try to dominate, painful past experiences, damaging social norms and values, destructively messaged music, poisonous media and entertainment, and toxic peer pressure. The enemy will use the desire for acceptance to coerce you into tolerating harmful influences. You do not have to follow the crowd. Many advertising slogans proclaim, "Be your own person, stand out from the crowd, and swim upstream," but ultimately, they all lead to conformity with the damaging sinful spirit of this world. Most people follow its current on the broad road leading away from God.[453] If you truly want to be different, truly live free, align yourself with God and His Word. The enemy offers many temptations, none of which promote health or freedom. The Scripture earnestly warns you to be watchful, prepared, and decisive in your stand against the enemy.[454] In order to preserve strength and draw from the potential of your inner world, you must continually fight negativity, temptation, and conformity.

Guard the Well of Your Heart

Protect the attitudes and perspectives of your heart; they are the wellspring of your life.[455] When my kids were little, they ran around quoting Woody, the sheriff toy from the movie Toy Story. When someone pulled the string on his back, he exclaimed, "Someone poisoned the waterhole!"[456] They loved repeating that quote. Unfortunately, in real life, the enemy continually tries to poison the waterhole of peoples' attitudes. He will use difficulties to make you think God doesn't care about you. He will use the offenses of others to make you skeptical, unforgiving, or bitter. He will use your desire for wealth or pleasure to make God seem less valuable. It's up to you to protect the water in your well.

From the beginning, the enemy successfully waged a campaign for people's hearts. Adam and Eve had everything. They enjoyed peace, prosperity, complete safety, and eternal life. Unfortunately, they allowed the enemy to turn their hearts from God with a lie. The serpent led them to believe everything wasn't enough. They took on a perspective that God was holding out on them. It is hard to believe they

---
453 Matthew 7:13–14
454 Ephesians 6:6–10, 2 Corinthians 10:4, 4:4, 2:11
455 Proverbs 4:23
456 John Lasseter, *Toy Story* (Burbank, CA: Walt Disney Pictures/Pixar, 2005).

took the bait. They had access to thousands of trees; only one was off-limits. Unfortunately, thousands weren't enough. The end of the story is well known. They were kicked out of Eden. They lost everything they took for granted and subjected themselves, their children, and all humanity to hard work, lack, danger, strife, and ultimately death.[457] If only they had trusted God rather than allowing the serpent to twist their minds.

Their children struggled as well. Adam's son Cain was angry and jealous. God tried to reason with him, but it was too late. He also believed the lie of the enemy—taking on the attitude that God was unfair, He played favorites. God's attempt to reason with him contains a warning just as relevant for you today, "If you do what is right, will you not be accepted? Sin is crouching at your door, it desires to have you, but you must master it."[458] Cain ignored God, allowing his warped, sinful perspective to control his thoughts. Driven by his passionate sense of injustice, he murdered his brother. Figuratively, God was on one shoulder speaking wisdom to Cain's mind, the enemy on the other speaking a message of self-gratification. We often see this imagery in cartoons. On one shoulder, a little red-suited, horned devil holding a trident; on the other, the little, white-robed angel holding a harp. Both try to influence our hero. In real life, this characterization is close to the truth. Unfortunately, the real-life devil is neither humorous nor harmless. He is a strategic, malevolent, lethal intelligence. He finds fertile soil in spiritually weak human hearts, pointing an accusing finger at God for the injustices in life. The same saga has repeated through the ages, from Adam through Cain up to the present day. People tend to believe the lies of the deceiver even though many deny he exists. Allowing the enemy to poison their perspectives and attitudes, people assign blame everywhere except where it belongs. You don't have to listen to the accuser's destructive voice. You can face life's struggles by listening to the voice of the Holy Spirit while embracing a positive, hopeful, trusting perspective.

Learn from the many tragic examples of people in Scripture, from Adam and Eve to Cain, to the people of Noah's Day, to the Israelites wandering in the wilderness, to Solomon, to the religious leaders of Jesus' day right up to the present time. You must protect the wellspring of your life. Your heart includes your emotions, attitudes, and perspectives. God wants to plant His truth, wisdom, and life into the soil of your heart. Jesus warned His followers to protect the seed of God's Word. Before it ever takes root, the enemy steals it away from some. He attempts to convince those who face troubles that God is unfair, sowing weeds of anger and bitterness. For those who start strong in their relationship with God, he attacks with worries or the love of wealth.[459] The enemy's goal is to poison the well of your heart. He really doesn't care which approach works. The poison could be unbelief or doubt, it could be disappointment, anger, and bitterness, or it could be the unhealthy love of things in this world. Only you can protect your heart. The test is simple: Are you growing closer to God, or are you allowing something in

---

457 Genesis 3
458 Genesis 4:6–7
459 Matthew 13:1–23

life to crowd Him out? Nothing is so valuable that you allow it to force God out of your life. Jesus asked, "What does it profit a man to gain the whole world and lose his soul?"[460] God's friendship is the ultimate treasure in life. Jesus warned, "Do not let the light in your heart become darkness."[461] Don't allow the enemy, or anyone else, to separate you from God by their words or actions. You don't want someone quoting Sheriff Woody over your life, "Someone poisoned the waterhole."

Guard the Gate to Your Mind

Be the gatekeeper of your mind and thought processes; they are the source of your livelihood. In the ancient world, the gate was the weakest point of a fortified city. The walls were thick rock reinforced with large cut stone. The gates were made of logs or iron, thinner and lighter, to allow for passage and commerce. Gatekeepers scouted for attackers and secured the gate while the city populace mobilized for battle. Scripture likens the self-controlled person to the strength of a city's fortifications.[462] Even the most fortified city is weak if the gates are unguarded. The same is true of your mind. Be careful what you allow through its gates. Through patience, mental discipline, and self-control, you can avoid many troubles and accomplish great things. You are not an animal driven by the basest needs and desires of the moment. You can make wise choices that lead to health and long-term benefits. Do not live like some who seek the moment of pleasure at the expense of their long-term health. I hate to confess I have seen and read things I wish I could permanently forget. Scripture offers profound wisdom for mental (and emotional) health, "Whatever is true, whatever is noble, whatever is right, whatever is pure, whatever is lovely, whatever is admirable—if anything is excellent or praiseworthy—think about such things."[463] You cannot totally insulate your life from the world's unpleasantness, but you don't have to treat your mind like a dumpster. So much of music and entertainment, even people's everyday speech, is pure trash. Don't allow the culture to fill your mind with its garbage. Close the gate for your own mental health and the well-being of the ones you love and can influence. According to Scripture, if it's true and noble and right and pure and lovely and admirable and excellent or praiseworthy, then it is okay to open the gate wide.

Clean eating is a popular term to describe a diet that focuses on fresh fruits and vegetables devoid of harmful chemicals, preservatives, or cooked with processes that reduce nutritional value. Apply the term clean eating to what you allow into your mind. You are not a raccoon that roots through the trash for food. First, do not let people use you to dispose of their emotional waste. Some people want to make themselves feel better by blaming you for bad things that happened. If you have committed a wrong, acknowledge it, ask their forgiveness, ask God's forgiveness, forgive yourself, and move on with your life.

---
460 Luke 9:25
461 Luke 11:34–35
462 Proverbs, 25:28, 16:32
463 Philippians 4:8

Sometimes, people want to blame you for bad things that happen, whether you had any responsibility. They want to bring you down to make themselves feel better or important. Do not take on any false guilt. The enemy will try to make you feel condemned. Scripture is clear. Condemnation is not from God.[464] If you ask God to forgive you, accept that He did and move on. Scripture promises He will always forgive.[465] If someone refuses to forgive you, you can still move on. Pray they will forgive you for their sake. You have done your part. The other part is up to them. Do not allow them to blackmail you (hold some past event over you) or use manipulation. You do not need to own any of these unhealthy thoughts.

Second, do not allow cultural influencers to sell you their trash so they can get rich. Some people will try to prey on you, like vampires; they feed on you for their needs and egos. If you buy their wares, they have reduced you to a loaf of bread.[466] You do not need to pollute your thoughts with messages that tear down faith and healthy love toward others. Take a moment to reflect on a few things with me. I love easy listening music from the 1970s, but so much of it is depressing or glorifies immoral sexuality. Do you and I really want to put stuff in our minds that's going to cause regrets or make us feel depressed? Recently, I went to bed singing a song in my mind that, when I really thought about the words, was all about a person's first sexual encounter with someone they didn't even know. Is that a healthy way to end the day? You may think right now, "That's just the way music is, it's no big deal." When you're facing adversity, you don't need the power of regret, negativity, or speculation about how your life may have turned out differently weighing on your mind. Truthfully, you're never strong enough to fill your mind with trash and thrive in life.

I grew up watching family hour TV with my parents and brother. I have fond memories of laughing together with the people I loved. That is a powerful force that most of our entertainment industry exploits to further their agenda and financial interests. You will struggle to find a fun, wholesome program today. So many portray violence and every kind of self-destructive behavior. Under the banner of artistic license, all forms of media push messages that are not noble, pure, lovely, admirable, or uplifting. While environmental pollution is a terrible thing, the air pollution of speech on the airwaves promoting fear, death, drug abuse, rape, robbery, deceit, adultery, and the disrespectful treatment of others is a national crisis. People are desperate to laugh, so desperate they will listen to the worst profanity and subjects imaginable. You are the gatekeeper of your mind. Think carefully about the content you allow into your mind and the amount of time you plug in. Consider how countless hours "plugged in" to all forms of questionable media affect your mind. The billions of dollars of advertising spent by companies every year are proof that media affects your thought processes. A countermovement has started to turn off (unplug) destructive media. You determine if an annual day of unplugging is just a day or if "unplugging"

---

464 Romans 8:1
465 1 John 1:9
466 Proverbs 6:26

is a normal part of your healthy lifestyle.[467] Protect the character of your heart. God has made you and only you, its guardian. You don't need to "follow others" or "get likes" to be accepted. You are accepted and loved by God.

Third, protect your mind from the inner threats of self-destructive messages. You can be your own worst enemy if you let unhealthy messages and thought processes from past experiences continue to rule your thinking. When my children were young, I used to wake up with visions of them injured in horrible accidents. I would remain awake for a long time, trying to recreate a different ending to the dream. This continued regularly for over a year. Sometimes the thoughts continued throughout the day. Eventually, I realized I don't have to live like this. God tells me to think on good things.[468] When the next nightmare came, I woke up and began to pray for God's blessings on my kids, family, and home. Remarkably, I quickly fell back to sleep. It seemed like the enemy would rather have me peacefully asleep than awake praying over bad dreams. After a month of praying after every nightmare, guess what happened? You're right; the dreams stopped completely. If I had started praying after these dreams a year earlier, I might have avoided a year of torment.

Yes, I have a negative track in my mental software. Throughout my life, I have regularly heard negative messages, especially when around other people. "People won't like you, so stay in the corner. You don't have anything of value to contribute, so stay quiet. You're worthless." I've had countless ruminations of embarrassing moments, hurts, or failures. The enemy uses each negative experience to build a higher, stronger mental prison that prevents you and me from experiencing more of God's fullness. God wants you to experience His fullness, but the enemy has another plan.[469] This is exactly what Jesus warned us about when He said, "The enemy comes to steal, kill and destroy."[470] The enemy uses your negative thoughts to destroy your future. Jesus went on to say, "But I have come that you might have life and more abundantly." God wants to demolish those walls of negative, self-destructive thinking and replace them with faith-filled, optimistic thoughts. You must resist the enemy's schemes as he uses your own voice against you. In the end, the inner battle is the one that matters most. You don't have to let anything said or done get on the inside of you. You don't have to take it personally or assign it any personal significance. However, you must first place that negative inner voice in captivity.[471] You must boldly, forcefully resist the enemy. The battle for your freedom requires forceful thoughts and action.[472] Place all those negative messages and the enemy inside the walls he meant to imprison you. Win the battle for your mind. Everything in your life flows from your mindset, attitude, and character. If the enemy can poison your mind, he can poison your life. Be a clean eater in your thoughts.

---

467 Global Day of Unplugging, Accessed April 19, 2021, National Day of Unplugging.
468 Philippians 4:8
469 Ephesians 3:19 (AMP)
470 John 10:10
471 2 Corinthians 10:5
472 Matthew 11:12

Job, the man who lost everything in the enemy's attempt to destroy his faith, made a radical commitment to guard his mind. He made a covenant with his eyes not to look at a woman with lust in his heart.[473] In a day when pornography addiction has wreaked havoc on human lives and relationships, every person would be wise to make the same commitment. Make a covenant with yourself not to allow toxic images and messages to pass the gateway of your senses. Perhaps it sounds very difficult, if not impossible. That is a lie of the enemy. What attainable goal can you make now to protect your mind? Even little steps can make a big difference. Is the Holy Spirit convicting you on this issue? Do you need to change the music you listen to, turn off videos, TV programs, or reign in your social media engagements? Do your entertainment choices hinder scriptural commands to love God and love other people? What can you do as the guardian of the gate of your mind? David guarded the gate of his mind in a moment of great vulnerability. You can do the same. The mind is vulnerable, but with God's strength, you can guard that gate.[474]

Practice Self-Awareness: Recognize the Weeds, Whack Them Down

You practice self-awareness when you consciously reflect on your own thoughts, feelings, and the patterns that link them. When you face difficult circumstances, it's easy for unhealthy thought patterns to crowd out optimism and hope. Recognize the signs and stop negative thinking as soon as it starts. Whack those weeds down! The Scripture counsels you to use prayer and petitions to replace anxious thoughts.[475] It promises you can walk in peace through significant problems as you ask and trust God to help. It promises that God will give you peace to guard your heart and mind.[476] I recently saw a church sign that read, "Prayer transfers problems to big shoulders." God always intended to carry the loads of your life on His shoulders.[477] He never meant for you to cope with struggles alone. Bad things happen to you, but you don't have to let the storm sink you. I love to fish. One afternoon, while fishing in my boat, a large thunderstorm hit the lake. Five-foot waves repeatedly rolled from bow to stern. Fortunately, my boat had two things going for it: it had a shell that forced water from the waves to roll right over the top and off the back; second, it had a bilge pump that pumped water in the boat back into the lake. My boat never swamped, and eventually, I made it to calmer waters as the storm subsided. Everyone faces storms in times of adversity. Let that water roll right over you and off your back just like a duck. Ducks don't worry about water. Their feathers force the water right over them and off the back. Use faith and prayer to pump the water out of your boat. Transfer the effects of the wind and waves to God's shoulders. Don't

---
473 Job 31:1
474 Philippians 4:13
475 Philippians 4:6
476 Philippians 4:7
477 Matthew 11:29

let the enemy overwhelm you with negative thoughts. Use self-awareness to identify weak spots in your patterns of thought, seek God's peace, and transfer your burdens to His shoulders.

An important skill to build strength in your inner being is the ability to recognize and cut down the weeds of unhealthy thoughts. Scripture repeatedly emphasizes the importance of being alert and watchful.[478] Nowhere is this more important than in your own thought life. In the Parable of the Weeds, Scripture shows how the enemy sows evil.[479] When applied to the human mind, it reveals how the enemy plants seeds of negative and destructive thoughts in your mind to steal from you, sap your energy, and destroy any good working in you. You can shape how painful experiences affect you in the long term. When emotionally hurt, people learn negative life lessons and develop unhealthy thought patterns that hinder future growth. If your thoughts drive a wedge between you and God, they are weeds. Weeds easily take root, but you don't have to let them grow unchallenged. Get your mental weed-whacker out and cut them down. Remember that person who made an insulting comment at work? You can rehearse that event in your mind, considering all the things you should have said. You can spend hours reliving the humiliation. Remember that costly mistake you made last week? If you had acted differently, you could have avoided the whole thing. You can spend hours condemning yourself for your mistakes. Don't do it! Stop those lines of thinking as soon as they start. You must recognize the trap of the enemy and change your thinking before you needlessly expend mental energy, waste precious time, and physically harm your body with worry and stress. In that moment, recognize your thoughts are in the danger zone. Through disciplined self-awareness, change your focus.

The enemy works overtime to ensnare your mind in destructive thoughts. He wants nothing more than to inject venom into your thought processes. If you allow him free reign, he will poison your mind, emotions, and physical body. Don't dwell on those destructive thoughts; bind them with God's Word. They may knock at the door of your mind, but you don't have to invite them for dinner. God does not bring evil to your life, but He will use your hardship to help you learn important spiritual lessons. God promises to take the bad things that happen, things the enemy meant to harm you, and turn them into fertilizer for personal and spiritual growth and gain.[480] You can interpret hardships as a failure of God's protection—letting the weeds take over your garden, or you can view them as an opportunity for spiritual growth and for a greater revelation of God's love and faithfulness. Would you profit more from God removing every obstacle out of your path or from walking with Him as you deal with the obstacles together? I would rather not have the obstacles at all, but I have grown far more spiritually by facing adversity than through the lack of it in my life. The battle will rage for your perspective. To win the battle in your mind, you must discern the spirit that sows weeds in your life from the *one* who helps you produce good fruit.[481]

---
478 1 Peter 5:8, 1 Corinthians 10:12, Colossians 4:2, Ephesians 6:18
479 Matthew 13:24–26
480 Romans 8:28
481 1 John 4:1, 1 Thessalonians 5:20–21

The battle for the mind involves two very important steps: recognizing your preoccupation with negative thoughts and redirecting your mind toward constructive ones.[482] I'm not suggesting you ignore your problems or pretend they don't exist. Rather, redirect your focus. I have heard preachers castigate those who "confess" they have any sickness or struggle. Be honest about your struggle. You don't have to cover it up or deny it. If you have a diagnosis, face a financial need, or experience trouble, share it with some wise, godly friends for prayer and support. However, don't let the problem be the end of your confession. Be sure to proclaim your faith in God and your expectation of His help. Faith makes God's Word more real and more powerful than your problem. There are always two reports: a report of natural sight for your current circumstances and a report of spiritual sight describing your situation from the perspective of Scripture, God's promises, and faith. Most people think the natural report, what you presently see with the senses, is more real or more relevant. God always has the final word. Your reliance on His promises can radically change your experience. The medical report says I am sick, but I proclaim, "I know God is my healer." You might say, "I'm facing a difficult situation, but I know God will provide. I'm facing a big mountain, but I know God can move mountains." Don't forget the "but" in what you tell others, and most importantly, don't forget the "but" in your own thoughts.

I used to be so fixated on my natural sight and senses I argued with God about my healing. Many years ago, I was in a church service in terrible pain from a back injury. The speaker ended the message, saying she was going to pray for healing, especially backs and shoulders, and that she would call on three people after the prayer to testify to their healing. As soon as I bowed my head to pray, I heard a voice in my mind say, "Stand up and testify you've been healed." I immediately countered, My back is in terrible pain; I'm not healed. The voice said again, "Stand up and testify you've been healed." I said, God, I'm in terrible pain; I can't stand up and say I've been healed. I even moved around a little bit to see if the pain left. It didn't. I heard God's voice repeat the same message a third time. At this point, the prayer was ending. I didn't believe I was healed, but I stood up anyway out of obedience. God has a sense of humor because in a sanctuary of over two thousand and me in the back corner, who was the first person to get called on to share? You guessed it: me. I was so concerned about not falsely stating my pain was gone I stated matter-of-factly, "God says I'm healed." The speaker replied, "Brother if God says you're healed, then you're healed. Stand on that word." I sat down and endured excruciating pain in my back for the rest of the event. Remarkably, within a week or so, I woke up, and the pain was completely gone. It had plagued me for months with no help from chiropractors or medicine. I have not experienced that type of pain or reinjured my back in over thirty years. What was more real in the moment God spoke to me, my pain or God's voice? Natural sight is like a polaroid photo, a snapshot in time. It is a fact you may be experiencing something in the moment. Spiritual sight is a window to the eternal. It reveals truth, recognizing the power and authority of God. So, which is more real? My pain was temporal; it existed

---
[482] 2 Corinthians 10:4–5, Colossians 3:2, Philippians 4:8, Isaiah 26:3

until God spoke, then its hold on my experience began to unravel. The thirty years pain-free was my reality the moment God spoke; I just didn't see it with my natural senses for a week or so. Was it any less true or any less real? Faith declares spiritual realities (truth) before you can see them with your senses. Delays don't make them any less real or true. Faith is the bridge between your natural sight (the present reality you see with your physical senses) and your spiritual sight (your belief in the future realization of God's promises and Scriptural truths). To walk by faith, not sight, means you make your spiritual sight more important than your physical senses in your thoughts, words, and actions. Your natural mind will scream your reality is here to stay. The devil will try to convince you your struggles and pain are here to stay. But you have another report, the report of spiritual sight tied to the reality of God's power, authority, and promises in your life. Include spiritual sight in every difficulty you face. God's people live by faith, by spiritual sight, not by natural sight.

You can dramatically help your mind by declaring your faith to yourself. Proclaim your healing, help, and provision. Wake up every day and proclaim you're expecting a miracle. Some talk so much about how big the problem is they forget to talk about the greatness of God. They repeatedly ruminate on the problem, neglecting to place the emphasis on God. When you focus on the goodness and faithfulness of God, you strengthen your inner being and release God's power to move on your behalf. I heard an advertisement on my local radio station a few years ago that said, "You can trust God, or you can worry. But you can't do both."[483] The degree you focus on God, His goodness, and His blessings in your life is the degree you will exclude stressful, negative thoughts from your mind. Faith and worry cannot coexist in your mind at the same moment. The battle for your mind is a literal knife fight to turn your thinking toward something encouraging, helpful, and profitable. You must commit to win. You must expend every possible effort to change your thinking. You cannot do yourself, others, or your circumstances any good by obsessing over negative thoughts. You cannot go back in time or change the past. Don't punish yourself with regret; life will do that well enough without your help. Learn from your past, grow wiser, and develop greater skill in recognizing the warning signs of an unhealthy thought life. You don't need to carry the extra burden in your thoughts and emotions. Choose to trust God in your hardship. Cut those weeds of negativity and direct your mind toward the peace of God.

This chapter is a reminder that you must guard your heart and mind. Your inner life, thoughts, emotions, attitudes, and perspectives are critical to how you face adversity. You are the gatekeeper, determining what you allow into your mind. If your experiences are like mine, many of the warm memories from your youth have a dark side that does not fully align with scriptural principles. Similarly, your painful past experiences may have negatively shaped your attitudes and perspective. To thrive through the ups and downs of life, your positive, healthy inputs must vastly outweigh the negatives. While many downplay the impact of cultural influences, do not be deceived. The enemy (aka the prince and power of

---
[483] K-Love Radio Station. Oakland, CA, 2017.

the air) heavily influences much of modern entertainment and media to shape your values and opinions in a negative way. A Scriptural worldview will help you identify ideas and arguments opposed to your spiritual and holistic health and enable you to counter destructive thoughts with positive, constructive strategies when times are tough. The issues addressed in many of the remaining chapters in this section, like deadly snakes, inject venom that corrupts the heart and mind. With the help of God's Word, the Holy Spirit, and spiritually mature friends/mentors, you can identify their poison, reject it, and replace it with something beneficial. As with many things in life, prevention is the best medicine. Guard your heart and mind. They are the wellspring of your life.

Chapter 2

Engage the Power of Faith

Now faith is confidence in what we hope for and assurance about what we do not see.[484]

Leverage the power of faith. Faith is critical to a strong and healthy inner life.[485] Spiritual resilience requires you to purge negative thoughts, replacing them with faith and hope. Spiritual hope is not wishful thinking; it is spiritual optimism. Faith builds on hope accessing the strength and power available through the spiritual life. Develop your faith, and you will strengthen your life. Faith is the key building block in your relationship with God, yet many don't understand it. What is faith? Hebrews 11, also known as the "Faith Hall of Fame," defines faith this way: "Now faith is being sure of what we hope for and certain of what we do not see."[486] Faith is an assurance, a certainty of something we cannot presently see. People often say, "Seeing is believing." Faith is different; it is the ability to believe before you see. In other words, "Believing is seeing." Faith has substance and surety that comes to you, but not from relying on your earthly sight. Faith allows you to see with spiritual sight, creating certainty in your vision for what is to come. Most people make decisions by only what they see with natural sight. You and I live by faith, incorporating spiritual sight into our decisions. A lot of people find it easier to believe in God's promise for another person. That is a good thing, but faith says, "God's promise is for you, right here, right now, today." The heroes listed in Hebrews 11 trusted God, believed in their hearts for the future blessing, and ultimately experienced mighty miracles because they saw with spiritual eyes what they could not see in the moment with their physical eyes. They walked by faith, trusting in their spiritual sight rather than following the crowd's "seeing is believing" philosophy.[487] Without faith, it is impossible to please God.[488] It is your faith that pleases God, that appropriates His blessing and favor to show up in your life as His reward. At the cross, Jesus paid for all the forgiveness, grace, love, blessing, fulfillment of His promises you will ever need. His resurrection power lives inside you.[489] So, the question for the manifestation of God's promises for your life is, "Why not you? Why not right here? Why not right now?" The prerequisite is your faith.

---

484 Hebrews 11:1
485 2 Timothy 1:7
486 Hebrews 11:1
487 2 Corinthians 5:7
488 Hebrews 11:6
489 Ephesians 1:18–22

Faith = Belief + Action

Many consider belief a synonym for faith. However, faith is not just belief. Scripture makes the point that merely believing in God is not faith, "Even demons believe that—and shudder."[490] Our enemy knows without a doubt God exists. He knows that Jesus is the risen Son of God, yet he has no faith—only knowledge. A key component of faith answers the question, "What are you doing with your knowledge and beliefs?" Are you serving and honoring God because of your belief? Scripture teaches several key points about faith.

> What good is it, my brothers, if a man claims to have faith but has no deeds? In the same way, faith by itself if it is not accompanied by action, is dead. But someone will say, "You have faith; I have deeds." Show me your faith without deeds, and I will show you my faith by what I do. You see that [Abraham's] faith and his actions were working together, and his faith was made complete by what he did. Abraham believed God, and it was credited to him as righteousness, and he was called God's friend.[491]

Faith is belief plus action. Your actions demonstrate your beliefs are sincere. They don't have to be major to confirm faith. Even seemingly small steps can be significant. Prayer is an act of faith. Faith leads you to pray *before* you exhaust other options. You firmly believe that God will answer your requests, so you make seeking Him your "go-to" response instead of your last resort. Trusting God rather than worrying in your time of trouble is an act of faith. Accepting His peace is an acknowledgment that you trust Him to take care of you. Giving to help those in need when you have your own financial needs is faith that God will provide. In each of these examples, belief in God, His character and promises, inspires an action that confirms your belief. This is the type of faith Abraham had, his actions inspired by his beliefs.

The definition of faith I prefer is "a belief in God, His Word, or promises that moves you to God-honoring action." This definition has two important distinctions. First, belief in God. Some people have faith in faith or faith in prayer. They say, "Faith helps," or "Prayer helps," as if the psychological benefits of using faith or prayer make the difference. Faith doesn't have power in and of itself. Prayer doesn't have power if you're not praying to God. The power of faith and prayer is the power of God at work through your faith and prayers. Second, the action must be God-honoring. Demons believe in God and act on their beliefs, but they don't serve God or His purposes. Your faith must honor Him, produce good works, spiritual fruit, and obedience. If you believe God will take care of you, you don't have to lie, steal, cheat, or kill (i.e., manipulate or take advantage of others) to get what you need. In sincere faith, you can love

---
490 James 2:19
491 James 2:14–25

God and other people the way Jesus described. Scripture clarifies anything not from faith is sin.[492] Sin or wrongdoing, by definition, is an act that harms you, someone else, or your relationship with God or others. Faith, by definition, does no harm. In contrast to sinful wrongdoing, faith produces wholeness and health. It draws you closer to God and others. Sin, the spiritual, technical term for wrongdoing, is self-centered and shortsighted. It takes advantage of others for short-term gain. Faith is God-centered with an eternal focus. Sin harms, faith heals.

Sin is alluring and attractive to the senses, but ultimately, it's a destructive force that delivers empty promises. The initial sensual pleasures are hollow; they drain your inner being and shackle your soul. One year on my birthday, my best friend John gave me a gift. It was a huge, beautifully wrapped package. John was always full of surprises. I remember thinking to myself at that moment what an awesome friend he was. I tore open the package and, much to my surprise, found another beautifully wrapped present. It was still a large package, so I didn't think much of it. My disappointment grew, however, as I opened several gift-wrapped boxes only to find smaller packages within them. Finally, I reached the last one, about the size of a ring box. Inside was a penny. John and his sister had a huge laugh. I felt foolish. The large gift and beautiful wrapping carried the promise of so much more. Wrongdoing initially looks attractive, initially very pleasurable. Later, once you unwrap all the packaging, you find you were deceived. It is not just an empty gift; it is often very destructive. Faith may be difficult at times, but it always enriches health, inner strength, and a solid foundation. Obedience to God may appear unrewarding and boring to your natural senses, but later, it proves far more satisfying.

Faith Believes God Is Good

Faith begins with a fundamental assumption about God—that He is good. Scripture states you cannot please God without faith because you must not only believe He exists, but you must also believe "He rewards those who earnestly seek Him."[493] Faith starts with the belief that God is good and He works for good in your life, He rewards every step you take toward Him, and He is repurposing evil or difficulties in your life for your benefit. Faith believes every good and perfect gift in this world comes from God and only God.[494] Scripture warns you not to be deceived about the inherent nature of God.[495] Some people believe God is angry and cruel, just waiting for the opportunity to punish them for wrongdoing. They interpret life's difficulties as God's vengeance. Those views of God often parallel their childhood experiences. We will discuss this connection in the topic of interpretation in the next chapter. If your family was not loving, it may be hard to believe God is a good father. Picture the best possible father on earth. If that father gives good gifts to his children, how much more will God give good gifts to you as his loved

---
492 Romans 14:23
493 Hebrews 11:6
494 James 1:17
495 James 1:16

child.[496] If God hurled lightning bolts from heaven for wrongdoing, every person on this earth would be a lump of human charcoal. Thankfully, that image of God is completely contrary to the God of love and mercy we see portrayed in Scripture. God is good. His core quality, His divine essence, is love.[497] It's not that God is loving or has love; God is love. Jesus told the Parable of the Prodigal Son, whose grieving father watched down the road for his son's return. The merciful father was quick to forgive, welcoming his son with a hug and kiss, restoring him to his place in the family and a great feast.[498] Scripture teaches that God's eyes roam over the Earth, not to punish your mistakes, but to strengthen those who are committed to Him."[499] God is good. He is looking for opportunities to encourage you. Scripture names God "the Father of compassion and the God of all comfort who comforts us in all of our troubles."[500] Like a parent, God is there to help in times of trouble, to bandage up the skinned knees of His children.

David's song vividly describes God's grace and mercy.

> The LORD is compassionate and gracious, slow to anger, abounding in love. He will not always accuse, nor will he harbor his anger forever; he does not treat us as our sins deserve or repay us according to our iniquities. For as high as the heavens are above the earth, so great is his love for those who fear him; as far as the east is from the west, so far has he removed our transgressions from us. As a father has compassion on his children, so the LORD has compassion on those who fear him; for he knows how we are formed, he remembers that we are dust.[501]

He is full of grace, giving you and I good things, we don't deserve. We do not have to earn them because they are a gift motivated by God's abounding love. They have no strings attached, but to fully appreciate them, we need faith." God is good. He does not accuse, nor does He treat us as our sins deserve. To treat us as we deserve is justice. To not treat us as we deserve is mercy. People don't want justice for themselves when they are guilty. They want to be let off the hook; they want mercy. However, in the moment of someone else's guilt, people want justice and punishment. If you want mercy, show mercy. Jesus was clear: the measure of mercy you use will be measured back to you.[502] You get what you sow. When I'm caught in the wrong, I want mercy. I'm sure you do as well. Sometimes, I have a heavy foot on the accelerator when I drive. About a year ago, I was speeding through a neighboring state, trying to pass another vehicle. As I came up over the hill in the passing lane, a police officer caught me in his radar gun. Sure enough, he turned on the lights and pulled me over. He caught me, guilty as charged. At

---
496 Matthew 7:11
497 1 John 4:8
498 Luke 15:11–32
499 2 Chronicles 16:9
500 2 Corinthians 1:3
501 Psalm 103:8–14
502 Matthew 7:1–3

that moment, I hoped that I would not have to face the justice of an expensive speeding ticket. I wanted mercy! I put on my most contrite face and apologized meekly. It was only partially successful. Instead of an expensive speeding ticket that would count as points and affect my insurance, he gave me a $94 ticket for a lesser charge. I'm thankful for the mercy of not getting a speeding ticket; however, I was hoping to get off with a warning. The ticket ruined the rest of my trip home; it was all I could think of that day. Mercy is precious in the here and now. Mercy is invaluable in eternity.

God relates to you with compassion and mercy because He values you beyond understanding. He knows you have an innate frailty passing quickly through this life. God is good. He doesn't want your fear. He wants your love. Some quote the Scripture saying, "Fear God."[503] There's a difference between the fear that causes stress and the respect and awe you have for someone who you greatly value and esteem. God desires your love and respect the way you desire it from those important to you. God is quick to forgive because He knows accusation is a barrier to close relationships. He wants to make it easy for you to approach Him. He doesn't keep a record of your wrongs because He wants you to relate to Him with freedom and confidence in His unconditional love. He is full of compassion to build you up, not break you. People use guilt and shame to manipulate for their advantage, but God always wants the best for you. I heard this quote, "God loves you, and everyone else has a plan for your life." Some people just want you to do what they want you to do—for their selfish interests. God's plan for your life always reflects His love for you. He's trying to lead you to the place of the best possible good, a place Scripture describes as blessing and favor. Can you accept God's attitude toward you? Either God is merciful toward your wrongdoings and desires good things for you, or He is a liar.[504] He cannot be both. Replace the image of a harsh, angry, vengeful God in your mind's eye with the picture of the Prodigal's loving father. Your life will change with this simple step.

Faith Appropriates God's Gifts

God has His hand extended with good things for you, but you must reach out and take them. Your faith appropriates the gifts God has already given you. It is wrong to think of faith as the tool to make God do things for you. Faith and prayer are not magic spells to make God move. God moves because he loves you. In His indescribable love, he has given you everything you need to live your best life.[505] In His amazing grace, God has given you numerous great and powerful gifts, sealed with promises in Scripture, to enable you to experience his divine nature while avoiding the corrosive effects of the world's evil.[506] These promises are a "Yes" for you in Christ and so you can say, "Amen" (literally, "let it be—I

---

503 Ecclesiastes 12:13
504 Jeremiah 29:11–13
505 2 Peter 1:3
506 2 Peter 1:4

agree").[507] In other words, you must take or appropriate by faith, the gifts God has given you through his grace. To say "Amen" is to take them boldly by faith not with timidity or doubt. Faith takes God's gifts from His hands; it does not wait for Him to drop them into your lap. Sometimes, the enemy tries to take good things God has given you. In one sense, the only thing the enemy tries to take are the gifts God has given you—why would he take what you don't have or doesn't belong to you? God wants you to boldly reach out and take what He has for you by faith, and if the enemy tries to take it out of your hands, God desires you fight courageously for it. Faith takes title to spiritual possessions God has already given you through Christ. Obviously, faith cannot appropriate what God has not given you, things opposed to Scripture. Some who misunderstand faith try to use it to make God do their will. He is not your genie in the lamp, He is your savior, Lord, and friend.

For instance, through faith in Christ, God has given you his Spirit to live inside your heart in all his resurrection power. You have his presence everywhere you go, all the fruit of the Spirit to live in the character of Christ, the power of God to serve him, you have peace from the Spirit through any struggle, courage, the promise of eternity with him, his forgiveness from all past, present, and future sins, justification against any spiritual charge or accusation, freedom from guilt and shame, the promises of healing, deliverance, protection, provision, and blessing. Numerous other promises can be named as well. You may not feel like you have any of these gifts. You do not live your life by natural sight, senses, or feelings. You live by faith. You don't base the truth on whether you feel it's true but rather on the truth of Scripture. Stand on the Word of God as the evidence you have God's gifts, envision the promises fulfilled in your life, declare out loud that you have them, and act as though they are already yours because they are. When you think about receiving one of God's promises, don't think of it as if you are waiting for God to give it to you. Think of it as if Jesus purchased the gift with His death and resurrection, and He already delivered it to you inside your spirit where His Spirit lives. To access it, you must accept by faith that God has already given it to you, that it belongs to you, envision its fulfillment in your life, proclaim it with your mouth, and patiently wait for it to be manifest in your life until you see it with natural sight. When your faith is a confident expectation, you can call things that are not yet visible naturally into being as though they were, taking a big step forward toward overcoming your difficulties. For example, you may not feel joy in the moment, but God has given you joy as a fruit of the Spirit. You have it. Act in joy with a glad and thankful heart, knowing it is yours, declaring you have it, thanking God for it, and envisioning yourself with an overjoyed heart because of what God has done for you. The joy of the Lord is your strength in good times and times of struggle. Laying hold of God's gifts by faith can help you experience more of God's promises, especially through adversity.

---

507 2 Corinthians 1:20

The Danger of Unbelief

In contrast to faith, unbelief is a toxic force in your life. Adversity tends to make people question God's reliability. Their faith lacks the depth to see them through the hardships that seem so formidable through natural sight. God seems so far away. Unbelief blocks God's gifts and will for your life. Because of unbelief, Israel turned a one-year trek to their Promised Land into an agonizing forty-year journey. Despite seeing God's amazing miracles in Egypt and throughout their journey in the wilderness, they grumbled, complained, and rebelled against Him. The final straw came when the spies brought back their report about the Promised Land. Ten of the spies emphasized the enemies, the obstacles, and the risks, seeing only with natural sight. Two of the spies, Joshua and Caleb, saw through the eyes of faith, declaring, "We can certainly do it."[508] Unfortunately, the people followed the report of the ten spies. Unbelief is the path of least resistance to human nature, leading people to base decisions on what they can see and touch over trusting the unseen God. Israel rejected God's leading based upon the exaggerated report of the ten, and every adult Israelite over the age of twenty lost their inheritance. God sentenced them to wander in the wilderness until the whole unbelieving generation perished.[509] They could have spent the next year watching God deliver their enemies into their hands as they moved into their new homes. That was His plan all along. Instead, they wandered in circles, homeless, and slaves to a new master, unbelief. Reject the exaggerations that come with an unhealthy focus on what you see and feel through your natural senses. Be part of the seventeen percent club, like Caleb and Joshua, who, with spiritual sight, can see the future outcome when God is involved.

Another story of the dangers of unbelief comes from the life of Jesus. After performing some amazing miracles, Jesus returned to His hometown. On the Sabbath, He began to amaze the people with His teachings; however, many took offense at Him. They could not get past the fact that He was the hometown boy, the carpenter, Son of Mary, and brother to men they knew very well. They could not spiritually see the coming of the Messiah to their town because they could not see through the man, they knew all too well from natural sight. Sadly, because of their unbelief, Jesus could not do many miracles there.[510] Jesus had just healed a man possessed by a legion of demons, a woman afflicted for twelve years, and raised a young girl from the dead (Mark 5), but because of unbelief, He could do very little to help the people He had known all His life. Jesus wanted to heal everyone in His hometown; instead, He accomplished very little. If unbelief can prevent a whole town from receiving the blessings of God, how much could you miss out on? Faith lays hold of the blessings in God's outstretched hands. Unbelief keeps your arms at your sides. You're not even turned toward God, let alone reaching out to Him. Jesus gave His life so you could be saved, a word that in the original language means saved, healed, delivered,

---
508 Numbers 13:30
509 Numbers 14:26–35
510 Mark 6:1–6

and prospered. He came that you might have life and more abundantly. Choose faith and take hold of the things God has provided for you. Don't let unbelief keep you controlled by your troubles.

Struggles can tempt you to accept unbelief, but you can embrace faith. During seasons of adversity, you should consider taking an inventory of your thought life and inputs. Recognize the negative influences that will try to lead you down the road of unbelief and refuse to allow them access. The culture promotes messages that undermine faith in God. It is interesting how movies of demonic possession/activity have flourished in the last few decades, but in nearly every case, people of faith (Christians, priests, the church) have little ability to defeat them. This message is completely contrary to the life, teachings, and ministry of Jesus. Demons do not have the last word. Submit to God, resist the devil, and he will flee.[511] Modern media directly opposes and contradicts the truth and teachings of Scripture. The influencers will sound wise, everyone applauds, the loudest voices will share how everyone believes this way, but do not be deceived. Don't go along with the crowd; they are headed over a cliff. If you fill your mind with these messages, you will struggle with unbelief. Your present circumstances may be another source of unbelief, leading you to doubt God can or will help, especially when you link them to lessons learned from difficult past experiences. If you're going to doubt, it is far more constructive to doubt your doubting thoughts than it is to doubt the promises of the God who believes in you. If the past is hindering your faith, perform an autopsy. Did you trust God, stand on Scripture, or pray with faith? Were your thought processes healthy and constructive? I can look back on many of my struggles and tell you plainly, I did not trust God or stand on His promises. I let my negative thoughts and feelings about the problem control my response. Unbelief had more control of my thinking than faith. You don't have to suffer with stress, fear, worry, and the physical feelings that come. Stop stinking thinking in its tracks.

Take captive every bad thought, every tempting message from the enemy, and silence your negative self-talk. If you are like me, you can ruminate over a stressful situation for hours. I can't tell you how many hours of my life I've wasted just mulling over difficulties. Hundreds? Thousands? Whatever the number, it is way too many. Sometimes, other people, even family members, can be a source of unbelief. Seek counsel from spiritually mature people who trust God and stand on His Word. Ignore the "good advice" of others if it counters faith. Remember Job's friends? In his darkest moments, his friends proved to be more of a discouragement than help. You may have to distance yourself from some people for a while if they do the same. If you are facing a health issue, the loudest voice of unbelief may be your symptoms. Remember, your senses and feelings are a snapshot in time, like an old polaroid photo. They are not your future. About fifteen years ago, I developed plantar fasciitis. Every morning, I would wake up in pain. I prayed and received prayer, but nothing happened. I began to hear a voice in my head say, "You will have this pain until you die." I pictured myself waking up for the rest of my life barely able to move my right leg. The feelings of pain shouted down faith every time. However, I continued to pray

---
[511] James 4:6

and believe I would be healed. One day, I woke up and the pain was gone. It has never returned. The point is my symptoms lied, the enemy lied, my own thoughts and vision of the future were a lie. You may experience severe pain or discomfort now, but it is passing. Do not let what you feel today be a reason for unbelief. God can heal all your diseases.[512] Faith is the bridge from your present to your better future, where you realize God's promises. Unbelief is the thief who steals your future. Instead of refusing to believe God, refuse to believe every source of unbelief. Let God always be true, and everything opposed to faith be a liar.[513]

This chapter is all about recognizing and replacing faith-less thoughts with faith-full thinking. In spiritual resilience, faith and trust describe an optimistic perspective. Optimism is an expectation of a positive future. It is hopeful, a crucial quality in contemporary discussions of resilience. Scientific evidence suggests that optimism contributes to good health by reducing one's sense of helplessness, engendering hope that bad situations can improve, and encouraging a person to develop supportive relationships. These qualities motivate people toward constructive action and studies link it to a longer, healthier life.[514] Science reinforces what Scripture has said all along: You must believe God is good and rewards faith with good things.[515] Fill your mind with the image of a good God who cannot wait to reward your sincere attempts to draw near Him. He always has good thoughts toward you.[516] As you orient your mindset to a positive, hopeful outlook, you will enjoy more peace and sense more of God's presence. Take steps of faith to honor and obey Him.

---

[512] Psalm 103:3–5
[513] Romans 3:4
[514] *Mental Help*, "Resilience: Optimism," accessed October 3, 2021, https://www.mentalhelp.net/emotional-resilience/optimism/.
[515] Hebrews 11:6
[516] Psalm 139:17

Chapter 3

Exercise the Power of Interpretation

"Can one accept good from God and not bad?"[517]

—**Job**

"God works all things out for the good for those who love him."[518]

—**Paul**

Exercise the power of interpretation. Be aware of and control thought processes, interpretations, and conclusions from your life experiences. No one can prevent adversity from happening in life. However, when troubles come, you can empower healthy thought processes to minimize their impact. Your negative thoughts can make your experience of troubles far worse. "Making a mountain out of molehill" is a well-known adage that describes the propensity of some to magnify problems by their attitude and speech. Your interpretations, evaluations, or explanations are the key factors in adversity. Life happens. Your experiences (the event, what happens) are facts. Your thoughts about the events, your interpretations of how and why they happened are not facts, they are your opinions and conclusions. Interpretations produce emotions that lead to your responses/actions/behaviors, which in turn produce consequences. Your thoughts are the critical point of self-control and intervention. You must recognize the importance of those initial thoughts (interpretations) and shape them in a healthy, constructive manner. They produce the emotions that directly contribute to your responses (actions/reactions) and produce consequences that can reinforce your initial (usually false) interpretation.[519]

---

[517] Job 2:10
[518] Romans 8:28
[519] Lisa Tams, "*ABC's of Changing Your Thoughts and Feelings in Order to Change Your Behavior*," accessed October 3, 2021, www.canr.msu.edu/news/abcs_of_changing_your_thoughts_and_feelings_in_order_to_change_your_behavior.

Figure 3a.
Event – Thought – Consequence Model

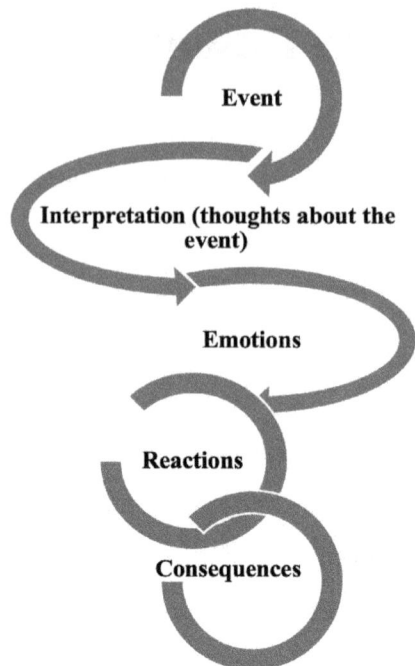

The *event* is something that happens to you. That is a fact. You experienced adversity. You cannot control everything that happens in life, other people, or your environment.

The *interpretation* is your conclusion or thoughts about how and why that event happened. Your thoughts and interpretation are completely in your area of control and are the focus of this discipline. They are not facts. We will see how your thoughts affect everything that follows.

The *emotions* you feel about the *event* are a result of your interpretation, not the actual experience. It is what you say about what happened that determines your *emotions* and *actions,* not the *event* itself. This is a very important principle to recognize and is the key to changing your attitude, stress level, and negative *action-consequence* cycle.

Consider this example:

Your co-worker, John, passes you in the hallway without smiling or greeting you. That is the *event*. You immediately think John is mad at you, and your mind races to determine why. That is your *interpretation*. It is not a fact that John is mad at you. The only fact is John didn't greet you. You feel stressed trying to figure out why John is upset at you, and you become offended and angry toward John.

Your *reaction* or *response* to the *event* originates in your *emotions* and the *interpretation* you gave of the event, not the facts themselves. You assume John is mad at you. You have no idea why John failed to greet you. Your actions or reactions have *consequences* as you relate to John, others, and your world.

The stress and negative emotions alone degrade your mental and physical health, mental focus, and productivity. Your preoccupation with negative thoughts and emotions limits your ability to relate well to others and perform the necessary constructive tasks. You interpret the negative consequences you experience from your *actions* as proof that your initial thoughts and interpretation were correct.

Back to our example: Later, in the breakroom, you make a comment under your breath when John enters. This is your reaction based on the negative emotions you feel toward John. Your co-workers look at you with a frown when John replies, "I guess someone is in a bad mood today." You immediately think, "John's comment proves your earlier conclusion was correct. John is mad at you for no reason. And now everyone in your office is on his side."

If you act on that thought and engage John negatively, you could end up in a major conflict. What if your interpretation of John's behavior was incorrect? Consider this scenario: John passed you in the hallway without smiling or greeting you. You immediately think, "That's not like John. Something must be bothering him today. I will have to check in on him." That thought produces emotions of care and concern, not anger. These emotions are selfless as you look to serve John, not selfish as you focus on your personal offense. When John enters the breakroom, you ask, "Is everything okay, John? You don't seem to be yourself today?" John is glad you asked and proceeds to tell you about his wife's bad medical report. It has weighed heavily on his mind all weekend. You pray together, and John is thankful for your friendship.

Figure 3b.
Event – Thought – Consequence Decision Matrix – Example of John

Event	Interpretation (Decision Pt)	Emotions	Action	Consequence	Next Thought	Next Emotion	Next Actions?
John didn't greet you	John is angry at me.	Offense/ Anger	Make provocative comment	John responds with a comment	I was right, John is a jerk	Greater offense/ anger	Escalate conflict?
	Something is bothering John	Care/ Concern	Ask John what is going on	John tells you his struggle, you pray together	I've been able to help John	Feel good, you helped John and you feel closer to him	Encouraged to help others

You face a choice with every experience, whether at work, in traffic, with family, or with your spouse. What interpretation will you give to the event? Will you assume the worst? You have thousands of thoughts a day. Identify and replace key thoughts that come when you face challenges or difficulties. Try meta-thinking, thinking about how you are thinking. Where is your mindset? Are you being reasonable? Are you giving people the benefit of the doubt? Do you have a preoccupation with the negative? Why? Are you honoring God in your thoughts? Your thought processes and conclusions are more important to your well-being than your experiences. It is tragically amazing that sometimes people can even take a positive event and make it negative.

Consider this true story. Jane received a pay raise and a strong evaluation of her work performance throughout the year. At the office party, her boss recognized her with a pen as a small token of appreciation. Jane was immediately offended. She lined her office shelves with mementos from previous supervisors who had given her extravagant gifts for her work performance. The pen did not satisfy expectations for recognition of her performance. She interpreted the event as a lack of appreciation. Jane harbored that offense against her boss and refused to speak to him. Her work performance quickly declined. Her refusal to talk to her boss and lack of response to his attempts to correct her performance led to a show down with the top manager in her department. She refused to speak to him until she finally stated emphatically that she would not do any work so long as her present supervisor was in charge. The manager gave her a letter of correction for her permanent performance record and placed her on suspension with loss of pay.

Figure 3c.
Event – Thought – Consequence Decision Matrix
Jane's Story (and What Could Have Been Jane's Story)

Event	Interpretation (Decision Pt)	Emotions	Action	Consequence	Next Thought	Next Emotion	Next Actions?
Jane's boss gave her a pen at the office party	Previous supervisors gave me much better gifts for my performance	Offense/ Anger	Refuse to talk to supervisor, reduce efforts at work	Supervisor correction and counseling	I was right, my boss doesn't like or value me	Greater offense/ anger	Refuse to work
	I received an outstanding rating and top pay raise. Maybe I should ask my boss about the pen gift.	Gratitude Pride in work	Maintain strong work efforts, discuss gift with supervisor	Supervisor explains his actions and gift limitations	My supervisor appreciates my work and did all he could to reward it	Feel good, you are a key part of the team	Keep working hard as part of office team?

You may think this example is extreme. Unfortunately, this is a true story that happened within an organization where I worked. Many interpersonal conflicts come from misunderstandings. They often spiral out of control far more than those involved ever expect. Scripture is clear about the importance of the inner thought life: "As a man thinks in his heart, so is he."[520] Scripture counsels you to focus on good thoughts with love; not expecting the worst.[521] Over time, your inner thought life will influence patterns determining who you are, your attitude, and character. In the present, your thoughts can powerfully influence your outcomes, as we have described in the *event—thought—consequence* process. Can you change who you are? Every person has basic qualities, strengths, and characteristics that will probably not change much. However, over time, as you consistently change the way you think, you can develop new behavioral patterns that will change the person you are.[522]

The *event—thought—consequence* cycle can work for you in a positive way but often contributes to a downward cycle when you allow negative thoughts to control. As emphasized above, your interpretation of the event is more important than the event itself. People tend to connect their interpretations so closely with the events they cannot distinguish between the facts and their assumptions. Something happens. A series of thoughts about how and why that event happened flood your mind, producing emotions that drive response. In a negative cycle, negative thoughts about the event produce negative emotions that cause a negative reaction. The unhealthy reaction produces negative consequences interpreted as justifying the original negative thoughts about the event. The downward cycle continues as the new negative interpretation produces further negative *emotions* that motivate new self-destructive *actions*, producing additional negative *consequences*.

The negative thoughts/interpretations come so quickly after the event happens, you think they are facts. You cannot distinguish the difference between the event and the interpretation, so you say to yourself, "My boss doesn't like me." That is not a fact. Your boss did not greet you when you walked in; that is the fact. The negative thought cycle reinforces itself as you hyper-focus on events that allow you to interpret them with a negative bias. You discount events that do not easily reinforce your negative thought patterns. This downward negative cycle is hard to break.

---

520 Proverbs 23:7 (KJV)
521 Philippians 4:8, 1 Corinthians 13:4–8
522 Romans 12:2

Figure 3d.
Event – Thought – Consequence Spiral

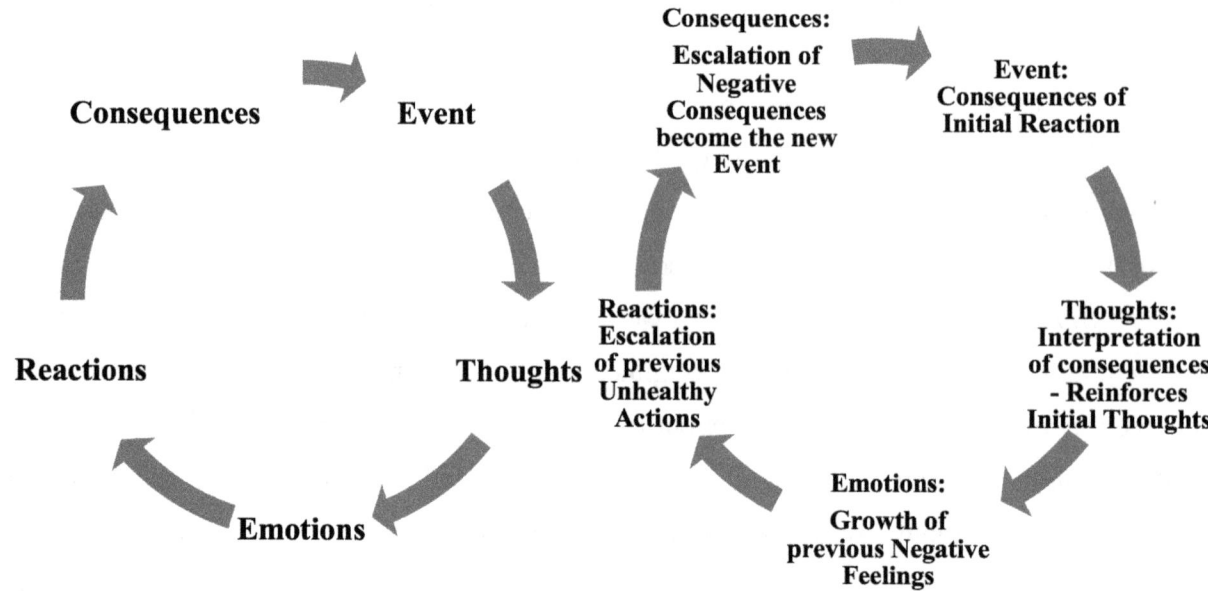

Scripture illustrates this principle with the account of the arrest of the apostles in Jerusalem.[523] Jewish officials arrested Peter and others as they preached the good news about Jesus. The priests had them imprisoned, tried, threatened, and flogged before they were finally released. The *event* was their arrest, imprisonment, and beating. These were the facts beyond dispute. What is interesting is their Interpretation or thoughts about this injustice. The Bible states they left the court "rejoicing because they had been counted worthy of suffering disgrace for the Name [of Jesus]."[524] This was an exceptional faith-filled response that buoyed their feelings. They interpreted physical torture and suffering as a privilege, identifying themselves with the suffering of Jesus. They continued their ministry, encouraged by the events renewing their commitment to spreading the good news. However, they could have made a negative interpretation of these events. The priests had them arrested, threatened, and flogged. They could have easily questioned God, asking, "Why didn't You protect us?" The thought would have produced negative emotions of doubt, fear, and self-pity. Those emotions could have led to less commitment to spreading the Gospel, with fewer people coming to salvation. Consider the decision matrix for the two scenarios below.

---
523 Acts 5:17–33
524 Acts 5:41

Figure 3e.
Event – Thought – Consequence Decision Matrix – Apostle's Arrest

Event	Interpretation (Decision Pt)	Emotions	Action	Consequence	Next Thought	Next Emotion	Next Actions?
Apostles arrested, threatened and flogged	We are honored to suffer as our Lord Jesus suffered	Joy, Pride	Refused to cater to rulers, continued to spread the Gospel more and more	People in synagogue and throughout Jerusalem heard the Gospel and were saved	We are honoring God and reaching more people	More Joy & Pride	Greater effort to share the Gospel and reach more people
	God didn't protect us from arrest and beatings	Stress, Fear, Self-pity	Intimidated by Rulers, reduce efforts to spread the Gospel	Less presentation of Gospel, less people are saved and helped	We are failing Jesus in our work	Guilt, More Stress, Fear & Doubts	Less effort to spread Gospel More hiding

Notice how important the initial thoughts about an event are in shaping the ultimate consequences from the stories of John, Jane, and the Apostles. The *event—thought—consequence* analysis reveals that outcomes are vastly different based upon a person's interpretations of life events. With an appreciation for the importance of your thoughts, can you think of a recent experience where the *event—thought—consequence* model described your outcomes? Write it out on paper using the format above.

The model highlights the critical importance of your interpretation in times of adversity. The stress that results from negative thinking is mentally and physically harmful. The negative emotions that result from undisciplined thoughts produce reactions that compound life's problems rather than helping. From a logical point of view, negative thinking is counter-productive to improving the difficult circumstances that challenge resilience. From an emotional point of view, the negative feelings produced by "stinking thinking" create a whirlpool of negative emotional energy, drawing you deeper into despair. As emotions are a key contributor to motivation and positive action, you must think in a way that fuels energy, hope, and action.

Difficult life circumstances can challenge your inner strength. However, you can help overcome these struggles by developing practical strategies to strengthen your mind and thought processes. Two people can face the same circumstances with very different interpretations, emotions, reactions, and results. The difference is the ability to shape their thoughts and interpretations in constructive ways. Some people make the situation worse by their negative thought processes. We call this "making mountains out of molehills." They take a relatively small problem and make it a huge problem. They do not have a high level of resilience. Other people "make molehills out of mountains." They cope with difficulties in constructive ways by leveraging self-discipline and optimism (faith) to reduce stress. The spiritual discipline is leveraging trust: spiritual knowledge, understanding, and relationship with God, to control your interpretation of life's events. Consider the example of Paul and Silas in Philippi. The magistrates arrested them, publicly stripped them naked, beat them, and locked them in stocks for the crime of healing a demon-possessed slave girl. Yet that night in jail, they prayed, sang hymns, and praised God while the other inmates listened.[525] They made a molehill out of a mountain! They could have complained to each other about God's failure to protect them and the unfairness of their situation. Many people immediately resort to self-pity when they face adversity. It reminds me of the quartet singing the old "Hee Haw" TV show song, "Gloom, Despair, and Agony on Me." "Gloom, despair, and agony on me, deep dark depression excessive misery. If it weren't for bad luck, I'd have no luck at all. Gloom, despair, and agony on me."[526]

The song was a catchy tune and fun to sing along with when I was a kid, but unfortunately, it illustrates how contagious self-pity really can be. Paul and Silas refused to indulge the weakness of their fallen nature. Instead, they replaced negative thoughts with praise. Their witness to the other prisoners could have sounded very different if they had poured out their complaints. Instead, the prisoners witnessed extraordinary faith and miraculous power as God opened the prison doors and broke the chains that held the prisoners. It wasn't the injustice of their imprisonment that appropriated the power of God to help Paul and Silas. It was their faith. Instead of trying to escape, Paul and Silas used the event to share the Gospel with the jailer. They recognized God's purpose in their arrest and led the Jailer's family and many others to salvation.

Your interpretations of life experiences carry tremendous power, dramatically influencing your life and the lives of others. Recognize the difference between what you can and cannot control, experiences vs. your interpretations of them. Steer your understanding of events toward constructive and God-honoring conclusions. Like Paul, pursue contentment in every situation.[527] You can leverage the *event—thought—consequence* principle to maximize your strength and resilience when troubles come.

---

525 Acts 16:22–25
526 Bernie Brillstein, Frank Peppiatt and John Aylesworth, *Gloom, Despair and Agony on Me*, recorded by Buck Owens and Roy Clark, Red Boot Records, 1969.
527 Philippians 4:10–12

Chapter 4

Include God's Purposes in Your Interpretation

Can we accept good from God and not evil?[528]
Our God can save us, but even if he doesn't, we will not bow down and worship your idol.[529]

You now recognize how your interpretation of events can be more important than the events themselves. That brings us to a very important spiritual lesson in times of trouble, recognizing God's purposes in the big picture. How does God's will figure in your interpretation of life's circumstances? If God chooses to lead you through a difficult situation, is it appropriate to conclude the circumstance is a negative in your life? According to the Bible, God's will is always the best course for your life.[530] What if God's will is difficult, painful, or seems to cause suffering? The biblical story of Job centers on the question, "How do you cope with the suffering of the righteous?" The answer: patiently trust God.[531] However, like Job, in the moment of trial, you may find God quiet, distant, and inscrutable. Job lamented that although he faithfully served the Lord, he felt alone in the storm.[532] He could not hear God's counsel or comfort in the moment of trial. When suffering makes you feel far away from God, how do you know for sure the struggle is truly His will? Discerning God's will can be a challenging quest. Unless you feel God is giving you specific direction on the source of the problem, continue to ask God to deliver you. As you walk through it, remember God's promise; He will work all things out for your good as you follow Him.[533] That means if you're walking through it, God will give you grace to stand, and ultimately, He will use it to produce good fruit in your life.[534] Scripture is clear God does not bring evil, troubles, or suffering into your life.[535] The enemy exploits human nature to cause much of the evil in this world.[536] The worst of human nature causes the rest. God will use these circumstances to provide opportunities to grow, help others, or both. He is the ultimate recycler. He uses the good, the bad, and the ugly of your life to accomplish His purposes and to draw you closer to Him. He will shape your character and lead you further into His purposes.

---

[528] Job 2:10
[529] Daniel 3:16–20
[530] James 4:15
[531] Job 42:1–2
[532] Job 13:24
[533] Romans 8:28
[534] 1 Corinthians 10:13
[535] James 1:17
[536] John 10:10

Consider an example from the life of David. When David volunteered to face Goliath in the Valley of Elah, King Saul heard of his comments and sent for him. The king immediately questioned his youth and his ability to face Goliath, a seasoned warrior trained to fight from his youth. David's reply offers some important insights.

> But David said to Saul, "Your servant has been keeping his father's sheep. When a lion or a bear came and carried off a sheep from the flock, I went after it, struck it, and rescued the sheep from its mouth. When it turned on me, I seized it by its hair, struck it and killed it. Your servant has killed both the lion and the bear; this uncircumcised Philistine will be like one of them, because he has defied the armies of the living God. The LORD who delivered me from the paw of the lion and the paw of the bear will deliver me from the hand of this Philistine." Saul said to David, "Go, and the LORD be with you."[537]

We discussed how David spent years in the open fields tending his father's flocks. During this time, he prayed, wrote songs, and developed an intimate relationship with God. David's responsibility from the time he was a boy was to protect the sheep and goats. By David's own admission, fierce beasts attacked the animals under his care. When he tried to rescue the sheep, the lion or bear turned on him in a fight for his own life. How could a loving God who deeply loved David—a young man after his own heart—allow him to be attacked by wild beasts? Surely, God would assign His angels to create an invisible fence around David and his flocks to protect them from harm! Could God truly have purpose in a boy fighting for his life alone in the wilderness? When you face trouble, the natural reaction is a feeling of betrayal that God would allow the situation to happen to you. Then the big question flies, "Why, God, why?" Would not a loving heavenly Father protect His child from every trial? We discussed the danger of the "Why?" question previously, but the answer is: God will not insulate you from every danger. Jesus was clear, "In this world you will have trouble but take heart, I have overcome the world [I will not abandon you]."[538] God has purpose in allowing you to face trials. He teaches you to rely on Him, expands your faith, and strengthens your courage and confidence in Him.

Could David have faced Goliath without the lions and bears? Short answer: no. Those wild animals proved to be the classroom, the laboratory, where God showed David all things were possible with His help. David learned that he was never alone, even in the darkest moments. He learned God was with him, would protect him, and would help him defeat every enemy he would ever face. Picture David as a small boy with God standing directly behind him. His enemies saw a small, vulnerable teenager, not realizing they were, in fact, fighting a young man of faith with God's power. King Saul didn't believe in

---
537 1 Samuel 17:34–37
538 John 16:33

him, his brothers ridiculed him, Goliath cursed him to his face, yet David was not dismayed. He knew God was with him regardless of how large the enemy. David boldly proclaimed his faith in the face of Goliath's taunting.

> David said to the Philistine, "You come against me with sword and spear and javelin, but I come against you in the name of the LORD Almighty, the God of the armies of Israel, whom you have defied. This day the LORD will hand you over to me, and I'll strike you down and cut off your head. Today I will give the carcasses of the Philistine army to the birds of the air and the beasts of the earth, and the whole world will know that there is a God in Israel. All those gathered here will know that it is not by sword or spear that the LORD saves; for the battle is the LORD's, and he will give all of you into our hands."[539]

What a declaration! Listening to this boy, I am ashamed that I've let much smaller challenges bring me to my knees. How did David face a fierce giant, trained in battle from youth and carrying massive weapons of war, with such assurance? God forged David's confidence in the fires of battles with lions and bears, standing watch over his father's flocks alone in the wilderness at night. In the *Wizard of Oz* movie, Dorothy sang, "Lion and tigers and bears, oh my!" David sang, "Lions and tigers and bears, I dare you to attack my flocks!" David had developed such a closeness with God in the wilderness that he literally armed himself on his way to face Goliath, where he picked up five smooth stones from a creek. He refused to take King Saul's armor and weapons. He didn't stand around waiting for Goliath to make his move. Scripture states he ran toward the battle line to engage his adversary, and he took the first shot.[540] Did God have a purpose in allowing David to face wild beasts in the wilderness? Absolutely! God used those challenges to prepare David to take down Goliath. Further, I believe Goliath was the laboratory that prepared David for the hardest trial of his life, Ziklag.

---
539 1 Samuel 17:45–47
540 1 Samuel 17:48

Figure 4a.
Event – Thought – Consequence Decision Matrix – David's Big Threats

Event	Interpretation (Decision Pt)	Emotions	Action	Consequence	Next Thought	Next Emotion	Next Actions?
David attacked by the Lion and Bear	God is with me and will protect me	Peace, Confidence	Bravely fought lions and bears to protect his flock	Rescued his sheep, killed lion and bear	God will be faithful Next time	More Peace Pride Courage	Set up to face Goliath
	God didn't protect me	Stress, Fear, Confusion	Intimidated by wild animals, didn't try to rescue sheep	Loss of sheep, flock not protected as well	I am failing my father	Guilt, More Stress, Fear & Doubts	Less effort to protect flock
David fights Goliath	God helped me kill the lion & bear, he will help me defeat Goliath	Courage Confidence	Volunteered to fight Goliath, made declaration of faith in God	Goliath killed, Israel rescued from the Philistines	God was faithful again	More Courage	Set up to trust God at Ziklag
	God didn't protect Israel from enemies	Stress, Fear, Confusion	Do nothing, return home	Israel subject to Philistine occupation	Should I have done more?	Guilt, More Stress, Fear & Doubts	Trust God less in life

Review the *event—thought—consequence* for David's battles with adversaries above. Can you recognize the positive cycle of faith that set him up for the next victory? David's life was on the line every time, but at Ziklag, David's life was at risk from his own men in their intense grief. At that moment, David was able to draw from his experiences in the wilderness, his victory over Goliath, and recognize that, once again, the battle was the Lord's. It was not going to be won by swords and spears but with the hand of the Lord. In the big picture, all the adversity, all the threats David faced to that point in his life, provided him the courage, confidence, and internal strength to overcome the crisis at Ziklag.

Look back on your life. What earlier crises has God used to help you face the next challenge? Several years ago, I started a journal of my "big answers" to prayer. It's amazing to look back and remember how difficult the challenge seemed at the time and how big God showed up to change those circumstances. That journal encourages my faith every time I face a new challenge. Could God be using your struggles to move you forward in His purposes? Consider the benefits you can reap through your trials: Problems present opportunities for positive change and growth. Problems serve as a pruning process stripping away the superficial distractions that hold you back.[541] Problems can move you to draw closer

---
[541] John 15:2

to God, re-prioritizing your relationship with Him. Problems produce godly character and perseverance.[542] Problems foster creativity and help you think out of the box about God and life. Problems cannot only increase your faith, but God can use them to position you for the next step in His plan for your life. Any of these purposes could be your silver lining. God will use difficulties to build your confidence that He is with you and has your back. Truthfully, in Christ, He is always with you. He lives within your spirit, with all the resurrection power of God. Your challenge is to know with certainty, without a doubt in your heart, that He is there and has your back. You must see with spiritual eyes the God who stands right behind you through life's journey, in the same way He stood with David. Some people think God is setting them up to fail. Resilient people realize God is setting them up for success—for the next big step forward. Consider the "Decision Matrix" below. Which *interpretation* is the most constructive for your life?

Figure 4b.
Event – Thought – Consequence Decision Matrix – Your Difficulty

Event	Interpretation (Decision Pt)	Emotions	Action	Consequence	Next Thought	Next Emotion	Next Actions?
Fill in your struggle. _____	God has a purpose: Change, New Growth, Draw closer to God, Perseverance Character, New ways of looking at life	Peace, Expectation	Seek God. React in ways that reflect your faith and trust in God. Focus outward to help others	God is honored, people are helped, God rewards obedience	I am making spiritual and personal progress	Greater peace, hope	Positioned to step out in faith and obedience as the Holy Spirit leads you, Greater effort to seek God, honor him and help others
	God has abandoned me	Stress, Fear, Confusion	React in ways that reflect less trust, withdraw from others	God is not honored. People are not helped	My problem is overwhelming me	Guilt, More Stress, Fear & Doubts	Lesser effort to seek God & help others. Not ready to step out as God leads

Your present struggle could be the greenhouse experience God uses to propel you toward His greater purpose for your life. Could God use it to move you to the next level in your spiritual walk? Regardless of the source of the problem, God can and will use it for your benefit. What Satan meant for evil; God

---
542 James 1:2–4

can turn to good. The key to this outcome is the ability to manage your thoughts with faith. One interpretation of your struggle is constructive and releases God's blessings on your faithfulness. The other is harmful spiritually, emotionally, and physically as fear and stress rule your mindset. As you pray, fast, and seek God's counsel, you encourage constructive action and create fertile ground for God to act on your behalf. The spiritual battle for your perspective may be more intense than for the problem itself. Your enemy knows how to fight strategically. If he can distance you from your support system, from your divine helper and godly friends, he maximizes his potential damage to your life. We already cited Scripture that God helps those who believe He is a rewarder of those who earnestly seek Him.[543] The key to God's help is faith, to think and act in ways that demonstrate your belief that God is good and that He intends to bring His goodness, blessing, and favor to fruition in your present circumstances. The faith-filled state of mind allows you to speak to the mountains, "Be moved." And your problems will begin to turn around as you exercise the authority God has given you.

Consider another biblical example. Joseph, the son of Jacob (also known as Israel), had a divine dream that he would rule over his family.[544] In jealousy, his ten brothers faked his death and sold him into slavery in Egypt. Joseph lost his family and freedom in one wicked act. His dream seemed an impossibility. Joseph continued to honor God in his life and became head of his master's household even as a slave. Once again, tragedy struck. Falsely accused of attempted rape, Joseph's master threw him into prison. His dream was over. Once again, Joseph honored God in his attitude and actions. God responded. Joseph became the right-hand man of the jailer, entrusted with access to the whole prison.[545] One day, the king jailed two of his officials. They had dreams that Joseph interpreted. The king restored one of the officials to his previous position. Unfortunately, the official forgot Joseph and neglected his promise to help him get out of prison. Finally, after two years, God sent Pharaoh a dream, and the official remembered Joseph. The rest is biblical history. Joseph became second only to Pharaoh in Egypt. Eventually, Joseph's family bowed before him. Scholars estimate Joseph spent thirteen years in servitude before he was elevated to court. Another seven-plus years passed before he saw his family again. Joseph experienced an extravagantly happy ending to his life. What about day one, when Joseph looked up from the bottom of a cistern, fearing for his life? What about year one, when Joseph was a slave in an Egyptian household? What about a few years later when he was imprisoned in a dark, damp cell? How did he feel after he was forgotten by the official he helped? At each of these moments and likely many more between, Joseph faced an *event—thought—consequence* decision point. Jacob's favored son could have descended into self-pity. Instead, he chose to trust, believing the same God who gave him dreams and

---

543 Hebrews 11:6
544 Genesis 37:5–8
545 Genesis 39

visions could deliver him from death, slavery, and a prison cell. Joseph had to wait thirteen years for his deliverance, although God's favor followed him in slavery and in prison. How long will you wait to see God's deliverance? Can you maintain faithful patience for a decade or more? Can you face beasts with fierce fangs or warrior giants? It is impossible to know how your specific circumstances will unfold, how long you will have to endure, or how God will reveal the answer. What you must know is God will never stop working for you no matter what unfolds or how long it takes. Patient faith is the cornerstone of spiritual resilience. The way to minimize the time required is to trust God, follow His Word, and use your spiritual authority in Christ as He commanded. In faith, continually command your mountains to move without giving up.

God challenged me with a passage of Scripture from Jeremiah. The prophet did not understand why God punished His people but allowed the wicked responsible to prosper. God answered, "If you have raced with men on foot and they have worn you out, how can you compete with horses? If you stumble in safe country, how will you manage in the thickets by the Jordan?"[546] Jeremiah, also known as the weeping prophet, struggled to trust God in his nation's moment of trial. God's answer: If you struggle with the challenges sent to train and strengthen you, how can you ever overcome the real trials? If we use David's story as a reference, God essentially said, "If you struggle with the lion or bear, how can you ever face Goliath?" Service to God can be difficult. One of the growth lessons of life is to trust God through the worst circumstances. Ziklag was not the end of David's trials. While your struggle won't be your last, it will be a building block God uses to increase your faith, refine your character, make you stronger, and move you forward in His plan and purposes for your life. It will become a multiplication factor in your ability to face the next battle. Remember David. God prepared him to fight Goliath in the protective laboratory of the shepherd's field, fighting lions and bears. "Protective laboratory" may seem like a stretch, but God was watching over David. He knew David's strengths, knew David was up to the challenge, and was on hand just in case. Picture a parent teaching a child to ride a bike. The parent recognizes when it's time to let go. The parent hovers nearby, far enough away so the child does the work but close enough to intervene. Picture God hovering over you in your circumstances the same way He hovered over David in the fields. God set him up for success. Then, God positioned him to be king over Israel through his victory over Goliath and, more immediately, by his victory over the Amalekites following Ziklag. Remember Joseph. God positioned him to be the number two ruler in Egypt using the worst of circumstances, betrayal, slavery, and prison. God was faithful. How might God be using your present struggles to position you for greater things? Make sure you include God's purposes in the meaning you assign to difficult events in your life. Your interpretations of life's problems have the potential

---

546 Jeremiah 12:4–5

to propel you forward in personal growth and God's blessings. They also have the power to mire you in a stagnant pool of self-pity and misery.

Chapter 5

Recognize and Contradict Thinking Traps

Your adversary the enemy is a liar and the father of lies.[547]

Recognize specific destructive thought patterns, called thinking traps, and contradict them with healthy, constructive thought processes! Thinking traps, also known as cognitive distortions, usually reinforce negative thoughts.[548] Your mind is your spiritual center of gravity. The enemy attacks peoples' minds with these common but very effective stratagems, leveraging the human tendency to focus on the negative and amplifying it with unhealthy patterns of thinking. These deeply ingrained thought processes convince people something is true when, in reality, it is completely false. They appear rational or feel realistic in the moment but find a basis in misconceptions or errors in judgment, usually generalizations and over-simplification. They contradict scriptural principles but appear true to believers because they feel true. Do not allow the power of your feelings to override your spiritual sight (faith). Like a venomous snake bite, thinking traps cause deadly poison to circulate through your heart and mind resulting in a self-destructive mindset. The thought patterns predominantly steer your thinking toward negativity and distrust. The pessimistic perspective inherent in thinking traps reinforces harmful misinterpretation of life's events. These patterns are contrary to faith and sap your ability to trust and serve God. They limit the growth of your relationship and set you up to make harmful Interpretations in the *event—thought—consequence* model. In fact, as we have shown in previous chapters, it's your response to the event—your mindset—not the event itself that causes negative feelings and leads to negative actions and consequences. Faith inherently contains optimism, expecting good things from God.

The consequence of wrongdoing (sin) is human suffering. In a dangerous world where people (in their fallen nature) strive to get what they want, sometimes at significant cost to others, everyone must be on guard. The natural response: protect yourself from pain. People focus on life's dangers and the negative information in their environment. Compound that dynamic with the lessons people learn from personal emotional wounds, and you have the perfect setup for a thinking trap. After a betrayal, you hear your friend say, "You just can't trust people. I'll never trust anyone again!" When faced with a series of setbacks, you hear, "Nothing good ever happens to me. I'm just a magnet for bad luck." Are these statements true? Are they constructive? No, but the negative thoughts produce intense emotions that empow-

---
547 John 8:44
548 Naoumidis, Alex, "*Thinking Traps: 12 Cognitive Distortions That Are Hijacking Your Brain*," Accessed October 3, 2021, http://www.mindsethealth.com/matter/thinking-traps-cognitive-distortions.

er self-destructive behaviors. They feel gratifying in the moment. Unfortunately, the negative thoughts quickly become patterns that continually seek out information to reinforce the original conclusions. This dynamic is a good example of the "self-licking lollipop (a self-sustaining system whose only purpose is to survive)." Like other patterns of sin, negative thinking uses your sympathetic fallen nature to dominate. The tendency to expand control in your mind is another destructive consequence.[549] Once negative thinking takes root, you must work hard to master it. Thinking traps contradict the clear teachings of Scripture. They violate the second great commandment to selflessly love one another.[550] Biblical love does not keep a record of wrongs or delight in evil.[551] Thinking traps fixate on evil and refuse to let go. Thinking traps also violate the commands to keep your mind pure.[552] Self-pity and the victim mentality are unhealthy, unproductive, and opposed to the work of the Holy Spirit in your life.[553] You cannot allow them to seize control. For years, I struggled with various thinking traps, such as preoccupation with the negative and assuming the worst. These have not only dominated my thinking in times of difficulty, but they also caused me to question God's goodness and promises. Unfortunately, negative thinking affected my fruitfulness as a church leader for two decades. My personal struggles to develop spiritually resilient thinking are a reason for this book.

The quest to make your thinking more faith-filled is a fist fight with your fallen nature to make it submit to the teachings of Scripture and leading of the Holy Spirit. You will be fighting the side of yourself that finds gratification in the negative as it finds sympathetic shelter deep within your belief system. The fight is critical to reset your thought processes on a healthy, constructive track. The prescription is simple but requires consistency to achieve. "Do not be conformed to this world (with its dark negativity) but be transformed by renewing your mind."[554] Recognize the errors in your thinking, then apply Scripture and wisdom to transform your thinking toward an optimistic faith-filled mindset. The first step, to recognize them in your thinking, can be difficult, as they appear so reasonable in the moment. Your interpretation of life experiences provides the camouflage. They look like facts. Second, to consistently challenge the inherent error of your thinking and replace it with a healthy, rational, and constructive thought process requires constant attention. You must consistently challenge your sympathy towards and self-indulgence of unhealthy thoughts to replace them with truth. Reading and speaking out truths of Scripture to replace bad thinking can be very effective. This is where faith comes; it requires faith to stand upon scriptural truth. This strategy contains numerous Scripture quotes to assist you. Write them down in obvious places. Begin your day quoting Scripture over your life. Over time, you can develop new habits of thinking to intercept destructive thought patterns before they produce negative emotions and harmful stress. It is

---

549 Genesis 4:7
550 Mark 12:31, John 13:34
551 1 Corinthians 13:4–8
552 Matthew 5:8, Philippians 4:8, 2 Timothy 2:21–26
553 Galatians 5:22–23
554 Romans 12:2

time to begin house cleaning. We will identify numerous common thinking traps people face, evaluate their fallacies based on scriptural counsel, and discuss how to recognize and replace them. Prepare to fight!

Thinking Trap #1: Jumping to Conclusions

The first thinking trap, *jumping to conclusions*, involves forming your opinions without enough evidence. Often referred to as *assuming the worst*, it involves some form of making poor, false, or extreme assumptions.[555] People have lied, so you assume someone is a liar. Love, a key component of faith, is the antithesis of assuming the worst. According to Scripture, love always trusts and always hopes.[556] Love gives others the benefit of the doubt. It believes for the best. It does not celebrate the negative, evil, or bad reports.[557] Some revel in the latest juicy gossip and share it quickly with no concern for the facts. *Assuming the worst* is a kindred spirit to *rejoicing in evil*.[558] Avoid them both like the plague. Ask yourself, "Have I made a snap judgment? Have I considered all the information in forming my opinion? What information exists that might contradict my initial view?" How does the new information bear on my initial thoughts? Give others the benefit of the doubt (grace). Train yourself to withhold judgment until you have considered complete information. How can God use this situation for His glory? Most thinking traps involve some form of *jumping to conclusions*, but two of the worst are *mind reading* and *fortune telling*.

Thinking Trap #2: Mind Reading

The second thinking trap, *mind reading*, assumes you know what others are thinking with no factual evidence to support your conclusion.[559] You may think, "I know my supervisor doesn't like me. He didn't smile at me in the hallway just now." The truth might be that he didn't smile at anyone or that he's so focused on his own problems he didn't think about how his behavior affected others. A wife may think, "My husband thinks I'm ugly. He hasn't said anything about how I look after I spent hours getting ready for our night out." Unfortunately, many men are slow to volunteer compliments, a quality that plagues their wives' thinking. The point of these scenarios is to highlight the danger of assuming you know what another person is thinking. You have no idea what is happening in the private life of another person, let alone the inner world of their thoughts and feelings. Many people are deeply troubled with their own fears, worries, and doubts, especially with the physical and economic concerns of a post-pandemic world dominated by inflation and recession. In most cases, it is not that people are against you (out to

---
555 Naoumidis, "Thinking Traps."
556 1 Corinthians 13:7
557 1 Corinthians 13:6
558 Ibid.
559 Naoumidis, "Thinking Traps."

harm you); it is that they are for themselves (self-centered). They center their thoughts and energy on their own well-being to the point they neglect to think about how their behaviors affect others—including you. Love is patient, kind, not boastful or proud.[560] *Mind reading* is not patient or kind. It is a snap judgment that assumes the worst, inherently based in the pride of thinking you know another's thoughts. Scripture counsels, "Be quick to listen, slow to anger."[561] *Mind reading* doesn't listen at all. It does not give the other person an opportunity to share their real thoughts; it is simply anger without listening.

Believing you can know the thoughts of others without any objective evidence will harm your relationships and bring unnecessary stress and angst to your mental-emotional state. You need relationships to strengthen your resilience and reduce stress. Taking on additional stress without a reasonable cause is self-destructive. Some reprimand their spouses for not having the ability to know what they are thinking. They say, "You should have known!" It is unfair to assume anyone can or should have been able to read your mind. Assumptions are dangerous in relationships. They place an unfair burden on others, and the perceived manipulation violates trust.

Another example of mind reading might be: "I know people are talking behind my back." If you feel uncomfortable in groups, you may be quick to assume that others look down on you. This is likely due to your own insecurities. As more of an introvert, I have personally struggled with feeling uncomfortable in large groups. I do not blend in quickly like some, so it is easy for me to assume that people have negative thoughts about me. Those assumptions make me feel awkward and embarrassed. Are those reasonable or helpful thoughts? It is impossible to gather enough information in the first few minutes with a new group of people to know what they think, but that fact does not stop the mind reading. I know my thoughts are not constructive because they impede my ability to get to know people in new situations. It takes energy and self-control to resist those impulses with new people.

You can change the way you think. Admit you are not a mind reader and the "ability to read minds" is neither healthy nor constructive. Identify the circumstances when you tend to use this thinking trap and quickly identify when you engage the behavior. When a negative situation occurs that stimulates mind reading, recognize your unhealthy response and refute it. A simple way to counter the thought is to ask yourself, "What other reasons (besides my hasty conclusion) may have caused the person to act or speak the way they did?"[562] The figure below shows a simple flow chart of the process.

---
560 1 Corinthians 13:4
561 James 1:19
562 Naoumidis, *"Thinking Traps."*

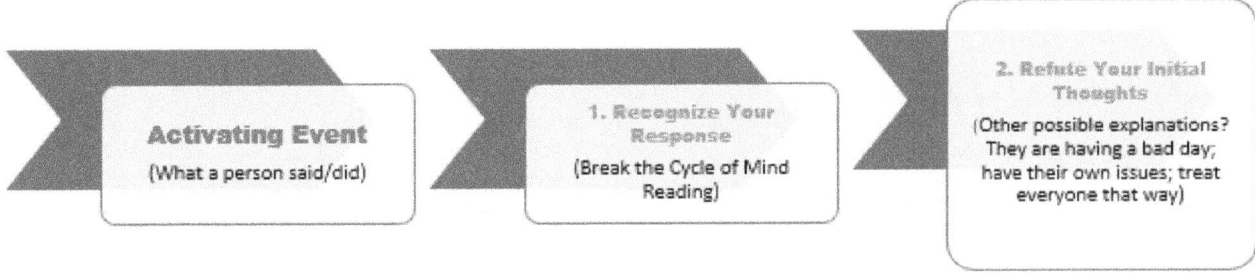

Figure 5a.
Mind Reading Intervention Flow Chart

Do not pride yourself in being a mind reader. You may have a sense of what someone is thinking from their non-verbal cues (posture, facial expression, tone, demeanor, etc.), but you can never be sure. Accept that this thinking trap does far more harm than good in your life.

Thinking Trap #3: Fortune-Telling

The third thinking trap, *fortune-telling*, is when you predict things will turn out badly.[563] It is an attempt to foresee the future with a very negative tone. You might say to yourself, "I will never get promoted at work. I could never speak publicly as well as Cindy, or I never win when I compete for something." Telling yourself something bad is going to happen before you attempt to affect the outcome is disempowering and destructive. You condition your mind by what you say to yourself. Negative conditioning thoughts produce feelings of weakness, fear, and hopelessness. The physical consequences of stress and these negative feelings can sap your physical strength. Your negative focus becomes a self-fulfilling prophecy as your bad feelings limit your motivation and effort, increasing the likelihood of a negative outcome. You cannot predict the future. Like worry, fortune-telling is a worthless expenditure of energy that creates mental, emotional angst. It not only saps your strength, it harms your body. Because you have no evidence to support your conclusion, fortune-telling is counter-productive and irrational. This mindset is the opposite of faith. Faith is optimistic, expecting good things from God.[564]

---

563 Ibid.
564 Hebrews 11:1,6, James 1:17

Figure 5b.
Countering the Fortune Telling Thinking Trap

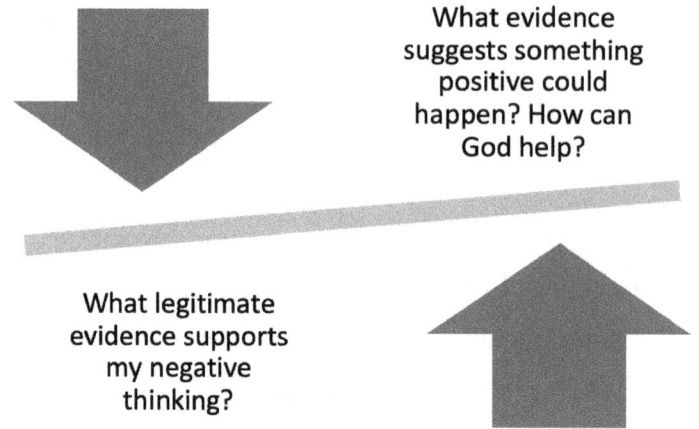

Scripture states, "Everything that does not come from faith is sin."[565] Faith is a confidence that God will help you with your needs. Fortune-telling contradicts faith. Faith urges you to expect and proclaim a positive outcome. To predict a negative outcome when you hope and pray for a good one is the kind of double-mindedness Scripture condemns.[566] To refute fortune-telling, ask yourself, "What legitimate evidence supports my negativity? What evidence suggests something positive could happen? How might God intervene? What friend/spiritual leader can join me in praying for good outcomes in this situation?" Some people curse themselves and their futures by proclaiming a bad outcome. A curse is a declaration that limits or restricts your future and potential. It becomes a self-fulfilling prophesy in the natural because it hinders your motivation for positive action. In a spiritual sense, the words become a prophetic stronghold the enemy uses to keep you bound. God has promised to prosper you, not harm you.[567] Do not curse what God has blessed. Instead, speak God's promises of blessing and favor over your life. Scripture declares these promises are a "Yes," through Jesus Christ that enables you to say, "Amen (let it be—literally "I agree.")."[568] If you are going to predict the future, predict one full of God's blessing and favor.

---

565 Romans 14:23
566 James 1:6–8
567 Jeremiah 29:11
568 2 Corinthians 1:20

Thinking Trap #4: All-or-Nothing Thinking

The fourth thinking trap, *all-or-nothing* thinking, is about thinking that something is either all good or all bad. Also known as black-and-white thinking, it leaves no room for the middle ground.[569] The negative bias associated with this trap declares one bad experience can mean your whole life is bad. This mindset takes a molehill and turns it into a mountain. You may think, "Nobody at work likes me," because you had a conflict with one person at work. You may think, "Everything I do fails," because you had one failure. As with fortune-telling above, predicting a negative future is contradictory to faith. One event or series of events is insufficient to predict that your whole future is lost. In Scripture, Job recognized life in a fallen world means people get a mixture of good and bad. Job was quick to recognize God's sovereignty over all.[570] Further, God can use bad experiences to strengthen your character and produce positive outcomes.[571] Adversity can literally set you up for a greater victory.

Things that appear negative at first can turn out to be the breakthrough you needed. An athlete suffered an injury several months before the championship event. It seemed like an end to his hopes and dreams. During those months, he continued training, strengthening other muscles that weren't usually worked as hard. He healed and won the championship primarily because he had increased his body's total strength. That conditioning would never have happened without the injury. David suffered a devastating loss at Ziklag, but within a short time, he was crowned King of Judah.[572] Could David have become king without Ziklag? Maybe, but Ziklag set him up to be the king Israel needed.

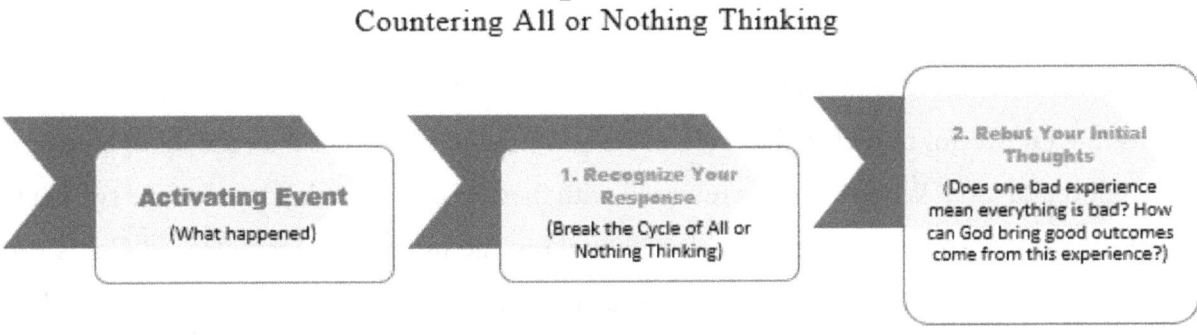

Figure 5c.
Countering All or Nothing Thinking

- Recognize and challenge your generalization.
- Ask, "What is my reality?"
- "What good things are happening?" "How is God blessing in this situation?"

---

569 Naoumidis, *"Thinking Traps."*
570 Job 2:10
571 Romans 8:28, James 1:2–4
572 2 Timothy 2:4

As with all thinking traps, it is important to recognize and rebut them. Challenge the generalization that one unpleasant situation means your future is doomed. In truth, life is a sampling of good and bad with everything in between. Ask yourself, "Is this truly my reality?" Does one difficult experience truly define your whole life? That type of thinking is an unhealthy exaggeration. Resilience allows you to maintain your perspective regardless of how difficult things get. You recognize, like Job, that life brings blessings and hardships. "Should God allow only good in life, insulating you from any bad?" What positive things are happening in your life? How is God blessing you?

Thinking Trap #5 Negative Brain Filters

The fifth thinking trap, Negative Brain Filters, is an unhealthy preoccupation with the negative, focusing on bad experiences to the exclusion of the positive.[573] Negative filters are a common thinking trap as people tend to be over-sensitive to negative stimuli in their environment. With a brain filter, you focus on your failures while ignoring your successes. For example, you beat yourself up for cheating on your diet, neglecting the fact that you have spent several days eating only healthy foods. Does one failure out of a week of disciplined choices make the whole week a bust? Does it justify all the harmful thoughts and emotions? Perhaps you get a "C" when you are normally an "A" or "B" student? Does one bad test justify feeling like a complete failure?

While a brain filter typically filters out the positive, Scripture encourages you to filter out the negative.[574] Human nature tends to accentuate the negative. The consequences of sin in our world create a wealth of negative reports. Whose report will you believe? Sometimes God will test you to determine if you will stand on His promises. God took Israel to a new home. He promised He would lead them safely into their inheritance after four hundred years of slavery. Unfortunately, even after God repeatedly demonstrated powerful miracles, they retained a slave mentality rather than the thought processes of beloved children of God. When the spies returned with their report of the land, ten of the twelve focused on the negatives (83 percent).[575] Ten of twelve filtered out the information that proved God's Promised Land was good and bountiful, instead exaggerating the threat of the people who lived there. When the spies presented their reports, Israel chose to ignore the optimistic reports of Joshua and Caleb, who assured the people, "We can surely take this land flowing with milk and honey."[576] Remarkably, the people saw the visible evidence of the fruit of the land with their own eyes yet refused to obey. Their negative filters resulted in thirty-nine more years of wandering in the desert until the last adult in that generation died.[577] Do you remember our earlier discussion of the qualities of child-like faith, mental flexibility,

---
573 Naoumidis, *"Thinking Traps."*
574 Philippians 4:8
575 Numbers 13:31–33
576 Numbers 13:27,30
577 Numbers 14:21–24

and lifetime learning? Of the twelve spies and remaining adult Israelites, only Joshua and Caleb entered God's Promised Land. They had turned away from a slave-victim mentality to a "God is able" mentality. Many people suffer from a poverty mentality, focusing on what they don't have while forgetting all the reasons to be thankful. Do not follow the crowd. You cannot experience God's fullness without retraining your mind.

To counter a *negative brain filter*, recognize your preoccupation with negative experiences. Identify the full spectrum of your performance, the good, bad, and in in-between. You may have missed a few shots in the game, but you played an exceptional game on defense. Occupy your mind with the good things that are going on in your life and be thankful. Shift your focus from what is wrong to what is going right.

Figure 5d.
Countering a Negative Brain Filter

Activating Event
(The Event or experience)

1. Recognize Your Response
(Break the Cycle of Filtering)

2. Rebut Your Initial Thoughts
(What good is happening? What is going right? What can I thank God for? What promises has God given?)

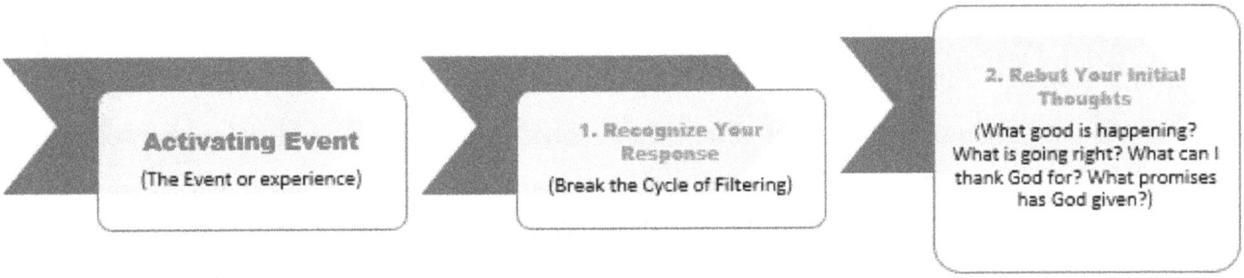

Thinking Trap #6 The Fallacy of Change

The sixth thinking trap, *fallacy of change*, is another common one. It involves the idea that you will be happy if people around you change.[578] For example, one might think, "If you really loved me, you wouldn't play video games for hours," or "If you really loved me, you would know what I wanted and just do it." Desiring people in your life to change is not a bad thought in and of itself. Everyone, including you, has room to learn, grow, and mature. The thinking trap exists when you condition your happiness on another person's change. You give control of your life to that person. You cannot control other people's actions, so you should not give them power over your inner peace and joy. When you think this way, you may be tempted to manipulate them to get what you want. This is not love. Your inner happiness should be a product of your own decisions, thoughts, and behaviors. Remember, change can be as difficult for others as it is for you.

Scripture recognizes the elusiveness of happiness.[579] The spiritual fruit of joy is an inner contentment and wellness of heart derived from the fellowship of the Holy Spirit and His work to produce Christ-

---

578 Julie Killion, "What Are Cognitive Distortions?" accessed October 4, 2021, www.mindpathcare.com/blog/what-are-cognitive-distortions/.
579 Ecclesiastes 4:4, 10–13

like values, character, and growth in your life.[580] When you make people the source of your happiness, you make them an idol in your life. Do not give people control of your happiness. They can never fully steward that responsibility. People can make a great contribution to your life, bringing you periods of happiness in a good relationship. Supportive relationships can strengthen your resilience. However, only God is worthy of being placed on a pedestal in your life, and only He can provide what your inner being fully needs. He designed you with a need for communion with Him.[581] His active work in your life will produce peace and joy.[582]

To counter the *fallacy of change* in your thinking, reflect on when and how you are relying on someone else's behaviors to make you happy. Understand that other people's behavior is not in your control. While you can help shape others' behaviors through healthy communication skills and your reactions, you cannot control them. Beware of trying to manipulate others into doing what you want. Give other people the same degree of choice you expect for yourself in the relationship. Communicate clearly what you want from others in your relationships but do so with the same kindness and respect you would want. Simply follow the *golden rule*, "Treat others as you want to be treated."[583] What if a person ignores your needs and desires? First, do not allow that situation to steal your peace and joy. Second, if your desires are reasonable, perhaps it is time to evaluate the level of importance you place on that relationship. You should not increase commitment to those who are not trustworthy. If the person is your spouse, your commitment should not be conditional. You may need to seek out a helper if you cannot make progress through your own problem-solving efforts. In summary, use these questions to help:

- Identify where you rely on someone's change to make you happy.
- Ask yourself, "Have I clearly, respectfully communicated what I want?"
- Ask yourself, "Is what I want reasonable? Would I think so if the shoe were on the other foot?"
- Ask yourself, "Have I given the other person the right to make their own choice about the change I want from them?"
- Recognizing you cannot control the person, find a healthy way to accept their decision.

---

580 Galatians 5:22–23
581 Ecclesiastes 4:11
582 Romans 14:17
583 Matthew 7:12

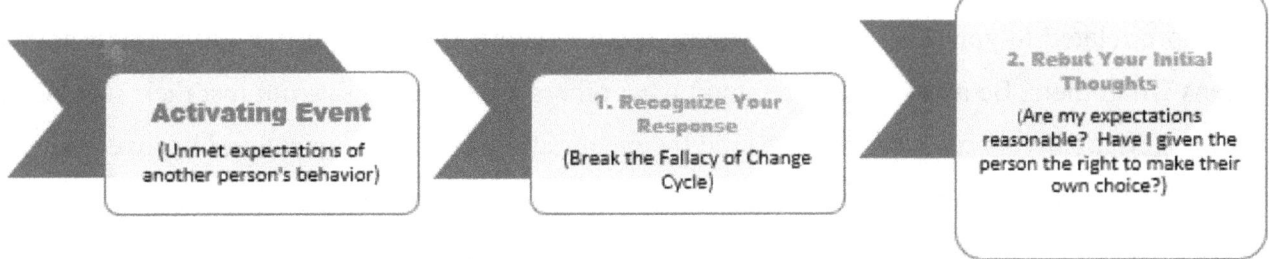

Figure 5e.
Countering the Fallacy of Change

Thinking Trap #7 The Need to Always be Right

The next thinking trap, *always needing to be right*, can seriously damage your relationships. This thinking trap is the way it sounds stopping at nothing to prove you are correct and the other person wrong.[584] "I know I'm right, and I'm going to prove it!" When you make every disagreement a court of law where you win the case at any cost, you communicate a lack of concern for others and their feelings. This is especially damaging to the ones you say you love, spouse, children, siblings, etc. You may think agreement is simple intellectual assent. However, many people experience agreement emotionally as relational resolution. You may have proved your point, but you left the other person feeling disrespected and less related. Agreement will be much harder to achieve next time because of their feelings, not to mention the damage to the relationship. Jesus said, "If you want to be first, you must be last."[585]

Scripture states two important rules, love others as you love yourself.[586] Second, treat others the way you want to be treated.[587] Do you want others arguing with you until they prove you wrong? Would that make you feel loved and valued? Would you rather be right or be happy in your relationships? Would you rather be right or be a positive force of encouragement in other people's lives? I call this being a "life-giving" force. Would God prefer you live the law of love or be right according to the law? You cannot do both at the same time. Jesus was very clear with the Pharisees, you painstakingly pursued being "right" according to the Jewish Law, but you became wrong because you neglected the higher priorities of love and compassion.[588] The truth is, you cannot always be right and please God because you cannot love others when you selfishly focus on winning. Always being right creates losers. There is no win-win scenario. This philosophy is the zero-sum game where there can only be one winner and everyone else loses, so you must win. You will be a loser in your relationships over the long term with this approach. Love looks out for the needs of others and creates opportunities for others to win, to get what they need

---
584 Naoumidis, "Thinking Traps."
585 Matthew 20:26–28
586 Mark 12:31
587 Matthew 7:12
588 Matthew 23:23

and want. Do you always have to win to feel good about yourself? The level of conflict in your life will drop dramatically if you seek the win-wins.

To counter always being right, recognize your most important personal victory is to leave others feeling more related to you. Get out of the "Who's right" game and look for the win-wins in your interactions with others. Be a listener. Understand what others are trying to say, not just their words; hear their hearts. Make it your mission to serve God by encouraging and communicating His love and value to others. Serve the people you love by helping them to see your love in positive words and actions. You can make a big difference in your relationships by simply changing your goal from winning (being right) to relating (being connected). You can greatly improve the mental, emotional health of the people you care most about by letting go of right. Your resilience will increase as your relationships improve.

Figure 5f.
Countering Always Being Right

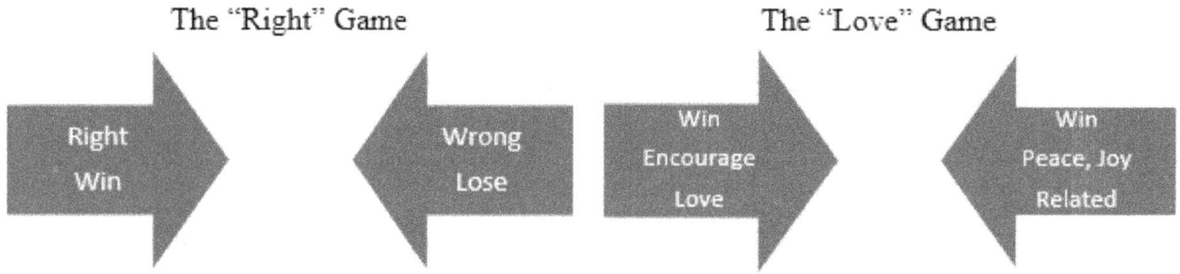

The "Right" Game | The "Love" Game

Right / Win → ← Wrong / Lose   Win / Encourage / Love → ← Win / Peace, Joy / Related

Thinking Trap #8 Labeling

The eighth thinking trap, *labeling*, is attaching a negative label to yourself or someone else.[589] Words have power, and the negativity associated with labeling becomes a self-fulfilling prophecy as you seek out information in your environment that reinforces the label you gave yourself. You may think, "I'm a failure." Not only does that make you feel bad, but it also hinders your efforts to succeed. Additionally, you increase the power of this label by overlooking your positive performance in favor of any information that reinforces the belief that you are a failure. This, in turn, increases the likelihood you will fail next time. You are subconsciously setting yourself up to fail. You may think, "I'm ugly." No matter how much you work out, change your hair, dress, etc., when you look in the mirror, you see ugly. It is less a matter of what is in the mirror and more about what is in your mind. To counter *labeling*, stop naming yourself with negative labels. Look in the Scripture and find out what God says about you. Scripture boldly states it is God who justifies, who has the standing to condemn (to contradict His declaration).[590] You do not have the spiritual authority to negatively label yourself when God has renamed you. Salvation means you no longer identify with your former fallen nature. It still influences your life, but the work

---

589 Naoumidis, *"Thinking Traps."*
590 Romans 8:33–34

of the Spirit inside your heart has made you a new creation; the old is gone.[591] Live like a new creation. Love does not dishonor self or others with negative labels.[592] Resist the harmful messages of the enemy. He is the accuser and a liar. He lacks the authority to dredge up your past. God has chosen to forget your past wrongs.[593] Do not let false guilt and condemnation rule your heart. The Spirit convicts, never condemns.[594] If Jesus told believers to bless and not curse their enemies, how much more should you bless and not curse yourself?[595] Speak positive messages over yourself. Find specific references, chapter, and verse. Start renaming yourself with God's words: beloved, blessed, forgiven, valuable, beautiful, highly favored, chosen, child of the king, righteous, redeemed, etc. Use positive, realistic words that will help you feel good about yourself and encourage positive outcomes in life.

Thinking Trap #9 Overestimating

The next thinking trap, *overestimating*, is inflating the possibility of a negative event occurring. A similar thinking trap, *catastrophizing*, will be discussed in detail at the end of the chapter. You catastrophize when you believe the worst-case scenario will happen. Overestimating is exaggerating the possibility that something bad will happen. You may think, "I know my boss is going to be mad at my poor work presentation tomorrow." You are exaggerating the possibility your boss will be mad. If you were catastrophizing, you would believe that you would be fired (worst case) tomorrow because of your poor presentation. By overestimating, you overstate the possibility your boss will be mad. The most likely scenario is your boss will appreciate the presentation. If you work hard, your boss may love the presentation. By overestimating, you inject needless stress and worry into the process. You lower motivation and effort by thinking the end is already determined regardless of how much work you do. Overestimating convinces your mind of a negative result, so you sabotage your efforts with your mind. You give up control of the situation. You may think, "If I drive my car that far, it will break down." You exaggerate the possibility the car will fail on the trip. If you have maintained the car, gas, oil, tires, etc., the car will probably have less chance of failing on a long trip without all the starting and stopping than experienced with the shorter distances of in-town driving. However, your negative mindset may cause you to do less to maintain the car, making a potential problem more likely. Exaggerating the chance of a negative outcome is the antithesis of optimism. If you choose to exaggerate, do so in a positive manner. It will benefit your health. Faith is not an exercise in pessimism. Faith contains the spiritual optimism of hope, being confident in God and His promises. As a church leader, I have observed too many believers treat pessimism as if it were holiness. God is not pleased with pessimism, especially overstating it. Pessimism

---
591 2 Corinthians 5:17
592 1 Corinthians 13:5
593 Hebrews 8:12
594 Romans 8:1
595 Luke 6:28, Romans 12:14

inherently believes God is not good to His people or a Rewarder of their efforts. It expects God to bring trouble and lack. That attitude is the slave mentality of Israel. Many people say, "God is good," but their pessimism says the opposite. Faith inherently believes God is good, the author of every good and perfect gift who rewards those who seek him.[596] Faith says, "Amen—I agree," to God's promises.[597] To counter overestimating, replace exaggeration with an evaluation of the real possibility of something happening. Make a quick backup plan, if necessary, but do not plan for exaggeration. Do not expend precious energy and effort for false imaginations in your mind. Pray and trust God to take care of your situation.

Thinking Trap #10 Generalizations

The tenth thinking trap, *generalizations*, is making broad conclusions about yourself, using the words "always" or "never," based upon a few negative experiences.[598] You may think, "I never get any good breaks" because someone else was promoted, or "I always get stuck with the work no one else wants" because the boss selected you for a difficult project. Neither of those statements is true. Negativity is contagious; you can easily make one or two bad experiences become proof of an incontrovertible rule of life. Couples are often guilty of this trap. You can say, "My spouse never thinks about what I want," because he or she insisted on a restaurant choice. Be very careful about the greater meaning you assign to any negative experience. You should not judge yourself or anyone else on one or two bad experiences. A good rule of thumb is, "Never use always or never in a criticism." Look for the good in yourself and others. No one is perfect. We all have good qualities and areas needing improvement. We all make good decisions as well as mistakes. Scripture states, love does not delight in evil but rejoices with the truth.[599] Do not magnify evil with gossip and slander. A generalization is never factual; it is a foolish judgment. As you assess your life, or others, make sure you see the whole picture. Avoid broad, sweeping judgments with the words "always" or "never." They only add to your negative emotions and sense of helplessness. They create bad feelings in your heart toward others that disrupt relationships.

Thinking Trap #11 Blaming and Shaming

The next thinking trap, *blaming and shaming*, is blaming others for negative experiences without accepting responsibility for your part. You can also unfairly blame yourself for others' behaviors.[600] When you blame others, you abdicate your responsibility and control. You take the role of the accuser in assigning it to others and often take on an unhealthy desire to manipulate or punish them emotionally (shaming). This trap can get you stuck on the past and powerless to influence future similar situations.

---

596 James 1:17, Hebrews 11:6
597 2 Corinthians 1:20
598 Naoumidis, *"Thinking Traps."*
599 1 Corinthians 13:6
600 Killion, *"Cognitive Distortions."*

Scripture encourages you to be gentle and patient with others, to use words to build them up.[601] We all make mistakes. Wrongdoing is not an excuse to treat others poorly. Show mercy, not judgment. We all need mercy.[602] Spiritual love covers a multitude of sins.[603] To counter this trap, resist the temptation to judge. Resist blaming others and taking revenge through shaming. Instead, take responsibility for your part, recognizing people usually share responsibility for bad situations. Show yourself mercy as well. Ask yourself how you can adjust your behaviors to influence better outcomes in the future.

Thinking Trap #12 Should've, Could've, Would've

The thinking trap, *should've, could've, would've*, is a focus on feelings of regret for negative experiences you might have avoided. Its focus is unmet expectations. You may think, "If only I had acted differently, I could have avoided that problem." The truth is your revised scenario is unknowable. You cannot be sure that something you did could have guaranteed the desired outcome. Regardless of the words you use—should, could, would—you are preoccupied with past regrets. The past is valuable to learn from mistakes and consider how you can improve next time you face a similar situation. The goal of learning from the past is to help you in the future; it is a forward focus. Overemphasis of the past is not constructive. Your thoughts of past regrets produce feelings of condemnation, sadness, and shame. They rob you of motivation and optimism. You feel less control over the future. It is not fair to place that burden on anyone else either. The accusation may continue to echo in another's mind with the same negative effect. The rear-view mirror in your car is far smaller than your windshield for a reason. You are meant to look forward as you drive. God did not mean for you to drive through life looking backward. Scripture makes an interesting comment, "Do not ask 'Why were the old days better than these?' For it is not wise to think on such questions."[604] You cannot move forward with regrets. Resist thoughts that draw you into rumination about the past. Avoid thoughts that include, "I should've," "I could've," or "I would've." You cannot change the past. The primary value in reflecting on past negative experiences is to learn lessons consistent with God's Word you can use to make better decisions in the future.

Thinking Trap #13 Beware of Magnification!

Avoid magnification of negative circumstances! You can train your mind to assume the worst regardless of how likely or realistic it is. This unhealthy thinking pattern is *magnification* or *catastrophizing*.[605] Literally, you can make minor things that happen appear catastrophic. We hear this commonly

---

601 Ephesians 4:2,29
602 Matthew 7:1–2
603 1 Peter 4:8
604 Ecclesiastes 7:10
605 Naoumidis, *"Thinking Traps."*

called "Making a mountain out of a molehill." It references those who magnify a difficult situation to the point it becomes impossible to overcome (aka. the end of the world). If you make every situation "the end of the world," you are catastrophizing. This unhealthy pattern of thinking causes excessive stress and promotes feelings of helplessness. Resilience equips you to take positive action to improve your situation. You must make realistic assessments to develop a plan of action. In catastrophic thinking, you accept the worst-case scenario without ever making an objective assessment of the situation and facts. You make the problem too big to handle. You magnify fears, weaknesses, or mistakes to the point they are insurmountable in your mind. For example, you might feel a financial setback means you will go bankrupt and lose your house. Your mind immediately begins to dwell on how you will live homeless without ever grounding your thoughts in the remote possibility of that happening. You may feel your shy nature will cause you to perform poorly during your work presentation. You agonize over the mental scene of your failure before it even happens and procrastinate on the project because you do not want to face the event. You live out the worst-case scenario in your mind before it ever happens. You treat your conclusion as if a full evaluation of the facts made it inevitable despite the remote possibility of the situation's occurrence.

Paul endured harsh persecution and injustice in his missionary journeys, yet he placed the events in perspective. He wrote, "We are hard pressed on every side, but not crushed; perplexed, but not in despair; persecuted, but not abandoned; struck down, but not destroyed."[606] He refused to admit defeat no matter how difficult the opposition became. Notice Paul did not deny the reality of his situation. He admitted his struggles, "hard pressed, perplexed, persecuted, struck down," but he placed them in perspective, refusing to give them more credit than they deserved. He specifically denied the worst-case, "crushed, despair, abandoned, or destroyed." Paul served God with a "bring it on" mentality. "Bring it on" means he would not magnify the trouble, and he would not back down. Instead, he chose to magnify God, proclaiming he was not abandoned. He was not in despair, crushed, or destroyed. He shared his testimony of God's protection and provisions, "You are more than a conqueror through Jesus Christ."[607]

You are an overcomer of all your troubles. Give God the praise with this thought, "I may be facing a battle, but the battle is the Lord's, and He will fight for me. The devil may have meant to bring me harm, but God is going to turn it for my good." Difficulties can fuel your motivation, encouraging you to double down on your commitment to fight through to the end. Never verbalize your surrender, as some do. They exaggerate the problem and capitulate without making a real effort to resist. Do not give the problem or the enemy extra power. God has given you the power of personal choice. Choice means you have control over your actions. Your faith-filled choices empower positive action that God blesses. Two laws are at work in your favor. The Natural Law of cause and effect means that good decisions normally

---
606 2 Corinthians 4:8–9
607 Romans 8:37

produce good results. With it comes an important corollary, "By the words of his mouth a man earns choice fruit."[608] What you speak forth (your decision) comes back to you (results). Make sure you choose positive, constructive things to say. Second, the Spiritual Law means that God blesses obedience in a supernatural multiplication of your godly decisions. Moses gave the Israelites critical words of encouragement before he passed the mantle of leadership to Joshua, "God blesses obedience, but brings curses down on disobedience."[609] Your faith-filled thoughts—thoughts that magnify God, not the problem—produce optimistic feelings that lead to wise decisions, releasing the fullness of God's power to work on your behalf. Faith-less thoughts—that magnify the problem rather than God—produce negative feelings that lead to fearful, weak, and poor decisions, creating a barrier to God's help.

Counter Catastrophic Thinking

Put your faith into action by choosing thoughts that honor Him. Magnify God instead of the problem. When you look at the situation through your mind's eye, what do you see? Does the problem fill your vision? Is God anywhere in the picture? Is your mind so preoccupied with the problem you cannot see anything else? Faith makes your vision of God eclipse the problem. The size of Goliath is legendary, but David was able to see the situation as it really was. With God, Goliath did not stand a chance. David saw Goliath spiritually, as a mouse, no match at all. He proclaimed the giant's future and ran toward the battle. Your view of the problem must be through your spiritual eyes. Envision what God's answer to your problem looks like. What does God's promise look like? What does God's miracle look like when He comes through? This is the view that must fill your vision. Consider how much God cares for you, that all things are possible for the one who believes and leverage the potential of faith, prayer, and other disciplines to release God's power on your behalf.[610] God can and will help you right here, right now. Magnifying assumes the worst case with little or no analysis of the situation. It is faithlessness in action. Put your hope in God by guiding your inner conversation, assessing your situation with optimism, and giving room for God to move on your behalf. Use faith in the mental exercise below to combat catastrophizing and see what God can do. Ask yourself, "What is the best-case scenario?" Write it down at the top of a sheet of paper or in your journal. Now ask yourself, "What is the worst-case scenario?" You probably already have an answer ready if you struggle with this trap. From an objective viewpoint, how likely is this scenario? Fill in your worst-case and its likelihood several lines below your best-case statement. Giving some thought to your response, ask yourself, "What is the most likely scenario?" The final step is to prayerfully, faithfully ask, "How do I want God to resolve this situation on my behalf (preferred scenario)?" Write that above the most likely scenario and add it to your daily prayer list. It may be your best-case scenario.

---
608 Proverbs 13:2
609 Deuteronomy 30:19–20
610 Matthew 19:26

Figure 5g.
Manage Catastrophic Thinking Methodology

1. Best-case Scenario?

4. My Preferred Scenario – Add to prayer list

3. Most likely Scenario?

2. Worst-case Scenario? How likely is it?

Conclusion: Thinking Traps

Thinking traps are strongholds of negativity that become deeply ingrained in your mental software. They are based on faithless and selfish lessons that you learn from life. The enemy uses them to keep you in bondage. You must use the truth of the Scripture and the leading of the Holy Spirit to expose these lies of the enemy. They are neither truth nor facts, despite what you might think. Remember, self-deception keeps you from seeing that you are deceived. You must exercise faith to accept Scripture as truth, truer than what you learned from life. Once you identify the negative, faithless patterns in your thinking, you must counter them with the Word of God. As you have read, there are numerous ways you can get stuck in your thinking. Like sand and water traps on a golf course, once you get in, it is very hard to get out. However, with God, all things are possible. You can take authority over the lies and free your mind. Reject them and embrace Scriptural truth. Jesus went to the cross to set you free.[611] He said, "You shall know the truth, and the truth will set you free."[612] It's the truth you know in your heart that you accept and proclaim as truth that will set you free. It's not enough to be familiar with the truth, to have read it once or twice, to be free. You must read that truth, let it sink from head knowledge into the "knower" of your heart where you proclaim, "I know as I know as I know this truth of Scripture, this promise of God

---
611 Luke 4:18, Galatians 5:1
612 John 8:32

is for me." When you know that truth in your heart, it will set you free. Once you identify the lies/traps of the enemy, countering them with the truth of Scripture, you can renew your thinking and transform your life.[613]

Thinking traps are like viruses in your computer software. They corrupt your thinking from the truth of God's Word. They are malware that allows the enemy access to weaknesses in your mind he exploits to lead you into self-destructive thoughts and actions. God's Word is like software protection. As you read, study, and proclaim it, it sweeps through your mind, identifying threats and eliminating them. It cleans up the stinking thinking, viruses, worms, and malware and provides protection for your heart and mind against future attacks. It gives you a software upgrade that renews your mind. Thinking traps can be a thing of the past when, by faith, you make Scripture and the leading of the Holy Spirit the authorities in your life. You can overcome adversity with faith-filled thoughts that produce faith-filled actions.

---

[613] Romans 12:2

Chapter 6

Be Alert for Icebergs: Identify the Real Issues

We demolish arguments and every pretension that sets itself up against the knowledge of God.[614]

Icebergs are big beliefs about you, your world, and your future. They often carry unwritten rules about how you should be, how others should treat you, and how the world should operate.[615] They are expectations. Big beliefs may exacerbate your reaction to adversity, especially since you may not be aware of how powerfully they affect your thoughts and emotions. Get beneath the surface of issues in your thinking. Your assumptions, beliefs, and values drive thoughts that produce perspectives and behavior. Scripture calls these arguments and pretensions that set themselves against the knowledge of God.[616] The battle in your mind is a fight for healthy and faith-filled thinking by which you demolish every stronghold that counters Scripture. As you reflect on your well-being, recognize most issues are resolved not in the visible events, behaviors, or actions but in the unseen inner forces that drive them. Ninety percent of an iceberg's mass is below the surface. You see only ten percent above the water. In the same way, your mental model composed of beliefs, values, and assumptions is the foundation for everything above.

**Figure 6a.
Iceberg Model**

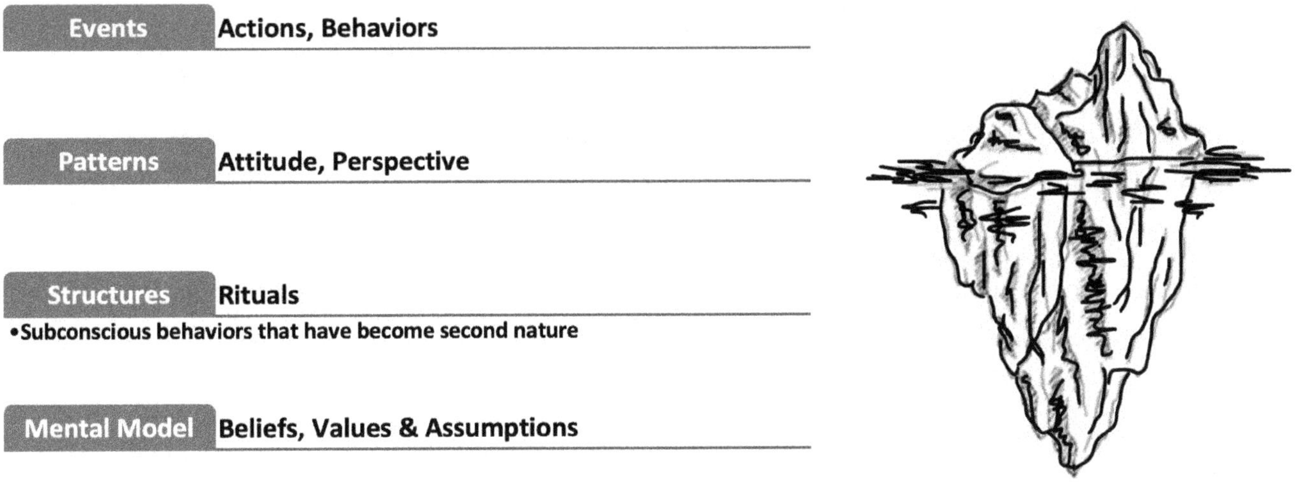

Events	Actions, Behaviors
Patterns	Attitude, Perspective
Structures	Rituals

•Subconscious behaviors that have become second nature

| Mental Model | Beliefs, Values & Assumptions |

---

614 2 Corinthians 10:5
615 Adaptiv, "*Navigating Around Icebergs*," accessed October 4, 2021, www.adaptivlearning.com/blog/bid/103406/Resilience-In-Recerssion-Tip-5–Navigating-Around-Your-Icebergs.
616 2 Corinthians 10:4–5

You can effectively identify icebergs in your thinking where you experience extremes. Do you have any extreme behaviors? What events push your buttons? Are you conflicted in any areas of your life—where your behaviors do not match your beliefs? Are you making unhealthy excuses for yourself? A simple method for recognizing mental models that may not be healthy, in line with Scripture, or consistent is the "Why?" question. As you recognize a possible iceberg, keep asking "Why?" until you have reached the level of your beliefs and values. Identify and explore it. Where does it come from? Is it consistent with Scripture?

For example, I get bothered by people leaving the lights on, the refrigerator open, or the air conditioning running when no one's home. Let's try to identify the big beliefs using the "Why?" method.

Why is that?

My response, "It's not right."

Why isn't it right?

"Because it's a waste."

Why is it a waste?

"Because it costs money to run the lights."

Why does the money matter that much?

"Because I grew up with very little. Every penny mattered."

Why does your childhood experience influence today?

"Because it is an enduring principle that you shouldn't waste what you have. There is no guarantee that you will have it tomorrow."

Have we reached the basic belief or value inherent in my behavior? Probably so. You couldn't hear it, but as I wrote the last "Why?" answer, I had a lot of passion and conviction in my heart. That is a good sign of a core belief or value. Is it scriptural? Probably so; you should not waste what God has blessed you with. Is it a good reason to be unkind, unloving, or judgmental toward others? No. I probably need to check my inner conversation and delivery when I feel bothered by what I consider someone else's wasteful actions.

Life may teach you lessons that do not line up with Scripture. You can develop unhealthy coping mechanisms to get what you need or want. Also known as "winning ways," they can help you win at the expense of others. For instance, you can use your good looks, charm, or outgoing nature to manipulate others into giving you what you want. The focus on your exterior appearance can limit the development of your inner character. Manipulative tactics are deceptive and can compromise your integrity for the favorable results you receive. Because these tactics help you "win" or get what you want, there is no motivation to change them. You can live your whole life using the same basic strategy you learned as a child. What about others? How do they feel about your manipulation? If you are winning, are others losing? Selfishness and pride drive you to take wins at the expense of others. Many people make it their life's pursuit to make losers out of others as if life is one big game. Do your "winning ways" line up with Scripture? Are you treating others as you want to be treated, or are you living by a different rule?[617] You can live by the golden rule, seeking "win-wins" with others where both parties receive something of value they feel good about.

When adversity comes, an iceberg may significantly magnify your reaction. You may not realize you hit an iceberg. How did your extreme reaction affect your present circumstances? Your reaction may have made your circumstances worse. Others find it difficult to respond to behaviors if they cannot identify a reasonable explanation. It takes a well-grounded, mature person to see past a person's way of being to uncover the deeper issues. Scripture states, "The purposes of a person's heart are deep waters, but one who has insight draws them out."[618] Few people I have met have this ability. You can save yourself a lot of trouble by identifying your iceberg beliefs and limiting your reactions when violated. Some common icebergs include:

I must be perfect.
Avoid conflict at all costs.
Family comes first.
You just can't trust people.
If you want it done right, do it yourself.
I must take care of the people I love.
People should follow the rules.
Never give up.
Winning is everything. If you're not first, you're last.
Failure is a sign of weakness.
I don't fly by the seat of my pants.
I must make people happy.
I must be right.

I have several icebergs on the list above. Can you identify one of yours? Do you have any not on the list? Has your present adversity caused an extreme reaction? Can you identify the icebergs that contributed? How can you restore what was damaged in the process?

---
617 Matthew 7:12
618 Proverbs 20:5

SPIRITUAL RESILIENCY

Use the *iceberg inventory* below to help you address unhealthy, false, or destructive beliefs and values. God made it possible for you to live your best life by following the principles of His Word. You probably have a strong emotional attachment to some of your iceberg beliefs. I know I do. However, you must identify those that contradict Scripture and retrain your thinking to align with its truths. Your icebergs set you up for failure and can complicate some of your present struggles. God's Word will help you avoid a nasty collision.

Figure 6b.
Iceberg Inventory

Do you have Icebergs in your thought processes?	How is the world different (How does it function differently) than it should be?
Recognize your extremes.	What pushes your buttons? What patterns exist in your interpersonal conflicts" Where are you inwardly conflicted or making excuses?
Identify/Inventory your core beliefs, values, morals, assumptions & expectations.	Ask the Why? Questions to identify your core beliefs and values. Get to the bottom of it—you may need to ask Why? Ten or more times.
Evaluate your beliefs	Do your core beliefs and values line up with Scripture?
Analyze the source.	What happened in life that taught you that lesson? Lessons from experience may not be Biblical. Can you identify the sin problem inherent in the event or your response? Are the coping skills (winning ways) you developed to meet your needs/wants in line with the Bible and the Golden Rule? Are your actions consistent with the beliefs and values you confess? If not, why are they different?
What needs to change?	Have you broadened your perspective? (less self-focused?) Consider where you can intervene in the thought process. Replace your icebergs with a Bible chapter and verse. Seek consistency in confronting and replacing mental models that don't work for you and are inconsistent with Scripture.

Chapter 7

Accept Your Identity in Christ, Welcome God's Cleansing River

A healthy spirit conquers adversity, but what can you do when the spirit is crushed?[619]

Accept your new identity in Christ and welcome God's cleansing river to your mind and emotions. Jesus stated, "Whoever believes in me, as the Scripture has said, rivers of living water will flow from within him."[620] The moment of salvation is a profound transformation. You are born again by the Holy Spirit of God.[621] You experience a radical change of identity: from lost to found, a child of God; included as an essential functional part of the body of Christ, the royal priesthood, the bride of Christ; a citizen of heaven and temple of the Spirit with the Holy Spirit living in your heart.[622] Your sinful past of guilt and shame replaced with righteousness, love, joy, peace, and every fruit of the Spirit. God gives you a new name that only He knows.[623] The river of God washes over you, into you, and through you. Your life will never be the same, or will it? It requires faith (faith that translates belief to action) to realize the transformation that has taken place in your spirit, mind, and body. The challenge lies in fully accepting the truths of Scripture in your journey toward knowing Jesus better, pursuing His character, and striving for greater obedience to His Word.[624] Spiritually you have radically transformed. Your decisions, responses, actions, and behaviors change as you submit them to the leading of the Spirit and the Word of God.[625] Faith in God and His Word allows that cleansing river to transform your life. Transformation gives you greater strength and resilience to stand amidst the trials of life. When you know who you are, you have confidence to weather the storms.

I once heard a quote attributed to Napoleon Bonaparte. "Never be a prisoner of your past. It was just a lesson, not a life sentence." God never faces backward. He is not hyper-focused on your past; He is interested in setting you free, so you don't live facing backward. I have met people who have spent forty and fifty years in bondage to their past. I believe God is grieved over lost decades of regret. I have seen the change God makes in people. As a child, I watched God radically change my parents. I noticed the difference in the lives of those who believe in God and those who don't in my extended family. When I

---
619 Proverbs 18:14 (MSG)
620 John 7:38
621 John 3:5–6
622 Galatians 3:26, 1 Peter 2:9, Philippians 3:20, 1 Corinthians 6:19
623 Revelation 2:17
624 Romans 13:14
625 Galatians 5:16–18

was a teenager, a school friend from a rough family life accepted Christ in a powerful spiritual encounter. She cried off and on for days, calling her tears, cleansing tears. She experienced such a large degree of pain and suffering in her life, she literally cried healing tears that washed away guilt, shame, and pain. When she finished, she smiled with a brightness I had never seen in all her life. That day, something changed on the inside; she assumed a new identity. She was no longer the abused, drug-using, drinking, smoking party girl. She knew she was loved, accepted, forgiven, wearing the spotless white robes of a daughter of God. You can experience the change of a cleansing spiritual river. God can wipe away the past with the power of His Spirit and the truths of His Word. Like seeds, His words will accomplish their purpose in bringing forth new life.

Earlier, we discussed icebergs, unhealthy patterns of belief that become strongholds. They keep you distracted from the truth of Scripture and stuck in unhealthy behaviors. In this chapter, we discuss icebergs you believe about yourself. These strongholds of belief will keep you from becoming the new you. You have been radically changed in your spirit when you accept Christ. By faith, that change will begin working its way through your mind into your physical body as you assume your new identity in Christ. You must accept that new identity and throw off those unhealthy, unscriptural lies the enemy has helped you view as wisdom from your past experiences. If your lesson contradicts Scripture, it is a stumbling block that will keep God's healing, transformational river of love and grace from fully flowing through your life. The problem with unhealthy beliefs about yourself is they are cloaked in self-deception. You view them as wise, personal discoveries that have helped you survive in this dangerous world. Your blind spots prevent you from seeing the beliefs that keep you from fully thriving and promote patterns of sin. This section identifies scriptural truths concerning your new identity in Christ and discusses some of the common contradictory beliefs that impede the transformational work of the Holy Spirit in you. You must rehearse the promises of God and the truths of His Word until they become true deep down on the inside of you.

You are a son/daughter of God.[626] Many who accept Christ find it difficult to believe their new identity; they struggle to believe God's promises or submit to His process of transformation. They remain stuck identifying with vestiges of the old self, never fully understanding or appreciating the true privileges they have as a child of God. Everyone struggles to live up to their new identity to some degree. Three false identities threaten the formation of your new identity in Christ: first, you are what you do (your value is in your performance); second, you are what you have (your value is in your possessions); and finally, you are what others think about you (your value is in your reputation and popularity).[627] In the same way Jesus was tempted in the wilderness, every person is tempted to view their identity and worth through the superficial lens of earthly pursuits. However, God views your innate value through

---
626 Galatians 3:26
627 Peter Scazerro, *Emotionally Healthy Spirituality* (Nashville, TN: Thomas Nelson, 2006), 75–77

His boundless love as your Creator-Father. You are precious apart from anything you will ever accomplish. Jesus told the Parable of the Prodigal Son as a poignant example of God's ever-present and unconditional love.[628] The son took an early inheritance and left his father's house to pursue the excesses of pleasure. When the money ran out, his fair-weather friends gone, he took the only job he could find, tending pigs. The farmer treated him so poorly, he had to eat from the pig's trough to survive. In his desperate state, a realization struck him like a beam of light in the darkness. His father treated his servants much better than this. He decided to go home and offer himself as a slave. While he was still far down the road, his watchful father saw him and ran to him. The prodigal offered himself as a slave, but his father ignored the proposal. He hugged him, kissed him, clothed him with a robe and sandals, and put his ring on his finger. The father received the prodigal with all the rights and privileges of sonship in a grand celebration. This parable illustrates how God receives every person who asks back home to His family.

Consider if the Prodigal's story continued after the father's celebration. Exploring the mindset of the son might provide insight into the mind of believers as well. The prodigal came home expecting his father to receive him as a slave. After the celebration ended, I wonder how much the prodigal would have struggled with guilt, shame, and unworthiness. How much did the enemy afflict him with the idea that he did not deserve to be a son, that he deserved slavery? His older brother certainly believed he deserved the treatment of a slave and probably repeatedly reminded his brother of the past. How much did the prodigal struggle with a slavery mentality despite the father's assurances of his restoration as a son? Even wearing the robe, sandals, and ring, the Prodigal Son might have looked in the mirror and seen a slave if he had not accepted the words of his father as truth. You face the same challenge today. Have you fully accepted your status as a child of God? Do you have a son/daughter mentality or a slave mentality? The beloved disciple, John, described the wonder of being called a son/daughter of God.[629] You've been given it, don't let anything take it from you.

You are accepted.[630] You may find it difficult to see yourself as a child of God because of a slave mentality—you may hear your inner voice telling you it cannot be true, you're not worthy, you're a slave. The enemy may whisper those accusations as well, reminding you of your faults and failures, maybe even your continued weaknesses and sin. Others, like the Prodigal's older brother, may be an impediment rather than a help. It is unfortunate that many churchgoers make it harder for new believers to feel loved by their unfriendliness, gossip, and lack of acceptance than the local bar. The TV show *Cheers* was a popular sitcom in the 1980s.[631] Part of the theme song was "you want to go where everybody knows your name." Whenever Norm walked into the bar, everyone shouted his name, "Norm!" People long for that kind of acceptance, especially those who recognize the hurt they caused others by

---
628 Luke 15:11–32
629 1 John 3:1
630 Romans 5:17
631 James Burrows, Director, *Cheers,* Season 1, Episode 1, "Give Me a Ring Sometime," aired September 30, 1982, on NBC.

the destructive nature of their former lifestyle. God loves you; He accepts you, and according to Jesus' Parables of the Lost Things, God shouts your name in a heavenly celebration when you return to Him.[632]

Do not let anyone or anything prevent you from seeing yourself as God's family. God knew every sin you would ever commit before you were born, yet He still forgave you. Why? Because Jesus paid for every single sin that day nearly two thousand years ago on a hill called Golgotha.[633] When God looks at you, He doesn't see your past or even your present failures. He sees the spotless sacrifice of Jesus, the Lamb of God.[634] The Prodigal's father didn't even acknowledge his son's confession. He saw repentance (change of direction) in each step of the journey home. You don't have to convince God or anyone else to accept you as a son. When you confess Christ as Lord, ask His forgiveness, and invite Him into your heart. God decrees you are a Son once and for all.[635] It is finished. You must let that decree fill your mind and sink into your heart. To get it into your "knower (you know as you know as you know)," you must confidently accept God's promise as truth, proclaiming it as fact and letting it change how you feel. God's mercy and grace are not a license to return to the old life with the promise of heaven; they are a reason to live free of guilt, shame, and condemnation.[636] You are family, so think like a member of the family! Look in the mirror every morning and tell yourself, "I am loved. I belong to God. God is working His blessings and favor in my life." When you see yourself as God sees you, you are confident God has accepted you as you are, His goodness and mercy will follow you every day of your life, and you know you will spend eternity with Him.[637]

You are still under construction; you can make mistakes, but your sonship is secured.[638] You enter this life with a fallen nature. Version 1.0 of your mental software has a corrupted operating system from birth. For good or bad, the interactions you have with the most important people in your life, the relationships, and experiences you have in those early years create an updated version of that software (Version 2.0) that will provide the basic operating system for the rest of your life. The hurts of those years provide many of the messages that replay in your mind and govern the emotions of your heart. They muddy the relatively clean waters of childhood innocence (although corrupted by fallen human nature). As you grow and mature, the negativity of your flawed mental software helps reinforce further negative interpretation from the pain and difficulties of life, partially overwriting your mental software to Version 3.0. The sin of those who were supposed to love you produces second, third, and fourth order effects that harm you and others involved. Your sin damages your mental, emotional, and physical well-being as well as others around you, creating another negative update to your mental software, usually reinforcing existing negative beliefs, interpretations, and coping mechanisms. The same dynamic happens to others.

---
632 Luke 15:32
633 Romans 3:22–23
634 2 Corinthians 5:21
635 1 John 3:1
636 Romans 6:1–4, Romans 8:1
637 Psalm 23:6
638 1 John 1:7–9, Romans 11:29, Philippians 1:6

The result is an inner river of negative thoughts and emotions masquerading as helpful lessons learned, enabling you to survive in the world. Where your thought processes conflict with Scripture, they lead you into sin, preventing you from thriving. Although they present themselves as wisdom for life, they function as thinking traps, icebergs, fear, worry, and other strongholds that hinder your relationship with God and limit your strength and resilience. They imprison you in a slave mentality, make you doubt God accepts or forgives you, and through the influence of the enemy, hinder your transformation from slavery to sonship. God's mercy toward you is a truth requiring faith; it is not an emotion.

You are righteous, approved, and commended.[639] From the moment of your salvation, God placed His Holy Spirit inside of you, releasing the resurrection power of Christ in you as a spiritual cleansing river to change your life forever. God intended for that river to transform your inner life and flow through you to touch the lives of others.[640] The river cleanses the muddy waters of your heart, but blockages impede the flow preventing its intended movement in and through your life. The blockages take many forms, including shame, low self-worth, an offended spirit, anger, unhealthy comparisons, lack of self-control, unbelief, and unforgiveness. One of the names of the enemy is "the accuser." The enemy will try to make you feel guilty and condemned to drive a wedge in your relationship with God. He will try to make you relive guilt from past sins. He will try to make you feel false guilt from confessed sin or wrongs that were committed against you. He will try to convince you that you are not worthy of forgiveness. The truth is none of us are worthy of forgiveness.[641] That is why Scripture calls it grace.[642] It is unmerited favor, an unearned gift from God. You received your cleansing from the Lord. Don't let the enemy make you feel that you never got it or don't deserve it. As with blame, the enemy will leverage condemnation from mistakes, failures, and defeats to make you feel worthless and ashamed. Jesus paid the price for all your sins, past, present, and future. In fact, when Jesus paid for them, all of your sins were future. He already paid for all the sins you will ever commit. If you confess your new sins, God will forgive them and cleanse you.[643] Your new failures cannot negate God's grace. God is looking for a perfect heart (one that places Him first in your priorities), not for a perfect track record of sinless behavior. If you say you have no sin, you make God a liar.[644] Your recognition of need for His presence and Lordship in your life counters the accusations of the enemy.[645] Shame can consume your mind as you ruminate on the past. Don't give it a chance. Reject condemnation, accusations, the whole blame and shame game, clearing those blockages as you stand on the Word of God. Scripture promises you have been justified by Christ and made free from all condemnation.[646]

---

639 2 Corinthians 5:21
640 John 7:38
641 Romans 3:23–26
642 Ephesians 2:8–9
643 Romans 6:23
644 1 John 1:10
645 James 4:10, James 4:7–8
646 Romans 8:1,35

You are valuable to God.[647] You may struggle with a low opinion of yourself. You may feel insecure. Your feelings do not reveal truth. You live out truth by your faith. I struggled with insecurity as a pastor. I felt personal rejection every time someone was upset or left the church. That burden was so heavy, but it was never mine to bear.[648] Jesus didn't ask me to make everyone like me or to carry their rejection. He asked me to follow Him. It is not popularity that matters to God; it is faithfulness and obedience He commends.[649] Every person has their own preferences and the power before God to make their own choices. Those choices may impact you, but they do not have to reflect on you, your character, or value. Other people's actions are really not about you; they are a reflection of their inner thoughts and emotions. As a mentor once told me, "It's not that people are against you; it's that they are for themselves." God values you despite what people say or do, despite your opinion of your own worth. Your negative feelings are merely a result of what you say to yourself when people reject you. If you think, "I am not good enough," you will feel deep hurt. Ensure your self-talk includes the value God has for you. Ensure you have a realistic expectation for people's reactions. Many people will like you; some will love you, but some people will struggle with you. Some will not appreciate what you offer. In every church I've ever been a part of, there have been people I knew loved me, people I was sure did not like me, and some I was not sure about. Even Jesus had one disciple betray Him, Judas, and almost all of them abandoned Him in His point of greatest need. Did this happen because Jesus was not enough? He was perfectly sinless, 100 percent God. You can see clearly the problem was in the disciples, not Jesus. How much more will you (like all of us) feel less than enough due to the reactions of others?

You are blessed.[650] When you embrace low self-worth, you prioritize your assessment and the message of the enemy over what God's Word says about you. Gideon is a great example of this mindset.[651] The angel of the Lord came to Gideon and said, "The Lord is with you, mighty warrior."[652] Gideon immediately questioned his plan and purpose. After further encouragement from the Lord, Gideon replied, "My clan is the weakest, and I am the least in my family."[653] Gideon did not think much of himself. He lived with an "insignificant" mentality. When God calls you a mighty warrior, it is rash to directly contradict him, regardless of how low you see yourself. Like Gideon, you may be tempted to contradict God's Word in your personal assessment. It's not humility to contradict God's Word when He declares your intrinsic worth. It is disobedience and lack of faith. It is spiritually dangerous to create a barrier to the flow of God's work in and through your life. Accept Scripture as truth and place yourself in agreement with God. Don't curse what God has blessed. Speak God's blessing and favor over yourself as His beloved. Resist the lies of the enemy and demolish those blockages of low self-worth. You don't stand

---
647 Luke 12:7, 1 John 4:9–10
648 Matthew 11:30
649 2 Corinthians 10:18
650 Ephesians 1:3
651 Judges 6–8
652 Judges 6:12
653 Judges 6:15

on your own merits but on the merits of Christ. He is your justification and defense.

You are an object of God's mercy and a mercy-giver. A wounded or offended spirit creates a similar blockage in the cleansing flow of God's river.[654] Are you easily offended (hurt) or incensed (angered) by others? How do you respond to correction, criticism, or counsel? Are you defensive or resentful? Past hurts may tempt you to be overly sensitive toward others. Criticism, when offered in love, is correction.[655] If you open yourself to correction, you are wise.[656] Confrontation is risky in a relationship, so friends who offer correction are rare and invaluable.[657] Few people love you enough to risk conflict. There are some people in your life who don't care about you and are happy to criticize. Their criticisms can still be profitable. Be teachable in spirit. It not only helps you excel in life, but it also gives you fresh insights into your circumstances. Be slow to anger.[658] Scripture states that those who respond with anger are foolish.[659] The feeling of anger is not a sin in and of itself, but when it motivates you to selfish, proud, or vengeful behaviors, it is extremely harmful. Do you fail to exercise self-control in your anger or restrain fits of rage?[660] Do you have malicious thoughts toward someone? Do not give the enemy a stronghold in your anger.[661] I experienced such rage from a church member one time I thought he was going to punch me in the face. That is a lot of rage. With that kind of rage, the issues are no longer the issue. He was a good guy at heart, but he had a severe anger problem. If you have an anger problem, pray, and use Scripture to clear that blockage out of your life. You may need a wise counselor to help you identify the foundational anger issues and agree with you in prayer for deliverance. Anger, hatred, and a desire for revenge will make your struggles worse.

Emotional health is arguably as important as physical health and is included in the healing provided at the cross. Believers can get so focused on spiritual growth and health they overlook its importance. There was a time when issues of mental and emotional health in the church were described as psychobabble. Today, we recognize the grievous effects of mental-emotional injuries and problems. Emotional health is characterized by a number of qualities that you are wise to consider in your pursuit of health, wholeness, and resilience, such as the ability to: recognize, identify and manage your own feelings; actively demonstrate compassion for others; develop and maintain close personal friendships; recognize and break free from self-destructive patterns; understand how your past has affected your present; clearly express your thoughts and feelings; respect and love others without having to change them; respectfully ask for what you need; accurately assess your strengths and weaknesses and share them with others; negotiate and maturely resolve conflict; openly consider the perspectives of others; appropriately

---

654 Matthew 6:15
655 Ephesians 4:15
656 Proverbs 9:8
657 Proverbs 27:6a
658 James 1:19
659 Ecclesiastes 7:9
660 Ephesians 4:26
661 Ibid.

express your sexuality; and grieve in a healthy manner.[662] Scripture provides counsel to help you develop greater health in each of these areas.

You are unique and irreplaceable. Unhealthy comparisons serve as another key blockage in your spirit. You are running a race through life against yourself; to become the best version of yourself you can be.[663] God has given you unique fingerprints, DNA, eyes, ears, teeth, voice, toeprints, and many other qualities. There is only one you, and only you can fulfill the puzzle piece shaped purpose that God specifically crafted you to fill. That truth is not sentimental nonsense; it is the clear teaching of many passages of Scripture.[664] If you are alive, your life has meaning and purpose. Scripture notes that David served his purpose in his generation.[665] King Saul first attacked David over jealousy. People praised David's military success more than the king's. He became so angry he tried to kill David on several occasions. He hunted David for years even though David's loyalty to Saul was unparalleled. When David twice had the opportunity to capture or kill Saul, he refused. King Saul could easily have been thankful for David's success. After all, David was his general. Instead, Saul made it a competition and lost the throne. Saul had his own purpose to serve in his generation, but he lost his way in his envious comparison to David. Caan had a similar problem. He was so blinded by jealousy he ignored God's counsel. He murdered his brother and became an outcast. God gave him a chance to serve his own purpose, but he chose to see himself in comparison to his brother Abel rather than finding his proper place in God. I recently heard someone remark how much pain people suffer because they hold on to something that was not theirs to begin with. Don't allow envy into your heart. Someone will have greater gifts, talents, and abilities than you; in the same way, someone else will have less.[666] It's okay. God asked you to be faithful with those He has given you. If you give God your best, you will find that it doesn't need to be better than everyone else's. It doesn't matter what your circumstances or experiences are. God factors it all into your reward. Some use hardships as an excuse to quit running their race or to do less than they can. Do not fall into that trap. When you stand before the Lord to give account for your life, your reward will derive from your love for God and your effort.[667] Self-pity, fear, unbelief are not excuses for giving up on your race. Do not let your pride distract you with how the race is going in the lane next to you. Envy is a spiritually destructive force that comes from a self-seeking heart of personal ambition. Do not get drawn onto a dead-end street. Unhealthy comparisons are a trap of the enemy.[668] You are valuable. God is watching you run with the heart of a proud father. Make Him proud by giving Him your best. Jesus already won the victory for you; all you need to do is finish the race. Victory lives inside of you; victory is in your blood.

---

662 Peter Scazerro, Healthy Spirituality, 45.
663 Hebrews 12:1–2
664 Psalm 139, 1 Corinthians 12
665 Acts 13:36
666 1 Corinthians 12:18–20,22,26
667 1 Corinthians 3:10–15
668 Bob Sorge, *Envy: The Enemy Within* (Ventura, CA: Regal Books, 2003), 21.

You are self-disciplined and victorious in the Spirit. Self-indulgence and lack of self-control can ruin your life. Not only do they bring destruction, but they also lead to a deeper downward spiral of self-destructive thoughts and behaviors. When you allow your fallen nature to control your life, you limit the work of the Holy Spirit. The excesses create greater and greater blockages in your life. Samson is a sad example.[669] Born into a special calling, God gave him supernatural strength as he lived under the Nazirite vow. Early in his adult life, he allowed spirits of sexual immorality and vengeance to take root in his heart. The impassioned desire for justice and self-gratification continued to consume Samson's focus throughout his life. Eventually, he betrayed his vow and ended up in captivity. One of the saddest statements of Samson's life is, "He did not know that the Lord had left him."[670] Samson had a mighty river of God's anointing running through his life. By the time his sensual desires had run their course, he was unaware the river had dried up. You must prioritize your spirit. If you consume yourself with feeding your fallen nature, it will eventually feed on you. David had a different spirit from Samson. He committed grave sexual sin (as well as others), but he humbly sought God in repentance. Psalm 51 records David's emotional plea for restoration to God's favor. Contrast his words, "Do not cast me from your presence or take your Holy Spirit from me," with Samson's seeming lack of sensitivity to God's presence in his life.[671] A focus on pleasure is all fun and games at the start, but in the end, people, including you, get hurt. Sin is a spiritual wrecking ball in your health and well-being. You can be victorious over the powerful and destructive lure of sin.[672]

You are faithful and full of faith. Unbelief is an especially grievous blockage. You may start strong in your relationship with God, but over time, you drift into a lukewarm state. If you do not feed your Spirit with the spiritual disciplines, you may find yourself slipping backward in shades of doubt and unbelief. You cannot welcome God's river to flow in your life if you doubt He exists or works in you. Similarly, you cannot find strength and resilience in your spirit if you doubt God's promises are true. Israel had a doubting, complaining, unbelieving heart problem in their journey out of Egypt to God's Promised Land. Their unbelief was so grievous to God, he would have destroyed them in the wilderness.[673] Fortunately, Moses interceded and saved them. Their attitude is remarkable, considering all the miracles they personally witnessed. Did they dismiss the plagues as coincidence? Did they think Pharaoh's change of heart was a natural choice? What about the Red Sea? Manna from heaven each morning? Water from a rock? During adversity, you may be tempted to dismiss past answers to prayer. Do not do it. Remember and record God's work in your life. Remind yourself of His past faithfulness as you reread your journal. Read of His faithfulness in the Scriptures and listen to the testimonies of others. David made a daily rit-

---

669 Judges 13–16
670 Judges 16:20
671 Psalm 51:11
672 Romans 6:12–14
673 Numbers 14:20–23

ual of remembering God's faithfulness at the end of each day.[674] This practice equipped him to persevere. Stand firm in your faith in the hard times for you have the faith of Christ.[675] Do not let unbelief choke out the river of your spiritual life.

You are forgiven, your wrongdoing forgotten, cast into the depths of the sea.[676] Unforgiveness is another especially grievous blockage. This issue is so important we will devote a chapter to a deeper discussion on the subject. Unforgiveness is so spiritually destructive, God states He will not forgive you if you do not forgive others.[677] That statement sums up its toxic effect on your spiritual life. Do not allow anyone's wrongdoing to affect you so deeply, you refuse to forgive. Some teach the opposite, but forgiveness is not an option. No matter how grievous the wrong, your journey to healing always passes through forgiveness. It may take time to forgive, to come to the point where you can give up your right for revenge entrusting justice to God, but you must keep pushing forward. Don't get stuck. God knows inner wounds fester without forgiveness. Bitterness and resentment feel good, but they work against you. He asks you to show the same kind of mercy that He showed you. One day, you will need forgiveness, and the measure you use will be returned to you. Since love is only made complete when you share it with others, the expression of forgiveness (as an expression of love) is also made complete in the sharing.[678] It is a singular method of identifying with Christ as Stephen did when stoned to death. His final words, "Lord, do not hold this sin against them."[679] In the same way, refusing to forgive is choosing not to identify with Christ nor to complete the circle of His love. Your unforgiveness chokes off the cleansing river of God's presence, allowing the muddied waters and blockages to remain.

You are a new creation. God's desire and purpose in your life is transformation, a new creation full of love, joy, peace, patience, kindness, goodness, gentleness, and every fruit of the Spirit. God wants to transform you with His life-giving Spirit so you, in turn, can be a life-giving force in the lives of others. We discussed the impact of negativity in your thought processes and damaged emotions that create blockages to God's life-giving healing work in your life. Human nature is our own worst enemy. We tend to the wrong thing, we want to sit in God's seat of authority, and we want to be in control—of our image, other people, our problems, our pain, etc.[680] The desire to call the shots not only works against the positive re-programming of your mind, but its consequences also produce additional baggage to deal with Take intentional steps to overwrite your software with an ever-increasing knowledge of the Word of God. Apply that knowledge to your life through faith to run the software update. Use the spiritual disciplines and Scripture to seek healthy thoughts and wholeness as you claim your new identity in Christ. Break up the strongholds that have created blockages. Open your heart to the truths of God's

---
674 Psalm 92:2
675 Galatians 2:16
676 1 John 1:9, Micah 7:18–19, Psalm 103:2–3
677 Matthew 6:15
678 1 John 4:12
679 Acts 7:60
680 John Baker, *Life's Healing Choices: Freedom from Your Hurts, Hang-Ups, and Habits* (New York: Howard Books, 2007), 14–17.

Word. You are a new creation; the old has gone the new has come.[681] You are changed. You have begun a spiritual journey of continuous transformation as the Holy Spirit reveals the character and ministry of Christ through your life.

As the Parable of the Prodigal Son shows, you are invaluable to God. God watched for your return from far off, always working and reaching out to welcome you home. God loves you beyond your ability to comprehend.[682] He is a Good Father working only to bring good and perfect gifts to your life.[683] His intent is to fill you with the whole measure of the fullness of God.[684] He wants to do immeasurably more than you can ask or imagine in your life.[685] He has placed you in the palm of His hand, thinking only good thoughts toward you. And He has seated you in heavenly places of authority with Christ.[686] Walk in the privilege and authority God has given you. Do not allow your sympathetic fallen nature to conform to the spirit of this world, continuing its self-destructive journey. Instead, pursue the high call of service to Christ. Do not let the enemy or anyone else drag you back into the destructive patterns of your painful past. Nothing, not shame, low self-worth, an offended spirit, anger, unhealthy comparisons, lack of self-control, unbelief, unforgiveness, nor anything else, can separate you from the love of God in Christ.[687] These forces lack the power to control you if you lean on Christ.[688] You have been born to transform, not to conform.[689] This transformation allows you to love God, to love yourself as God loves you, and to love your neighbor as you love yourself.

You are salt and light in this world.[690] Do not let the heart issues above be a stumbling block to your life's purpose. As the cleansing river washes through your heart, it will bring refreshment to others as well. Do you have a generous spirit? Are you quick to encourage, help and bless others? As you adopt God's attitude towards others, you can live in a spirit of blessing, rejoicing over God's work in their lives as well. God can and will use you. Jesus' mission was to reconcile humanity to God through His sacrifice on the cross.[691] That message belongs to you as His ambassador.[692] Everything you do can reflect God's glory as you continue Christ's work. Make it your primary mission in life to shine the love and light of Christ through your life. You don't have to be faultless to accept this calling. Submitting yourself to God's cleansing work in your life and allowing the river of God's Spirit to flow through you to touch others is enough. God will complete His work in you as His mighty, cleansing river of blessing touches others.[693]

---

681 2 Corinthians 5:17
682 1 John 3:1, Ephesians 3:17–18
683 James 1:17
684 Ephesians 3:19
685 Ephesians 3:20
686 Ephesians 2:6
687 Romans 8:38–39
688 Romans 8:37
689 Romans 12:2
690 Matthew 5:13–16
691 Mark 10:45
692 2 Corinthians 5:20
693 Philippians 1:6

Chapter 8

Fight off Fear

God has not given us a spirit of fear, but a spirit of power, of love, and of self-discipline.[694]

When you are about to go into battle, the priest shall come forward and address the army. He shall say: "Hear, O Israel, today you are going into battle against your enemies. Do not be fainthearted or afraid; do not be terrified or give way to panic before them. For the LORD your God is the one who goes with you to fight for you against your enemies to give you victory."[695]

Fight off fear. Fear blocks spiritually resilient thinking. It keeps you from trusting God in your circumstances, instead relying on your natural sight, senses, abilities, and resources to cope. Faith relies on spiritual sight, God's power and promises. As the figure below illustrates, faith and fear cannot coexist; they function on opposite ends of the faith spectrum. One will crowd out the other. The degree to which you make faith rule in your mind, fear will be limited. If you let fear control you, faith will be crowded out. The spirit of fear will try to dominate your mind. It will keep you from stepping out in faith, from healthy risk-taking, to change your situation. Fear says, "It is too risky, God's not big enough. The giants are just too big." Faith says, "The resurrection power of Christ lives within me. I can do all things through Christ, who gives me strength.[696] Nothing is impossible with God." At some point in your struggle to overcome, you must choose between the two messages. You will have to demonstrate the courage of faith to trust God's Word. It is a simple choice but challenging because fear shouts in your mind. Faith speaks with the still, small voice of the Holy Spirit.[697] Courage does not mean you don't feel the emotion of fear; it means you do not let fear control your decisions. You trust God to handle the risks associated with your thoughts and feelings of fear. You let God's peace rule in your heart.

---

694 2 Timothy 1:7
695 Deuteronomy 20:24
696 Philippians 4:13
697 Psalm 46:10

Figure 8a.
The Faith Spectrum

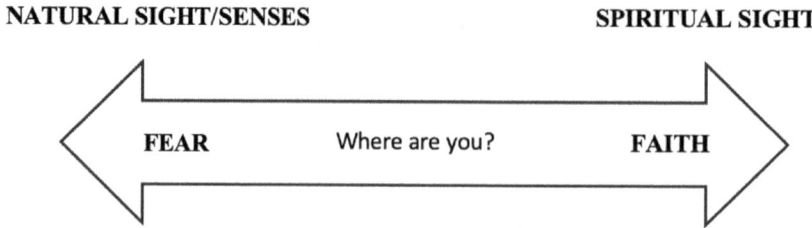

Some emotions of fear are helpful in situations where your physical safety or well-being is at risk. Fear prepares you to respond to danger by releasing hormones that elevate heart rate and increase adrenaline, among others. It is helpful in moderation. When you constantly experience fear, these responses can be destructive to the body, your immune system, cardiovascular system, gastrointestinal organs, fertility, and the aging process and even lead to premature death.[698] Fear affects the mind as well, negatively affecting memory, thinking, ethical decision-making, and emotional regulation, causing you to misread communication cues and making you susceptible to impulsivity. Long-term fear can lead to fatigue, depression, and PTSD.[699] In times of trouble, it can keep you stuck, draining energy, and paralyzing constructive action. Obviously, fear can be a powerful source of manipulation by the enemy and others. Major media outlets effectively use fear as a reason to stay tuned for the latest information, and advertisers use it to sell their products. Fear can be a powerful persuader in public discourse, motivating people to comply with the message to avoid threats to their well-being. Today, the media frequently uses warnings of an existential threat (a threat to humanity's survival) in news reporting, and Hollywood uses it extensively in movie plots: aliens, meteors, zombies, global floods, etc. Scripture provides peace in the face of all existential threats. It reveals how God brings His kingdom to the Earth and promises some cataclysms, such as a global flood, are not in our future.[700] The COVID-19 pandemic produced a level of public panic I've never experienced before in my lifetime. You don't have to fear what others fear because God is with you. Fear is meant to serve you, not be your master. Don't let fear become a stronghold.

As a child, I would occasionally have this dream that a monster was chasing me around the car in the driveway. I tried to always keep the car between us, but I was so afraid my feet wouldn't move right. They were so heavy and clumsy; the monster would catch up to me as I tried to circle the car. The fear paralyzed me, draining the energy right out of my body. Thankfully I always woke up before it caught me. Now I realize the monster was fear. Don't let it control your thinking.

---

698 University of Minnesota, *"Impact of Fear and Anxiety,"* accessed October 11, 2021, www.Takingcharge.csh.umn.edu/impact-fear-and-anxiety.
699 Ibid.
700 Genesis 9:15

Scripture is clear: fear is not from God.[701] In fact, God assures you that trusting in His ever-present and protective love will drive away fear.[702] Nearly thirty verses of Scripture encourage you not to fear.[703] Faith, by nature, is protective against fear in all forms: being afraid, phobias, worry, anxiety, stress, doubts, dread, panic, fear of rejection, fear of making mistakes/failing. Choosing to trust God for His help and protection rejects the helpless feelings that often accompany fear. Scripture teaches anything not from faith (absolute trust in God) is sin.[704] The enemy effectively uses fear to control and manipulate. In my opinion, fear (in some form) is one of his most powerful weapons against individuals. Fear, like a nuclear device, is a weapon of mass destruction. It is the root of all kinds of wrongs against other people: manipulation, deceit, theft, adultery, murder, coveting, etc. Fear subjects you to harmful stress that damages relationships limiting another source of help and strength in hard times, friends. Do not accept God is using fear to some righteous end. Healthy natural fear is momentary to help you avoid danger. God promises peace, not fear, as the abiding sign of His presence and guidance in your mind.[705] God may trouble your heart as a temporary check to your present course of action, but your permanent state is always peace—along with all the fruit of the Holy Spirit's work in your life.[706] The enemy may try to use fear to manipulate you, expect your Good Father-God to lead you into right decisions, joy, and peace in the Spirit.[707]

David's life was on the line at Ziklag. His men blamed him for their loss. David could have slipped away from the camp to hide out until things cooled down. He could have abandoned them entirely in resentment for their disloyalty. Both courses of action would have betrayed his faith. His future as king could have been in jeopardy. Instead, David trusted God to protect him from his men and restore his leadership. David's courage during great loss only further added to his battle-hardened reputation. He engendered greater confidence and loyalty in the days ahead as he took courageous action. Ziklag transformed his men from complainers and blamers into the mighty men of great exploits listed in Scripture. The same can happen for you. You can become a mighty warrior as you courageously face your feelings of fear. The 23rd Psalm reflects David's confidence as he trusted God. "Even though I walk through the darkest valley, I will fear no evil, for you are with me."[708] Like David, you can be fearless in your dark times. God, the Shepherd, protects you with His Shepherd's staff. The staff can be used to block attempts to do you harm; it can also be used to inflict damage upon your enemy. David used the threat of death (the valley of the shadow of death) as the worst possible scenario to illustrate the depth of God's protection. He faced death numerous times, but God always came through. Psalm 23 is a "theme psalm" for your life in your darkest valleys.

---

701 2 Timothy 1:7
702 1 John 4:18
703 Psalm 34:4, Isaiah 35:4, Psalm 27:1, Psalm 118:6, Deuteronomy 31:6, Matthew 10:28, Romans 8:15, Hebrews 13:6, 1 Peter 3:14
704 Romans 14:23
705 John 14:27
706 Galatians 5:22–23
707 Romans 14:17
708 Psalm 23:4

I heard a preacher once say, "You never get free of anything by running from it." Fear says, "Run!" Fear says, "Hide!" Feeling the emotion of fear does not mean you are weak or cowardly. True courage is having the strength to face your obstacle despite feelings of fear. The enemy uses your fears to bully you, to make you feel small and weak. Intimidation is a powerful force. You can watch its effects all around you, such as on social media's battlefield of "The Like Wars." Users pressure young people to conform to popular opinion to receive "Likes" on their posts. "Dislikes" or few "Likes" can make impressionable minds feel ridiculed and rejected. Fear of rejection is a powerful motivator to conform. Does getting "Likes" or fitting in really promote freedom, growth, and strength in your life? Scripture calls fear of people a snare.[709] This is one example of numerous ways the enemy uses fear to herd people into conformity with his will. You, however, are called not to conform but to be transformed by the renewing of your mind in Scripture and in faith.[710]

As a teenager, I decided to skip my senior year of high school football so I could focus more on practice time for the basketball team. The football coach wasn't too happy, so he came to see me. He threatened to have the superintendent open an investigation into my basketball coach if I didn't play. I was less inclined to play football after that, but I signed up, fearing that not playing would bring trouble on my basketball coach. I was not happy playing football and considered quitting. The football coach continued his manipulation, threatening to write a letter to my college admissions boards saying I was a quitter. Eventually, I did quit the team over several issues, but the season was almost over before I finally got the courage to do it. I should not have played football, to begin with, but I never fully confronted the coach's manipulation. The more you let fear control you, the more of you it wants. It also gets harder to break free of it the longer you submit to its power. You can continue to live in slavery to fear, or you can face it, reject it, and trust God to take care of you.

Face Your Fears

Adversity may create additional fears in your life; maybe a difficulty keeps you awake at night. I never experienced anxiety or panic attacks. Then, I encountered a major setback. For the next year, I woke up in the middle of the night, consumed with anxiety and regrets about things I should have done to prevent it. I could not have foreseen the circumstances; the situation was unknowable. I tortured myself with fears that literally soaked my body in sweat. Did any of that fear and anxiety help? None of it changed my circumstances, although my hair got a lot grayer that year. What do you do when you experience attacks of fear? Face your fears and fight back.

---

709 Proverbs 29:25
710 Romans 12:2

Jesus made an interesting statement, "The Kingdom of God is forcefully advancing, and forceful people lay hold of it."[711] God's work violently collides with the spirit of evil in this world. People of faith need to be forceful in the spiritual battles they face. You must face fear like an enemy in the field of battle. Show fears no mercy, for they will show you none. Some may question how love and forcefulness can coexist in the believer. You show love toward people, but you must resolutely confront the work of the enemy. Do you doubt the violence? Look at the problems in this world, sickness, hatred, greed, addiction, immorality, etc. Do not tell me there are no deaths in this war. Sickness is violent. I watched cancer reduce my brother from a strong man in his prime to an emaciated shell of his former self before he died. Disease is a widow maker. God doesn't cause cancer. Sickness comes from the enemy. Division and strife destroy communities, addictions consume people from the inside out, and the second, third, and fourth order effects of sin and evil in this world continue. Four of my extended family members died in the violence of evil that plagues this world. You must fight the enemy without hesitation, without a sign of weakness, without fear. You must be strong and courageous.[712] Get angry at how the enemy uses fear to afflict you and your loved ones. Take decisive action in faith. Refuse to let the enemy manipulate you. Refuse to let him win. If you continue to stand, you win.[713] The devil is described like a lion seeking whom he may devour, but you can overpower him.[714] David killed the bear and the lion; you can too.[715]

The enemy tries to shape what you perceive to magnify fear. In the book, *The Lord of the Rings: Return of the King*, the Steward of Gondor, the city's leader, had an all-seeing stone that the former Kingdom of Numenor used to communicate between leaders of nearby cities, modern-day FaceTime. After the fall of Numenor, evil Lord Sauron captured one of the seeing stones and used it to control what others who used the stones could see. Sauron allowed the Steward of Gondor to only see negative visions of the war that was coming to Gondor. Because the Steward could only see the bad reports, he refused to defend the city, ultimately ending his life. Gondor was saved in the war, but the Steward never saw the help that would deliver Gondor from Sauron's attack.[716] He did not consider the possibility of victory because his mind was consumed, undermined really, by fear. When you look at your situation, refuse to hyper-focus on the negative reports. Do not make the mistake of the Steward, allowing fear and despair to take root in your mind. With God, all things are possible.[717] Make room in your mindset for God to deliver you. Fight fear with a vision of God who is bigger than your problems, who can do miracles for you—right here, right now.

The enemy uses deception and intimidation to overwhelm you with fear, but you can fight back. First, when you face adversity, you may need to find out more information. Fear of the unknown is

---
[711] Matthew 11:12
[712] Joshua 1:9
[713] Ephesians 6:13
[714] 1 Peter 5:8
[715] 1 Samuel 17:34–36
[716] J.R.R. Tolkien, *The Lord of the Rings: The Return of the King* (Boston: Mariner Books, 2004), 181–183,186.
[717] Matthew 19:26

common. Eliminate as many of the unknowns as possible by digging into the problem. When Moses led the people to the Promised Land, he sent twelve spies out to gather information. Moses tried to find out what they were facing. Counting the cost of a commitment is an important principle.[718] Understand your situation and debunk the unreasonable fears. Unfortunately, when the spies returned, only two believed it was possible to conquer the nations residing there. The other ten were afraid and spread a bad report among the people. "The land we explored devours those living in it. All the people we saw there are of great size. We seemed like grasshoppers in our own eyes, and we looked the same to them."[719] The fear in the ten spies spread like wildfire. Two of the spies recognized that God was far bigger than the enemies in the land. They had no fear of taking it. You choose the report you believe in—choose to accept the report of faith. Second, ensure you address any unhealthy magnification (catastrophizing) of the problem. Obviously, the spies were not the size of grasshoppers compared to the people of the land. That would make the Canaanites over two hundred feet tall. Fear magnifies the problem, depletes courage, and paralyzes constructive action. You are gathering information to enable your response, not hinder it. Maybe the information shows you have a weakness. Third, you may need to develop a plan to address a weakness, need, or implement a solution to the problem. If the spies had returned with some constructive intelligence about the weaknesses of their enemies, Moses could have developed an informed plan of attack. Instead, the spies' fear provided nothing of value. Their report was not factual. Fear begets other negativity, such as the thinking trap of magnification. Do not let it rule your mind. Years later, when Joshua led Israel into the land, he formed a brilliant plan of "divide and conquer," attacking in the middle to separate the northern kingdoms of the Canaanites from the southern kingdoms. Courage enabled him to plan and execute God's will for Israel. These three steps promote discipline in dealing with fear as you face difficulties.

The fourth principle is to leverage spiritual disciplines for strength. Fight fear with Scripture, seeking its vital encouragement. Remember, fear is not from God. God's work in your life produces a sense of security, confidence, and mental strength.[720] Faith is the key to fighting fear. Use Scripture to stir up confidence God is with you. God repeatedly reminded people in Scripture that He was with them.[721] Joshua saw numerous miracles on the journey out of Egypt. Yet when he assumed the leadership mantle of Moses, he needed additional encouragement. Moses talked to God face to face. Moses was so close to God, the glory shone in his face—it was so powerful, the people asked him to cover his face with a veil when he came out of the tent.[722] I'm sure Joshua felt a little inadequate to follow in Moses' footsteps. How could he replace Moses? God sent the angel of the Lord to tell him to be strong and courageous.[723]

---
718 Luke 14:28–32
719 Numbers 13:32–33
720 2 Timothy 1:7
721 Isaiah 41:10,13–14, Joshua 1:9, Deuteronomy 31:6
722 Exodus 34:31–34
723 Joshua 1:6

In the same way God was with Moses, the angel assured Joshua God would be with him. It wasn't Moses that made the difference; it was God's presence. The special ingredient in the secret sauce you need to overcome your challenge is the presence of God. He is Emmanuel, God with you.[724] God loves you so much, He will present Himself as your refuge (protection) and strength (source of power); as a light (illumination) and a stronghold (protection), and as a helper in times of trouble.[725] Bottom line, God is everything you need in your circumstances. Do your part with constructive action. You may doubt that your efforts can help. God will make up the difference. Remind yourself that God makes a way where there seems to be no way.[726]

Fight fear by trusting God is with you in the worst of circumstances. Keep fear from overwhelming you by remembering His protection.[727] The twenty-third Psalm stands out in Scripture as a declaration of faith producing spiritual strength and resilience for each day of your life. I encourage you to pray and proclaim it daily. Like a shepherd watching over the herd, God watches over you. God miraculously saved my life when I was nine years old. It was a snowy day, and a friend and I walked up the country road to our favorite hill to go sledding. We were in the middle of the road when we saw a car approaching. The driver honked his horn and spooked both of us. I ran to one side, but my friend ran to the other side. Because he was older, I tried to cross back over with him. I got to the middle of the road and realized I was safer back on my side. I spun around and began to take a step. My body froze as I felt a hand on my chest. The driver never slowed down as he approached, and, at that moment, the speeding car passed right in front of me less than two feet from where I stood in the middle of the road. If I had stepped forward, I would have been hit. I heard the voice of God speak to my heart, "You're not going to die until my work for you is done." That day, an angel from God reached out its hand and kept me from stepping into the path of that car. I'm sure the angel saved my life as the car never slowed down. In fact, the driver startled me again, beeping his horn as he passed in front of me. Maybe the devil was driving that car. Scripture references guardian angels in several places.[728] Your guardian angel protects you with the staff of the Lord. Be fearless, knowing God works tirelessly behind the scenes to protect you. He is always present as your Good Shepherd.

Fight fear in prayer, believing your prayers will remove fear and usher in the sense of His presence and peace as you trust Him.[729] This Scripture passage is a recipe with several key ingredients to replace fear with peace. Do not be anxious about anything. Instead of allowing useless fear to pervade your thinking, present your needs to God. The caveat is to approach God with an attitude of thanksgiving. I don't know how you feel about ungrateful people, but I confess that attitude is one of my icebergs. I

---

724 Matthew 1:22–23
725 1 John 4:8, Psalm 46:1–2, Psalm 27:1, Psalm 118:6–7
726 Isaiah 43:16
727 Psalm 23:4
728 Acts 12:15, Daniel 9:21, Hebrews 1:14, Matthew 18:10, Psalm 34:7, Psalm 91:11
729 Philippians 4:6–7

cannot stand when my kids fail to show appreciation for acts of kindness—to anyone. I am not predisposed to be generous in that situation. I know God is gracious, but thankfulness is an important spiritual attitude as well as essential for healthy thought processes. You must direct thankfulness, like faith, toward God. When you pray, don't allow fear into the conversation. Tell God what you need and pray like you are expecting Him to answer. That makes God smile. You are expecting your Good, Good Father to reward your trust in Him. When you petition God this way, God will send his peace to protect your mind from fear, anxiety, and all negative thoughts. This peace transcends understanding because after you pray, your situation has not improved by natural sight. However, your spiritual sight recognizes that God is with you, He knows your need, and He is working for you. Spiritually, your situation has improved dramatically. All that remains is to see how God is going to work your situation out for His glory and your well-being.

Fight fear by remembering God is personally involved in the details of your life and specifically working to provide you peace that transcends your circumstances.[730] It is easy when you're not seeing any progress in your situation to feel all alone and unimportant in the universe. God knows the number of hairs on your head. He keeps a constant count because it changes every moment. What a great metaphor for God's attention to your life! I love the scene in the movie *Bruce Almighty* where God opens the file drawer to the details of Bruce's life.[731] It shoots open, extending to the far side of the room, dragging Bruce along with it. In that drawer is every detail of his life. God was with him every step of the way, even when he felt like God abandoned him. Bruce repeatedly tests God throughout the movie. By the end, he understands the measure of God's power and love and his need to patiently trust. Like Bruce, it would be nice to talk to God face-to-face during adversity. Spiritually, you are talking to God face to face. Further, you are blessed when you don't physically see Him yet believe.[732] By faith, talk to God as you would a person you can see because He is listening. When you read Scripture, hear the words as His personal words to you. Receive peace in the conversation.

Unfortunately, after they received the report of the spies, the people of Israel did not seek God in prayer according to the spiritual principles above. Along with ten of the spies, they rejected faith as a solution to their challenge. In fear, they refused to follow Moses into the land, turning away from their promised home. On numerous previous occasions when the Exodus journey became difficult, the people declared they were better off in Egypt. They were determined to run in fear rather than fight. You cannot effectively battle anything with your back toward it. You must face adversity to get to the next level of growth in your life. One recent study showed the brain must face repeated exposure to fear to get over it.[733] We see that principle in Scripture. David faced bears and lions to prepare for Goliath. David

---

[730] Isaiah 43:1, Luke 12:7, John 14:27
[731] Tom Shadyac, Bruce Almighty, United States: Universal Pictures, 2003.
[732] John 20:29
[733] O. Khalaf, S. Resch, L. Dixsaut, V. Gorden, L. Glauser, and J. Graff. "Reactivation of Recall-induced Neurons Contributes to Remote Fear Memory Attenuation," Science, 360(6394): 2018, 1239–1242.

faced Goliath to prepare for Ziklag. David faced Ziklag to prepare for the throne. God worked all these obstacles for David's good. David's life was no more important than the lives of those heading into the Promised Land. God gave the people repeated exposure to their fears to prepare them for the next battle. Unfortunately, they rejected God's training. Victory is impossible if you never face the battle. Because Israel refused to trust God, he refused to bless that generation. They spent the next thirty-nine years wandering in circles in the wilderness until the last one died. Then Joshua led their children to conquer the Promised Land.[734] Do not let the enemy intimidate you with the size of your problems. David dropped Goliath with one small stone and then killed him with the giant's own sword. God can do the same for you.

Fight fear with a firm resolve to persevere until you overcome.[735] As Gandalf the Wizard told Frodo, "All you have to decide is what to do with the [difficult] times you have been given." You must decide that you will not quit, you will get back up when you are knocked down and stand when it feels like you cannot get up again. God will give you the strength. Don't get sidetracked by the personal cost, negative consequences, or the worst-case scenario. The enemy will use all these to make your problems appear enormous and to make you feel like a grasshopper in comparison. The truth is, how you view yourself in comparison to your problems is the critical factor. Israel's army saw a giant and believed they didn't have a chance. David saw the giant as insignificant, so he had no fear. Both saw the same giant with their physical eyes; only David used his spiritual eyes. If we could have seen David and Goliath spiritually, we would recognize David was the giant, Goliath was the boy. Goliath didn't have a chance. Trust God to make you more than enough. You and God are a majority. Trust God to give you your sling and stone to bring down the giant problem. Scripture provides a long list of those who went before, who conquered big problems (and their fears) with faith.[736] Fear saps your resilience. Don't let the enemy magnify your problems to the extent they become bigger than your God. God will use your struggles to reveal your courage, to make you stronger in faith. The more you face your fears, the stronger you grow, and the greater the conviction that comes to you. Get angry that the enemy is trying to use fear to keep you from God's blessing. Use that anger to fuel your resolve to overcome.

---

[734] Joshua 1:1–6
[735] Hebrews 10:36
[736] Hebrews 11:1–40

Chapter 9

Drive Away Worry

Therefore, I tell you, do not worry about your life.[737]

—Jesus

Drive worries out of your mind. Worry is a relative of fear, a negative pattern of repetitive thoughts and feelings focused on problems and potential consequences causing stress and anxiety. Adversity can serve as a catalyst to numerous worries as you focus on negative possible outcomes or create unrealistic scenarios (thinking traps). One pastor called worry a meteor shower of what-ifs.[738] You, as many people do, may tend to worry during difficulties. I have battled worry all my life, primarily from a tendency to overly attend to negative information. Worry impedes faith-filled, spiritually resilient thinking. Like fear, it keeps you from trusting God, instead relying on your pessimistic natural sight, senses, and abilities to assess your situation. Faith is optimistic, relying on spiritual sight, God's power and promises. As the figure below illustrates, faith and worry cannot coexist; they function on opposite ends of the faith spectrum. I heard a radio announcer share a thought on worry several years ago. "You can trust God, or you can worry, but you can't do both." One will crowd out the other. The more faith rules in your mind, the more peace will replace worry. If you let worry dominate your thinking, you will lack faith. Worry is a dark cloud that tries to permeate every corner of your mind. It tries to shield the mind from the light of hope. Faith speaks wisdom and peace to the worry. Fill your mind with God's Word. It will breathe a fresh wind into your thinking, clearing out the dark cloud of worry.

The Faith Spectrum

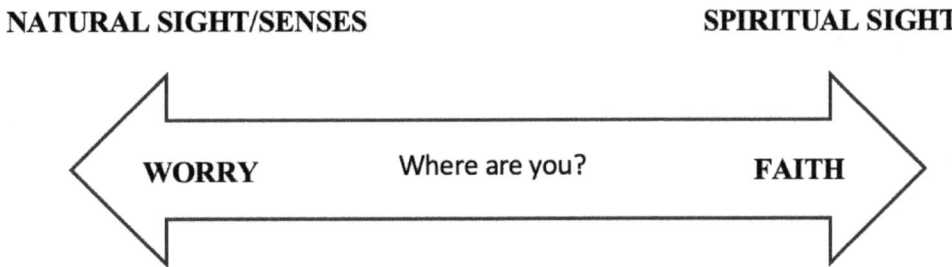

---

737 Matthew 6:25
738 Max Lucado, *Anxious for Nothing: Finding Calm in a Chaotic World* (Nashville, TN: Thomas Nelson, 2017), 4.

David had a lot to worry about at Ziklag. He was initially distressed (worried) because his men talked of stoning him. In their grief, they focused their bitter anger on David.[739] He could have retreated to his tent, worrying that every noise he heard was the footsteps of those coming to kill him. He could have worried his men would abandon him. He could have ruminated on the fate of his wives and children. Worry would have drained his strength and motivation to act. Instead, David chose the Lord. We know that David did not sink into worry because the same verse states, "David found strength in the Lord his God."[740] He went to God in prayer and nourished his spirit, reflecting on the nature of "his God" and His past faithfulness. David chose to commune with God rather than brood over his worries. This prepared him for constructive action.[741] You will have the same choice in your difficulties.

Scripture is clear, "Do not worry."[742] This is a simple statement, but when troubles preoccupy your mind, the spiritual battle rages for control. Will you fret or have faith? Military leaders have learned throughout the ages, even the simplest thing is difficult in battle.[743] Spiritual battles are no different—you must fight for inner peace. Fortunately, after encouraging people not to worry, Jesus offered some important principles in how to do it: get perspective, recognize God will provide for you, worry is counter-productive, centering your life on material things is futile, find reassurance in the nature of God, make God your priority, and live life one day at a time.[744] The bottom line for Jesus, faith is better for you than worry, every single time. Faith is optimistic and empowering. Worry indulges your fallen nature's tendency toward pessimism and abdication of responsibility. Simply, it is easier to worry and do nothing than to face your problems and take constructive action. Worry reproduces more negative thoughts and emotions, overestimates problems (remember thinking traps), and emotionally spawns more intense emotions of self-pity and victimization. While these emotions may feel good in the moment with their self-indulgence and some short-term victories in manipulating others to get what you want, they are destructive to you and others in the long-term. Worry, like fear, is harmful to your health, producing chemical stress reactions that damage the mind and body over time.[745] Stress-related ailments cost the United States $300 billion every year while spending on anti-anxiety medications more than doubled in less than a decade. People are three times more likely to experience depression than the preceding generation.[746] Obviously, our society faces a stress epidemic. How do you fight off worry? Consider Jesus' words below.

---

[739] 2 Samuel 30:6
[740] 2 Samuel 30:6
[741] 2 Samuel 30:7–8
[742] Luke 12:22
[743] Clausewitz, *On War*.
[744] Luke 12:22–31
[745] Harvard Health, "*When to Worry About Worrying,*" accessed October 12, 2021, www.health.harvard.edu/mind-and-mood/when-to-worry-about-worrying.
[746] Lucado, *Anxious for Nothing*, 6.

First, Jesus encouraged the perspective: "Is not life more than food?"[747] As in fighting fear, objectively evaluate its source. Worry draws you into a false reality, that the negative outcome you fear is inevitable. Worries do not reflect facts. They do not even reflect an objective assessment of the facts. Research from the University of Cincinnati showed that eighty-five percent of the things people worried about never came true, and for the fifteen that did, people were surprised at how well they coped.[748] By worrying, you make your body and mind suffer as if enduring the worst-case scenario. Why are you worrying? Are your reasons valid? Consider what is most important in your life. Search out information and consider possible solutions. Does it really make sense to worry? In the big picture, life is more than your needs. God created you with meaning and purpose. You have needs just as a car needs gasoline and oil. You did not buy a car just to provide it gas and oil. You made an investment to help you get where you need to go. In the same way, God created you to get where He wants you to go. He predestined you for eternity with Him in heaven, and His greater purpose involves serving others, helping them find their way home along the way.[749] God knows what you need and promised to provide it. Your worth to Him is far more than food, clothing, and other needs. The world measures you by the fancy clothes you wear, your house, your car, God values you for who you are, His child. Perspective puts God, not your problems, in focus.

Second, recognize God is your provider. When He went to the mountain, Abraham discovered God was Yahweh (Jehovah) Jireh, "the Lord will provide."[750] God sustains all of creation by His invisible power.[751] We recognize life on Earth exists in a delicate balance of conditions that enable living things to thrive. If Earth moved closer to the sun, it would burn up, if it moved further away, it would become an ice planet. God set up natural laws at creation to provide sustenance. In fact, by the time Adam was formed from the dust on the sixth day, God had already created everything humans would ever need to perpetuate life on this earth. Even after Adam's rebellion damaged the natural order, God protected Earth's ability to sustain humanity. When you consider world hunger, the problem is not supply. The world produces enough food to feed everyone on the planet. Conflict is the number one disruptor of people's access and availability to food resources in the world.[752] This is a sin problem, not a God problem, as people and groups vie for power over others.[753] You do not live in a zero-sum game scenario where someone else's blessing takes away from yours. God has provided the resources for everyone to have enough. Everyone can be blessed abundantly.[754] On a more personal level, Scripture promises God will

---

747 Matthew 6:25b
748 Don Joseph Goewey, "*85% of What We Worry About Never Happens*," accessed 19 April 19, 2021, https://www.huffpost.com/entry/85–of-what-we-worry-about_b_8028368.
749 Philippians 1:11
750 Genesis 22:14
751 Luke 12:24
752 UN World Food Program, "*Causes of Hunger*," accessed December 30, 2022, www.wfpusa.org/drivers-of-hunger/.
753 James 4:1–2
754 Psalm 50:10–12

supply all your needs.[755] The word "all" actually means *all*—every single one. Jesus stated plainly, "The enemy comes to steal, kill, and destroy. I have come that you may have life and more abundantly."[756] Jesus pointed at the birds flying above and the flowers on the hillside as He posed the question, "If this is how well God takes care of creation, how much more will he take care of you?" You are far more valuable to God than the creatures He sustains. Jesus tried to assure His listeners, "You don't have to worry about your future." God will take care of you.[757] Faith in God and His promises to provide will negate worry.

Third, realize worry is counterproductive.[758] Worrying is like fighting your shadow. You can consume yourself by throwing punches, but in the end, you have only depleted your own strength. Perhaps you are a person who struggles with a fear of flying. You can spend the entire flight with a white-knuckled grip on your armrests, worrying about every bump or sound, or you can trust the pilot to handle the flight, sit back, relax, and enjoy the ride. In truth, once you are in the air, there is little you can do to affect the outcome, so your worry is in vain. The Serenity Prayer attributed to Reinhold Niebuhr states, "God grant me the serenity to accept the things I cannot change; courage to change the things I can; and wisdom to know the difference."[759] The first part of the prayer, you have no business worrying about something you cannot change. Ask God for wisdom to recognize the less obvious challenges in life you cannot control. Some problems simply require prayer and your trust in the Lord for the outcome. If the outcome doesn't appear to be favorable, trust God to bring something good from it as promised.[760] Do not waste your mental and physical energy with worry; you have a limited amount each day. You will need it for those things you can control. You want a sunny day for your party, but it may rain. You pray for sun, but someone may be praying for rain. Develop a backup plan. Do not spend your night drowning your mind and body in the destructive chemicals of stress. Accept whatever weather you get with a thankful heart.

Regarding the second part of the prayer, worry is not a helpful way to affect the things in life you can change. Constructive action can positively influence many of your problems. As Jesus noted, worry is unproductive, you cannot change a thing by worrying.[761] However, you can reduce the chance of a favorable outcome by worrying. Not only is it not helpful practically, but it also obstructs mental clarity and drains valuable physical, mental, and emotional energy.[762] Feelings of worry result from negative thoughts. Instead of viewing your problem through your natural senses, ask yourself what God thinks and says about your problems. Exercise your faith in His promises to see with spiritual sight—how

---

755 Philippians 4:19, 2 Corinthians 9:8, Psalm 145:15–16
756 John 10:10b (KJV)
757 Jeremiah 17:7–8
758 Luke 12:25
759 Beliefnet, "*Serenity Prayer*," accessed October 12, 2021, www.beliefnet.com/prayers/protestant/addiction/serenity-prayer.aspx.
760 Romans 8:28
761 Matthew 6:27
762 Harvard Health, "*When to Worry*."

things can change with God's help. If you redirect your thoughts, you will change your emotions. Instead of indulging in the emotional drain of worry, consider leveraging the positive emotions of worship and prayer. If plagued by worry, fasting can provide a helpful distraction to the physical feelings accompanying stress. It may seem like stepping on your toe to distract yourself from the pain in your finger, but fasting has many other constructive benefits besides distraction. Max Lucado offers the acronym CALM to help worriers redirect their thinking: Celebrate God's goodness, Ask Him for help, Leave your concerns with Him, and Meditate on good things.[763] Worry is not a helpful or healthy coping mechanism. In fact, it makes your problems worse. Faith, not worry, is the key to moving forward.

Fourth, recognize the futility of centering your life on material things. Things do not add meaning or value to your life. God observes humanity scurrying over the earth in vain pursuits like kids watching ants in an ant farm. Or maybe it's like watching a hamster in a spinning wheel. The hamster runs like crazy, but he doesn't go anywhere. Human pursuits have a futility. Ecclesiastes lists numerous human pursuits, wealth, fame, power, accomplishments, knowledge, that all have an expiration date. In the words of the teacher, they end up, "Meaningless!"[764] God designed you to make an eternal impact, to invest your life in others and the kingdom of God. You have probably heard of famous people who seem to have everything but take their own lives. Common goals for life are wealth, fame, or position, but they ultimately leave the soul empty. Only through Christ can we turn earthly pursuits into heavenly gain. The ancient Egyptians tried to take wealth to the grave, but today we know they only provided treasures for the grave robbers. A popular bumper sticker read, "He who dies with the most toys, wins." It is a superficial definition for "winning," at best. As the old saying goes, "You never see a hearse pulling a U-Haul trailer." Only the investments of love in others can cross with you to eternity.[765] Do not worry about meaningless things. Recognize what is most important to God with eternity in focus.

Fifth, find reassurance in the nature of God. God is love. Your mind cannot conceive the full depth of God's love for you, yet He is continually revealing it. Scripture describes Moses as one who talked to God like you talk to a friend. The Lord revealed Himself physically to Moses, passing by with these words, "The Lord, the Lord, the compassionate and gracious God, slow to anger, abounding in love and faithfulness, maintaining love to thousands, and forgiving wickedness, rebellion, and sin."[766] Scripture uses the words "heavenly Father" to describe God's nature—He is like a father.[767] Jesus used the same comparison in another passage contrasting the care of earthly parents, "How much more will your Father in heaven give good gifts to those who ask."[768] If you are a parent, think about how much you want to help your children. The heart of a parent is boundless. You would probably be willing to do

---

763 Lucado, *Anxious for Nothing*, 150–153.
764 Ecclesiastes 12:8,13–14
765 Matthew 5:44–46, 6:19–21
766 Exodus 34:6–7
767 Matthew 6:32
768 Matthew 7:11

almost anything for your child in need—maybe even offer your life in place of theirs if it was necessary. God is not the kind of parent who abuses His children. His heart for His human children is far more loving than the most loving earthly parent.

In Christ, you are a spiritual child of God. He already offered His life through Christ for you. If He would not spare Himself, how will He not graciously give us all things?[769] Many believers do not have because they do not ask.[770] They do not believe God is always good. Faith, by definition, expects good from God as the giver of everything good in this life.[771] The truth from John 10:10 is simple: God is good; your enemy, the devil, is bad. Do not assign evil to God. He does not kill, steal, or destroy. He did not afflict you with sickness or trouble. He did not take your loved one. When my son was young, I repeatedly told him to hold my hand, not to run away near a roadway. In one instance at a gas station, I told him to wait for me, and we would cross the lane to the mini mart together. He pulled out of my grasp and ran across the drive into an oncoming car. I watched in horror as I vainly leaped to stop him. Thankfully, the car braked in time and merely knocked him down with no other injuries. When I picked him up and made sure he was okay, I used the moment as a teaching point. "I gave you this rule to keep you safe. You must listen to the rules, so you don't get hurt." I did not want my son hurt, nor did I cause him to be hit by the car. However, I did use the moment to explain the importance of my rules and their purpose. God is no different. His rules are meant to keep you from harm, not fun. He doesn't bring evil into your life—that comes from someone's wrongdoing (maybe yours) or the work of the enemy, but He will use the experience to teach you wisdom for the future. The essence of God's nature is goodness and love.

Faith is critical in rejecting worry. Jesus' words were a clear appeal to faith, "you of little faith."[772] Trust in the core nature of God to take care of your needs. You do not need to worry about the issues of life. God created you; He is committed to caring for you, and He will provide all you need. Scripture states those who trust in the Lord lack no good thing.[773] Sometimes, your worries have to do with your wants. Sometimes, they relate to timing. I have regularly struggled with God's timing in my life. Honestly, I still look back and wonder why things happened as they did. Life is not always fair. We live in a fallen world infected with the dark designs of the prince and power of the air (our enemy). I accept that without illusions. I also know this God is fair, just, and good. He has earned my trust. He is worthy of yours. Do you trust in the fundamental nature of God, His love, grace, mercy, and justice? Use your confidence in God's nature to resist worry.

Sixth, prioritize serving God in your life. When you prioritize material goals, you increase your self-focus and invite many cares. You become like the man in Jesus' Parable of the Rich Fool, who con-

---

769 Romans 8:32
770 James 4:2
771 Hebrews 11:6, James 1:17
772 Luke 12:27–28
773 Psalm 34:10

sumed himself with earthly wealth but did not consider eternity.[774] Hold the things of this world loosely. You can own stuff, but do not let your stuff own you. Be careful what you love. Many people love stuff and use people. Envy, jealousy, and the desire for the lifestyle of the rich and famous steal peace and joy. Work hard, trust God to bless you, and be content with what you have. You do not need all the excess. Compared to most people on the planet, you are rich. If you live in America, you are probably in the top 80–90%. Love God, love people and use stuff. Use your possessions to serve God and others. When you give to help others, God promises to bless you abundantly so that in all things, at all times, you will have all you need.[775] When you make serving God your mission in life, deepening your walk with Him, many of the normal cares of life shrink in importance. I would love a new luxurious car, but for driving to work every day, the car I own works great. With a new, expensive car, I would be worried about scratches, dents, or it being stolen. I would want to wash and wax it regularly. I would pay expensive fees to maintain it. I do not worry much about my present car. It has a few marks, but it runs well with very low maintenance and good gas mileage. It has few extra costs and few worries. My point is, more stuff, expensive stuff, brings more work and more cares. I do not need a new car to be happy. When you make loving God and others your life mission, the cares of this world (that haunt so many people) just do not seem to matter as much. Many people today are finding peace and joy in simplicity and minimalism. They have found materialism and excess to be a heavy burden. You can have peace, joy, and contentment as Paul did. He learned the secret of contentment in every situation.[776] What did he reveal? "I can do all things through Christ who gives me strength."[777] You can find everything you need in Christ. Make God's priorities your priorities. Love God and love others. Your life will get simpler, happier, and more worry-free.

Finally, take life one day at a time. The Lord's Prayer is an affirmation of this principle, "Give us this day our daily bread."[778] Jesus encouraged people to ask God to provide one day at a time. Plan for the future but live in the present. Don't get so caught up worrying about tomorrow you lose today. In truth, the only day you have is today—yesterday is gone, and tomorrow is not guaranteed. I have listened to people share they could not wait for a better day to come, only to hear them years later wish they could go back to the way things used to be. You can spend so much time in anticipation or regret that you miss the only time you really have. God fed the Israelites manna when He brought them out of Egypt. He only allowed them to gather food one day at a time (except for the Sabbath). He wanted to teach them to trust Him for their needs every single day. Unfortunately, they never quite learned the lesson of trust. Instead of faithfully following Him, they complained and rebelled. God already had a plan for everything they needed on that journey, but they refused to follow. They romanticized the past

---
774 Luke 12:16–21
775 2 Corinthians 9:8
776 Philippians 4:11–13
777 Philippians 4:13
778 Matthew 6:11

despite the fact they were slaves in Egypt. Do not be like them. Speak to the worry as God spoke to Israel when a foreign army threatened to invade, "It will not take place, it will not happen."[779] Use God's Word to drive worry out of your mind. A common worry today is global flooding due to climate change. I care about pollution and the proper stewardship of what God has given us. However, I do not worry about global flooding. Why? Because God promised Noah the Earth would never again be flooded.[780] Global floods make for blockbuster movies, but the premise contradicts Scripture. I refuse to worry about anything that clearly contradicts the Word of God. You will need your energy to handle the challenges of today. Do not squander it catastrophizing about tomorrow. Take one day at a time. Enjoy it to the fullest. Recognize each day is a gift from God.[781]

The key to submitting your mind to God is accepting Scripture as fact. I used to see a bumper sticker on a neighbor's car, "God said it, I believe it, that settles it." However, scriptural truth is not dependent on anyone's belief. It is true because God says so. "God said it, that settles it." However, you can only overcome with the Scripture you believe deep in your heart. It is the truth you know (that you believe unequivocally) that will set you free. Get in agreement with God's Word. The enemy uses doubt and unbelief to his strategic advantage. He conceals his intelligent, strategic, and malevolent offensive against humanity in the conceptual camouflage that he does not exist while suggesting that God is the author of all that is wrong with the world. At best, God is irrelevant; or worse, God Himself is at fault for having failed humanity. From the beginning, he asserted God's Word is false.[782] Don't fall for the enemy's schemes. Scripture promises that God will always be faithful, not allowing anything to test you beyond your limits.[783] Scripture is your sword, your weapon to fight the enemy, and the negative sympathetic thought processes in your own mind. Use it to drive away worry. As Scripture states, you must demolish (utterly exterminate) any thought that sets itself up against the knowledge of God.[784] Worry has no problem destroying your physical and mental health or making you live in misery. Crush it completely without compromise.

Jesus never promised you a life free of trouble. He stated the opposite: "In this world you will have trouble. But take heart! I have overcome the world."[785] You will have problems, like every one of us who lives in this fallen world. One day, Jesus will return and wipe away every tear—no more death, pain, sorrow, or suffering.[786] You will live in the peace, joy, and the beauty of God's manifest presence, the way God originally created this earth. Right now, you live in a fallen world heavily influenced by the malevolent, destructive intelligence of the enemy. Bad things happen but be encouraged God is

---
779 Isaiah 7:7
780 Genesis 9:9–16
781 Ecclesiastes 3:12–13
782 Genesis 3:1–5
783 1 Corinthians 10:13, Hebrews 13:5
784 2 Corinthians 10:5
785 John 16:33
786 Revelation 21:4

on your side. Together, you can handle anything that happens. Life is not always fair, but God is fair, and He has a way of working things out to pay you back.[787] Two years ago, I suffered a big loss. I felt heavily stressed, condemned, and discouraged. As I prayed and read my Bible, a verse jumped off the page, "Isn't God able to restore what was lost?" I felt in my spirit it was a word from the Lord. I wrote it down and taped it to the bottom of my computer screen. People might say, "That verse has nothing to do with your situation." Normally, that may be true. However, when God speaks it to your heart, the original context is re-contextualized to your situation. How do I know that is true? Because last year, God restored what was lost. He not only restored what was lost—He restored seven times what was lost. God is faithful. I rarely understand God's timing. Frankly, my timing was yesterday. In this situation, I am thankful it was quick. I look back over my life and realize God has regularly challenged me to be patient. I also look back over my life and see God has been faithful—He has been good to me. I am no more special than you. God will be faithful to you as well. Trust Him for your today. Do not waste time worrying about a day that may never come.

I mentioned my personal struggles with worry at the beginning of the chapter. After months of waking up stressed out, consumed by worry, I got sick of it. My worry came from a failure to trust God. I had to learn to walk by faith. I can worry my life away, stressed out thinking about problems for hours in the middle of the night, or I can fight worry with a disciplined mind. I have chosen to fight. God has earned my trust. When I wake up with thoughts of worry, I choose to start praying. Every negative thought that comes to my mind I contradict with Scripture. If I succeed in refocusing my mind on prayer, I go back to sleep quickly. If not, I battle to refocus on praying. Worry is the demand signal (like a warning light) that it's time to pray. Trouble getting back to sleep is now my call to prayer. On the worst nights, I may open my Bible and begin reading. If worry comes during the day, I refute it with Scripture. I'm not going to lie; some nights are a real battle to stay focused on prayer. However, I choose to fight worry with Scripture and prayer. Do not let worry get the best of you. Battling worry is a brutal fistfight sometimes. Reject it, replace it with faith and eliminate a major threat to your resilience.

---

787 Romans 8:28

Chapter 10

Get Prepared for the Battles

"The kingdom of heaven has been forcefully advancing, and forceful people lay hold of it."[788]

Whether you realize it or not, you are engaged in a spiritual war. The enemy will try to use difficulties to drive a wedge in your relationship with God. He will try to undermine your authority, purpose, and meaning in life. The conflict may be subtle at times, but the effects of defeat are devastating, agonizing losses in your life. Scripture describes the enemy as a roaring lion looking for someone to devour.[789] He is opportunistic with dark designs, but he is not invincible. You can resist him and stand firm in the fight. These battles rage every day, primarily in your thoughts. The battles come in the form of sinful influences, doubts, unbelief, ideas, and arguments opposed to God's truth, negative thought processes (such as thinking traps), wounds and flawed conclusions from the past, fear, worry, and other thoughts contrary to God's nature and Word. To defeat these schemes, recognize the lies and replace them with the truth of God's Word.[790] You must be prepared, as Scripture warns.

> Finally, be strong in the Lord and in his mighty power. Put on the full armor of God, so that you can take your stand against the devil's schemes. For our struggle is not against flesh and blood, but against the rulers, against the authorities, against the powers of this dark world and against the spiritual forces of evil in the heavenly realms. Therefore, put on the full armor of God, so that when the day of evil comes, you may be able to stand your ground, and after you have done everything, to stand. Stand firm then, with the belt of truth buckled around your waist, with the breastplate of righteousness in place, and with your feet fitted with the readiness that comes from the gospel of peace. In addition to all this, take up the shield of faith, with which you can extinguish all the flaming arrows of the evil one. Take the helmet of salvation and the sword of the Spirit, which is the word of God.[791]

Although he works tirelessly to camouflage his destructive schemes against humanity, the enemy is

---
788 Matthew 11:12 (GW)
789 1 Peter 5:7–9
790 2 Corinthians 10:4–5
791 Ephesians 6:10–17

very real. When I was fifteen, I heard a sermon on this passage. I re-read it and scoffed at the notion of demons and dark spiritual forces. I lay down in bed and shut off the light on my nightstand. Instantly, I had a vision of a dark face in the window of my room. It had a wicked smile like the face of the Cheshire cat, and I knew it was the enemy. It laughed and smiled, "You don't believe." It made the hair stand up on my arms. Dark evil shapes began to pour into my room through that window. They filled every inch of my room, hovering over my bed. I froze, afraid to move in any way, lest I brush against one of them. In the next second, I saw four angels at the corners of my bed and a bright shield of white light between me and the dark shapes. Instantly, the vision was gone, and my room looked normal again. I stayed frozen for the next five to ten minutes, afraid I might accidentally break through the shield of light. Since that day, I have accepted the passage above as fact. Demons survived the period of the New Testament, they are just as destructively active as they were in Jesus' day, perhaps just better concealed in our sophistication.

The enemy is destructive, but your authority in Christ is greater. You have authority and power over every dark spiritual force.[792] This is why the Scripture above starts with, "Be strong in the Lord and in His mighty power." You prepare for battle by recognizing the spiritual significance of each piece of armor in protecting you against the lies of the enemy. The spiritual principles that govern your relationship with God, identity as a believer, understanding of the truths of His Word, faith and moral choices equip you to fight and win the battles. The Scripture is your sword, your offensive weapon. Truthfully, your war has already been won by Christ through His death and resurrection. Your enemy is defeated.[793] All it takes for you to realize the victory is to stand against Him. If you outlast Him, you win.[794] You don't have to knock Him out, you don't have to be perfect. If you get knocked down, you win if you get back up and stay in the fight. If you submit yourself to God and keep resisting the enemy, he will be forced to flee.[795]

Understand the enemy's tactics: he is a liar and the father of lies.[796] A friend of mine described deception as the enemy's weapon of mass destruction. I agree; it has been a wrecking ball in people's lives throughout human history. In the digital age, the lies have evolved, becoming more wise sounding with greater altruism than ever before. People justify their violence toward others with words like human rights and tolerance. They explain their disrespect and mistreatment of others with an appeal to justice. And no wonder, Scripture warns, Satan masquerades as an angel of light.[797] In this culture of information overload, it is more important than ever to filter messages through Scripture and a scriptural worldview. John, the beloved disciple of Christ, warned the church, "Do not believe every spirit, but test them to see if they are from God."[798] You must examine every message to discern the spirit behind it.

---

792 Ephesians 1:18–21
793 Luke 10:19, John 16:11, Colossians 2:15
794 Ephesians 6:10–18
795 James 4:7
796 John 8:44
797 2 Corinthians 11:14
798 1 John 4:1–3

Many spirits operate as influencers and activists, cloaking themselves behind noble causes. The key test is how these efforts treat Jesus. An example is environmentalism. When legitimate concern for taking care of the planet becomes, in essence, worship of the planet, there is a spiritual problem. Many people regard nature as divine rather than honoring the divine creator of it all. The new morality is love for the planet rather than love for God and others. Scripture clearly warns of this error.[799] Another issue, when human rights infringe on the right of people to openly profess and practice their religious beliefs, there is a spiritual problem. In fact, the well-being of societies is extensively connected to the contribution of religious institutions.[800] Religious freedom is the guardian of all other human rights. In societies where religious freedoms are restricted, basic human rights follow.

It is an interesting historical fact that movements "for the people" that resulted in centralizing government power always resulted in intense physical persecution of religious groups. This continues today in places like North Korea, China, Nigeria, and many others. What spirit is concealed behind revolutionary human rights movements that lead them to crush the perceived threat of individual religious expression? The worldwide persecution of Christians continues to grow at an alarming rate.[801] You must carefully test the information you allow to shape your beliefs and values. The enemy is shrewd and calculating, leading the world away from God in the spirit of antichrist, under a banner of "good causes."

A review of the deception of Adam and Eve provides a good illustration of how many spiritual battles unfold. God clearly told them not to eat from the Tree of the Knowledge of Good and Evil, limiting the access to only one tree of thousands. Yet Satan sowed seeds of doubt with the words, "Did God really say you must not eat fruit from any tree in the garden?"[802] He twisted God's words in this question for God had only restricted one tree. When Eve explained God's command, Satan replied, "You will not certainly die, for God knows when you eat of it you will be like him." In this response, he both contradicted God's words and accused God of unfairness, of withholding something good from them. The deception worked, Eve ate the fruit and gave it to Adam also. They gained knowledge but they lost far more, they lost their immortality and caused every creature and all of creation to suffer with them in the new hostile creation caused by their sin. Harmony on the earth and among its inhabitants has been lost until it is eventually restored by Christ. Bottom line, they did die. God didn't hold out on them in the Garden; He had given them everything they needed for a fantastic life together. They traded the eternal harmony and peace of the Garden for the world as it exists today. Ever since, mankind has tried to recreate the utopia of Eden, but they always fall well short. The battle is real, and the enemy's primary weapon is deception. Beware of fine-sounding arguments intended to lead you away from God.

---

[799] Romans 1:18–25
[800] Paul Marshall and Timothy Shah, "Why People Need Religious Institutions and Why Religious Institutions Need Freedom." Religious Freedom Institute, 2021, 13.
[801] Emily McFarlan Miller, Christian Persecution Higher than Ever as Open Doors' World Watch List Marks 30 Years, (Bethesda, MD: Religion News Service, January 17, 2023.
[802] Genesis 3:1–7

Your primary weapon in battle, the sword of the Spirit, is truth from the Word of God. To figuratively sharpen that sword and have it "at the ready" for battle, you must be familiar with, know, and be ready to use Scripture. The enemy engaged Jesus in battle after forty days of fasting in the wilderness.[803] All alone and at one of His physically weakest moments, Jesus took on the enemy with one weapon: the Word of God. The enemy came at Him, twisting God's Word, but Jesus recognized the lies and fought back with scriptural truth. You can do the same. The enemy desires to mire you down in worry, fear, doubts, guilt, shame, anger, and similar forms of stinking thinking. Block these attacks with your knowledge of Scripture. Prepare yourself for spiritual warfare.

You must have spiritual weapons to fight a spiritual battle. It may seem crazy to some, but the Word of God has divine power to counter the deceptions of the enemy and to empower you to maintain control of your thought life so it is healthy, constructive, and honors God.

> For though we live in the world, we do not wage war as the world does. The weapons we fight with are not the weapons of the world. On the contrary, they have divine power to demolish strongholds. We demolish arguments and every pretension that sets itself up against the knowledge of God, and we take captive every thought to make it obedient to Christ.[804]

Recognize, the battle is real, you have been given power and authority to win that battle, and your armor and weapons (through faith in the Word of God) are all you need to overcome an already-defeated enemy. The strategic factor in your readiness to fight is your knowledge and understanding of the Word of God. Identify the key Bible verses you need to know to fight the attacks you will experience. Add these to other favorites or "life" verses that will help you overcome. Write out your key verses and keep them available for easy access. Study so Scriptures are not merely words you know about; they are words you understand and live in your heart. Memorize key verses you need to have ready in the moment when you don't have time to get your Bible.

God has given you spiritual armor to stand against the enemy as shown at the beginning of the chapter. According to Scripture, standing is winning. The belt of truth holds the sword of the Spirit and supports the breastplate of righteousness. Both the sword and the breastplate spiritually require truth. Truth helps you parry the deceptive attacks of the enemy as Jesus did in the wilderness and protects you against every accusation in your legal standing before God. The breastplate of righteousness protects the vital organs both in the righteousness provided legally by Christ your justification and by the protective effects of doing the right thing before God. Moral decisions prevent the many second and third

---
803 Matthew 4:1–11
804 2 Corinthians 10:3–5

order effects of sin the enemy uses to drag you into spiritual affliction and bondage. Having your feet fitted with readiness from the Gospel of peace is the spiritual preparation to engage in battle. No soldier wants to fight barefoot; it undermines stability and movement. Shoes take precious time to lace and tie addressing the importance of always being ready for the inevitable spiritual battles. The shield of faith, trust in God and His word, provides key protection against the many schemes the enemy uses to wound you, everything from offense to condemnation and more. These flaming arrows can cause you serious spiritual damage without true faith. The helmet of salvation protects your most vulnerable part, the head. Your status of salvation; forgiven, redeemed, and belonging to God prevents the enemy from striking a death blow in one fell strike. Your head is always protected by the work of Christ. Finally, the sword of the Spirit, the word of God, is your offensive weapon to rebuke the activity of unclean spirits and cause the enemy to flee. Your knowledge of the scripture provides the spiritual skill by which you wield your sword. That is why this book relies so heavily on scripture and repeatedly uses key verses to reinforce your understanding of spiritual truths. With your armor, you have no need to fear any dark spirit or any of the enemy's schemes. You are victorious in submission to Christ and only need to stand to assert your authority and claim your victory.[805]

The sections below are lists of topical verses that will equip you for battle. Some will strengthen you as you declare them over your life every morning. Some will parry specific attacks of the enemy. Mark these pages and refer to them as needed. As you continually read and reflect on Scripture, you will add to this list and have your sword sharp and ready for the battles in your mind.

If You Need Comfort

Job 14:7–9 (NIV)

At least there is hope for a tree: If it is cut down, it will sprout again, and its new shoots will not fail. Its roots may grow old in the ground and its stump die in the soil, yet at the scent of water it will bud and put forth shoots like a plant.

Psalm 9:9 (NIV)

The LORD is a refuge for the oppressed, a stronghold in times of trouble.

Psalm 23:1–6 (NIV)

The LORD is my shepherd, I lack nothing. He makes me lie down in green pastures, he leads me beside quiet waters, he refreshes my soul. He guides me along the right paths for his name's sake. Even though I walk through the darkest valley,I will fear no evil, for you are with me; your rod and your staff,

---
[805] Ephesians 6:10–17

they comfort me. You prepare a table before me in the presence of my enemies. You anoint my head with oil; my cup overflows. Surely your goodness and love will follow me all the days of my life, and I will dwell in the house of the LORD forever.

Psalm 30:11 (NIV)

You turned my wailing into dancing; you removed my sackcloth and clothed me with joy.

Psalm 34:17–20 (NLT)

The LORD hears his people when they call to him for help. He rescues them from all their troubles. The LORD is close to the brokenhearted; he rescues those whose spirits are crushed. The righteous person faces many troubles, but the LORD comes to the rescue each time. For the LORD protects the bones of the righteous; not one of them is broken!

Psalm 34:19 (NLT)

The righteous person faces many troubles, but the LORD comes to the rescue each time.

Psalm 55:16–17 (NIV)

As for me, I call to God, and the LORD saves me. Evening, morning and noon I cry out in distress, and he hears my voice.

Psalm 55:22 (ESV)

Cast your burden on the Lord, and he will sustain you; he will never permit the righteous to be moved.

Psalm 91:5–6 (NIV)

You will not fear the terror of night, nor the arrow that flies by day, nor the pestilence that stalks in the darkness, nor the plague that destroys at midday.

Isaiah 42:3 (NIV)

A bruised reed he will not break, and a smoldering wick he will not snuff out. In faithfulness he will bring forth justice.

Isaiah 54:17 (NIV)

No weapon forged against you will prevail, and you will refute every tongue that accuses you. This is the heritage of the servants of the LORD, and this is their vindication from me," declares the LORD.

Lamentations 3:22–25 (NIV):

Because of the LORD's great love we are not consumed, for his compassions never fail. They are new every morning; great is your faithfulness. I say to myself, "The LORD is my portion; therefore I will wait for him." The LORD is good to those whose hope is in him, to the one who seeks him;

Zephaniah 3:17 (ESV)

The Lord your God is in your midst, a mighty one who will save; he will rejoice over you with gladness; he will quiet you by his love; he will exult over you with loud singing.

Matthew 11:28–30 (NIV)

"Come to me, all you who are weary and burdened, and I will give you rest. Take my yoke upon you and learn from me, for I am gentle and humble in heart, and you will find rest for your souls. For my yoke is easy and my burden is light."

Philippians 4:19 (NIV)

And my God will meet all your needs according to the riches of his glory in Christ Jesus.

Hebrews 12:1 (CEV)

Such a large crowd of witnesses is all around us! So we must get rid of everything that slows us down, especially the sin that just won't let go. And we must be determined to run the race that is ahead of us.

1 Thessalonians 4:13–18 (NLT)

And now, dear brothers and sisters, we want you to know what will happen to the believers who have died so you will not grieve like people who have no hope. For since we believe that Jesus died and was raised to life again, we also believe that when Jesus returns, God will bring back with him the believers who have died. We tell you this directly from the Lord: We who are still living when the Lord returns will not meet him ahead of those who have died. For the Lord himself will come down from heaven with a commanding shout, with the voice of the archangel, and with the trumpet call of God. First, the Christians who have died[c] will rise from their graves. Then, together with them, we who are still alive and remain on the earth will be caught up in the clouds to meet the Lord in the air. Then we will be with the Lord forever. So encourage each other with these words.

Romans 15:13 (NIV)

May the God of hope fill you with all joy and peace as you trust in him, so that you may overflow with hope by the power of the Holy Spirit.

2 Corinthians 1:3–4 (NIV)

Praise be to the God and Father of our Lord Jesus Christ, the Father of compassion and the God of all comfort, who comforts us in all our troubles, so that we can comfort those in any trouble with the comfort we ourselves receive from God.

If You Feel Fearful, Anxious or Need Courage

Hebrews 13:6 (NIV)

So we say with confidence, "The Lord is my helper; I will not be afraid. What can mere mortals do to me?"

Deuteronomy 31:6 (KJV)

Be strong and of good courage, do not fear nor be afraid of them; for the LORD your God, He is the One who goes with you. He will not leave you nor forsake you.

Joshua 1:9 (NIV)

"Have I not commanded you? Be strong and courageous. Do not be afraid; do not be discouraged, for the Lord your God will be with you wherever you go."

1 Chronicles 28:20 (NIV)

David also said to Solomon his son, "Be strong and courageous, and do the work. Do not be afraid or discouraged, for the LORD God, my God, is with you. He will not fail you or forsake you until all the work for the service of the temple of the LORD is finished."

Psalm 27:1 (NKJV)

The LORD is my light and my salvation; Whom shall I fear? The LORD is the strength of my life; Of whom shall I be afraid?

Psalm 46:1–3 (NIV)

God is our refuge and strength, an ever-present help in trouble. Therefore we will not fear, though the earth give way and the mountains fall into the heart of the sea, though its waters roar and foam and the mountains quake with their surging.

Psalm 56:3–4 (NIV)

When I am afraid, I will trust in you. In God, whose word I praise, in God I trust; I will not be afraid. What can mortal man do to me?

Proverbs 12:25 (NIV)

Anxiety weighs down the heart, but a kind word cheers it up.

Isaiah 41:10 (NIV)

So do not fear, for I am with you; do not be dismayed, for I am your God. I will strengthen you and help you; I will uphold you with my righteous right hand.

Isaiah 41:13 (NIV)

For I am the LORD, your God, who takes hold of your right hand and says to you, Do not fear; I will help you.

Isaiah 54:4 (NKJV)

Do not fear, for you will not be ashamed; Neither be disgraced, for you will not be put to shame; For you will forget the shame of your youth And will not remember the reproach of your widowhood anymore.

Matthew 10:26–28 (NLT)

"But don't be afraid of those who threaten you. For the time is coming when everything that is covered will be revealed, and all that is secret will be made known to all… Don't be afraid of those who want to kill your body; they cannot touch your soul. Fear only God, who can destroy both soul and body in hell."

Matthew 11:28–30 (NIV)

"Come to me, all you who are weary and burdened, and I will give you rest. Take my yoke upon you and learn from me, for I am gentle and humble in heart, and you will find rest for your souls. For my yoke is easy and my burden is light."

Romans 8:15 (NIV)

The Spirit you received does not make you slaves, so that you live in fear again; rather, the Spirit you received brought about your adoption to sonship. And by him we cry, "Abba, Father."

1 Corinthians 16:13 (NIV)

Be on your guard; stand firm in the faith; be men of courage; be strong.

2 Corinthians 4:8–11 (NIV)

We are hard-pressed on every side, but not crushed; perplexed, but not in despair; persecuted, but not abandoned; struck down, but not destroyed. We always carry around in our body the death of Jesus, so that the life of Jesus may also be revealed in our body. For we who are alive are always being given over to death for Jesus' sake, so that his life may be revealed in our mortal body.

Philippians 1:12–14 (NIV)

Now I want you to know, brothers, that what has happened to me has really served to advance the gospel. As a result, it has become clear throughout the whole palace guard and to everyone else that I am in chains for Christ. Because of my chains, most of the brothers in the Lord have been encouraged to speak the word of God more courageously and fearlessly.

2 Timothy 1:7 (NLT)

For God has not given us a spirit of fear and timidity, but of power, love, and self-discipline.

Hebrews 13:5–6 (NKJV)

For He Himself has said, "I will never leave you nor forsake you." So we may boldly say: "The LORD is my helper; I will not fear. What can man do to me?"

1 Peter 5:7–9 (NIV)

Cast all your anxiety on him because he cares for you. Be alert and of sober mind. Your enemy the devil prowls around like a roaring lion looking for someone to devour. Resist him, standing firm in the faith, because you know that the family of believers throughout the world is undergoing the same kind of sufferings.

1 John 4:18 (NIV)

There is no fear in love. But perfect love drives out fear, because fear has to do with punishment. The one who fears is not made perfect in love.

If You Feel Discouraged or Depressed

Joshua 1:9 (NIV)

Have I not commanded you? Be strong and courageous. Do not be afraid; do not be discouraged, for the Lord your God will be with you wherever you go.

Nehemiah 8:10 (NIV)

Nehemiah said, "Go and enjoy choice food and sweet drinks, and send some to those who have nothing prepared. This day is holy to our Lord. Do not grieve, for the joy of the Lord is your strength."

Psalm 5:11 (NIV)

But let all who take refuge in you be glad; let them ever sing for joy. Spread your protection over them, that those who love your name may rejoice in you.

Psalm 34:17–19 (NIV)

The righteous cry out, and the LORD hears them; he delivers them from all their troubles. The LORD is close to the brokenhearted and saves those who are crushed in spirit. A righteous man may have many troubles, but the LORD delivers him from them all.

Psalm 37:7 (NIV)

Be still before the Lord and wait patiently for him; fret not yourself over the one who prospers in his way, over the man who carries out evil devices!

Psalm 46:10–11 (NIV)

Be still before the Lord and wait patiently for him; do not fret when people succeed in their ways, when they carry out their wicked schemes.

Proverbs 3:4–6 (NIV)

Trust in the Lord with all your heart and lean not on your own understanding; in all your ways submit to him, and he will make your paths straight.

Proverbs 4:25 (NIV)

Let your eyes look straight ahead; fix your gaze directly before you.

Job 17:9 (NIV)

Nevertheless, the righteous will hold to their ways, and those with clean hands will grow stronger

Isaiah 42:3 (NIV)

A bruised reed he will not break, and a smoldering wick he will not snuff out. In faithfulness he will bring forth justice.

Isaiah 43:18–19 (NIV)

"Forget the former things; do not dwell on the past. See, I am doing a new thing! Now it springs up; do you not perceive it? I am making a way in the wilderness and streams in the wasteland."

Lamentations 3:22–25 (NIV)

Because of the Lord's great love we are not consumed, for his compassions never fail. They are new every morning; great is your faithfulness. I say to myself, the Lord is my portion; therefore I will wait for him." The Lord is good to those whose hope is in him, to the one who seeks him.

Haggai 2:4–5 (NIV)

But now be strong, Zerubbabel,' declares the Lord. 'Be strong, Joshua son of Jozadak, the high priest. Be strong, all you people of the land,' declares the Lord, 'and work. For I am with you,' declares the Lord Almighty. 'This is what I covenanted with you when you came out of Egypt. And my Spirit remains among you. Do not fear.'

John 14:1 (NIV)

Do not let your hearts be troubled. You believe in God; believe also in me.

Romans 8:31–35 (NIV)

What, then, shall we say in response to these things? If God is for us, who can be against us? He who did not spare his own Son, but gave him up for us all—how will he not also, along with him, graciously give us all things? Who will bring any charge against those whom God has chosen? It is God who justifies. Who then is the one who condemns? No one. Christ Jesus who died—more than that, who was raised to life—is at the right hand of God and is also interceding for us. Who shall separate us from the love of Christ? Shall trouble or hardship or persecution or famine or nakedness or danger or sword?

Romans 8:28 (NIV)

And we know that in all things God works for the good of those who love him, who have been called according to his purpose.

Romans 12:2 (NIV)

Do not conform to the pattern of this world but be transformed by the renewing of your mind. Then you will be able to test and approve what God's will is—his good, pleasing and perfect will.

Romans 15:4–5 (NIV)

For everything that was written in the past was written to teach us, so that through the endurance taught in the Scriptures and the encouragement they provide we might have hope. May the God who gives endurance and encouragement give you the same attitude of mind toward each other that Christ Jesus had.

2 Corinthians 5:7 (NIV)

For we live by faith, not by sight.

Galatians 6:9 (NIV)

Let us not become weary in doing good, for at the proper time we will reap a harvest if we do not give up.

Philippians 3:13–14 (NIV)

Brothers and sisters, I do not consider myself yet to have taken hold of it. But one thing I do: Forgetting what is behind and straining toward what is ahead, I press on toward the goal to win the prize for which God has called me heavenward in Christ Jesus.

Philippians 4:6–7 (NIV)

Do not be anxious about anything, but in every situation, by prayer and petition, with thanksgiving, present your requests to God. And the peace of God, which transcends all understanding, will guard your hearts and your minds in Christ Jesus.

Colossians 3:2 (NIV)

Set your minds on things above, not on earthly things.

1 Peter 5:7–8 (NIV)

Cast all your anxiety on him because he cares for you. Be alert and of sober mind. Your enemy the devil prowls around like a roaring lion looking for someone to devour.

If You Feel Guilt

Psalm 32:1–5 (NIV)

Blessed is the one whose transgressions are forgiven, whose sins are covered. Blessed is the one whose sin the Lord does not count against them and in whose spirit is no deceit. When I kept silent, my bones wasted away through my groaning all day long. For day and night your hand was heavy on me; my strength was sapped as in the heat of summer. Then I acknowledged my sin to you and did not cover up my iniquity. I said, "I will confess my transgressions to the Lord." And you forgave the guilt of my sin.

Psalm 139:23–34 (NIV)

Search me, God, and know my heart; test me and know my anxious thoughts. See if there is any offensive way in me, and lead me in the way everlasting.

Proverbs 28:13 (NIV)

Whoever conceals their sins does not prosper, but the one who confesses and renounces them finds mercy.

Isaiah 43:25 (NIV)

"I, even I, am he who blots out your transgressions, for my own sake, and remembers your sins no more."

Jeremiah 33:8 (NIV)

I will cleanse them from all the sin they have committed against me and will forgive all their sins of rebellion against me.

Romans 5:20–21 (NIV)

The law was brought in so that the trespass might increase. But where sin increased, grace increased all the more, so that, just as sin reigned in death, so also grace might reign through righteousness to bring eternal life through Jesus Christ our Lord.

Romans 8:1 (NIV)

Therefore, there is now no condemnation for those who are in Christ Jesus.

2 Corinthians 5:17 (NIV)

Therefore, if anyone is in Christ, the new creation has come: The old has gone, the new is here!

2 Corinthians 7:9–10 (NIV)

Yet now I am happy, not because you were made sorry, but because your sorrow led you to repentance. For you became sorrowful as God intended and so were not harmed in any way by us. Godly sorrow brings repentance that leads to salvation and leaves no regret, but worldly sorrow brings death.

Galatians 3:1–3 (NIV):

You foolish Galatians! Who has bewitched you? Before your very eyes Jesus Christ was clearly portrayed as crucified. I would like to learn just one thing from you: Did you receive the Spirit by the works of the law, or by believing what you heard? Are you so foolish? After beginning by means of the Spirit, are you now trying to finish by means of the flesh?

Philippians 3:13–14 (NIV):

Brothers and sisters, I do not consider myself yet to have taken hold of it. But one thing I do: Forgetting what is behind and straining toward what is ahead, I press on toward the goal to win the prize for which God has called me heavenward in Christ Jesus.

Hebrews 8:12 (NIV)

"For I will forgive their wickedness and will remember their sins no more."

Hebrews 9:14 (NIV)

How much more, then, will the blood of Christ, who through the eternal Spirit offered himself unblemished to God, cleanse our consciences from acts that lead to death, so that we may serve the living God!

Hebrews 10:22 (NIV)

Let us draw near to God with a sincere heart and with the full assurance that faith brings, having our hearts sprinkled to cleanse us from a guilty conscience and having our bodies washed with pure water.

Hebrews 12:2 (NIV)

Fixing our eyes on Jesus, the pioneer and perfecter of faith. For the joy set before him he endured the cross, scorning its shame, and sat down at the right hand of the throne of God.

Hebrews 12:5–7 (NIV)

And have you completely forgotten this word of encouragement that addresses you as a father addresses his son? It says, "My son, do not make light of the Lord's discipline, and do not lose heart when he rebukes you, because the Lord disciplines the one he loves, and he chastens everyone he accepts as his son." Endure hardship as discipline; God is treating you as his children. For what children are not disciplined by their father?

Revelation 12:10 (NIV)

Then I heard a loud voice in heaven say: "Now have come the salvation and the power and the kingdom of our God, and the authority of his Messiah. For the accuser of our brothers and sisters, who accuses them before our God day and night, has been hurled down."

Ephesians 6:11 (NIV)

Put on the full armor of God, so that you can take your stand against the devil's schemes.

James 4:7 (NIV)

Submit yourselves therefore to God. Resist the devil, and he will flee from you

If You Need Healing

Exodus 15:26 (NIV)

"If you listen carefully to the Lord your God and do what is right in his eyes, if you pay attention to his commands and keep all his decrees, I will not bring on you any of the diseases I brought on the Egyptians, for I am the Lord, who heals you."

Psalm 30:2 (NIV)

Lord my God, I called to you for help, and you healed me.

Psalm 41:3 (NIV)

The Lord sustains them on their sickbed and restores them from their bed of illness.

Psalm 103:2–4 (NIV)

Praise the Lord, my soul, and forget not all his benefits- who forgives all your sins and heals all your diseases, who redeems your life from the pit and crowns you with love and compassion.

Psalm 107:19–20 (NIV)

Then they cried to the Lord in their trouble, and he saved them from their distress. He sent out his word and healed them; he rescued them from the grave

Psalm 147:3 (NIV)

He heals the brokenhearted and binds up their wounds.

Proverbs 4:20–22 (NIV)

My son, pay attention to what I say; turn your ear to my words. Do not let them out of your sight, keep them within your heart; for they are life to those who find them and health to one's whole body.

Isaiah 58:8 (NIV)

Then your light will break forth like the dawn, and your healing will quickly appear; then your righteousness will go before you, and the glory of the Lord will be your rear guard.

Jeremiah 17:14 (NIV)

Heal me, Lord, and I will be healed; save me and I will be saved, for you are the one I praise.

Matthew 8:19–17 (NIV)

When evening came, many who were demon-possessed were brought to him, and he drove out the spirits with a word and healed all the sick. This was to fulfill what was spoken through the prophet Isaiah.

Matthew 9:35 (NIV)

Jesus went through all the towns and villages, teaching in their synagogues, proclaiming the good news of the kingdom, and healing every disease and sickness.

Mark 5: 34 (NIV)

He said to her, "Daughter, your faith has healed you. Go in peace and be freed from your suffering."

Luke 8:50 (NIV)

Hearing this, Jesus said to Jairus, "Don't be afraid; just believe, and she will be healed."

John 9:2–7 (NIV):

His disciples asked him, "Rabbi, who sinned, this man or his parents, that he was born blind?" "Neither this man nor his parents sinned," said Jesus, "but this happened so that the work of God might be displayed in his life…Having said this, he spit on the ground, made some mud with the saliva, and put it on the man's eyes. "Go," he told him, "wash in the Pool of Siloam" (this word means Sent). So the man went and washed, and came home seeing.

James 5:16 (NIV)

Therefore, confess your sins to each other and pray for each other so that you may be healed. The prayer of a righteous person is powerful and effective.

1 Peter 2:24 (NIV)

"He himself bore our sins" in his body on the cross, so that we might die to sins and live for righteousness; "by his wounds you have been healed."

If You Need Peace

Psalm 4:8 (NIV)

In peace I will lie down and sleep, for you alone, Lord, make me dwell in safety.

Psalm 119:165 (NIV)

Great peace have those who love your law, and nothing can make them stumble.

Proverbs 3:23–24 (NIV)

Then you will go on your way in safety, and your foot will not stumble; when you lie down, you will not be afraid; when you lie down, your sleep will be sweet.

Isaiah 26:3 (NIV)

You will keep in perfect peace those whose minds are steadfast, because they trust in you.

Isaiah 32: 17 (NIV)

The fruit of that righteousness will be peace; its effect will be quietness and confidence forever.

John 14:27 (NLT)

I am leaving you with a gift—peace of mind and heart. And the peace I give is a gift the world cannot give. So don't be troubled or afraid.

John 16:33 (NIV)

"I have told you these things, so that in me you may have peace. In this world you will have trouble. But take heart! I have overcome the world."

Romans 8:6 (NIV)

The mind governed by the flesh is death, but the mind governed by the Spirit is life and peace.

1 Corinthians 14:33 (NIV)

For God is not a God of disorder but of peace—as in all the congregations of the Lord's people.

Philippians 4:6–7 (NIV)

Do not be anxious about anything, but in everything, by prayer and petition, with thanksgiving, present your requests to God. And the peace of God, which transcends all understanding, will guard your hearts and your minds in Christ Jesus.

Philippians 4:9 (NIV)

Whatever you have learned or received or heard from me or seen in me—put it into practice. And the God of peace will be with you.

Colossians 3:15 (NIV)

Let the peace of Christ rule in your hearts, since as members of one body you were called to peace. And be thankful.

2 Thessalonians 3:16 (NIV)

Now may the Lord of peace himself give you peace at all times and in every way. The Lord be with all of you.

James 3:18 (NIV)

Peacemakers who sow in peace reap a harvest of righteousness.

If You Feel Worried or Stressed

Matthew 11:28–30 (NIV)

"Come to me, all you who are weary and burdened, and I will give you rest. Take my yoke upon you and learn from me, for I am gentle and humble in heart, and you will find rest for your souls. For my yoke is easy and my burden is light."

John 14:27 (NIV)

Peace I leave with you; my peace I give you. I do not give to you as the world gives. Do not let your hearts be troubled and do not be afraid.

1 Peter 5:7 (NIV)

Cast all your anxiety on him because he cares for you.

Colossians 3:15 (NIV)

Let the peace of Christ rule in your hearts, since as members of one body you were called to peace. And be thankful.

2 Thessalonians 3:16 (NIV)

Now may the Lord of peace himself give you peace at all times and in every way. The Lord be with all of you.

Matthew 6:25–34 (NIV)

"Therefore I tell you, do not worry about your life, what you will eat or drink; or about your body, what you will wear. Is not life more than food, and the body more than clothes? Look at the birds of the air; they do not sow or reap or store away in barns, and yet your heavenly Father feeds them. Are you not much more valuable than they? Can any one of you by worrying add a single hour to your life?" And why do you worry about clothes? See how the flowers of the field grow. They do not labor or spin. Yet I tell you that not even Solomon in all his splendor was dressed like one of these. If that is how God clothes the grass of the field, which is here today and tomorrow is thrown into the fire, will he not much more clothe you-you of little faith? So do not worry, saying, 'What shall we eat?' or 'What shall we drink?' or 'What shall we wear?' For the pagans run after all these things, and your heavenly Father knows that you need them. But seek first his kingdom and his righteousness, and all these things will be given to you as well. Therefore, do not worry about tomorrow, for tomorrow will worry about itself. Each day has enough trouble of its own.

Psalm 55:22 (NIV)

Cast your cares on the Lord, and he will sustain you; he will never let the righteous be shaken.

Philippians 4:6–7 (NIV)

Do not be anxious about anything, but in every situation, by prayer and petition, with thanksgiving, present your requests to God. And the peace of God, which transcends all understanding, will guard your hearts and your minds in Christ Jesus.

Luke 12:25 (NIV)

Who of you by worrying can add a single hour to your life?

Jeremiah 17:7–8 (NIV)

"But blessed is the one who trusts in the Lord, whose confidence is in him. They will be like a tree planted by the water that sends out its roots by the stream. It does not fear when heat comes; its leaves are always green. It has no worries in a year of drought and never fails to bear fruit."

Psalm 94:19–20 (NIV)

When anxiety was great within me, your consolation brought me joy. Can a corrupt throne be allied with you- a throne that brings on misery by its decrees?

Luke 10:41–42 (NIV)

"Martha, Martha," the Lord answered, "you are worried and upset about many things, but few things are needed-or indeed only one. Mary has chosen what is better, and it will not be taken away from her."

If You Feel Grief or Loss

Genesis 37:34–35 (NIV)

Then Jacob tore his clothes, put on sackcloth, and mourned for his son many days. All his sons and daughters came to comfort him, but he refused to be comforted. "No," he said, "I will continue to mourn until I join my son in the grave." So his father wept for him.

Deuteronomy 34:8 (NIV)

The Israelites grieved for Moses in the plains of Moab thirty days, until the time of weeping and mourning was over.

2 Samuel 12:16–17 (NIV)

David pleaded with God for the child. He fasted and spent the nights lying in sackcloth on the ground. The elders of his household stood beside him to get him up from the ground, but he refused, and he would not eat any food with them.

Ecclesiastes 3:1–4 (NIV)

There is a time for everything, and a season for every activity under the heavens: a time to be born and a time to die, a time to plant and a time to uproot, a time to kill and a time to heal, a time to tear down and a time to build, a time to weep and a time to laugh, a time to mourn and a time to dance.

Ecclesiastes 7:4 (NIV)

The heart of the wise is in the house of mourning, but the heart of fools is in the house of pleasure.

Psalm 77:2 (NIV)

When I was in distress, I sought the Lord; at night I stretched out untiring hands, and I would not be comforted.

Psalm 119:92 (NIV)

If your law had not been my delight, I would have perished in my affliction.

Proverbs 15:13–14 (NIV)

A happy heart makes the face cheerful, but heartache crushes the spirit. The discerning heart seeks knowledge, but the mouth of a fool feeds on folly.

Isaiah 41:10 (NIV)

So do not fear, for I am with you; do not be dismayed, for I am your God. I will strengthen you and help you; I will uphold you with my righteous right hand.

Isaiah 42:3 (NIV)

A bruised reed he will not break, and a smoldering wick he will not snuff out. In faithfulness he will bring forth justice.

Lamentations 3:22–25 (NIV)

Because of the Lord's great love we are not consumed, for his compassions never fail. They are new every morning; great is your faithfulness. I say to myself, "The Lord is my portion; therefore I will wait for him." The Lord is good to those whose hope is in him, to the one who seeks him.

Philippians 3:13–14 (NIV)

Brothers and sisters, I do not consider myself yet to have taken hold of it. But one thing I do: Forgetting what is behind and straining toward what is ahead, I press on toward the goal to win the prize for which God has called me heavenward in Christ Jesus.

James 4:7 (NIV)

Submit yourselves, then, to God. Resist the devil, and he will flee from.

Psalm 116:15 (NIV)

Precious in the sight of the Lord is the death of his faithful servants.

Psalm 119:50 (NIV)

My comfort in my suffering is this: Your promise preserves my life.

Isaiah 51:11 (NIV)

Those the Lord has rescued will return. They will enter Zion with singing; everlasting joy will crown their heads. Gladness and joy will overtake them, and sorrow and sighing will flee away.

Romans 8:18 (NIV)

I consider that our present sufferings are not worth comparing with the glory that will be revealed in us.

1 Corinthians 15:54–55 (NIV)

When the perishable has been clothed with the imperishable, and the mortal with immortality, then the saying that is written will come true: "Death has been swallowed up in victory." "Where, O death, is your victory? Where, O death, is your sting?"

1 Thessalonians 4:13 (NIV)

Brothers and sisters, we do not want you to be uninformed about those who sleep in death, so that you do not grieve like the rest of mankind, who have no hope. For we believe that Jesus died and rose again, and so we believe that God will bring with Jesus those who have fallen asleep in him. According to the Lord's word, we tell you that we who are still alive, who are left until the coming of the Lord, will certainly not precede those who have fallen asleep. For the Lord himself will come down from heaven, with a loud command, with the voice of the archangel and with the trumpet call of God, and the dead in Christ will rise first. After that, we who are still alive and are left will be caught up together with them in the clouds to meet the Lord in the air. And so we will be with the Lord forever. Therefore encourage one another with these words.

Revelation 14:13 (NIV)

Then I heard a voice from heaven say, "Write this: Blessed are the dead who die in the Lord from now on." "Yes," says the Spirit, "they will rest from their labor, for their deeds will follow them."

Revelation 21:4 (NIV)

'He will wipe every tear from their eyes. There will be no more death' or mourning or crying or pain, for the old order of things has passed away."

If You Feel Angry

Leviticus 19:17–18 (NIV)

"'Do not hate a fellow Israelite in your heart. Rebuke your neighbor frankly so you will not share in their guilt. "'Do not seek revenge or bear a grudge against anyone among your people but love your neighbor as yourself. I am the Lord.

Proverbs 10:12 (NIV)

Hatred stirs up conflict, but love covers over all wrongs.

Proverbs 12:16 (NIV)

Fools show their annoyance at once, but the prudent overlook an insult.

Proverbs 14:29 (NIV)

Whoever is patient has great understanding, but one who is quick-tempered displays folly.

Proverbs 15:1 (NIV)

A gentle answer turns away wrath, but a harsh word stirs up anger.

Proverbs 20:3 (NIV)

It is to a man's honor to avoid strife, but every fool is quick to quarrel.

Proverbs 29:11 (NIV)

Fools give full vent to their rage, but the wise bring calm in the end.

Mark 7:20–23 (NIV)

He went on: "What comes out of a person is what defiles them. For it is from within, out of a person's heart, that evil thoughts come—sexual immorality, theft, murder, adultery, greed, malice, deceit, lewdness, envy, slander, arrogance and folly. All these evils come from inside and defile a person."

1 Corinthians 13:4–5 (NIV)

Love is patient, love is kind. It does not envy, it does not boast, it is not proud. It does not dishonor others, it is not self-seeking, it is not easily angered, it keeps no record of wrongs.

Ephesians 4:26–27 (NIV)

"In your anger do not sin": Do not let the sun go down while you are still angry, and do not give the devil a foothold.

Ephesians 4:31–32 (NIV)

Get rid of all bitterness, rage and anger, brawling, and slander, along with every form of malice. Be kind and compassionate to one another, forgiving each other, just as in Christ God forgave you.

James 1:19–20 (NIV)

My dear brothers and sisters, take note of this: Everyone should be quick to listen, slow to speak and slow to become angry, because human anger does not produce the righteousness that God desires.

If You Feel Lonely

Deuteronomy 31:6 (NIV)

Be strong and courageous. Do not be afraid or terrified because of them, for the LORD your God goes with you; he will never leave you nor forsake you."

1 Samuel 12:22 (NIV)

For the sake of his great name the LORD will not reject his people, because the LORD was pleased to make you his own.

Psalm 25:16 (NIV)

Turn to me and be gracious to me, for I am lonely and afflicted.

Psalm 27:10 (NIV)

Though my father and mother forsake me, the LORD will receive me.

Psalm 68:5–6 (NIV)

A father to the fatherless, a defender of widows, is God in his holy dwelling. God sets the lonely in families, he leads out the prisoners with singing; but the rebellious live in a sun-scorched land.

Proverbs 18:24 (NIV)

One who has unreliable friends soon comes to ruin, but there is a friend who sticks closer than a brother.

Isaiah 41:10 (NIV)

So do not fear, for I am with you; do not be dismayed, for I am your God. I will strengthen you and help you; I will uphold you with my righteous right hand.

Isaiah 42:3 (NIV)

A bruised reed he will not break, and a smoldering wick he will not snuff out. In faithfulness he will bring forth justice.

Lamentations 3:22–25 (NIV)

Because of the LORD's great love we are not consumed, for his compassions never fail. They are new every morning; great is your faithfulness. I say to myself, "The LORD is my portion; therefore I will wait for him." The LORD is good to those whose hope is in him, to the one who seeks him.

Matthew 28:20 (NIV)

"…and teaching them to obey everything I have commanded you. And surely I am with you always, to the very end of the age."

Romans 8:31–38 (NIV)

What, then, shall we say in response to these things? If God is for us, who can be against us? He who did not spare his own Son, but gave him up for us all—how will he not also, along with him, graciously give us all things? Who will bring any charge against those whom God has chosen? It is God who justifies. Who then is the one who condemns? No one. Christ Jesus who died—more than that, who was raised to life—is at the right hand of God and is also interceding for us. Who shall separate us from the love of Christ? Shall trouble or hardship or persecution or famine or nakedness or danger or sword? As it is written: "For your sake we face death all day long; we are considered as sheep to be slaughtered." No, in all these things we are more than conquerors through him who loved us. For I am convinced that neither death nor life, neither angels nor demons, neither the present nor the future, nor any powers, neither height nor depth, nor anything else in all creation, will be able to separate us from the love of God that is in Christ Jesus our Lord.

1 Corinthians 10:13 (NIV)

No temptation has overtaken you except what is common to mankind. And God is faithful; he will not let you be tempted beyond what you can bear. But when you are tempted, he will also provide a way out so that you can endure it.

1 Peter 5:7 (NIV)

Cast all your anxiety on him because he cares for you.

To Renew Your Purpose and Meaning

Psalm 139:13–17 (NIV)

For you created my inmost being, you knit me together in my mother's womb. I praise you because I am fearfully and wonderfully made; your works are wonderful; I know that full well. My frame was not hidden from you when I was made in the secret place, when I was woven together in the depths of the earth. Your eyes saw my unformed body; all the days ordained for me were written in your book before one of them came to be. How precious to me are your thoughts, God! How vast is the sum of them!

Romans 12:4–8 (NIV)

For just as each of us has one body with many members, and these members do not all have the same function, so in Christ we, though many, form one body, and each member belongs to all the others. We have different gifts, according to the grace given to each of us. If your gift is prophesying, then prophesy in accordance with your faith; if it is serving, then serve; if it is teaching, then teach; if it is to encourage, then give encouragement; if it is giving, then give generously; if it is to lead, do it diligently; if it is to show mercy, do it cheerfully.

1 Corinthians 12:4–7 (NIV)

There are different kinds of gifts, but the same Spirit distributes them. There are different kinds of service, but the same Lord. There are different kinds of working, but in all of them and in everyone it is the same God at work. Now to each one the manifestation of the Spirit is given for the common good.

Ephesians 2:10 (NIV)

For we are God's handiwork, created in Christ Jesus to do good works, which God prepared in advance for us to do.

Ephesians 4:11–13 (NIV)

So Christ himself gave the apostles, the prophets, the evangelists, the pastors and teachers, to equip his people for works of service, so that the body of Christ may be built up until we all reach unity in the faith and in the knowledge of the Son of God and become mature, attaining to the whole measure of the fullness of Christ.

Philippians 1:4–6 (NIV)

In all my prayers for all of you, I always pray with joy because of your partnership in the gospel from the first day until now, being confident of this, that he who began a good work in you will carry it on to completion until the day of Christ Jesus.

Chapter 11

Use Distractions to "Change the Channel" in Your Mind

We take captive every thought.[806]

When you're stuck in negative thinking, use distractions to quickly change the channel of your mind. Sometimes the problem is so big, it casts a shadow over every minute of your day. Your thinking can become so fixated on the gravity of your circumstances that you get stuck. This can include the stress of the moment, thinking traps, or ruminating about a situation (what you should have done, etc.). Scripture warns against futile thinking.[807] If you continue to dwell on unhealthy thoughts, you will contaminate your outlook with damaging anxiety. Your mindset acts as a filter to everything you experience, causing your perceptions to be skewed by negativity. You must discipline yourself to recognize harmful thoughts, restore peace, and promote healthy thought patterns. When you experience persistent negative thoughts, treat it like a call to prayer or worship. Build a habit of automatically seeking God to reset your mind. Scripture advises you to renew your mind in the Spirit.[808] I have wasted hours driving or mowing the lawn worrying about problems, ruminating on events of the past (what I should have said or done, what went wrong, reflecting on my feelings, second-guessing, regrets) with no constructive end. In moments like these, you need a quick change of focus. Think of it as changing the channel on your TV or radio. The idea is to quickly refocus your mind on something engaging so you can break free of the negativity. Once you are re-focused, you can steer your thinking toward something positive and healthy. You can use many different methods, such as simple mental games, to create the necessary distraction. The first step is to recognize your thinking is in an unhealthy, unproductive place. Second, take action to change your channel. Several simple mental games are listed below.

1. Counting games: Count backward from twenty-five, count to hundred by fives, or if it is too easy, count to hundred by threes. It must work your mind enough to distract it from negative thinking.
2. Say the alphabet in reverse order.
3. Think of three to five words that begin with a letter of the alphabet. Work from A to Z, speaking them out loud.

---
806 2 Corinthians 10:5b
807 Ephesians 4:17
808 Ephesians 4:23

4. Name the Books of the Bible (in order if you can), break it into Old and New Testament, or try to list ten to twenty books from each if easier.
5. Name as many of the twelve disciples as you can. Name as many of the Tribes of Israel as you can.
6. Read a passage of Scripture out loud. Focus on each word as you read it. Think about what God may be trying to say to you.

Ensure you occupy your mind with the exercise. If it's not sufficiently challenged, your mind will continue its negative track while going through the motions of the mental game. You also want to ensure you stay engaged long enough to allow your mind to jump to a new constructive train of thought. You may need to start new mental games several times to redirect your focus.

Other Methods to Distract the Mind

Several activities can help distract your mind when you are stuck in negative thinking. Put your mind to work reading a book, engaging in a hobby, physically exercising, or completing a task sufficient to redirect your focus. The goal of any of these activities is to break you out of the negative thoughts dominating your mind. Many of the previous chapters focused on breaking thought processes and cycles. Mental distractions are meant to quickly transition your present mindset from a negative focus to something constructive.

Some music can be a helpful distraction. Music is powerful; however, caution is necessary. It engages the emotions and the mind, making you feel very happy and uplifted or bringing you down. I grew up listening to music from the 1970s and '80s. I still love these eras of music, especially the smooth sounds of the '70s. Several years ago, I noticed that many of the messages of the music I love are not positive. Sometimes, listening to this music makes me feel sad and nostalgic. While this may seem okay, when you are already feeling down, you do not need to add weight to your heart by listening to depressing music. Listening is probably not okay anytime. Many segments of music promote destructive behaviors such as violence, drug and alcohol abuse, greed, and unfaithfulness. You don't need to hear messages promoting unhealthy coping behaviors when you are trying to overcome adversity. I have personally found that listening to praise and worship music is positive, strengthens my faith, and builds hope. I don't feel down after listening to it. I encourage it all the time but especially when you are facing struggles. Many Christian radio stations advertise the benefits of the positive and faith-building messages in their music. Praise is a powerful weapon during spiritual battles. Remember Joshua in the Bible. He brought down the immense walls of Jericho with shouts of praise.[809] God can do the same for you.

---
809 Joshua 6:5,

Ask God for help with your "Jericho" and start praising God for the victory.

Videos, television, and video games may be a helpful distraction. However, videos and gaming can seriously affect your mindset with negative messages. I grew up in the era of movie theaters, drive-ins, and family time around the TV. Many of the warm family memories I have with my parents and brother are seated together in the living room, watching sitcoms during what used to be called the "family hour." As a result of these experiences, I associate movies and TV with warm experiences. I raised my kids, centering family time on movies. Regrettably, Hollywood has not lived up to the trust we have given them. Over my lifetime, they have pushed the boundaries of morality, contradicting biblical values whenever possible. The present level of violence, sexual immorality, denigration of the Christian faith, disrespect toward others, and horrible language make it hard to find anything worth the investment of time. It is exceptional to find something positive and constructive. Sometimes, I've had to do something else to cheer myself up from a terrible move or video. Those are not the type of distractions you want to use during difficulties. Thankfully, recent faith-based movies with encouraging and faith-building messages have become more prevalent. Many have encouraged me. Games and videos are equally violent, promote a "win at any cost" mentality filled with profanity in the game and among online players. Porn is a contagion, poisonous in relationships, enslaving people in addiction, and making unrealistic demands of relationships. The world will say, "These forms of entertainment will help you and your relationships." Not only is this false, but you will also find yourself less related to those around you by trying to escape in unhealthy forms of media. During your times of struggle, you must consider your viewing choices carefully. Talking to friends or sharing activities together can be another way to distract your mind.

Your thoughts can become so toxic, they lead you to self-destructive behaviors. You can preempt this dynamic by quickly recognizing harmful thoughts and changing the channel of your mind. Use caution in how you distract your mind, focus on healthy positive inputs. Much of the media focuses on negative and divisive messages. The news has always used controversy and fear to sell their news product. In my years, I have never seen the degree of negativity in the news that is evident in recent years. Do not allow outside sources to drag you into a negative state of mind. If it isn't helping you, consider turning it off. You need something to promote peace and well-being. Talk to God. How does He feel about your present situation? How might God want you to "be" in this time—your mindset, perspective, and attitude? Faith in God means you trust Him for help and hope. The fruit of the Spirit, God's work in your inner being, nature, and character, does not change with life's circumstances. According to Scripture, the fruit is love, joy, peace, patience, kindness, goodness, gentleness, faithfulness, and self-control.[810] Cultivate these qualities in your inner being. Don't let outside voices hijack God's purposes for your life. Paul continued in his discussion of the fruit to admonish believers who live by the Spirit, "to keep

---
810 Galatians 5:22–23

in step with the Spirit."[811] If the inputs you are using to fill your mind do not promote life and growth in the Spirit, perhaps they should be limited or excluded. Don't be afraid to quickly change the channel in your thinking. This is especially true when life's difficulties challenge you.

---

[811] Galatians 5:25

Chapter 12

Leverage Your Strengths

So, in Christ we who are many form one body, and each member belongs to all the others. We have different gifts, according to the grace given us.[812]

Leverage your strengths (in a constructive way) to help you overcome adversity. You may wonder why this is in the spiritually resilient thinking section. Because awareness of your strengths and confidence in your God-given abilities are patterns of thinking. Your perception of your capabilities may reinforce weakness, especially if important people in your life contributed to these negative messages. This is one reason Scripture emphasizes the importance of encouraging one another. You may be tempted to focus on skills and capabilities that you lack during difficulties. Preoccupation with weaknesses not only switches your mind into a negative thinking pattern—the glass is half empty—and amplifies your sense of helplessness, but it also discourages you from drawing on your strengths to solve problems. God gave you, and every person, a unique set of talents, skills, abilities, and spiritual gifts. Scripture is clear: while you were in the womb, God poured His creativity into your being. He determined your make-up and plan for your life.[813] He equipped you in advance with everything you need to make a positive impact in this world.[814] God made you a unique, wonderful masterpiece. He not only describes you as such, but He has countless thoughts of good toward you and your future.[815] He positioned you in His family as a unique, invaluable, irreplaceable part.[816] Scripture compares your place in God's family to the parts of a human body.[817] Your unique abilities, strengths, and other characteristics make you comparable to some body part in God's family. I do not know what that specific part is or even if it matters. The point is you are a part, you have a practical, indispensable role, and most relevant for this section is the irreplaceable nature of the abilities within you. I cannot think of a single body part I want to live without. You matter to God and to the family of believers regardless of whether they (or you) acknowledge it. Like David, you have a purpose to fill for your generation.[818] God created you to serve others in your sphere of influence. You may have no idea what your strengths are, but Scripture states they are worthy of honor.[819]

---

812 Romans 12:5–6
813 Psalm 139:13–18
814 Ephesians 2:10
815 Psalm 139:17–18
816 1 Corinthians 12:12–14
817 1 Corinthians 12:12–31
818 Acts 13:36
819 1 Corinthians 12:19–24

You can access free online resources to help discover your spiritual gifts, abilities, and strengths.[820] Your talents provide you with tools to overcome adversity in your life. Trust them.

David's life provides a great example of how God can use your talents. David, the youngest son, was looked down on by most of his family. He often took care of his father's sheep by himself, even though he had seven older brothers. He overcame loneliness in the shepherd's field by using his creative writing skills and musical talent. He was also good with a sling, a projectile weapon like a slingshot. I can picture him as a boy practicing with that sling out in the fields. He probably set up targets, tried to hit a tree, or maybe even took a shot at a passing bird. It reminds me of my childhood shooting cans with a BB gun. How amazing that a childhood skill became a weapon to take down a giant! David had courage and knew how to defend himself. The battles he fought protecting the sheep in the fields produced the skills he used to bring down Goliath with a sling and one stone.[821] King Saul wanted David to use his armor and weapons, but David refused. He was not comfortable with them.[822] This highlights an important spiritual truth. Others may pressure you (or you may pressure yourself) to cope with your struggles relying on someone else's strengths. God has given you abilities, and like David, you should follow God's leading, even if it looks very different from what others expect. David faced Goliath with his staff, sling, and five stones he picked from the stream. More importantly, David squared off against Goliath with faith, the confidence that the God of the shepherd field was with him on the battlefield. Goliath never realized he was outmatched. When you offer yourself to God, no matter how little it seems, He can multiply it to meet the needs of your circumstances. Later, David's courage and skill caused him to excel as a general in King Saul's army. The people sang songs of his military prowess.[823] As king, he would lead Israel to subdue her foes and influence the whole region. It all began with a sling and a stone.

Remember those musical talents? David used the solitude of the fields to write and sing numerous songs to the Lord. He wrote many of the Psalms in Scripture. I can picture David in the field with his lyre, playing common songs of the day and creating new melodies. When King Saul was tormented by an evil spirit, his attendants searched for a skilled musician to make him feel better. They heard of David's musical abilities with the lyre and brought him to the palace. How interesting that music set David up in his future home. In the palace, he built relationships that would help him navigate many of his future troubles. How might your strengths help you overcome? Do not underestimate the potential God placed inside you.

Your strengths are God's impartation of a unique blend of attributes and abilities. Only you can make the "you-shaped" impact in your field of influence. You are the missing piece in the puzzle. Like David, you have talents. They may not be musical, but you are not David. You may be an artist or a

---

[820] Lifeway.com. Mintools.com. Gifts.churchgrowth.org.
[821] 1 Samuel 17:34–37
[822] 1 Samuel 17:38–40
[823] 1 Samuel 18:5–7

designer. You may have other abilities, be a great cook, funny, witty, mechanically minded, good with people, or a great problem-solver. You may have other skills you can develop through practice. God can use your abilities to bless other people by serving, helping, giving, or encouraging. People tend to value some strengths more than others. I've always wanted to play the piano, but I'm not gifted with it. My son took some lessons as a young child. He can just sit down and play. He has the talent, I don't, but I can sing; I can follow melody and rhythm. Be careful not to devalue what God has given you. I have heard people say numerous times how they wish they had other abilities. They look at someone else and admire their accomplishments. Be cautious of placing an unhealthy value on others' gifts. Scripture accentuates the importance of diversity.[824] The body needs every spiritual gift of strengths and functions. It is not complete without them. Do you want a body with five eyes, no ears or nose? Would you trade an arm for another leg or a foot for more fingers? These are ridiculous questions, yet some people routinely devalue their importance relative to others. Do not look down on yourself. You have a specific set of strengths, abilities, and characteristics because God gave them to you with the measure of grace (aptitude) that he imparted. People with similar talents do not have the same level of ability. Artists have a wide range of style and ability to paint. Some pianists are exceptional beyond their peers. This spiritual truth is critical. It's not the level of ability you have that matters to God. It is the level of your faithfulness with the ability you have.[825] Honor God by faithfully using the strengths you have been given without comparing yourself to others.[826] God is your provider; you have everything you need to overcome.[827]

Don't let your purpose get sidetracked by difficulties. They don't mean that God is against you, God is not the author of bad things in your life, nor does He tempt you to evil.[828] As we have repeatedly noted, difficulties can set you up for the next big blessing of God in your life. God's deepest desire is for you to know Him personally.[829] He is for you, working to move you closer to Him and shaping you to make a greater impact in this world. Some feel discouraged by trials, becoming embittered toward God. They refuse to acknowledge their true spiritual identity and purpose, using their talents and abilities in opposition to God or in selfish service. It is the immoral use of their strengths that causes so much pain and suffering in the world. This milieu of human rebellion, self-indulgence, and surrender to the enemy's destructive influence wreaks havoc. While God calls people to loving service, he is not unprepared for the consequences of rejecting his purpose. You are not at the mercy of the world's evil.[830] God will always use adversity for your good.[831] At a minimum, He will shape and strengthen your character and abilities, equipping you for greater effectiveness and preparing you to take advantage of the next oppor-

---

824 1 Corinthians 12:15–20
825 Matthew 25:14–30
826 2 Corinthians 10:12
827 Psalm 23:1
828 James 1:13–17
829 Ephesians 1:17
830 John 10:10a
831 Romans 8:28

tunity. Scripture promised God will continue His work; He will never give up on you.[832] Don't descend into self-pity, and don't cut off your lifeline to God. God has given you everything (skills, abilities, and resources) you need to get through this tough season, and His grace will prove sufficient for you to persevere.[833] He has His hand on the emergency "stop" switch in your circumstances. Scripture promises you will not be tempted/tested beyond what you can bear, and that God will always provide a way out so you can stand up under it.[834] I have repeatedly experienced God's help in struggles. I have experienced God's "way out" right in the middle of a temptation. God will make a way.[835] He is leading you to victory with the strengths He deposited in you.

Ignore the comments of anyone who would devalue your strengths. Scripture addresses this error in the body as well.[836] They deprecate those who don't fit their ideal. Some people enjoy putting others down for no reason at all. If you are an ear, the eye may want you to be an eye. The hand may want you to be a hand; the foot may want you to be a foot. This is immature and unspiritual. God made you and the other person as He designed you to be. One is not better than the other; no one gets to choose or criticize. Instead, God commands every part to value and honor every other part. Some parts are in the spotlight. Some work behind the scenes. Each part deserves equal honor. Some parts that appear less important are indispensable. Some parts may do more than others because they contribute differently. Even though the parts are not equal in their level of ability or in their contribution to the whole, they have equal importance and equal honor. Can the conductor create awe-inspiring music without each team of instruments? A group of world-famous conductors would make for a lousy symphony. You are playing the music for God. You offer your talents and abilities to an audience of one. You answer to God for your faithfulness. People do not always hear the music or see the beauty of God's people at work. God always hears the music created by faithfulness. God always sees the bigger canvas of millions of brushstrokes creating a masterpiece of love and worship.

Some of the same body parts may function with more ability than others, but all have equal value. I have heard better preachers, observed better leaders in my lifetime. I used to wish I could be like them. You do not have to be the best. You must do your best with the strengths and level of ability God has given you. You are running a race for the Lord, not for the crowd. God does not measure success the way humans measure it. His thoughts are not our thoughts, and His ways are not our ways.[837] God does not use human standards to value you. Remember how God chose David for kingship. The Prophet Samuel came to the house of Jesse to anoint the next king of Israel. Samuel told Jesse to present his sons; however, Jesse left David in the fields with the sheep. What kind of message does that send when your

---
832 Philippians 1:6
833 2 Corinthians 12:9
834 1 Corinthians 10:13
835 Isaiah 43:19
836 1 Corinthians 12:21–26
837 Isaiah 55:8–9

father leaves you out of the family lineup? Samuel thought the oldest looked like a king. God spoke to his heart, "I don't judge the way men judge. Men judge by appearances, I judge by the heart."[838] Samuel walked down the line of sons, but God was silent. Samuel asked Jesse if he had more sons. "I have one more, the youngest, but he is out tending the sheep." Other people may not value your gifts or think you have much to offer. You don't answer to them. They don't determine your future. God is the master, the provider, the promoter. Samuel wouldn't even let the group sit down until David came to the banquet. God has a way of honoring those who honor Him despite the bad behavior of others. When David came in, God said, "Rise and anoint him. He is the one."[839] David was just a young, harp-playing, stone-slinging shepherd boy. He was the least of his family. God called him a king. Do not get caught up in a competition with others. Be the best you that you can be. Use your gifts to the best of your ability for God without unhealthy comparisons. God calls you blessed and highly favored.

Some of your strengths may be speaking gifts like prophecy or teaching. Some may be serving gifts like helping, administration, or leadership. You may be a giver. Everyone has a mix of spiritual gifts that fits them into God's family, the body of Christ. Scripture provides several lists, but you may have any possible combination of other strengths, talents, and abilities.[840] Identify your strengths. Ask others, family, friends, and coworkers; you can trust for their assessment of your strengths. Spiritually and relationally, God's family suffers and rejoices as one connected community. It cannot maximize functionality without you doing your part. If the community is a puzzle, your gift mix forms a missing puzzle piece that only you can fill. The world is the lesser for every person who neglects to use their unique blend of strengths to serve God and others. While God gave you spiritual gifts and abilities for the good of the spiritual community and God's kingdom, your strengths, talents, and abilities are given to you to provide for your needs and your family as well. The ox has great strength and can turn the mill wheel, but the Scripture states, "Don't muzzle the ox during his labor."[841] In other words, the ox should get a share in the profits of his labor. In the same way God gives you seed—financial and other resources—to sow, serving Him and others, God gives you seed to eat for your own needs.[842] Eat the seed you need, and remember to serve God and others by sowing the seed given you to sow. You will help your situation by properly balancing the time, energy, and effort you use to constructively resolve your problems and what you use to help others in need around you.

People tend to coach others by pointing out weaknesses for correction and improvement. Another school of thought encourages coaches to point out strengths, provide help in developing those strengths and guidance for using them to achieve success. This principal lines up with Scriptural counsel to cel-

---

838 1 Samuel 16:7
839 1 Samuel 16:12
840 Romans 12, 1 Corinthians 12, Ephesians 4
841 1 Timothy 5:18
842 2 Corinthians 9:10–11

ebrate what you have rather than criticize yourself for what you lack.[843] Over-emphasizing weaknesses is not the optimistic approach that resilience requires. Develop your strengths. You will be happier and more effective doing what comes naturally. The old saying goes, "There's more than one way to skin a cat." You're probably not interested in skinning a cat (neither am I), but the point is, you can effectively accomplish tasks using many different approaches. People want you to do things their way. The leadership principle is, "Let the people who are doing the task determine their own way to do it." The spiritual principle is, "Use your divinely given abilities as you are led by the Spirit to do it in a way that honors God." The practical principle is, "Use what you have to do it as efficiently and effectively as possible." The strength-focused principle is, "As much as possible, draw on your strengths to accomplish the task." To summarize, "Use your strengths to overcome difficulties as effectively and efficiently as possible, in healthy, constructive, Spirit-led, and God-honoring action." Reject any preoccupation with what you or others wish you had.

Knowing your strengths can help you recognize and develop strengths in others. You don't live for self alone; you live with the responsibility to look out for others with the concern you have for self.[844] As you appreciate your place and value in the body of Christ, you are better equipped to help others. People have a common need for meaning, significance, and purpose in life. Many people undervalue their strengths or wrestle with criticism of their abilities from others. Life has a way of making people feel worthless and unloved. The enemy uses this idea to oppress and enslave people. Scripture presents a solution; you can find both purpose and meaning through service together with others in a spiritual community of faith. God designed the members of the body of Christ to lift each other up as they labor together. You can play a key role in helping others appreciate and leverage their strengths for success in life. Think of yourself as a coach or mentor. As you help others with their struggles, you will be empowered to face yours.

We used scriptural principles to describe how differing members of the community of faith (called the body of Christ, the church) work together to help you leverage your abilities.[845] The same principles apply to the effective operation of teams and groups. Modern organizational theory uses the term diversity to describe them. Diversity recognizes that people are very different in their background, experiences, perspectives, talents, skills, and abilities. The most effective teams draw from the strengths of different people to solve problems, drive innovation, and accomplish tasks. People tend to prefer to work with others like them. This reflects the adage, "Birds of a feather flock together." People flock together with people like them as well. People tend to be more comfortable with people like them, but they may not find it more advantageous. Groupthink, the tendency for people to approach problem solving from a common mindset, hinders the creative thinking that produces success. Teams, like faith communities

---

843 1 Corinthians 12:15–18
844 Philippians 2:3–4
845 1 Corinthians 12

need to recognize and value the strengths of each member, support their individual identity and contributions, work to ensure each one is treated with dignity and respect, and recognize that the group succeeds or fails together. People need your differences, and you need theirs to overcome your struggles.

You may feel that you are walking through adversity alone, but the strength principles remain just as relevant. First, you are never alone. The God who made you is with you. No matter what situation you face, you and God are enough. Paul experienced a serious affliction. He never received deliverance, but God told him, "My grace is sufficient for you, for my power is made perfect in weakness."[846] God can use what you think is insufficient and make it enough. Second, seek out spiritual mentors in addition to your own circle. You can use their encouragement and unique perspective to help you move forward. As a young man, I began a major career transition. I wanted to return to my home state, so I limited my inquiries. A spiritual mentor encouraged me to consider opportunities where I lived at the time. Although it wasn't my first choice, I listened to his counsel. Within a month, I had a job offer. Eventually, I transferred close to my home and family when God's timing was right. My mentor could see my situation from a different angle, enabling me to follow God's path. Seek help and counsel to augment what God has given you. Finally, draw from the gifts, abilities, talents, and other qualities God has given you. When you discount your capabilities, you give the enemy power over your situation. Don't give up your power to choose a course of action. The enemy wants to keep you from trying. If he succeeds, you lose before you ever start. Scripture encourages you to resist the devil and he will flee.[847] As you submit yourself to God, you cannot lose. Press through the trouble with confidence in the gifts and abilities God has given you, trusting Him to make up the difference wherever needed. His strength is more than enough in your weakest moments.

Like many of God's gifts, strengths, abilities, and talents are useless if they are not leveraged to overcome your current difficulties. The mind is the gatekeeper for these resources. You cannot use what you don't know you have or understand how to use. Don't undervalue what God has given you and don't let anyone else do so either, especially the enemy. Recognize the strengths you have were put there by God for such a time as this. Difficulties do not mean God has abandoned you, they mean God is giving you an opportunity to develop your strengths, with His help, in the laboratory of adversity. Don't make the mistake of comparing yourself or your abilities to others. The challenge you face is to do your very best with the strengths God has given you. Develop your abilities and work with others to help you become better. Always remember, with God's grace, your strengths, abilities, and talents are more than enough. You don't need to be perfect; you don't need to knock the enemy out, you only need to keep fighting to win the battle. God has appointed you to win, and He has given you the tools to do so. He is already preparing the victory party (the table) in the presence of your enemies, anointing your head with oil, and filling your cup until it overflows.[848] Use your God-given strengths to overcome every adversity.

---
846 2 Corinthians 12:9
847 James 4:7
848 Psalm 23:5

Summary: Spiritually Resilient Thinking

This section focused on the importance of your thought patterns and processes to your inner strength and resilience. You alone are the guardian of your inner life. The strategic warfare for your wholeness, health, and well-being happens on the battlefield of your mind. The key to victory is healthy, constructive, faith-filled thinking. Faith is the discipline that will see you through; it is how you appropriate everything God has already given you: His promises, His indwelling Spirit containing Christ's resurrection power, and His authority to exercise that power. Faith gives you the wisdom and discipline to overcome everything you experience in life. Spiritually resilient thinking allows you to recognize and replace faulty thought patterns called thinking traps with healthy, constructive ones. It allows you to examine your beliefs and past through the lens of Scripture and restore biblical values and worldview in your thinking. It enables you to combat fear, worry, and numerous other unhealthy thinking patterns and feelings as you stand against principalities and powers of darkness. Finally, it allows you to recognize the importance of talents, abilities, and gifts God has given you. God lives within your spirit making you a temple of the Holy Spirit. Your mind is the valve controlling how much you embrace God's word as truth, obey Scripture, and choose to live by the Spirit. For this reason, your mind is your spiritual center of gravity: key to your relationship with God, your spiritual growth, your ability to overcome adversity and defeat every tactic of the enemy. Section III will focus on the outward manifestation of what's happening in your inner world, spiritually resilient, faith-filled action.

Section III

Spiritually Resilient Behaviors/Actions/Practices

Section I addressed key spiritual disciplines that strengthen your spiritual life and relationship with God. Section II used the foundation of your spiritual disciplines to develop spiritually driven, healthy, and faith-filled thought processes. Section III covers twelve constructive actions that position you to overcome adversity. The first set focuses on healthy speech (Chapters 2–4), and the second on other practical strategies such as problem-solving and conflict resolution (Chapters 5–12).

Use healthy speech to reinforce a healthy mindset and prepare the environment for the actions that follow. At the beginning of time, darkness covered the earth. It was formless and empty.[849] God prepared to bring forth His creative power to remedy the situation. He didn't look at the void and curse the darkness. Scripture states, "God said, 'Let there be light.'"[850] He didn't focus on the problem. He called forth the solution, light came forth, and it was good. God never used His words to belabor how bad the situation was. He never told His servants to describe the depth of their problems. He told them to call forth the answer. Jesus healed by commanding miracles.[851] He didn't waste any time describing symptoms or the medical condition. He commanded it to leave. In the same way, focus on the possibilities of God's power as you speak. When you focus on the problem, you accentuate the negative and drain motivation and strength. When you declare God's goodness, you release faith for positive action. Use your words to prepare your thoughts and the environment for miracles.

Direct your energy and efforts toward healthy and constructive action. People tend to orient their thoughts and speech in a negative direction. This undermines their attempts at progress. Scripture highlights the consequences of double mindedness.[852] You cannot expect good results when you think one way and behave another. You cannot ask God to move on your behalf and then speak doubt and unbelief that He will do so. Adversity can sap your motivation. You can rise above these feelings by determining to act regardless of how you feel. Your actions determine, in large part, the outcomes of your life. Positive, God-honoring actions result when you let faith lead your choices, not emotion. If your life is a train, faith is the engine, feelings are the caboose. Don't let the tail of the train determine its direction. Emotions are powerful influencers of your decisions, but the caboose has no power to drive your life along a meaningful path. Your life will end up tossed back and forth by the feelings of the moment. Choose faith to drive wise and constructive actions that change your difficult circumstances.

---

849 Genesis 1:2
850 Genesis 1:3
851 Matthew 8:3, Mark 5:34, Mark 9:23–25
852 James 1:8

David Takes Action at Ziklag

These principles played out in David's life as well. Consider the incredible emotional challenges David faced in our case study. David renewed his strength by seeking the Lord. With a sound mind—not mired in emotionalism, regrets, self-pity, or doubts, he quickly developed a plan. The solution was simple: track the Amalekite raiding party, defeat them in battle, and recover everything stolen. However, the most critical step, Step 1, was to seek God's counsel. This is an essential step for success, often neglected by people of faith. With his mind prepared for action, David went to the priest to inquire of the Lord. "Should I pursue the raiding party? Will I overtake them?"[853] Inherent in these questions was a third, could his men win the ensuing battle? God provided a clear answer, "Pursue them, you will succeed in the rescue."[854]

You may think, "If God would answer me that clearly, I could easily overcome my problems just like David." It can feel harder to sense the leading of the Spirit than having David's priest simply give you the answer. It always seems simpler after the trouble has passed, as things usually get worse before they get better. It is in the moment you decide to trust God the enemy throws his best punch. If he can make you quit, he wins. What do you do when the enemy's punch lands and things get worse? That is the gut-check moment. David refused to succumb to the flurry of emotions; he sought God. Do you see it through with God or cave to the intense feelings? This is the moment you must choose to seek God and see it through. The crucial first step is to ask. Scripture warns, "You do not have because you do not ask God."[855] Some people become cynical, thinking it is useless to ask God because he does not answer. This may come out of past disappointments or the severity of the trial. The nation of Israel had the same destructive thinking pattern after they returned from captivity in Babylon. "It is futile to serve God; what do we gain by carrying out his requirements?"[856] God promised them a day when the seeming futility of faith and life's injustices would be set right.[857] I cannot explain your experiences. Scripture shows us devout Godly people wrestled with the same tensions. What I can say is, faith is your solution; so, make faith the fix. Some go to God as a last resort when they exhaust every other possibility. Be like David, who chose God as his first option. He made faith the solution when it looked like God had abandoned him. God proved faithful to David, and He will for you as well.

The second step is to cultivate a listening ear. Jesus ascended to Heaven so the Holy Spirit could dwell personally in each believer.[858] Hearing the leading of the Spirit is an art, it develops over time. You have some clear actions required on your part, such as to ask (seek and knock).[859] You must demonstrate

---
853 1 Samuel 30:8
854 1 Samuel 30:9
855 James 4:2
856 Malachi 3:14
857 Malachi 3:17–18
858 John 14:15–18
859 Matthew 7:7

persistence, ask until you get an answer.[860] Persistence reveals the importance of the issue to you and God. Search for a clearer sense of God's will as you persevere in prayer.[861] Much of the time, continuing in prayer is more about how God is shaping you than it is about his answer. He wants to answer you.[862] He wants to help you in your troubles. He also wants to help you become stronger, more mature, and more like Christ. The art of hearing God is sensing the leading of the Spirit within your inner being. You can read a passage of Scripture and feel a strong inner witness that God is speaking directly to you. Sometimes that comes through the counsel of a spiritual mentor, prayer partner or friend. Something in the discussion may ignite a spark inside of you. An experience may be a catalyst in your heart that God uses to impress you to act. As you pray or worship, you may sense God leading in a powerful thought that comes to mind. Any of these inner impressions, thoughts, or feelings, especially peace, may be the leading of the Holy Spirit. Over time, you will gain a stronger conviction of when these leadings truly are from God.

Scripture is clear: you must test your sense of God's will.[863] Any sense of God's leading must line up with the clear teaching of the Word. God will not lead you to do something opposed to the clear guidance of Scripture. You must also test the spirit behind your sense of God's leading.[864] Some claim God is leading them to take an action that is clearly vengeful, jealous, full of anger, or spiteful, etc.[865] God leads in the fruit of His Holy Spirit.[866] The difference between the spirits of this world that lead to lawlessness and the Holy Spirit is clear by their fruit. James provides a clear distinction between the wisdom that comes from God and that which is earthly, unspiritual, and from the enemy.[867] These passages will help you find clarity. Sometimes, a friend may come claiming they have a word from God. Not only do the two previous tests apply (Does it line up with Scripture? Does it pass the test of the spirit behind it?), I urge you to consider a further test, a confirmation. A word from others should only confirm something God is laying on your heart. It should never be the sole source of your direction. God speaks to you for your life. He is your counselor. Some people are great at hearing direction for others but struggle to find their own direction from God. Each of us must bring order to our own spiritual house before we try to order the actions of others. You must protect your inner sense of God's leading from confusion that might come from another's spiritual immaturity. One final consideration: let your inner peace be your guide. God confirms His leading with a sense of inner peace and rest. I love how the Amplified Version states this important Scripture, "Let the peace of Christ (the inner calm of one who walks daily with Him) be the controlling factor in your hearts (deciding and settling questions that arise)."[868] Let peace in your

---
860 Luke 18:1–8
861 1 John 5:14
862 John 15:7
863 Romans 12:2
864 1 John 4:1–3
865 Galatians 5:17, 19–21
866 Galatians 5:22–23
867 James 3:13–18
868 Colossians 3:15

heart settle the questions that arise in your life. God speaks in a still, small voice."[869] You must quiet your mind, turn off the background noise and your devices, and be patient. You can cultivate a listening ear, pursuing prayer, the reading of God's Word, seeking the counsel of others, and listening for the peace that passes understanding.

David developed the ability to hear God over the years alone in the shepherd's field. While evading Saul's murderous traps, he instinctively went to God first. When the priest gave David the answer, he did not hesitate. He decisively rallied his men and set out after the Amalekites. Some question God's answer, wanting irrefutable proof of God's help. The angel of the Lord visited Gideon with clear instructions to deliver Israel, addressing him as mighty warrior. Yet Gideon required several further proofs that God was truly with him.[870] When God speaks, like David, move forward. Action takes courage and usually involves risk. As the adage states, "Luck favors the bold." David followed the Amalekite trail with four hundred men of questionable loyalty (two hundred of the men were left behind, overwhelmed by their emotions, and too exhausted to continue the chase). Only hours prior, his men considered stoning him. In the pursuit, David fortuitously found a sick Amalekite slave left behind by the raiding party. In compassion, David cared for the man who had been without food or water for three days. Because David promised he would not return him to his master, the man agreed to guide David to the Amalekite camp. Note how David's faith-filled action led to the next breadcrumb needed to retrieve his loved ones. God did not give them all the information upfront, as many expect God to do. Rather, He gave them the next step to follow in faith. David and his men were led directly to the enemy camp. The warriors immediately attacked and fought the large Amalekite force for twenty-four straight hours, all through the night to the end of the next day. At the end of the battle, David recovered everything they had taken, including a large amount of plunder stolen from the Philistines.[871] What a comeback. David went from zero to hero in the span of a few days. A short time later, David was crowned king of Judah. Ziklag could have been the end of David's story, because of his spiritual resilience, it became his springboard to the throne of all Israel. Your difficult situation can become the spark for your brighter future when led and empowered by God.

Ziklag is not the only story of bold victory. The faith hall of fame found in Hebrews 11 repeatedly lists the power of faith-filled action in bringing about God's will and blessing in people's lives. Your life is no different. Choosing to live by faith is risky, but it has great rewards. The risks are easier to take when you are close to God; hence, the need for spiritual disciplines. They are easier to take when your mind is optimistic, focused, determined, committed, and full of God's Word; otherwise known as faith-filled. Because David knew God intimately, because he stood with unwavering confidence upon God's Word, he boldly moved forward with his plan to find and attack a much larger army. Every hero from the

---
869 1 Kings 19:11–13, Psalm 46:10
870 Judges 6–8
871 1 Samuel 30:16–20

faith hall of fame took a risk to follow God. In truth, if the end is guaranteed, do you even need faith? Faith sees the risks and chooses to follow God anyway. Organizations continuously seek to mitigate risk as they conduct business. Spiritual resilience sees God as the great Mitigator of all risk. With God, all things are possible. With God, your difficulties become one more opportunity for God to reveal His power in your life. He is the ultimate insurance policy for every situation and eternity (heaven). That is not to say that all your problems will work out exactly as you desire, but rather that with Christ, all your problems will serve your well-being. This outcome is not automatic. Overcoming adversity is a battle that requires your faith-filled action and perseverance. Use the power of your words to shape the spiritual atmosphere and your circumstances, then, follow up with courageous obedience (action). This is the prescription for victory over adversity and every spiritual battle: get closer to God, renew your mind with Scripture and constructive faith-filled thinking, and boldly take faith inspired action that reflects the wisdom and character of God."

Chapter 1

Get the Quick Wins

Rejoice always, pray continually, give thanks in all circumstances; for this is God's will for you in Christ Jesus.[872]

Take immediate action to accomplish some quick wins. Gaining some positive traction in your situation provides hope and energy to ultimately overcome. The wins don't have to be major victories, small, simple steps forward can provide a major boost in the bigger picture of change in your circumstances and victory in the spiritual battles. It is amazing how much of a difference seemingly small wins can make. Identify and execute simple action-steps to make positive, healthy, and constructive changes in your life. Include the spiritual disciplines and healthy thought processes as part of your plan. As you make progress with smaller steps, you will build motivation, confidence, and momentum to tackle larger ones.

Make a list of easy actions that will help you accomplish your goals and start doing them. You can make a big difference in your life by making disciplined choices. What steps do you want to take immediately? Follow through for several weeks and you will turn them into habits.

Some quick, easy, and impactful decisions in your spiritual life could be to:
1. Read one chapter in your Bible every day.
2. Start and end your day in prayer. Consider praying the Lord's Prayer (This is Jesus' model for prayer), followed by praying Psalm 23, the Psalm of personal resilience.
3. End your day thanking God for three blessings you received that day. Make it the opening to your evening prayer to thank God for your top three. Everyone can thank God every day for something off this list: family, a job, a house, food, clothing, health, friends, salvation, and God's mercy. What good things happened today?
4. Start a search for a healthy, Scripture-based spiritual community.
5. Start your day with worship music or a sermon on your way to work. Forget the depressing news or other music. Fill your mind with something that strengthens your inner being.
6. Compliment people around you. Refuse to vent your anger or frustration on others.

---
872 1 Thessalonians 5:16–18

Some quick wins in your personal growth:
1. Find some passages in your Bible that help you face fear, stress, worry, or other challenges and write them down where you can easily see them.
2. Prepare your self-talk. Have a plan to support your key Scripture verses with positive statements that will encourage you with strength, hope, and optimism.
3. Look for an opportunity to be kind to someone every day. Compliment or encourage someone each day.
4. Look for ways to give and help those in need.
5. Listen to solid scriptural teaching to reinforce your knowledge and faith.
6. Look for opportunities to practice your faith and demonstrate the fruit of the Spirit.
7. Try the seven-day mental diet. Allow no negative thoughts or speech for one day. If you have a negative thought invade your mind, replace it immediately with something positive. Once you can do one day, set a goal for three days. After you achieve three days, work up to seven days.
8. Join a small group or Bible Study.
9. Listen daily to sermons and Scripture teachings.
10. Read a book to help you grow.
11. Eliminate negative inputs in your life.
12. Inventory your thought patterns to eliminate thinking traps, icebergs, and unhealthy thoughts.

Some quick and easy decisions in your physical health:
1. Take a walk every day.
2. Drink eight glasses of water each day.
3. Reduce sugar, caffeine, and other chemicals in your diet.
4. Eat some good foods every day, like fresh fruit and vegetables.
5. Try to get more sleep and make time to relax.

Some quick wins in your relational health:
1. Hug those you love every day.
2. Tell them you love them every day.
3. Be a good listener.
4. Make a point to smile at everyone you meet.
5. Laugh and have fun.

List some potential action steps. Start with quick, easy, and sustainable actions that will produce immediate results. If something is not working as planned, scrap it for now and add something else. Make a personal list from the suggestions above or add something you feel led to include to generate quick wins and build momentum for change.

Goal-setting is a planning process to accomplish complicated goals that take longer to achieve. A later chapter will discuss this process as a constructive approach to making progress in difficult times. This chapter addresses actions that are too simplistic for goal-setting. Quick wins are simple, easy-to-achieve actions that can generate progress in the short term. Quick wins get the momentum moving in your favor and demonstrate that you are not stuck. Goal-setting helps you develop plans that will help you make progress with complex long-term problems. Quick wins help you make immediate progress, energize motivation, and demonstrate that progress is possible with hard work, perseverance, and God's blessing.

Chapter 2

Leverage the Power of Your Words

From the fruit of his mouth a man's stomach is filled; with the harvest from his lips, he is satisfied. The tongue has the power of life and death, and those who love it will eat its fruit.[873]

Leverage the power of your words to strengthen you in hard times. Your words can bring you great benefit or do you great harm. Most people do not appreciate their power. Scripture describes the disproportionate power of the tongue with several practical illustrations.[874] Although horses are almost half a ton of pure muscle, a small bit in the mouth can turn the animal in the direction a rider wants him to go. Similarly, a rudder on a ship is very small compared to the huge vessel it steers. Powerful winds may be driving its sails, but the rudder ultimately controls the ship's direction. Scripture compares the destructive power of the tongue to the small spark that starts a massive forest fire. A few years ago, over six hundred fires in California destroyed nearly one million acres. State leaders called fifteen thousand firefighters from around the nation to battle what started as small sparks. Like fire, the tongue has influence far beyond its relative size in the body. Foolish words can quickly spread, making your difficult situation far worse. Once ignited, you may need to go to great lengths to get the fire back under control. The resources expended to control the California fires highlight the similar challenge of recovering from hasty speech. Your words have the power to determine the whole course of your life (or someone else's). I recently listened to a man share his account of rescuing people caught in a volcanic eruption. They were severely burned by the incredibly hot steam. He moved back and forth among the dying people, providing encouragement and helping them to be as comfortable as possible while they awaited rescue. He remarked after the rescue, "When people are down and out, nearly gone, words are tremendously powerful."[875] Encouraging words helped renew hope in people on the brink of death. Your words truly have the power of life and death. Use that power for your benefit.

Unfortunately, people have a natural tendency for unhealthy and destructive speech. Scripture acknowledges this tendency, calling the tongue a world of evil among the parts of the body.[876] It is a corrosive force, like rust or decay, and, spiritually speaking, is "set on fire by hell (evil)." In addition to the powerful "dark side" of the tongue, it is very difficult to control. Many people struggle to discipline

---

873 Proverbs 18:20–21
874 James 3:1–2
875 Kennedy, Rory, The Volcano: Rescue from Whakaari. Netflix, 2022.
876 James 3:1–6

their speech (known as taming the tongue).[877] Simply, your tongue is a lethal weapon. Countless hours go into training on the proper use of a weapon. Before a person receives a hunting license, he must take a Hunter's Safety class, including hours of weapons safety. In our military, soldiers complete annual weapons training in the classroom and on a firing range. Weapons themselves have safety mechanisms to help limit the possibility of accidental discharge. In comparison, the average person receives little or no instruction on how to control their speech. Words could be the most pervasive damaging form of violence in the average family, school, and workplace. Flip the safety mechanism on your speech. Your words have a tremendous influence on your life and the lives of others. Carefully guard what you say, refusing to weaponize the power of your tongue.

Just as your thought-life has incredible power to work for or against you, your words affect your outcomes. In fact, faith is voice activated, your words being a fundamental component. The message of faith in Christ requires believing in your heart and proclaiming with your mouth.[878] Your belief works in tandem with your confession, releasing the power of salvation when you act upon your beliefs with speech. This spiritual principle applies to faith in general; even in the Old Testament, people believed and spoke. Therefore, your faith must include speaking forth what you believe.[879] Your speech is powerful. In a natural example, the psychological term "self-fulfilling prophecy" describes how people's beliefs or predictions consciously and subconsciously cause their behavior to align in a way that produces the originally expected outcome.[880] When you speak these thoughts out, you strengthen their control of your future thoughts and behaviors. For example, you state, "I never get recognized for my hard work on the job." Because you believe your success, recognition and promotion are outside of your control—you do not put forth the effort. Your supervisor refuses to reward your weak performance resulting in the fulfillment of your original prediction. By speaking out your pessimistic belief, you increase the possibility the negative outcome becomes your reality. Faith can work for or against you; if you proclaim negative things over your life, you exercise your belief in negative outcomes. If you exercise spiritual faith in God and His promises, you release the spiritual power but also increase the chance of a positive outcome based upon the natural principle of cause and effect. How much more important is it, then, that you should leverage the power of faith-filled speech to overcome difficulties? The suggestions for constructive speech described below can help reinforce positive action. They include both dos and don'ts, strategies to use your speech as a life-giving force and behaviors to avoid. Ask yourself, "How is your speech helping you overcome your struggles and serve God's purposes in your life? How is it hindering you?" Take time every day to listen to what you say. Are you strengthening yourself and others? Are your words a destructive force? As Scripture observes, "The wise person builds their house, the foolish

---
877 James 3:8
878 Romans 10:8–10
879 2 Corinthians 4:13
880 R.K. Merton, "The Self-Fulfilling Prophecy," The Antioch Review, 8(2), 193–210.

one tears it down with their own hands."[881] One could easily replace the word "hands" in this passage with "tongue." Many people use their speech in a self-destructive manner. Your words have tremendous power that works for or against you. Use the disproportionate power of your tongue to lift yourself and others. You will significantly strengthen your ability to overcome the difficulties you face.

Use Your Speech to Build Yourself Up

Use your speech to lift yourself. Bless (speak good things about) yourself. Refuse to speak negatively about your character, abilities, or potential. Whatever you do in faith is constructive and spiritually healthy, so speak about your life in faith. God has blessed you in many ways. Right now, you may struggle to remember them, but God continues to work His plan for good in your life.[882] He is not against you, nor is He punishing you because you didn't measure up. He is for you, and His mercies endure forever.[883] The twenty-third Psalm is clear, "The Lord is your Shepherd, his goodness and mercy will follow you every day of your life."[884] Get in agreement with God. Align your speech with His Word. You may have heard important people in your life put you down. Someone may have cursed you with phrases like, "You're worthless. You will never amount to anything." These messages become part of your mind's software as you grow older. They may play on repeat in your mind over and over again. They shape your beliefs and expectations. They make it hard to believe you are worthy of God's blessing and favor, so you may struggle to speak it. It is time to update the software that runs your speech. Use your words to overwrite your thinking. Jesus noted that speech comes out of your heart.[885] When your heart is infected with negativity, how do you change your speech? You can attack the negativity from both directions. Renew your mind in the truths of Scripture to change the way you think, but also speak those same truths of Scripture over yourself to reinforce a new way of thinking. You don't have to wait until they align.

I used to think if I didn't feel the truth of what I was saying, it was a lie. The enemy used my own honesty to stifle the power of my speech for decades. Do not fall into this trap. Scripture reveals truth regardless of whether you or I believe or feel it. I don't always feel like God loves me, but that does not change the fact that He does. In hard times, you may question whether He is with you. Your uncertainty does not change the spiritual truth that in Christ, He is always with you. He lives inside your heart; technically, the Holy Spirit dwells in your spirit. Recognize that what you think or feel with your senses is not truth, nor is it always true and accurate. Your eyes and senses can deceive you. Scripture is truth and always true. This is not wishful thinking. It is not faking it until you make it. It is not denying your present difficult circumstances.[886] To live in faith is to live by spiritual sight. It is to believe and proclaim

---
881 Proverbs 14:1
882 Jeremiah 29:11–13
883 Psalm 136:1
884 Psalm 23:1,6
885 Matthew 12:34
886 2 Corinthians 4:18

things that are spiritually true and very real, although presently unseen, over your life and circumstances. The other option is to trust your senses that the only real things are the things that you can see or feel. To live this way is to deny the spiritual part of your being, a part that has been scientifically proven to exist. To live that way is to deny who you really are. You are body and soul (mind, will, emotions), but you are also spirit. To be true to who you really are, you must acknowledge the eternal aspect of your being and recognize the eternal Creator who made you. Everything that exists in the physical world came from the Spirit; therefore, the spiritual world is higher.[887] What God says about you and this life is true and truth. It supersedes what you presently see and feel because spiritual truth is always true. What is true in the Spirit will eventually transform the physical. When you say, "I am loved, valued, forgiven, righteous, never alone, strong, etc.," you are declaring spiritual truth that can change your present circumstances, what you see and feel. It is not a lie to speak spiritual truth over yourself. Feelings are never truth; in fact, they are often wrong. The only thing true about your feelings is to acknowledge in the present moment what they are. And that is only true for a snapshot in time because, in the next moment, they could change. Speak spiritual truths over yourself. Proclaim what God says about you and your situation. It will change your experience of life.

Refuse to speak anything negative about yourself or the circumstances. You may say, "I'll never amount to anything. All I have is bad luck. Nothing good ever happens to me." Do not entertain such thoughts in your mind, and absolutely never speak them over yourself. Statements like these function as curses, limiting your potential and future well-being. Deny them any further influence over your life. Refute the lies of your spiritual enemy by rejecting any agreement with him or those he uses to tear you down. Refuse to become your own worst enemy. The foolish person tears his life to the ground with his own speech. God is a re-builder at work in your life to raise you up from the ashes. His will is to bless and prosper you.[888] He is making the bad things in your life, things the enemy meant to harm you, profitable for you.[889] Speak good things over your future. Put the enemy on notice that you trust God and you will never quit. The Lord's Prayer contains these words, "And lead us not into temptation but deliver us from the evil one (or evil)."[890] It is double-minded to pray "deliver us from the evil one" only to turn around and walk right into his trap by putting yourself down. Such a prayer will never work because you don't agree with yourself, let alone with God. It is not from faith. Instead of binding yourself by such statements, use your faith to bind the enemy. I pray this section of the Lord's Prayer this way, "By the blood of Jesus and faith in his name, I bind every dark and unclean spirit that has come against me." With this type of prayer, you not only refuse to speak negatively about yourself, you bind the enemy's attempts to speak against you.

---
887 John 1:1, Colossians 1:15–17, 2 Peter 3:3–5
888 3 John 1:2, James 1:17
889 Romans 8:28
890 Matthew 6:13

Empower Yourself with Positive Self-Talk and Declarations

Start your morning with positive, Scripture-based self-talk. Self-talk is your inner conversation, the things you say to yourself, especially when stressed. It is frequently negative reflecting negative thought processes but gets verbalized under your breath or spoken loudly when alone. It may be accompanied by a slap on the head or a fist to the steering wheel. You may berate yourself for what you did or should have done. It may be self-criticism. God does not want you belittling anyone, especially yourself. He doesn't want you condemning yourself, not even under your breath.[891] Everyone has faults. All believers are in the process of character change. You don't have to live under your own unrealistic standards. Tearing yourself down doesn't help you become better. Transformation comes through renewing your mind in Scripture. When your inner conversations take a negative turn, or if you want to reinforce faith in your self-talk, it is time to use your words. Remember who you are in Christ, keep drawing near to God, and tell yourself what He says about you.

In Section II, we discussed the faith-filled thinking strategy of recognizing your new identity in Christ. You cleansed your mind by identifying as a new creation. Now it is time to remind yourself, speaking aloud, what you know from the Word. Tell yourself you are a temple of the Holy Spirit who lives within you.[892] You are a child of God, dearly loved and valued by Jesus, who expressed His ongoing commitment to you by offering His life in your place.[893] You are worthy and impervious to accusation, not because you deserve it, but because God loves and justifies you.[894] You are an object of His grace, mercy, favor, and blessing, all of which are renewed every day.[895] You are righteous, not because you always do the right thing, but because Christ's righteousness is imputed to you.[896] In Christ, all the sins you have ever committed and will ever commit have been forgiven.[897] Because Christ lives inside of you by the Spirit, you contain the resurrection power of Christ.[898] You are seated in heavenly places with Christ and given authority over every power of darkness on this earth.[899] You are already victorious, guaranteed a place in God's triumphal procession and a reservation in eternity with Him.[900] You are part of a royal priesthood, an integral part of the spiritual community known as the body of Christ, the church.[901] You have irreplaceable gifts, talents, abilities, and characteristics that help complete God's family.[902] God

---

891 Romans 8:33–34
892 1 Corinthians 3:16–17, 6:19–20
893 1 John 3:1
894 Romans 8:31–34
895 Ephesians 1:3, 3:20, Philippians 4:19, James 1:17
896 Romans 3:22, Philippians 3:9
897 Colossians 2:13–14, Hebrews 10:10,14,17–18, 1 John 2:12
898 Ephesians 1:18–21
899 Ephesians 1:21, 2:5–6
900 2 Corinthians 2:14
901 1 Peter 2:9
902 1 Corinthians 12:12–27

made you unique, with distinctive identifying marks, such as eyes, nose, ears, voice, fingerprints, and other characteristics that reflect your life's purpose and meaning.[903] These declarations are not mantras meant to superficially make you feel good; these are truths from Scripture. Anything you tell yourself that is opposed to God's Word must be rejected and overwritten by the words of your mouth. You cannot wait for someone else to tell you what God has already told you. You must proclaim it yourself.

Speaking these truths aloud not only helps block the negative, destructive self-talk that may be your normal pattern, but it also keeps your thoughts aligned with the Word of God. Your character is not perfect, but you have a sincere desire to become more like Christ. That is the making of a perfect heart. Tell yourself you have all the fruit of the Spirit who lives in your heart. The fruit of the Spirit is in you already; you do not have to ask God to put them there. You must choose to let them show as you submit to the leading of the Spirit rather than your desires. You don't have to respond in the way someone mistreated you or give someone a piece of your mind. You are better than that. The enemy may call you a liar. It is not a lie to prophesy the Word and will of God over yourself. He is a liar and the father of lies, so ignore him.[904] You are not prideful to call yourself what God calls you; you are faithful (full of faith). God calls all His people blessed and highly favored. Faith is courageous and bold. It can sound prideful, but pride is valuing yourself above others, not being confident in the Lord.

"I Can Do This."

Recently, I watched my five-year-old granddaughter climb an indoor rock wall. She got about halfway up the wall and paused a second. It was obvious she was afraid. It was a high wall for a five-year-old. Then she started shouting, "I can do this!"

With each handhold she grabbed, each step she made, she shouted again, "I can do this!"

I was amazed as she easily climbed to the top. At the top, she paused again and looked down. I'm sure it looked very high to her.

She said to her dad, "Help me down!"

"Climb down a little bit," he replied. "Now, climb down a little bit," he said again. "Look back at me; you can jump now."

She jumped the last few feet to the mat.

I was amazed by the whole thing, so I asked my daughter who taught her to talk to herself like that. It was her dad, my son-in-law, who taught her to tell herself, "I can do this," whenever she faces a difficult situation. What a powerful lesson for a five-year-old. In the same way, your heavenly Father has given you numerous "I can do this" words in Scripture. In a very real sense, He watches as you face your obstacles, and the Spirit within is reminding and guiding you with the truths of Scripture. Something

---
903 Psalm 139:13–18
904 John 8:44

powerful happens when you move these words from the page of Scripture and your mind, through your speech, into the atmosphere. Your words will build you up and maximize your potential to overcome. Your Scripture-based, "I can do this!" will enable you to climb the walls of adversity in your life.

Make scriptural declarations over yourself every day! Declarations are faith-based statements you make about yourself and life. They set the tone for how you think, speak, and act for the day and proclaim hope (spiritual optimism) and expectation for your future. They are founded in the Word of God. With God, all things are possible.[905] Start your day reading the Word, then proclaim His promises over your life.

Last year, I began a practice of declaring Psalm 23 over my day. Here are some of the declarations I made:

> The Lord is my Shepherd.
>
> Today, I have everything I need.
>
> God restores my inner being.
>
> He guides me in wisdom to do the right thing.
>
> I will fear nothing today, for God is with me.
>
> He exalts me in the face of my enemies.
>
> He anoints me with His Spirit, peace, and joy.
>
> His blessings and favor will follow me today, tomorrow, and every day of my life,
>
> And I will spend eternity with Him in heaven.

I have used these simple declarations as a great source of encouragement for my struggles.

Scripture states, "No matter how many promises God has made, they are 'yes' in Christ."[906] God's promises are not a maybe. As you continue to read this passage, realize you must exercise faith, coming into agreement with God by saying, "Amen" (literally, "let it come to pass").[907] God wants you to speak forth your agreement. By faith, you reach out and take the gifts God holds in His outstretched hands. The gifts are there, bought and paid for by Christ. Even though they have your name on them, they are not practically yours until you reach out and take them. You take hold of them by forcefully declaring them over your life. You proclaim the truth you see with spiritual sight until it becomes the manifestation you see with natural sight. That is your agreement, your "Amen."

If You Have Faith, You Can Say…

Faith has a voice control feature. Your words, when combined with faith, can change your circum-

---

905 Matthew 19:26
906 2 Corinthians 1:20a
907 2 Corinthians 1:20b

stances. You may think you lack the faith to make that work. Your words can help. The disciples asked Jesus to increase their faith. In response, He encouraged them, "If you have faith as small as a mustard seed, you can say to this mulberry tree, 'Be uprooted and planted in the sea,' and it will obey you."[908] Notice, it does not take a large quantity of faith to tip the scales—mustard seeds are tiny, but when you have the faith to speak, things happen. Your words are a result of faith, but they also move your faith from a neutral position into action. Faith and speech powerfully combine to bring change. Amplify your faith with your words. Jesus made another radical statement, "Truly I tell you, if anyone says to this mountain, 'Go, throw yourself into the sea,' and does not doubt in their heart but believes that what they say will happen, it will be done for them."[909] In this verse, we see the perfect combination of faith and speech. If anyone "says" to this mountain and believes… If you have faith, you can say, "Mountain be moved," and it will be done for you. That may seem like a stretch for you, especially right now in your season of adversity. However, have you tried it? Faith is what happens in the middle of the problems before you see the answer. Now is the time to try. Maybe it has not worked for you because you never tried. I don't mean just once and give up. Make it a daily discipline to command your problems to be removed/resolved in Jesus' name. Jesus' words produced miracle after miracle. Your words of faith can change your reality as well.

Apply the faith principle above to declarations. When you make positive statements of faith over your life, you align your thinking with God's heart and will. You agree with His promises, and you release your belief in the constructive action of speech. People with little faith in God's promises do not speak them out. They are doubtful, unbelieving, timid, or fearful. Declarations require courage, boldness, and confidence. Jesus made a profound observation, "The kingdom of God has been forcefully advancing and forceful people have been seizing it."[910] You must become bold and forceful in the battles for your future well-being. You may not feel these qualities or see yourself as a faith-filled person. It is time to change that. Use your speech to reinforce what you know you should be in obedience to God. Gabriel came to Mary with the words, "Greetings, you who are highly favored. The Lord is with you."[911] She was an unremarkable teenager in her town, but God saw it differently. What God says about you is far more important than what you or others think or say. The spiritual power of words is in alignment with God's Word. In another example from the time of Israel's judges, the angel of the Lord greeted Gideon with the words, "The Lord is with you, mighty warrior."[912] In his own eyes, Gideon saw himself as nothing, the least in his family. God saw Gideon and said something very different. You cannot call something nothing that God says is favored and mighty. You don't have the authority to do that, even when it concerns yourself. It is interesting in both accounts that God spoke words of blessing before

---
908 Luke 17:6
909 Mark 11:23
910 Matthew 11:12 (God's Word)
911 Luke 1:28
912 Judges 6:12

either Mary or Gideon ever took a single step of obedience. God calls out things before they ever come to be.[913] If you want to please God, if you want to agree with God, if you want a breakthrough, you must, with faith, call things into being in your own life and circumstances before you see them with your physical eyes.

Your speech can reinforce your faith. Some say, "I have to be true to myself and speak what I really feel." Your feelings are not truth, nor do they help you to be your true self. Your true self is genetically hard-wired to connect with God. Your feelings are a fleeting response to what's happening in the moment and how you interpret it. To be true to yourself, you must act with regard for your spirit. Feelings follow; they do not lead you to your best life. Faith leads your life, and eventually, your feelings will catch up. I am not suggesting you should never say what you feel. It is important in healthy relationships to share how you feel. It is probably more important to consistently share what you want in your relationships as well. Rather, I suggest that speaking out declarations of faith over yourself is far more helpful than telling yourself how you feel, especially when you face adversity.

I Will Say of the Lord

Declare God's promises over yourself every day. Faith agrees with God. I continually find it amazing how impactful Scripture can be when reading or speaking it aloud. Scripture declarations will nourish your spirit and sustain you in the same way that healthy food nourishes your body. The psalmist wrote, "I will say of the Lord, he is my strength."[914] Throughout history, people of faith have been unafraid to boldly state, "I will say of the Lord…" They trusted God for their help, and they declared who He was: savior, healer, deliverer, helper, counselor, comforter, provider, banner, righteousness, etc. Faith happens in the middle of your adversity before you see even the glimmer of a chance that things are turning around.[915] Faith is about what you do when your senses show you the negative report. That is when faith speaks with confident words of trust. You may not feel confident, but you do not rely on your feelings. You decide in faith, "I will say of the Lord…" You may be thinking it, you may be reading it to yourself, but something special happens when you declare it to yourself, the spiritual realm, and to anyone else who may be listening.

A good place to identify helpful verses to proclaim is to use favorites from your daily reading plan. Another source is to use common topical passages that encourage you to face your present challenges. If you are struggling with fear, use a keyword search to find relevant verses on fear. Personalize these verses and speak them over yourself, such as, "God has not given me a spirit of fear but of power and love and a sound mind."[916] A list of topical verses is provided at the end of this book. Read the Scripture

---

913 Romans 4:17
914 Psalm 91:2
915 Hebrews 11:1
916 2 Timothy 1:7

passages aloud to yourself. They can renew your mind, transform your thinking, and powerfully shape your emotions and behaviors.

To speak God's Word over yourself is to proclaim your trust in the one who lifts you up. It is absolutely not faith (or humility) to tear yourself down. You do not have to belittle yourself to prefer others. With God, there is no zero-sum game. You are not taking blessings away from others to receive your blessings from God. He has an infinite supply. You are no better than anyone else, but you are no less, either. In their fleshly self-indulgence, people try to tear others down and elevate themselves. Biblical wickedness is to push someone else down to get what you think you need. The last six of the Ten Commandments forbid this kind of behavior. These commands prohibit deception, manipulation, theft, or brute force to take what you want at another's expense. In Christ, you can help your neighbor get what they need as you reach for it yourself. The command is to love your neighbor as you love yourself, not more or less than.[917] To love someone is to value them, to commit to value them in your actions. We will discuss loving speech at length in the next chapter. It is hard to share kind words with others when you cannot share them with yourself. Build yourself up. When you tell yourself words that God thinks and speaks over you, you have aligned yourself with Scripture and positioned yourself to receive and share God's blessings.[918]

The enemy tries to make you believe the worst-case scenario in the circumstances you face. Worst-case scenarios are not facts. They are a negative prophecy, also known as catastrophizing. If you are going to prophesy, it may as well be in your favor. The Holy Spirit works through Scripture to encourage you and promote a faith-filled perspective. I remember an old Beetle Bailey cartoon from our newspaper where Sarge and Beetle had a ping-pong tournament. Sarge won, but Beetle had to notify the newspaper. The next day, the headlines read, "Beetle Almost Wins." Even in defeat, Beetle denied Sarge the headline.[919] In the same way, deny the enemy the headline. You control the interpretation in your mind. Transform your interpretation with thoughts anchored in the Word of God. Reinforce it by declaring them out loud, informing your mind and any who can hear. The sword of the Spirit is the Word of God. With the two-edged sword, you can demolish arguments (reasoning and logic that oppose trusting God), pretensions (negative, faithless assumptions), and strongholds (seats of power that bind and imprison) that set themselves against the knowledge of God.[920] Speaking scriptural declarations over yourself is a way of swinging that sword, parrying the strikes of the enemy, and weakening his position against you. Jesus used the Scripture in the same way when Satan tempted Him.[921] He did not just think about the verses. He refuted Satan's temptation by boldly proclaiming them. This is not just another Bible story. It is a model for training in spiritual warfare from Christ Himself. God gave you a sword. You are in a

---
917 Mark 12:31
918 Psalm 115:12
919 Mort Walker, Beetle Bailey, June 3, 2007, King Features Syndicate, NY, 1950.
920 2 Corinthians 10:4–5
921 Matthew 4:1–11

battle whether you realize it or not. Use it every day to encourage and strengthen yourself and fend off the attacks of the enemy.

Every morning on my drive to work, I pray, "Good morning, Father. I thank You for Your love today. I thank You for Your peace in my heart today, no matter what happens. I thank You for Your joy today that will encourage others. I thank You for the anointing of Your Spirit so I can be a blessing to others." I do not always feel anointed, loving, joyful, or at peace. My natural inner voice highlights the negatives. I struggle with difficulties and troubles in this world. I force my flesh to think and speak with faith. I tell myself, "You already have love, joy, peace, patience, kindness, goodness, gentleness, faithfulness, and self-control." I consider this, "How can I call myself a God-follower if I cannot rise above troubles to be a blessing to others in hard times?" I commit, "I will bless someone today." These declarations encourage me to find strength in God, regardless of difficulties. I proclaim Psalm 23 over myself every day. It is amazing how the spiritual power in this Psalm, and many others, can make such a difference in my soul (mind, will, emotions). I go to work with a far more positive mindset when I exercise positive self-talk. You will, too.

Describe Your Struggles In Words of Faith and Expectation

Troubles can seem bigger than God. You may be tempted to talk too much about the problem. After all, physical sight is more concrete and believable. People get a diagnosis from a professional. The doctor said, "I have cancer." My boss said, "The company is downsizing, and my job is being eliminated." The teacher says, "My child is struggling." So many bad reports, but whose report will you prioritize? Some people talk so much about the problem, how big and bad it is, they make it impossible for faith to have a chance. Your words of faith in the problem can be just as effective at giving it the victory as your words of faith in God. Has your problem eclipsed the Lord? For the Israelite army, Goliath was the biggest. His threats, his weapons, and his presence were all they could see. For David, Goliath looked very different. He was a mosquito to be squashed. David used his words to describe Goliath as he was spiritually. He used his words to describe himself spiritually, in the strength of the Lord. In truth, spiritually speaking, Goliath didn't stand a chance. You have the same choice with your problem. You can describe it with your natural senses the way Israel's soldiers did, or you can describe it spiritually as David did. I encourage you to trust the possibilities in Christ. Choose God's power and promises over your problems.

It can be helpful to know your problem, but it is more important to know your God. You do not need to know how remote the chance of healing is when you have the Creator of the Universe on your side. God defies all the odds. He trumps every possible negative outcome. You do not have to deny your situation; just prioritize your faith and spiritual sight. Speak out, "I'm facing a struggle, but God is my hope and deliverer. He is bringing good things to me. He is turning everything out for my good. God is making a way where there seems to be no way. He is lifting me up and causing me and my family to prosper." Speak the words out, even if no one is around. Sometimes, you must convince yourself. Your natural mind (sometimes referred to as the flesh in Scripture) needs to hear from your spirit. If God speaks a specific word of encouragement to your heart, speak that blessing over yourself. Record it in your journal. If God tells you, He is healing you, say so, "I am healed." You do not have to ignore your problem in denial. Magnify God instead of the problem. "The doctor says I have an illness, but I know God is my healer. "In truth, he has already provided for your healing. By Jesus' stripes you are healed."[922] He will completely heal me. My bank statement says I do not have enough, but God is my provider. With God, all things are possible." You are facing some challenges. Speak to those problems like Jesus instructed His disciples to speak to the mountains, "Be moved." Your trust in God honors Him, so be bold. Speak to your life, straighten your pathway, level the mountains, and fill in the valleys in your way.[923]

I have seen repeated miraculous healings and provision. God restored hearing to a person who had been deaf in one ear for over fifteen years. I didn't even know she couldn't hear, but many others did. The night before, her husband was told God would give their family a sign that would bring salvation to their home. The whole family accepted Christ the next day after the healing. I experienced major healing in my back when, in agony, God told me I was healed. I didn't believe it because the feelings of pain were still there. But God's word prevailed. In a few days, my pain was gone and has never returned. My aunt, who was terminal with cancer and on hospice, saw a vision of Jesus smiling at her. Immediately, all pain left her body. She stopped taking all her pain medication and continues to do well two years later. In the last few months, several prominent cancerous tumors disappeared from her body. Family friends once needed tires for their car but had no money. They came home from church to find four brand-new tires on the lawn. They were just the right size. They never knew where they came from, and neither do I. Did God send an angel with tires? God knows. These are just a few examples of how God works in people's lives every single day. All things are possible with God, so do not be afraid to shout it from the rooftop. The voice of cynicism may say they were special, but that can never happen for me. God doesn't play favorites. He is simply looking for those who will trust Him. Refuse to accept negative pronouncements over your life. You may hear them but don't allow them into your heart. Absolutely do not prophesy them over your life. Use your words to describe faith-filled expectations of God's goodness. Remember, faith believes God is a rewarder of those who seek Him.[924] Put that belief into action by speaking out your agreement with God's Word. Proclaim blessings over yourself and your needs.

---

922 Isaiah 53:5
923 Mark 11:23
924 Hebrews 11:6

Use Slogans to Help You Overcome

Slogans are words or phrases that provide a positive focal point for action. They motivate you to persevere, as energy and motivation are critical aspects in overcoming adversity. Any constructive means you can use to harness them is important. Slogans may seem simplistic, but they can be powerful. They may directly reflect Scripture, or they may be a word you feel God personally provided to encourage you in your struggle. Difficulties can discourage you and make you want to quit. In the faith, quitting is the only way to lose. If you keep running the race, you win. You may fall, do not stay down, get back up and keep moving. Scripture says, "Stand."[925] You do not have to destroy the enemy to win. All you must do is get back up when life or the enemy knocks you down. Endure: God's grace will help you cross the finish line. As a regular runner, I used to approach the difficult physical effort required to run up hills with the words, "You're an ox, be the ox. Step by step, keep pushing forward." I literally spoke it out to myself as I ran. By thinking about conquering the steep hill, one step at a time, I was able to keep moving, get over the top, and continue my run. Through some severe circumstances where I could not see a way out, I quoted, "God can make a way where there seems to be no way."[926] Stated another way, "God's got this!" How amazing that a few simple words can be so encouraging. In hard times, God has given me Scriptures to use as slogans. Recently, I was impressed by the verse, "Let nothing move you." I used it as a slogan, "Nothing will move me." That simple statement gave me peace through several struggles. Sometimes you just need enough inspiration to get you over the hump. The battle can become intense right before you reach the turning point, and slogans can help. If you can hold on long enough, you will be victorious.

As I develop my annual prayer and read-through-the-Bible plan each year, I normally receive a goal or slogan. God uses these words as themes to encourage me through the coming year. A few years ago, the words were, "How will God turn this situation for my good?" I used that question to confront every difficult and discouraging situation. Rather than getting stuck on the problem, I was constantly looking for how God would make each trouble profitable. It helped me to see past the short-term pain, to trust God for His sovereign work. In 2021, while reading the Bible, a sentence burned in my heart, "God can restore what was lost." In a year when so much was lost from COVID-19, it encouraged me to trust God for restoration. At one point, I became discouraged by a string of setbacks. However, in one day, God restored everything that had been lost over the last year. I still have obstacles and losses to overcome, but I am continually encouraged to look past the present with high expectations for a better future. Slogans can help remind you troubles are temporary, but God is faithful. It is normal to face struggles. You may have to endure some afflictions your whole life. Paul prayed to be healed of his "thorn in the flesh"

---

925 Ephesians 6:13
926 Isaiah 43:16–19

throughout his life.⁹²⁷ God did not deliver him from the problem, but He was faithful. He told Paul, "My grace is sufficient for you and my power in you is made perfect when you are weak.⁹²⁸ That statement is a slogan God gave Paul. You can use it as well, "God's grace is sufficient for me. I have the most power when I am weak, utterly dependent on God." God is an encourager and comforter. Slogans are one way He will lift you up. He is the God of all comfort.⁹²⁹

God can encourage you through thoughts He gives you, Scripture verses He impresses on your heart, encouraging words from friends, and countless other ways. A friend once encouraged me during a hard time in ministry. He said, "God has called you to this position, and if you can't do it, no one can." Somehow, that loving counsel ignited a fire in my heart that helped me to press through to victory. I repeated those words every time I hit a wall. Without them, I am not sure I would have made it. I am again reminded of the wise counsel Gandalf the Wizard gave Frodo Baggins that opens this book. Frodo lamented that he lived to see such evil. "So do I," Gandalf replied, "and so do all who live to see such times. But that is not for them to decide. All we have to decide is what to do with the time given us." You, like every person before or after you, must decide whether you will be overcome by your troubles or whether you will overcome them with the Spirit who lives within you. These thoughts are not just empty platitudes. Divinely inspired slogans are words of hope that encourage you to keep running your race. Find what works for you, use it to your advantage, and keep pressing forward.

Use Your Tongue to Praise God In Tough Times

Sometimes it seems like God is silent. You may not get much out of reading the Bible, your prayers may seem uninspiring, or you feel spiritually empty. Most believers experience this specific season of testing. The spiritual life is lived in faith, not feelings, so it is critical to engage faith in the discipline of praise. David went through a difficult time like this as well. He wrote how he used to rejoice in going to the house of God, but now he was empty. He asked himself, "Why are you so downcast, oh, my soul, why so disturbed within me?"⁹³⁰ He was discouraged, depressed, and felt like God had forgotten him. Yet David did something remarkable that helped him through this difficult time. He made a declaration. Amid his inner conflict, he exhorted himself, "Put your hope in God. For I will yet praise Him, my Savior, and my God."⁹³¹ In times like this, remember where your help lies. Remind yourself. Speak it loudly. Order yourself to look to God and praise Him. Praise takes the focus off yourself and your circumstances and places it on God. Sometimes you must praise your way out of a situation. Put on some worship music, read, and pray through some of the Psalms or go to a worship service and focus on praising God.

---
927 2 Corinthians 12:7
928 2 Corinthians 12:9
929 2 Corinthians 1:3
930 Psalm 42:5
931 Psalm 42:11

Make God the center of your world and make Him your solution. Praise until you get your breakthrough. This may take time, but it is a sure prescription. You could use your tongue to complain as the Israelites did time again in the wilderness.[932] Unfortunately, that is the absolute wrong approach and ultimately caused them to miss God's blessing. The abuse of their tongues precipitated judgment despite numerous second chances. Use your tongue to magnify God, not your discomfort, not your problem. God responds to praise. One of the challenges believers face is to see if they will bless God when there is no earthly reason to do so. Job faced the same test and refused to quit.[933] Your praise will see you through. Praise will build you up in your inner being when nothing else seems to help.

---

[932] Numbers 14:22
[933] Job 2:10

Chapter 3

Use Your Speech to Strengthen Others

Gentle words bring life and health.[934]

Speak life-giving words to others and be positive when talking about them. You have just read how your words can powerfully impact your own life. These same principles apply in the way you speak to others. Review every principle of Chapter 2 and consider how you can apply it in your relationships with others. Life-giving words communicate love, value, and appreciation for others. You can help someone more than you know by simple words of encouragement. In the process you will lift yourself as well. Countless Scripture verses describe the importance of positive words, especially Proverbs.[935] I encourage you to study through the book, reading only those verses that address speech. Some have special beauty, such as these below.

> Gracious words are like honeycomb, sweet to the soul and healing to the bones.[936]
> Gentle words bring life and health.[937]
> An honest answer is like a kiss on the lips.[938]
> A word aptly spoken is like apples of silver in settings of gold.[939]

People crave kind words. The devastating effects of sin on the mind and emotions leave people hungry for affirmation.[940] Encouragement is a way of powerfully serving others with the strength of your speech. Anyone can exercise a ministry of encouragement. Even a greeting with a smile can significantly impact someone's day. Never underestimate your ability to bless others as you serve. It is difficult to know what others are going through, but recognize they are likely struggling with their own issues. You may wrestle with compassion for someone who seems cold, distant, or unkind. People act this way when they are trying to hide their own issues. Be a safe person in your home, workplace, and other areas of influence. The ministry of kindness can be far more impactful than you realize. Love reaches places you never imagine. Your encouraging words can elevate others, strengthen relationships, and encourage yourself as well.

---

934 Proverbs 15:4a
935 Proverbs 16:24
936 Proverbs 16:24
937 Proverbs 15:4a
938 Proverbs 24:26
939 Proverbs 25:11
940 Colossians 4:6

Living and speaking as a life-giving person involves radiating the fruit of the Spirit; love, joy, peace, patience, kindness, goodness, gentleness, faithfulness, and self-control.[941] It means demonstrating an appreciation of others' eternal spirit and value in how you talk to them. This is not easy in today's sin-soaked world. In the beginning, humanity lived in perfect harmony with God, the created world, and each other. Adam and Eve were immortal with access to the fruit of the Tree of Life. Had they not disobeyed God, they would have lived forever in the harmony of paradise. However, Adam and Eve chose to violate their relationship with God by doing the only thing they had to do to demonstrate their love and commitment to Him—they ate from the fruit of the Tree of the Knowledge of Good and Evil. The immediate result was the shattering of the harmony humans had with God. Right on the heels of that divide came the loss of harmony between Adam and Eve. Our present dissension between men and women, aka the "war between the sexes," finds its beginning with them.[942] Following the loss of harmony with nature came the splintering of harmony between each and every human being.[943] Cain killed Abel with the words, "Am I my brother's keeper?"[944] After thousands of years of envy, lying, manipulation, theft, murder, and war, we recognize Adam and Eve made a bad trade. Knowledge isn't everything it's cracked up to be. We keep trying to get back to paradise with its eternal life (or at least a lot longer lifespan). We invented the internet, smartphones, and more technological advancement than many thought possible. Unfortunately, we feel a lot less love, relatedness, and harmony. World peace is almost a laughable dream. The world is in bad shape. Knowledge and technology aren't going to help you love God and others any better. This is the social backdrop for serving others with life-giving speech. Demonstrate by your words (and actions) that God loves all people beyond possible description. In Christ, you are God's ambassador, as though He was making His appeal through you.[945] Put down your phone, look people in the eye, and speak words of life to them. You are planting seeds of hope that will bear fruit in your own spirit as well.

What If Someone Is My Problem?

Another person(s) may be contributing to your present problems. You can change the relational dynamic by changing the way you think and act toward them. Use your words to communicate esteem, value, and appreciation. In a dyad (a relationship with one other person), you have tremendous influence to shape the interactions. You can speak to them through eyes of faith, calling into being things that are not present in the relationship right now. You can refuse to rise to the conflict with the name-calling, criticism, cursing, and other negative speech. Replace these tactics with healthy speech. In some cases,

---
941 Galatians 5:22–23
942 Genesis 3:16
943 Genesis 3:17–19
944 Genesis 4:9
945 2 Corinthians 5:20

the person is so toxic, you just need to separate yourself from them, especially if you or loved ones are physically at risk. If that is not an option and you must deal with some level of toxic behavior, this is the time for faith. Keep your speech healthy and positive but go to war in your prayers. Speak to your mountains and bring some trusted prayer warriors (if possible) into agreement with you to change the circumstances. You do not have to internalize the negative words of others. Section II, on faith-filled resilient thinking strategies, equipped you to deal with such messaging. Remember, you do not have to wait for someone else to change to resolve the problem. You can be the change in the situation, and using the power of your words, you can reduce/neutralize the impact another person has on your life and well-being.

Use Your Words to Bless and Do Not Curse

Use your words to bless everything and everyone around you. Right now, the priestly blessing of Israel is a popular worship song. The Lord commanded Moses to have the priests speak this blessing over the people because He is always good and wants the best for you and all people.

> The Lord bless you and keep you;
> the Lord make his face shine on you and be gracious to you;
> the Lord turn his face toward you,
> and give you peace.[946]

Is there a good reason not to bless everyone you meet? You have no idea what events are shaping people's lives. You have read how sin brings harm to people. Who will bless what the enemy has cursed? How many opportunities per day will any person have to receive a blessing from one of God's people? How many believers intentionally start their day with a plan to bless and do good to others? In a world of evil, Scripture counsels you, "Don't be overcome by evil, rather overcome evil with good."[947] Jesus commanded His followers, "Love your enemies, do good to those who hate you. Bless those who curse you and pray for those who abuse you.[948] Be a light in the darkness and bless those around you. The good deeds you do will light up your inner being and give you strength in your hardships."

Speak the same kinds of scriptural declarations over others as you do yourself. Use Scripture to call forth God's will for others, speaking what can be, not what you see now. Speak God's promises over your children and family members. Scripture warns fathers, "Do not exasperate your children (with your words) instead bring them up in the fear and admonition of the Lord."[949] You want your kids to

---
946 Numbers 6:22–26
947 Romans 12:21
948 Luke 6:28
949 Ephesians 6:4

have the best possible life and to serve God. Yet harsh criticism and lack of gentleness with their feelings can serve as a contradictory example that drives your kids further away from God. Love is better than the Law. This is the message of the New Testament. What the Old Covenant could not do through all its rules and regulations, Jesus did under the New Covenant by offering Himself on the cross as the perfect sacrifice of love. Offer yourself in love and allow obedience to follow from a willing heart. Harshness or criticism can build greater resistance to the positive behaviors you want to encourage. Rules are important but mercy and grace triumph over the law. Your children will be more emotionally healthy through love and acceptance than through harsh, rigid legalism. Love is more important than the rules. If you can combine them in your home, with love being most important, you will see fruit. Reinforce this atmosphere with prayer and declaration of Biblical promises over those you love. God's thoughts towards your loved ones will help you temper your heart and attitude. Your family is an important place of strength in difficult times.

Use Your Words In Active Listening

Active listening is an important skill. Scripture states, "Be quick to listen."[950] As people share important experiences, it is necessary to be actively engaged in verbal and non-verbal cues. People, including close family members, who do not see your engagement may interpret those cues as not caring and slowly stop sharing their joys and sorrows with you. Active listening is the key. Ensure you make eye contact, display engagement in your non-verbal cues, and respond verbally with questions and comments that invite the person to share more. Simple generic responses in the conversation indicate lack of interest. Active listening is more difficult today with the distractions of phones, social media, and other technology. I regularly watch families sit around the table in a restaurant each one fully engrossed in their phones. I recently watched a couple do the same on Valentine's Day. There is not a lot of sharing happening in these relationships. Mealtime used to be a time for family members to share what happened that day. It is vitally important to make time to listen. Celebrate with others, especially those close to you, and grieve with them as well.[951] Active listening will deepen your relationships, providing a stronger bond when you need to lean on the strength of friends and family.

Make a Plan to Encourage Someone Every Day

Encourage others at every opportunity. Scripture reminds followers to be encouragers. "Therefore, encourage one another and build each other up, just as in fact you are doing.[952] Do not let any unwholesome talk come out of your mouths, but only what is helpful for building others up according to their needs, that it may benefit those who listen."[953] Your encouraging words build others up, providing

---
[950] James 1:19
[951] 1 Corinthians 12:26
[952] 1 Thessalonians 5:11
[953] Ephesians 4:29

stability in a person's heart and mind while making an investment in their emotional well-being. These are not empty platitudes. Words have power beyond the time and energy invested. Make a plan to encourage someone every day. Start by reminding yourself to encourage everyone you meet. Set a goal for how many people you will speak to or identify a person the Lord lays upon your heart to encourage. Look for opportunities to lift others throughout the day. As you serve others with the gift of encouragement, you will feel stronger emotionally and physically. The positive feelings created by serving others will help you face your troubles. The wisdom of Proverbs profoundly states this truth. "A generous man will prosper; he who refreshes others will himself be refreshed."[954] What you give away, you will receive in the same measure.

Tell Others "Thank you!"

Be quick to thank others.[955] Express your appreciation when they do good things for you. Positive reinforcement is a powerful force. The more you recognize the good others do with thanks, the more apt people are to repeat the behavior. You can help others make the world a better place. Section I describes this discipline in detail. I recently received a thank you card in the mail from a friend. Inside the card was a quote attributed to William Arthur Ward, "Feeling gratitude and not expressing it is like wrapping a present and not giving it." On the other side were the handwritten words, "I am grateful for you." No one knows how thankful you are until you tell them. Saying thank you makes people feel loved and valued. Those two simple words will return to encourage you in your times of need.

Tell the Truth (Speak the Truth In Love)

Scripture states, "Speaking the truth in love, we will grow up in all things."[956] Speaking the truth supports your moral fortitude while lying undermines your conscience and weakens your character. Lying also creates stress by forcing your mind to exert the additional energy required to maintain the web of deception. Truth can be difficult to share with others, but dealing with adversity requires honesty and loving confrontation. Sharing your perspective and feelings with others is the prescription for progress. As my high school literature teacher once told me, "Truth is a hard pill to swallow." That is true for all and a good reminder of why you always need to wrap the truth in love. Put yourself in the other person's shoes and ask yourself, "How would I want them to share this truth with me?" When you have considered the wording and tone of your message with the intent of communicating the value of the other person, you are ready to have the conversation.[957] When people give their pets medicine, they often wrap

---

954 Proverbs 11:25
955 1 Thessalonians 5:18
956 Ephesians 4:15
957 Matthew 7:12

it in something appealing like cheese or bacon. It gives the pill a desirable flavor and makes it easier to swallow. Wrap your truth in the bacon of love. Everyone has feelings and an innate need to be valued. Demonstrate the love of God in your speech, and you will minimize the second and third-order effects of criticism. Many people share their truths like a hand grenade. They pull the pin and toss it; whatever happens, happens. It is on them to deal with it. Tossing people the truth, or the truth about your feelings/opinions, like a grenade is not speaking in love. No one wants to be riddled with the explosive shrapnel of another person's feelings and frustrations. That approach only exacerbates the problem and conflict. Avoid the victim mentality. That thinking trap robs you of power and control in the situation. Speak the truth in love and maximize your potential to make progress. There are no guarantees when you relate to others. Even when presented in love, a person can take offense at the truth. If you face a negative reaction, it is best to try to lovingly end the conversation and give the other person time to think. Some people process better with alone time to think through the message and its implications. Unfortunately, I have had to confront numerous individuals in my life and ministry. Some have handled it well. Some have been defensive, some angry, some hurt, some a combination of many feelings. I have also been confronted. It is difficult to give or receive. Confront only when you must. There is no spiritual gift of confrontation. When you can show grace and mercy, do so. When confrontation is necessary, do so. Love is the key.

Tell Others What You Want

In your struggles, you may develop the temptation to expect those around you to read your mind. After all, if they really cared, they should know what you need. Unfortunately for everyone, that is not true. Only God knows your thoughts and feelings. Expecting others to know what you need is a thinking trap. Be open, honest and tell those you love what you want. This practice has many benefits. First, you may not be fully sure what you want. Listening to yourself speak out what you want will help you clarify your thoughts. I have heard some who use this practice repeatedly say, "What I mean is..." As they listened to themselves, they were able to describe their need more clearly. Try to boil down your statement to a specific measurable request. Consider this example of a couple's conversation in counseling.

"What I want is more '*me* time.'"

"*Me* time?" the spouse replies.

"What I mean is I just need some time to relax."

"Relax?" the spouse asks.

"You know what I mean. I want to have some time away from the kids, where I can just relax and do what I want to do."

"So, you want me to watch the kids?"

"Yes, I need a couple of hours on Saturday to get out of the house and pamper myself."

"How do you want to pamper yourself?" the spouse asks.

"Maybe a massage or a mani-pedi, and someone else's coffee."

"Okay, so you want me to watch the kids on Saturday for a few hours while you grab a coffee and some '*me* time.'"

The original "*me* time" request could mean a lot of things. Additionally, frustrations could make it difficult for the conversation to reach its necessary conclusion. Patience is critical to achieving full understanding.

A second benefit of sharing what you want is the building of trust. Your statement demonstrates trust in the other person and your relationship to share something deeply important to you. Loved ones will value your openness in a healthy relationship. Third, by stating openly what you want, you give the other person an opportunity to address it in a fair, reasonable, and loving manner. A healthy discussion and negotiation can begin. Scripture instructs you to present your requests to God in this way. It reads, "You do not have because you do not ask." [958] Asking is a model for other relationships as well. You cannot blame others for not helping you if you do not ask.

Know When to Say Nothing

Sharing what you want does not mean you share everything you think or feel. Some thoughts and feelings towards others, especially the negative ones, are best kept to yourself. Sometimes less is more. The old proverb says, "Silence is golden." Listening can be the best prescription to help others.[959] Let them talk. Do not try to refute their observations or take over their conversation. Listen to understand their perspective and affirm their feelings and vulnerability.[960] You may not agree with everything they say, but you can recognize and agree that they have been hurt. You do not have to accept that the person's view is correct or accurate to listen. In fact, it is a great exercise of self-discipline to let someone else share their perspective while everything inside you wants to debate or argue the points they are making. If you listen without speaking (or asking only clarifying questions), it can help you understand the other person more fully and soften your responses. Treat other people's feelings as gently as you want them to treat yours. Gentleness is a fruit of the Holy Spirit.[961] Some people are quick to say, "Quit being a whiner. Suck it up and keep going. Put on your big boy/big girl pants." Yet those same people can be the quickest to push back when their feelings are hurt. Biblical wisdom warns, "When words are many, sin is not

---

958 Philippians 4:6
959 James 1:19
960 Proverbs 18:13
961 Galatians 5:22–23

absent."[962] Not only is listening often the best approach, but it can also keep you out of trouble. Scripture observes, "Fools find no pleasure in understanding but delight in airing their own opinions."[963] Some people are very good at filling up the room with their persuasion. They can easily say too much and do more harm than good. Oftentimes, less is more. I heard a humorous story attributed to Mark Twain. He went to church to hear a missionary speak. After the first five minutes, he wanted to give the missionary fifty dollars in the offering. After fifteen minutes, he wanted to give the missionary twenty dollars, and after over thirty minutes of listening to the missionary ramble on, he wanted to take money out of the plate as it went by. You may not realize you are saying too much. Too many words can become selfish and manipulative. Usually, only a few of your words make the biggest impact in others. Listening is serving. Scripture notes, "Even the fool is thought wise when he remains silent."[964] Saying nothing can be very profitable and prevent you from making your situation worse.

---

[962] Proverbs 10:19
[963] Proverbs 18:2
[964] Proverbs 17:28

Chapter 4

Refuse to Use Your Speech as a Negative Force

It is not what goes into the mouth that defiles a man, but what comes out of the mouth.[965]

Check your speech. Don't get drug into the muck with people who use their tongues to destroy others. Value your relationship with God too highly to let your relationships with others sour to the point where it hinders your spiritual life. Scripture provides a checklist of actions to avoid. Your speech can be a venomous destructive force in your life and the lives of others. The enemy will tempt you to vent your anger by verbally attacking others. Don't fall for that trap. Malicious, critical, and disrespectful speech may feel good in the moment, but it harms your heart and can prevent the flow of God's blessings in your life. Jesus taught his disciples the mouth speaks out of the overflow of the heart.[966] The key to cleansing your heart and speech is to give hurtful, unjust circumstances of the past to God. When you rehearse, repeat, and seek revenge for past wrongs, you re-wound yourself and make it harder to heal. The bitterness of heart that feeds destructive speech is like a cancer in your spirit that grows and spreads its poison throughout your system. You don't want to add to your struggles by allowing your inner being to be infected this way. The pressures of stress and struggles make it much harder to maintain positive speech. Use the spiritual fruit of self-control to restrain your natural impulses, loose kindness and gentleness in your speech, and release past hurts that can harden your heart. Maximize your mental, emotional, and relational health as you seek a right heart and a pure spirit.[967] Refuse to use your speech to wound others in any of the destructive means described below.

Criticism

There are six things the Lord hates...feet that run swiftly to evil {so bent on revenge they feel like what they are doing is right}[968] *A scoundrel plots evil, and his speech is like a scorching fire.*[969]

Do not use criticism to wound others. Some people behave like venomous snakes. They look for opportunities to strike, delivering venom deep into the flesh of people's hearts. Unfortunately, people who claim to love God often function like snakes in their faith community. They wound and divide. They

---
965 Matthew 15:11
966 Luke 6:45
967 Psalm 24:4
968 Proverbs 6:16 (AMP)
969 Proverbs 16:27

criticize everything, from the clothes people are wearing to the sermon that day. I know families who spend their Sunday dinner together criticizing everything that went on in the worship service that day, as well as each other. The sad truth is they have largely harmed themselves, allowing the enemy unfettered access to their hearts. While some criticize in their homes, others are unafraid to infect others with their bitter spirit, openly proclaiming their opinions to anyone who will listen to gossip and strife. Still, others have a critical spirit and strike at anyone around them, including loved ones. Nothing meets their standard. They become a tool of the enemy for blame, shame, and condemnation. Criticism is destructive to others as it can deeply wound the heart, but it is especially dangerous to the one who wields it. Jesus rebuked the Pharisees not for failure to observe the minute details of the Jewish law but for their lack of mercy. The Pharisees, not the prostitutes and thieving tax collectors, received His harshest rebukes.[970] His rebukes serve as a warning about the damage criticism does to the heart of the speaker.

Use criticism sparingly, surgically, and always in person. Everyone is a child at heart. That means even the seemingly hardest people on the outside have inner vulnerabilities. Some people use their hardness or indifference to protect themselves emotionally. Scripture advises you to "tell the truth in love."[971] When you must provide improvements as part of your constructive feedback, ask yourself, "How would I want to hear this criticism if I was on the receiving end?" The answer is probably, "As lovingly as possible." In other words, have the best interests of the other person in mind before the conversation. Then, using precise language, gently engage the discussion. This is laser surgery, not "clear-cutting" like loggers do in a forest. No one wants to have their emotions trampled callously. If you cannot find a way to speak what you see as truth in a loving, gentle, and constructive way, then it's not the time to share it. Pray about it. Ask for God's direction and timing. Sometimes, God will use another means to challenge people. Sometimes God will use you. When someone asks what you really think, be courageous and loving as you share your perspective.

Moses just led God's people across the Red Sea. The waters crashed in over the Egyptian Army. His sister Miriam picked up her tambourine and led the people in the famous song of victory.[972] Soon after, she became critical of Moses because his wife, Zipporah, was not Jewish. Perhaps it was spiritual pride after her role in leading Israel's song of triumph, perhaps a conflict she had with Zipporah. God heard Miriam criticizing Moses, and she developed leprosy. God's truest nature is love. He rejects harsh criticism and opposes the proud. Miriam now found herself opposed to God. Fortunately, Moses was a humble and merciful person. He asked God to heal Miriam and remove her sin. God heard his prayer and healed her. She spent an additional week outside the camp to ensure she was healed. You do not want to stand in agreement with the accuser (Satan). God is not seated on that side of the courtroom. Speak to (and about) others with dignity, always remembering their value to God. Show everyone respect, at

---
970 Matthew 23
971 Ephesians 4:15 (MSG)
972 Exodus 15

a minimum, despite your disagreement with their actions, beliefs, or lifestyle. People do not come to salvation because you show them how wrong they are. God's kindness leads people to repentance.[973] Be cautious of looking down on others. You may be right, but your critical spirit makes you wrong. You may feel superior, but your lack of mercy may be a greater sin than the person you are attacking. Don't let the enemy lead you into a critical spirit that hardens you to the heart of God.

One day, a young man (Tim) visited the church. He had been kicked out of several churches, and I sat down with him and listened to his story. He claimed to have a prophetic gift with the ability to recognize the strongholds of sin in others. He shared how his ministry had led him to continually be rejected. I asked him about his manner of sharing his gift and what he felt the ultimate purpose of confronting others was to the kingdom of God. He centered on exposing sin regardless of the cost. I shared how the gifts of the Spirit, including prophecy, were meant to strengthen, encourage, and comfort others and should always be exercised in love. He found it hard to accept any counsel on the use of his gifts, nor could he recognize the strongholds of sin in his own life. I realized I was not really helping Tim, so I prayed for him and arranged a ride home for him with a good friend of mine, Steve. Steve was about five years older than Tim, married, and a very down-to-earth, likeable guy. An hour later, I got an urgent call from Steve. He was agitated and upset thinking about things Tim had told him while they drove home together. "Tim knew every sin in my life!" Steve exclaimed. "He even called out my biggest struggle, greed. He told me I'm going to hell if I don't get my life straightened out!" Tim had thrown him a hand grenade. I spent the next hour calming Steve down, trying to help him understand salvation, God's grace, forgiveness, and a constructive way to use his understanding of his sinful struggles that would help him grow closer to God and mature spiritually. As I look back now, knowing Steve, it strikes me kind of funny. Tim had pulled a negative "Jedi mind trick" on a sincere albeit imperfect believer. Back then, it was not so funny. It illustrates how even good things like spiritual gifts can be damaging to people and the kingdom when they lack love. That is the point of the "love chapter" found in 1 Corinthians 13. Correction, criticisms, and rebukes require humility and love to be edifying.

The Pharisees are an example of righteousness gone wrong (what we call self-righteousness). Jesus repeatedly condemned their sinful heart attitudes.[974] In the scriptural account of the man born blind, the Pharisees interrogated the man about his miraculous healing.[975] The man had enough. Standing up for Jesus, he said, "I don't know whether He's the Messiah or not, but how could someone not from God do such an incredible miracle?" When they heard the man's response, they replied in rage, "You were steeped in sin at birth. How dare you question us?" They assigned his blindness as God's indictment against him and his parents. Interestingly, the disciples had asked Jesus a similar question right before His healing, "Is it this man's sin or his parents' that has left this man blind?" Jesus was quick to answer,

---
973 Romans 2:4
974 Matthew 23:1–36
975 John 9

"Neither. This blindness will be used for God's glory." This healing miracle was a powerful witness in the city, for the man had been blind for forty years and was known by everyone in the city. The Pharisees should have been the first to recognize and welcome the Messiah, but their critical spirits and lust for power blinded them to the truth. Their hard hearts made them blind while the blind man could see. Refuse to use your words to tear others down.

Proverbs 16:27 (NIV)

A scoundrel plots evil, and on their lips, it is like a scorching fire.

Proverbs 17:5 (NIV)

Whoever mocks the poor shows contempt for their Maker; whoever gloats over disaster will not go unpunished.

Proverbs 22:10 (NIV)

Drive out the mocker, and out goes strife; quarrels and insults are ended.

Proverbs 26:2 (NIV)

Like a fluttering sparrow or a darting swallow, an undeserved curse does not come to rest.

Lying

There are six things the Lord hates...a lying tongue.[976]

Thou shalt not lie. The ninth commandment reveals a critical requirement for loving other people. Scripture says, "The enemy is a liar and the father of lies, lies are his native language."[977] He uses deception, his weapon of mass destruction, to manipulate and control. Lies are a very selfish response to life's circumstances. Using deception to get what you want at the expense of someone else is the definition of biblical wickedness. You might be tempted to lie to help you cope with your present struggles. Don't fall for it. Lying will only complicate and amplify your problems. One lie ends up spawning more lies until you end up caught in your own web of deceit. You don't need to make your challenges worse. You need healthy constructive coping mechanisms. Scripture tells the story of Ananias and Sapphira, who donated the proceeds from the sale of a field apparently to win the approval of others.[978] Regrettably, they decided to hold some of the money back for themselves, but wanting to appear more generous, claimed

---

[976] Proverbs 6:16
[977] John 8:44
[978] Acts 5:1–11

they gave everything they earned. Peter asked Ananias for the truth, but he lied. Instantly, he fell dead. A short time later, Sapphira arrived. Peter asked her the same question. Not knowing of her husband's fate, she lied and died as well. Scripture describes lies as the arrow in the bow of the mouth.[979] Lies kill; they are both lethal and self-destructive. You cannot profit yourself with the weapon of the enemy without consequence. You can lie to yourself or others, but God always knows the truth. Eventually, it will become known. Refuse to allow your tongue to be used against you in this manner. You cannot overcome adversity this way.

Proverbs 16:13 (NIV)
Kings take pleasure in honest lips; they value the one who speaks what is right.

Proverbs 17:20 (NIV)
One whose heart is corrupt does not prosper; one whose tongue is perverse falls into trouble.

Proverbs 18:17 (NIV)
In a lawsuit the first to speak seems right, until someone comes forward and cross-examines.

Proverbs 19:5, 9 (NIV)
A false witness will not go unpunished, and whoever pours out lies will not go free. A false witness will not go unpunished, and whoever pours out lies will perish.

Proverbs 21:28 (NIV)
A false witness will perish, but a careful listener will testify successfully.

Proverbs 24:26 (NIV)
An honest answer is like a kiss on the lips.

Proverbs 26:18–19 (NIV)
Like a maniac shooting flaming arrows of death is one who deceives their neighbor and says, "I was only joking!"

Proverbs 19:28 (NIV)
A corrupt witness mocks at justice, and the mouth of the wicked gulps down evil.

---

[979] Jeremiah 9:3

Isaiah 28:15 (NIV)

You boast, "We have entered into a covenant with death, with the realm of the dead we have made an agreement. When an overwhelming scourge sweeps by, it cannot touch us, for we have made a lie our refuge and falsehood our hiding place."

Jeremiah 9:3,5–6 (NIV)

"They make ready their tongue like a bow, to shoot lies; it is not by truth that they triumph in the land. They go from one sin to another; they do not acknowledge me," declares the LORD. Friend deceives friend, and no one speaks the truth. They have taught their tongues to lie; they weary themselves with sinning. You live in the midst of deception; in their deceit they refuse to acknowledge me," declares the LORD.

Malice

There are six things the Lord hates ...a heart that plots evil.[980]

Keep your tongue from evil and malicious speech. Some people spew hate, ridiculing others, mocking, and tearing them down. Often, their hatred is focused on things that people cannot change: their looks, height, hair, color of their skin, race, sex, socio-economic status, religion, and other superficial qualities like weight, speech, mannerisms, etc. Do not allow malice into your spirit. The Scripture says, "Blessed is the one who does not walk in the counsel of the wicked or stand in the way that sinners take or sit in the seat of mockers."[981] Wickedness seeks personal advantage at the expense of others. Some people like to make themselves feel better at the expense of others. They stomp others down with their words to lift themselves up. They ridicule and mock, enjoying the pain they cause. Scripture is clear, "Love does not delight in evil."[982] Do not let cruelty into your heart. Be sensitive about the feelings of others. Some people carry a chip on their shoulder. They look for weaker people to vent their frustration—like an emotional punching bag. Others hold such strong negative opinions about other people or their beliefs, they look for any opportunity to put them down. When these views involve God and religion, it often becomes religious persecution. It has become culturally correct behavior to publicly demean, ridicule, and criticize people of sincere faith. No one should have their sincere religious beliefs mocked, regardless of their religion. Many people feel alone, unimportant, and forgotten in modern society. They can be easy targets. In our social media-centric society, the "Like" wars have left many young people feeling this way. People weaponize likes and dislikes on social media to bully others. Some who

---
980 Proverbs 6:16
981 Psalm 1:1
982 1 Corinthians 13:4–8

have experienced malice become hateful offenders themselves. Do not let meanness, prejudice, or any other form of malice have a place in your heart or speech. You cannot let the enemy infect you with a bitter heart; you must overcome the evil with good (love).[983] When you show love to those who are down, God will lift you up.[984] The power of hateful emotions will not serve you well. It is another weapon of the enemy to ensnare your mind, will, and emotions. Love can set you free and empower you to overcome your struggles.[985] You will feel better, you will nourish the healthy side of your personality, and you will release God's blessings in your life.

Proverbs 17:4 (NIV)

A wicked person listens to deceitful lips; a liar pays attention to a destructive tongue.

Proverbs 19:1 (NIV)

Better a poor man whose walk is blameless than a fool whose lips are perverse.

Proverbs 26:24–26 (NIV)

Enemies disguise themselves with their lips, but in their hearts they harbor deceit. Though their speech is charming, do not believe them, for seven abominations fill their hearts. Their malice may be concealed by deception, but their wickedness will be exposed in the assembly.

Gossip

There are six things the Lord hates ...a false witness who pours out lies [even half-truths].[986]

Gossip is another destructive use of your tongue. Avoid it like the plague. Scripture says, "A gossip separates close friends."[987] Love covers a multitude of sins. Some people cannot wait to share the latest juicy news. People have a fascination with gossip, like gawkers driving by a car accident.[988] Gossipers revel in the attention they get from others by trafficking negative information. Gossip promotes misunderstandings, offense, and conflict. It destroys relationships. In a time of struggle, you need relationships to strengthen your inner being and empower you to overcome. You don't need to exacerbate your problems by promoting conflict. Scripture records the consequences of gossip in the story of Noah.[989] After the flood, in a moment of weakness, Noah became drunk. Not to excuse Noah, but I can only imagine how he felt. It must have been very lonely realizing your family was all that remained of humanity.

---

983 Romans 12:21
984 Matthew 5:7–9
985 1 Corinthians 13:13
986 Proverbs 6:16
987 Proverbs 17:9
988 Proverbs 18:8
989 Genesis 9:20–27

Ham found him naked and passed out. Instead of covering his father, he went to the rest of the family and shared the gossip. Shem and Japheth refused to participate. They immediately rushed to Noah and walking in backward out of respect, covered him. When Noah awoke, he cursed Ham and his offspring but blessed Shem and Japheth. In the first year after the flood, division and strife came to the remaining eight people on earth because of gossip. Gossip has vast destructive power. It truly is the fire of the tongue referenced earlier in Scripture. Do not let the enemy start a fire in your backyard through this trap. Gossip will, at best, complicate your present struggles. Refuse to spread gossip. Be a peacemaker promoting harmony in your circles of influence.[990] The rewards will return to you.

Proverbs 16:28 (NIV)

A perverse person stirs up conflict, and a gossip separates close friends.

Proverbs 17:9 (NIV)

Whoever would foster love covers over an offense, but whoever repeats the matter separates close friends.

Proverbs 18:8 (NIV)

The words of a gossip are like choice morsels; they go down to the inmost parts.

Proverbs 26:20 (NIV)

Without wood a fire goes out; without a gossip a quarrel dies down.

Strife

There are six things the Lord hates ...a person who stirs up conflict in the community.[991]

The enemy uses division as another weapon of mass destruction, especially in groups of people. Don't let the enemy use your words to sow seeds of strife. Scripture clearly shows the origin of quarreling and strife; the selfish desires that war within.[992] You want something and are willing to sacrifice peace to get it. Scripture encourages believers to maintain the unity of the Spirit through the bond of peace.[993] Love is willing to overlook an offense to preserve the community. Scripture states, "Warn a divisive person once, after that have nothing to do with him. You can be sure he is self-condemned."[994]

---
990 Matthew 5:9
991 Proverbs 6:16
992 James 4:1–2
993 Ephesians 4:3
994 Titus 3:10–11

Some people love to stir up trouble. One of its problems: once it starts, it is hard to stop.[995] It takes on a life of its own. God views strife like a cancer in the body of Christ. Don't spread the cancer. Strife is one of the sins that can hinder God's blessing in your life. You can't be close to God and be at war with your neighbor. You especially need to be close to God in times of trouble. The enemy uses quarreling and strife to cause people to hurt one another. If people attack each other, he has less work to do—other people are doing it for him. On top of that damage, strife hinders God's blessings. It's a win-win for the enemy. Everyone else loses when God's people fight each other. When my kids were young, the two oldest came and sat on my lap. They began to fight with each other. I corrected them several times but finally said, "You cannot sit on Dad's lap and keep fighting with each other." I made them get down. Immediately God spoke to my heart and affirmed the same truth for His children. Do not use your speech to promote strife, be a peacemaker.[996] You will strengthen your stand against the enemy by living in peace.

Proverbs 16:28 (NIV)

A perverse person stirs up conflict, and a gossip separates close friends.

Proverbs 17:14 (NIV)

Starting a quarrel is like breaching a dam; so drop the matter before a dispute breaks out.

Proverbs 21:19 (NIV)

Better to live in a desert than with a quarrelsome and nagging wife.

Proverbs 26:17 (NIV)

Like one who grabs a stray dog by the ears is someone who rushes into a quarrel not their own.

Proverbs 27:15–16 (NIV)

A quarrelsome wife is like the dripping of a leaky roof in a rainstorm; restraining her is like restraining the wind or grasping oil with the hand.

Proverbs 24:29 (NIV)

Do not say, "I'll do to them as they have done to me; I'll pay them back for what they did."

---

995 Proverbs 17:14
996 Matthew 5:7–9

SPIRITUAL RESILIENCY

Boasting

There are six things the Lord hates—no, seven things he detests…a proud look [the attitude that makes one overestimate oneself and discount others].[997]

Do not engage in boasting. Boasting overstates your importance relative to others. It makes you feel better about yourself at someone else's expense. Scripture states, "Love does not boast, it is not proud."[998] You don't need to puff yourself up to be important. God already thinks you're important. You are His beloved child. Some people use information to gain power over others. Scripture states, "Knowledge puffs up, but love builds up."[999] Love strengthens others. As you serve, God fills your heart. You feel better about yourself. Love is a win-win. On the other hand, some people think they know everything. They make boastful statements and air their opinions as if their words are more important. God values humility. Scripture says, "God opposes the proud but gives grace to the humble."[1000] Do not think more highly of yourself than you should. It's good to think well of yourself, just not at the expense of others. You don't need to manipulate others to make them think highly of you or make them feel less of themselves. God will take care of your reputation. Let Him lift you up as you follow the example of Jesus, who humbled Himself and took the nature of a servant. The disciples argued about who would be greatest in the kingdom of God. Jesus rebuked them, "If you want to be great in God's kingdom, learn to be the servant of all."[1001] Use your words to serve others, not yourself. Your humility will release God's favor into your situation and will strengthen your relationships with others.

Proverbs 27:2 (NIV)
Let someone else praise you, and not your own mouth, an outsider, and not your own lips.

Proverbs 18:2 (NIV)
Fools find no pleasure in understanding but delight in airing their own opinions.

Use your spiritual disciplines, such as self-control, to restrain your tongue from these negative and destructive behaviors. Your tongue has great power. It can be a weapon to fight the enemy, declaring the Word of God, your faith, and other constructive messages. With it, you can also harm yourself and others. Refuse to play into the schemes of your enemy. Put your life and reputation in God's hands and let Him fight your battles. Do not get drug into verbal exchanges with others that is exactly what the devil wants you to do. You don't have to do his dirty work for him. Flick the safety switch on your tongue when not in use. Do not switch it off until you are ready for positive, healthy, godly, constructive speech.

---
997 Proverbs 6:16 (AMP)
998 1 Corinthians 13:5
999 1 Corinthians 8:1
1000 James 4:6
1001 Matthew 20:26, Matthew 5:7–8

Chapter 5

Use Your Spirit to Strengthen Your Body

Physical training has some value...[1002]

Use your spirit to strengthen your body. Scripture states, "Physical training has some value, but godliness has value for all things."[1003] Take intentional steps to improve your physical health. The physical and spiritual parts of your being are very different, yet holistically inseparable and interdependent. Your spiritual being is primary and eternal. Everything physical proceeds from the spiritual. God created the universe from His spoken word. The Word brought forth life and every aspect of physical creation. God continues to sustain creation by the Spirit.[1004] In the same way, you can find the strength to endure great physical suffering through your spiritual life. Your spiritual disciplines can protect you from things that drain your physical strength such as stress, negative emotions, and addictions. Paul and Silas endured beatings yet sang and praised God while chained in their prison cell.[1005] Their spirits sustained them through severe torture. Your physical health is important to your spiritual life as well. Under normal circumstances, you may find it hard to practice spiritual disciplines when your body is sick or hurting. Before you experience stressful times (or during difficulties), do everything possible to fortify your body so it can support your spiritual focus. Scripture describes how the spiritual dimension is the foundation of life, holding promise for this physical world and the eternal one to come. As you look to the eternal, do not neglect the importance of your physical well-being. Scripture counsels you to steward your physical well-being to the best of your ability.[1006]

At the same time, Scripture teaches life has a far greater purpose than just meeting your physical needs (food, clothing, shelter, etc.) and desires. Jesus instructed His followers not to worry about them, for God knows them and will provide.[1007] If you prioritize your relationship with God, He will take care of your needs, including the physical ones.[1008] This is a great comfort in times of trouble; it can give you confidence and hope. The enemy may fight you for this promise, so you must be prepared to stand on it, proclaim it, and speak to obstacles in the way. For example, sickness is often a weapon of the enemy to oppose the realization of God's promises. Be a good steward of your body but also be ready to speak to

---
1002 1 Timothy 4:8
1003 Ibid.
1004 Hebrews 1:3, Colossians 1:17
1005 Acts 16:22–25
1006 1 Corinthians 6:19–20
1007 Matthew 6:34
1008 Matthew 6:33

the sicknesses in your life to be removed in the same way you speak to any other obstacle. By the stripes of Jesus, you were healed.[1009] If Jesus were on the Earth today, He would be traveling around, doing good, and healing all those under the power of the enemy.[1010] Guess what? He is here, living inside of believers with His resurrection power. You can command sickness to depart in His power in the same way He did.[1011] Your faith in God can radically change your physical condition. Your faith can also change other circumstances in your life.

God created humanity with interconnectedness between spirit, soul, and body. The truth of Scripture is, in Christ, your body is a spiritual temple.[1012] The Spirit of the living God lives within you as a believer.[1013] This is the reason to be a good steward of your body. You are commanded in Scripture to make moral choices that protect both your body and spirit. You should take positive steps to improve your physical health but recognize that obedience to Scripture is the best protection for your health, wholeness, and well-being. Sin is like smoking. It produces a short-term pleasure, but over time it will destroy your health. My grandmother smoked from age fourteen—not uncommon in her day. I remember her coughs and the effects of the smoke ageing her face. Years before she died, she had to push an oxygen tank wherever she went in order to breathe. It doesn't matter what you are smoking, drinking, or shooting into your body—that is not God's best. You have one physical life on this earth. What you do with it determines eternity.[1014] Your physical health, how you treat your body, is a representation of how your moral choices determine your spiritual health. The Apostle Paul reiterated the primacy of spiritual disciplines, but he also affirmed the value of physical training and the efforts made to improve your physical health. While the Christian community tends to emphasize the protective commands of Scripture with the list of *thou-shalt-not*'s, the list of positive steps to fortify the body is just as important. Loving others and living in peace with others are examples of commands that powerfully impact mental and emotional health, relational health, and significantly affect physical health as well. In a day when the culture fails to value Scripture, it is interesting that society continues to emphasize teachings on rest, diet, and exercise clearly noted in Scripture.

Rest

Ensure you get adequate sleep and time off from work. Sleep is essential for health and healing, specifically circulation, hormone production, respiration, metabolism, immunity, thinking, and memory. Foremost in the scriptural emphasis on physical stewardship is the command to rest. The fourth com-

---

1009 Isaiah 53:5
1010 Acts 10:38
1011 John 14:12–14
1012 1 Corinthians 6:19–20
1013 1 Corinthians 3:16
1014 Hebrews 9:27

mandment states, "Remember the Sabbath Day by keeping it holy, on it you shall not do any work."[1015] Keeping the Sabbath holy means to set it apart as a day of rest in the same way God rested from the work of creation. Even Jesus often rested, withdrawing from the crowds to get alone and pray.[1016] You need rest, relaxation, and recreation. Growing up in a farming community, I often heard people say, "All work and no play makes Jack a dull boy." It also makes Jack stressed, burned out, and prone to physical injury. The body needs regular rest. You need enough sleep every day. You need at least one day off from all work every week, whether it be professional or personal labor, and you need time every year to rest and recharge. In the Jewish Old Testament Law, every Sabbath or seventh day was a day of rest. Several holy days (holidays) were set apart every year for public remembrance, celebration, and worship. Three of these involved national gatherings for worship and sacrifice. Every seventh year was a Sabbath year, a year of rest for the people and the land.[1017] Every fiftieth year, the year of Jubilee (after seven Sabbath years), was an additional year of rest for the land and the forgiveness of all debts and indentures. Additionally, the Law required the return of all property sold to pay debts to its original owners.[1018] The point of listing these rules is to illustrate rest for humans and all of creation is very important to God. Rest is not inactivity; it is an intentional, proactive means of healing and restoring your whole being. In Scripture, God promised people would be more productive if they observed His requirements for rest. You reduce your effectiveness and productivity by working when you should be resting. Note the connection between requirements for rest and times of worship. Rest involved a focus on the centrality of God to life, health, and wholeness. Because of Israel's neglect of worship and the Sabbath, God forced the people out of the land until they repaid every unobserved Sabbath year.[1019] As people neglect the spiritual aspect of life, they neglect rest. God knew what He was doing when He prioritized rest. Make sure you get adequate sleep every day, take at least a day off every week, and make time for a vacation. Do not be the person who faces self-inflicted adversity because of burnout. You must regularly recharge to maintain your strength and overcome during times of difficulty.

Proper Diet

Eat foods that fuel your body and keep it healthy. Scripture contains numerous dietary laws.[1020] While these found their root in God's commands for spiritual purity, they also served a practical purpose of protecting the community. We know today that improperly cooking certain foods makes you susceptible to sickness and disease. Many of our popular foods are quick, easy, and taste good but have little nutritional value contributing instead to weight gain and disease. Resist the temptation to make taste the

---
1015 Exodus 20:8–11
1016 Luke 5:16
1017 Leviticus 25:1–7
1018 Leviticus 25:8–55
1019 Jeremiah 25:3–11
1020 Leviticus 11:1–47

sole factor in your diet. What tastes great is not the measure of a healthy diet. I grew up in a farming community where the four food groups were meat, potatoes, bread, and desserts. My favorite meals still contain foods from those four groups. Unfortunately, the way most of those foods are prepared limits their health benefits. While much debate and rancor rage over proper food choices, I appeal to the Scripture and God's original intentions. In the beginning, when God declared creation "very good," He gave humans and animals only plants to eat (specifically seed-bearing plants).[1021] Highly nutritional foods such as fruits and vegetables function as medicine for your body. In fact, eating the right foods: seeds, nuts, vegetables, fruits, and some fish, can help your body fight many diseases including infection, diabetes, and cancer. The right diet can also improve allergies, mood, memory, and brain function.[1022] This is not to say you must be vegetarian; rather, a diet that promotes your physical health requires a large portion of vegetables. God gave Peter a vision declaring all foods clean in the New Testament.[1023] The vision does not propose all foods are healthy, only that they were made permissible to God's followers. New Testament faith proposes all things are permissible to you (you are not under law); however, not all things are beneficial.[1024] God gives you the wisdom to choose what is constructive, profitable, and wholesome. Apply this principle to your dietary choices. This is not meant to over-spiritualize eating or make it legalistic. I consider this a matter of conscience, a decision between you and God. The spiritual life is not about what you eat; it is about righteousness, peace, and joy in the Holy Spirit.[1025]

At a conference I attended, a respected church leader laughingly stated, "Eating is the one thing believers can do and not worry about sinning." It was funny at the time but untrue. You can do many things without worrying about sinning, and you can sin in eating if you are gluttonous.[1026] As a captive and potential leader in Babylon, the king ordered Daniel to eat the delicacies of the Babylonian king's tables. I am sure it was like one of our modern all-you-can-eat buffets. Instead, Daniel asked to eat only raw fruits and vegetables. The king's servants were surprised to find that after ten days, Daniel looked healthier than those who ate from the king's buffet.[1027] This story illustrates what we already know—overeating and eating rich foods is not constructive. Excessive weight damages health and wholeness. Eat healthy foods to provide healthy fuel for your body, not merely for taste. Ensure you prioritize healthy foods like fruits and vegetables, eat high-fat healthy foods in moderation, and limit everything else. Avoid over-processed foods with lots of additives and preservatives. You might think, "That's easy for him to say; he probably loves all those veggies." The truth is ice cream and chocolate chip cookies tie for first on my top favorite foods list, then seafood, meat, potatoes (especially chips), bread, and pasta dishes. Unfortunately, as I grow older, I have found that most of the foods on my list of favorites taste great on

---

1021 Genesis 1:29–30
1022 Your Body Can Heal Itself: Over 87 Foods Everyone Should Eat (Peachtree City, GA: FC&A Medical Publishing, 2008), 326–362.
1023 Acts 10:9–16
1024 1 Corinthians 6:12, 10:23
1025 Romans 14:7
1026 1 John 2:15–17
1027 Daniel 1:8–16

the way down but leave me feeling a little queasy once they are inside. Those experiences have led me to eat more for health than for taste. As a kid, I was often told, "An apple a day keeps the doctor away." I liked most fruits but hated vegetables. Now, I have expanded my diet to prioritize all kinds of fruits and vegetables. A "quick win" for eating is to start the day with a glass of water, eat a low-fat, low-sweet, and low-processed breakfast such as oatmeal, fruits and vegetables, or a smoothie. Fuel your body with lots of water and healthy foods that nourish it without the negative long-term effects. Losing weight will help you feel better physically, will help you feel better about yourself, and will give you the needed energy to face adversity with strength.

Exercise

Keep your body healthy through proper exercise. Paul's recognition of the value of physical training to one's total well-being says it all. The body works best when you regularly use it. In ancient times, much of people's daily routine involved physical exertion: walking long distances, working in agricultural vocations or necessary trades, and household chores. With today's modern conveniences, you may find yourself in a sedentary job and lifestyle. My job requires little physical exertion, primarily using a computer and telephone. A friend recently gave me a book on how to remain youthful through the aging process. The majority of the top ten recommendations included some form of exercise. Exercise is essential to health and wholeness. Paul likened the life of faith to an athletic event and believers as athletes. Through discipline and conditioning, athletes prepare themselves to compete.[1028] They stretch for flexibility, use weights to build strength, and perform aerobic conditioning. In the life of faith, you require these same qualities of resilience: flexibility to adapt to life's difficulties, strength to face spiritual battles, and endurance to stand against evil, overcoming it with goodness (good deeds and a good attitude). Exercise is part of the training required to stay strong. Numerous resources exist online to help you condition your body. An easy place to start is walking. After just two weeks, a twenty to thirty-minute daily walk can help improve your heart, circulation, and mood. Walking is a great start for the "quick wins" discussed in the previous chapter. Work your heart, flex your muscles, and stretch. These will enhance your ability to bounce back. I have found physical exertion, such as lifting weights, running, or bicycling provided me a needed distraction and relief in my body from the stress of my circumstances. Essentially, you're replacing a negative stress with a positive stress. Sweat the negative feelings and their accompanying stress chemicals out of your system with physical activity. Your physical health will help you stand up under hard times and will maximize your motivation and ability to press into the spiritual life. If your difficulty is an illness or health condition that limits exercise, in addition to finding some possible activity to work your body, rest and proper diet will be crucial. You will also have to lean into the other spiritual disciplines to effect change in your health.

1028 1 Corinthians 9:24–27

Breathing

While diet, exercise, and rest are the big three factors you can leverage to improve your health, breathing can be a valuable tool to reduce stress and enhance your performance.[1029] The body's response to feelings of stress can be helpful in reacting to traumatic events, such as fight or flight responses. However, when stress becomes your typical response to normal life events, its physiological symptoms can damage your body and overall health. Breathing exercises can be a powerful tool to ease its effects on your body. Stress reduction skills are an essential part of a larger strategy to increase your inner strength and overcome life's struggles. When you feel the physiological effects of stress, use controlled deep breathing to reduce its impact on your body. Take a slow, deep breath using a ten-second count, fully expanding your diaphragm. At its peak, use a measured ten-second count to exhale all the air from your lungs. Repeat this practice three to five times. You should feel your breathing and heart rate return to normal, and other extreme physiological symptoms of extreme stress subside. You may continue this practice for approximately five minutes to relax your body in more extreme instances. For years, I have used this practice to quickly reduce the effects of stress, such as increased heart rate, stressful emotions, and racing thoughts. I usually follow this quick breathing exercise with prayer and reciting of Scripture. It has proven very effective in taking my thoughts off the problem and reorienting them on God.

Recently, a friend taught a class on drug abuse prevention. She grabbed everyone's interest by saying, "In this class, I will make you feel high." What followed was a breathing exercise. Place the tip of your tongue behind your upper front teeth. Inhale for four seconds, hold it for seven seconds, and exhale for eight seconds. The exercise was repeated four times. I've never been high, so I didn't know if I did it correctly, but I definitely felt better. Numerous breathing techniques can effectively temper physiological reactions to stress. Find one that works for you and be ready to use it when you experience stress. Another breathing exercise that has shown potential for those under extreme stress or coping with a highly traumatic past event is quick breathing, almost like hyperventilating. While seated, take deep but very quick breaths over a period of thirty to forty seconds. Take a fifteen to twenty-second break and repeat for a total period of two to two and a half minutes. If you feel like you are going to pass out, you may need to adjust your technique. Quick breathing is not for everyone, so make sure you are seated and/or safe from falling before you try it. Breathing can also help enhance performance. Before public speaking, competing, or some other type of performance, use a deep breath to calm your nerves and oxygenate your brain. Simply take a deep breath, hold it for a few seconds, and then slowly release it. Believe it or not, many athletes use a yawn before they compete. A yawn helps oxygenate the brain and calm the body. Try it to enhance your performance. Breathing regulation can be a great intervention to reduce stress and protect your body from its harmful effects.

1029 University of Michigan Health, "*Stress Management: Breathing Exercises for Relaxation,*" accessed 02 January 2022, Www.uoFmhealth.org/health-library/uz2255.

Protect Your Body from Self-Destructive Activities

When facing difficulties, some people try to "escape" by engaging in harmful behaviors. A common escape is alcohol and other drugs. I do not believe Scripture commands abstinence from alcohol, although I strongly recommend it. However, Scripture condemns drunkenness and overuse of alcohol.[1030] Supporters of drug and alcohol use like to say that it is harmless. They promote marijuana use as a healthier option than smoking and designate other drugs as recreational. Unfortunately, I have seen the devastation of drug and alcohol use from these "harmless" escape strategies. Alcoholism, physically, emotionally, and financially ravaged my family. I had a front-row seat to the devastation of drug and alcohol abuse. A man high on marijuana killed my great-grandmother in a car accident and severely injured my aunt. Several family members committed suicide while under the influence of drugs and alcohol. I watched marijuana use destroy the lives of childhood friends. These are just some of the physical consequences of addiction; the mental/emotional effects are just as destructive. It is not a pleasant sound to hear a 6-foot 3-inch, 250-pound man whine for beer like a little child. It leaves an impression. Don't attempt to use self-destructive and addictive activities to meet your needs. They are not an ally. Whether drugs, gambling, pornography, sexual immorality, etc., they will take control of your life if you open the door. I know many people who claim they have no addiction problem when it obviously controls their lives. The enemy is a master deceiver who uses your weaknesses against you. The biggest problem with self-deception is you do not realize you are deceived. You must recognize negative influences and master the desires in the same way athletes master their bodies in training. They make their bodies slaves to accomplish their competition goals. If you do not make your body your slave, something else will. Do not open the door to any of these influences. If you have opened the door, shut it, and never open it again. If you are addicted, you must take radical action. Ask God for help, seek a godly support system, get in a program or accountability group, and do whatever else it takes to rid yourself of the influence.

You only get one body. Everything you subject it to will accumulate in an aggregate effect as you age. Things that seem harmless in today's youthful ignorance will reveal themselves in time. If you don't believe me, look at before and after pictures from people's twenty-five-year class reunions. Everything you eat, drink, and ingest in your body will show up later. You will recognize the effects of exercise and rest. I went to my twentieth-class reunion some years back. It was good to catch up with some old friends, but by the time the night was over, my heart just hurt. The same classmates who lived the party life in high school were stumbling around the dining room, running into people in the bathroom hallway, and throwing up in the parking lot. It was a great way to celebrate getting together with old friends. The moral is, what you start in your youth will follow you to the grave if you don't take control. Today is the day to stop taking orders from your body. Every time it wants a snack or to be lazy, you set the agenda.

[1030] Ephesians 5:18, Galatians 5:21, Proverbs 20:1

SPIRITUAL RESILIENCY

Avoid hand and mouth disease by being cautious about what foods you let your hand put in your mouth. Get some exercise, lift weights, do some stretching, and go for a walk. Make sure you turn off the TV or phone and get the rest you need. Your inner being needs a strong body, especially when you are struggling with difficulties. You can also prevent future physical health issues by choices you make today.

Chapter 6

Use Joy to Strengthen Your Being

A merry heart doeth good like a medicine.[1031]

Laugh often. Scripture describes the power of humor in life; it is like a medicine. A friend gave me a sketch of Jesus laughing as a gift. It was weird to think of Jesus that way. I typically think of Him in a sober, serious mood. I have often heard friends say, "God has a sense of humor." I guess we just don't think He laughs at His own jokes. But laughter is important to you and me. We need to rest in the peace and joy of the Spirit. "Don't take yourself too seriously" is an important rule for life. Too many people walk around with a sour attitude and a sour look on their faces. Some Christians act as if a frown is a badge of holiness. Misery is not a fruit of the Spirit. Who wants to know a God whose followers live like that all the time? Joy, humor, and fun provide powerful emotional tools to overcome adversity. One of the powers of joy is its mysterious capacity to be felt amid suffering.[1032] As discussed in the thinking traps section, your best strategy for managing circumstances out of your control may be humor and laughter rather than anger, frustration, and flawed thought processes. Many of the most stressful circumstances in my past have become my funniest stories. If only I had realized that in the moment!

Be joyful. Scripture describes the importance of joy in the return of the Jewish exiles. Ezra read the Scripture to those Israelites who had returned to Jerusalem from captivity in Babylon. As the people heard God's commands, they wept aloud (grieved over their guilt). You might think God would want them to feel ashamed for all the evil they committed in abandoning Him for wickedness and false religion. Instead, Ezra and the priests went through the crowd, encouraging people not to weep for "it was a holy day." They encouraged the people to eat, drink and celebrate with the words, "The joy of the Lord is your strength."[1033] God wanted them to begin their new lives in the land with joy. Many people equate God's holiness with an angry, harsh God. This account shows that holiness is about joy, peace, and freedom. Those are the marks of people who live under God's rule. Your best life begins with God's lordship over it. The exiles faced many stressors as they began their new lives. Joy from God provided the strength to endure their hardships. Joy enables you to bypass the negative emotional effects that can weigh down your mind and discourage positive action. Scripture states, "A merry heart doeth good like a medicine." Sometimes, laughter truly is the best medicine. It lifts the spirit, sends positive chemicals through the body, increases motivation, and encourages action. During adversity, you need that positive energy to move you toward constructive action.

[1031] Proverbs 17:22
[1032] Angela Gorrell, The Gravity of Joy: A Story of Being Lost and Found (Grand Rapids, MI: Wm B Eerdmans, 2021), xvii.
[1033] Nehemiah 8:10

Enjoy this season of life. Solomon, the wisest man who ever lived, wrote in Scripture, "I know that there is nothing better for people than to be happy and do good while they live."[1034] Many people are so intent on pursuing happiness in their life and career they never truly find it. To find contentment in your work is a gift of God.[1035] Ultimately, accomplishments, wealth, and happiness are not the purpose of life. You find purpose in knowing and serving God. When you seek God first, the other things you desire are more likely to come as God blesses.[1036] God will bless you with joy and happiness as you place Him first in your life. Many people live with the thought, "When I get this job, I'll be happy. When I get this promotion, I'll be happy. When I become a company vice president or a partner, I'll be happy." Unfortunately, when they get what they want, the happiness is fleeting, so they look to the next big accomplishment to bring them happiness. By so doing, they live their whole lives largely without it. Multitudes of people look for happiness in their next big accomplishment but never find it. You cannot string a long line of pleasurable moments together to feel good about life. One author on joy wrote, "The majority of our time is spent living on Saturday in the space between death on Friday [Christ's crucifixion] and the indescribable joy of Sunday morning [His resurrection]. It is the space in between."[1037] Faith is all about how you cope with your present sufferings on Saturday before your deliverance comes. Eventually, you will be left alone with yourself and your sufferings/pains/regrets. But you can find joy in life prioritizing your spiritual connection with God. When God is in the right place in your life, you will find joy. It is not just a matter of accepting Christ into your life; long-term joy comes when you let Him lead.

Parents can make a similar mistake, thinking happiness will come in the next stage of life. "I'll be so glad when this kid is out of diapers. I cannot wait until this kid goes to school and I have some time to myself. I'll be glad when my son can drive himself to his games and practices. I'll be so glad when my daughter is off to college and out of the house." Then the parents look back and lament, "I wish I could go back to when they were little! The time flew by so quickly." By always living for the future, they never fully appreciate and live in the moment. Life works in seasons. Enjoy the season you are in because it will pass, and you will never get back there. By nature, happiness is fleeting—it's an emotion tied to the moment. Joy is the inner source of peace and contentment based on your inner condition, not external circumstances. "I can do all things through Christ who gives me strength."[1038]

Promotion, pleasure, wealth, position, fame, power, etc., only provide temporary happiness. Like a drug, they leave you wanting the next fix. If you lack inner joy, you will never find it in these pursuits. You must find contentment in your relationship with God and your place in service to Him. Scripture records how Paul learned this secret to joy, independent of his circumstances. It reflects the recognition in all of Scripture that God just keeps showing up. In truth, God is always with you by His indwelling

---
1034 Ecclesiastes 3:12
1035 Ecclesiastes 3:13
1036 Matthew 6:33
1037 Gorrell, Gravity of Joy, 132.
1038 Philippians 4:11–13

Spirit, but sometimes that presence is felt in a moment of breakthrough where the God who lives within reveals Himself in a special way, like when believers gather for worship. Your natural senses see Him in the beauty of the moment and feelings of peace, joy, and awe. Sometimes, those moments are unexpected, so be ready. This is another important reason to be thankful always. You will face adversities throughout your life. There will also be blessings. Recognize, enjoy, and thank God for the blessings, regardless of the difficulties. Like Paul, as you seek him, you will find strength and joy in God. Solomon wrote, "There is a time for everything and a season for every activity under the heavens."[1039] Enjoy the season you are in, live it to the fullest for God and others. It will probably have some negative aspects. Do not get preoccupied with them. Focus on the positive and enjoy the season so you do not have regrets later. Finding joy in the trials will help you benefit from them.

Find an Oasis In the Desert

Find an oasis (place of refreshing) in your desert times. As discussed above, focus on the positive aspects of your life when you face hard times and search for God's special provision. Scripture records how the Israelites endured harsh conditions in the desert during the exodus from Egypt. After leaving the victory at the Red Sea, they traveled for three days without finding water. When they finally came to water, it was bitter and undrinkable, so they called it Mara. At this point, the people reached their limit and grumbled against Moses.[1040] God healed the water and made it drinkable, using it as an important teaching moment. Sometimes hardships are an "Ah-ha" moment where God reveals Himself in a special way. The next stop in the desert was Elim, a beautiful place of refreshing with seventy palm trees and twelve springs.[1041] The community camped there under the trees with abundant water. Deserts have hidden treasures. Likewise, times of great difficulty hold special blessings from God. One year, my work took me far from home to a hot, remote, desolate location with austere living conditions. It was a difficult situation, but one day as I walked around the area, I stumbled upon an indoor swimming pool. That pool became part of my daily routine. At night after work, I exercised, swam laps, and showered at the pool. It was a great morale booster and became my Elim in a difficult season. Unfortunately, the pool closed about a month after I arrived. I was bummed. I could have gotten stuck mourning the loss of my Olympic-sized indoor swimming pool, but I trusted God to lead me to the next Elim. Look for an oasis in the middle of your desert time. I don't know what it might be—a new friend, a beautiful park, a song, etc.—but I am certain God will bring something into your life to uplift you in your difficulty. God can bring you to an Elim, or He can throw a healing branch into your Mara (bitter waters), restoring something you thought was lost.

1039 Ecclesiastes 3:1
1040 Exodus 15:22–24
1041 Exodus 15:27

SPIRITUAL RESILIENCY

Another way to find joy in difficult times is to find a new hobby or source of recreation. It is helpful to have a healthy, constructive activity for fun and distraction. Just as you may find it necessary to distract your mind with mental activities, it is important to have physical activities to change your frame of mind. I spent several years in an intense, structured academic environment. It was extremely stressful and seemed like it would last forever. One of the administrators asked our class, "How do you eat an elephant?" The answer, of course, is "one bite at a time." I found ways to brighten my routine. I regularly stopped by our chapel's office to grab a soda, snacks and get to know other people needing encouragement. I became a Sunday school teacher, joining the teaching team each week. I faithfully attended church and midweek Bible study. These activities became bright spots in my week that I looked forward to with anticipation. After the first year, I became involved in horseback riding. I had fond memories of having horses as a young child, so I got actively involved. Riding, taking care of the horses, and enjoying the change of scenery off campus became my new hobby. In truth, God used horseback riding to bring a lot of joy and good to my life in a difficult time. It also provided opportunities to serve Him. You never know how God will show up in your hard times. It may not be as elaborate as horses or a swimming pool but expect Him to provide blessings. At the same time, look for opportunities to serve God and others. God can use every hobby and recreational activity to encourage, help, and bless others. As you open yourself up to new opportunities and service, you will find strength in unexpected places and see God reward your obedience.

Joy is an action, a byproduct of faith. When you know God, know He is a giver of good gifts, and a helper in times of trouble your heart is buoyed. You feel lighter in the storms. Joy is an expectation for good things to come your way and a willingness to watch for them, welcome them, and embrace them in the moment. It walks hand in hand with gratitude. Some people get so soured by their struggles they treat the moment of blessing with cynicism or miss it altogether. Some people, by their behaviors, take a "yes" and make it a "no." They miss out on the small but powerful blessings that provide an updraft for open wings. Be watchful, open, and take steps to discover God's hidden treasures in the middle of the struggles. Enjoy the season you're in, not because everything is going perfect, but because you know who walks with you. Those who wait upon the Lord (the spiritually resilient) will renew their strength. They will rise on wings like eagles.

Chapter 7

Build Connections with Others

Pity the one who falls and has no one to help him up.[1042]

Invest in supportive relationships in your life. You need other people to strengthen you when you face struggles. The power of relational support is what makes the social dimension an important pillar of resilience. Encouragement from others will help strengthen your resilience and increase your emotional health. Like sheep, we are "people of the flock." You need others to thrive. Studies show that those with a larger social network, at varying levels of closeness, demonstrate a greater capability to endure hardship.[1043] On the other hand, loneliness is a key risk factor, especially with health issues. God gives you His Spirit, your Counselor and Advocate, to make Jesus' name Emmanuel— "God with us"—a daily reality. You are never alone. God will never leave you nor forsake you.[1044] He gives you another gift as well—His people, commanded to live in *koinonia*, the Greek word for sacrificial friendship and fellowship. God knows you cannot go it alone. He always planned that you should have an unconditionally loving community to share the ups and downs of life. One of the Greek words used to describe love in the Bible, *philos*, describes the mutually supportive, sharing (give and take) love of friendship. The body celebrates together and cries together. Life brings both good and bad, but believers never have to walk alone. Part of the responsibility is on you to find a biblically based community that loves God, loves people, and will love you. The other half of the responsibility is for you to be a selfless, loving member who will do the same for others. The strategies in this chapter can help you strengthen your relationships. A faith community presents an important opportunity to develop them.

In addition to faith communities, look for encouraging people in your present social circle. Draw mature encouragers closer to you. Encouragement is an important spiritual gift God gives people to support others, especially in times of trouble. Invest time to get to know them better and share your burdens with those who are willing and able to walk with you. Apply these same principles to those with the spiritual gifts of wisdom and intercession. You cannot have too many people praying for you.

You may find that some of your present friendships drag you further into discouragement or set you up for moral failures. Exercise the principle of "multiplication by subtraction" to move unhealthy and destructive relationships to the fringes of your relational circle. The Scripture warns, "Do not be

---
[1042] Ecclesiastes 4:10
[1043] Steven M. Southwick, Lauren Sippel, and Robb Pietrzak, "Why are Some Individuals More Resilient than Others: The Role of Social Support," *World Psychiatry*, Feb: 15(1) 77–79, 2016, accessed February 25, 2023, Https://www.ncbi.nlm.nih.gov/pmc/articles/PMC4780285/.
[1044] Hebrews 13:5

deceived, bad company corrupts good character."[1045] Some people will use your friendship to drag you into their self-destructive behaviors. You cannot afford to add the weights of other people's poor choices when you are trying to overcome your own. Lifeguards train to protect themselves from being drowned by the persons they are trying to save. At some point in your life, you will return to lifeguard status and will be strong enough to help others. If you're at a low point in your life or overwhelmed by struggles, this is not your time. Non-swimmers never get sent into the water to rescue drowning people. Make sure your relationships are healthy and constructive. Invest in existing positive relationships and look to develop new relationships to increase your number of mutually supportive friendships.

You need close relationships to strengthen your resilience and overcome hard times. Vulnerability in sharing your needs with others (mature persons capable of supporting you) is worth the risk. If you do not have deep friendships, intentionally seek out experiences to meet new people and develop friendships. Social media is not a replacement for true friendship. Those who relate solely on social media are losing or never developing the emotional intelligence and other social skills necessary to form strong friendships. This is evident in the way people relate in the virtual world. People are quick to take offense, quick to air their opinions, and quick to ridicule others. Scripture states the opposite, "Everyone should be quick to listen, slow to speak, and slow to anger."[1046] Scripture has over four hundred "one another" verses of counsel for treating others with respect, dignity, and love. You are hard-wired for community, finding a purpose in serving outside yourself. An effective way to make friends is to be a friend. Seek to deepen authentic relationships with others, especially those who reinforce your spiritual beliefs and values.

The pandemic made building relationships more challenging. Experts wrongly coined "social distancing" as the magic bullet in fighting COVID-19 and other infections. "Physical distancing" is the proper term to describe the behavior medical experts seek to encourage. Social isolation is one of the worst solutions when you are facing difficulties and uncertainty. People need connection and community. An important aspect of the Christian faith is the familial connectedness with brothers and sisters in Christ. A spiritual bond forms between you and God at salvation that becomes a triangle in your relationships. The bonds require believers to share God's love with others. The faith calls you to love everyone, but a few will walk with you through the hard seasons of life. You need a few close friends for mutual support and other friends who can encourage you through life's challenges.

1045 1 Corinthians 15:33
1046 James 1:19

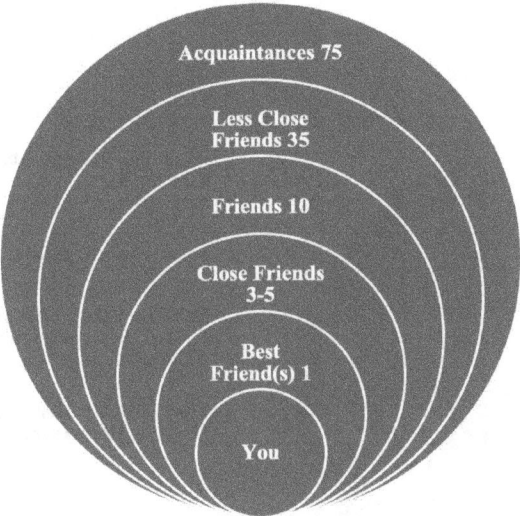

**Figure 7a.
Network of Supportive Relationships**

A counselor once shared the average person needs twenty-four supportive relationships to help overcome adverse life events. The figure above shows numbers of friends in each level of relationship that a healthy adult can maintain.[1047] One study shows that adults with four to five friends enjoy the highest levels of satisfaction, and those with three are close behind. If you have one person considered a best friend, satisfaction in life is significantly higher than those who do not.[1048]

What does your social network look like? Can you visually graph your social circle? As an example, consider David's social network. David had six hundred loyal warriors who followed him through numerous battles and the exile he faced from King Saul's court. They were faithful through the many years Saul and his army sought his life. Inside his community, David had thirty mighty men known for the great exploits they performed on his behalf.[1049] Of those thirty, three had a special place in his inner circle. They carried the special title, "The Three." Of his warriors, the most dependable, capable, and closest to him was called Chief of the Three. David's best friend was Saul's son, Jonathon, who supported him in several critical moments of his life. David also listened to the counsel of his wives, who provided wisdom and support through difficult events in his life. If we chart David's social network, we recognize a significant web of support at various levels of relationship.

[1047] Kate Leaver, "How Many Friends Do We Need to Be Happy," accessed October 13, 2021, www.google.com/amp/amp.abc.net.au/article/everday/12589694. Based on Research by Dr. Robin Dunbar, Oxford.
[1048] Suzanne Degges-White, "How many Friends Do You Need in Adulthood?" accessed October 13, 2021, https://www.psychologytoday.com/us/blog/lifetime-connections/201908/how-many-friends-do-you-really-need-in-adulthood.
[1049] 2 Samuel 23

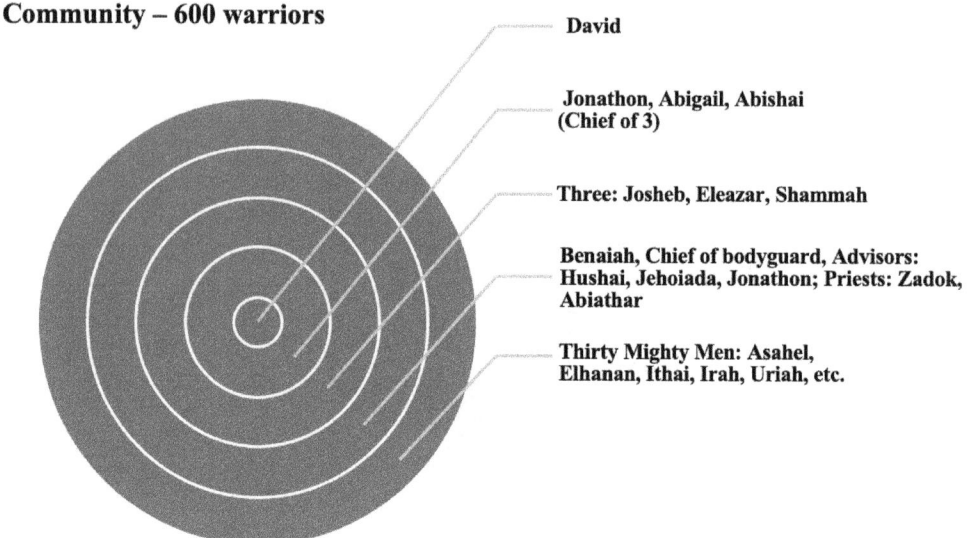

**Figure 7b.
David's Social Network**

You only have so much time, energy, and effort to sustain your most intimate relationships. Some have illustrated this concept with toy Legos. Most Legos have four to six connection points. In the same way, you have a limited capability to sustain your closest relationships. David had three to four in his closest circle. However, you can expand your network through those connected to those close to you. David connected closely with the Three (Josheb, Eleazar, and Shammah) and their Chief (Abishai) but was also connected closely to the Thirty Mighty Men through the supportive influence of the Three. In turn, the Thirty helped David wield influence over his six hundred warriors. Relationships are mutually supportive. David was able to positively impact his inner circle, his succeeding relational rings (The Three and Thirty), and, ultimately, his community (600 warriors) through encouragement, leadership, wise counsel, and direction. His military prowess, combined with the legendary feats of his inner circle, gave him extraordinary influence. It is human nature to love winners. Victory gives people momentum and exponential influence. In the hard times, as David found, you distinguish between those in your circle who truly care about you and those who are along for their personal benefit.

Do not expect to find the perfect community, family, workplace, or faith community. Even Jesus did not have one. The disciples were a mixed bag of victories, frustrations, joys, and sorrows. That is the experience for all human beings in this world as we seek to live out the character and mission of God. Remember, the same things you need in others: unconditional love, friendship, mercy, sharing, joy, grace, trust, and commitment are the same things others need from you. Spiritual community is an airplane constructed in flight. You create it while you're walking through the joys and sorrows of life. It is a learning organization and living organism shaped and growing through the joy of victories and the agonies of defeats. Some get disillusioned because their faith community failed them. Judas wanted Jesus to liberate his fellow Jews from Roman oppression. He expected a conquering hero Messiah who would rule an earthly political kingdom. When he realized Jesus had a different vision, he quit. Judas gave up on Jesus, but Jesus never gave up, even when His disciples betrayed Him. You learn mercy and forgiveness, how to be a better teammate through disloyalty.

People today demand justice. As a society, we absolutely need to treat all people with dignity and respect. Treat others the way you want to be treated. However, I will confess; when I do wrong, I want mercy. I don't want justice (what I deserve). I want a break. It is unfair to demand justice when people do you wrong but seek mercy when you fail others. Relationships require you to expect the best but to readily give mercy when they fail. Do not get cynical and disillusioned when people fail you. Use it as an opportunity to show them the love that Jesus showed His friends. In extreme cases, a relationship may be so toxic (abusive, a person who leads you into illegal or destructive behaviors, or strongly opposes your new spiritual direction) that you may need to distance yourself from them. Bad company can derail you.[1050] Sometimes multiplication happens by subtraction when you separate from a friend who refuses to change their behaviors.

Don't be discouraged by betrayal. Jesus was God in the flesh, lived a perfect, sinless life, and was empowered by the Spirit beyond understanding, yet He was betrayed by most of His inner circle. Judas betrayed Him for a year's wages, Peter denied knowing Him three times, and all but one of the remaining disciples scattered at His arrest. The happy conclusion to this story is that all but one of His twelve disciples (Judas) was restored. Consider Jesus' social circle more closely. Jesus had a best friend, John, who described himself "as the one Jesus loved."[1051] Of the twelve, Jesus had three in His inner circle: Peter, James, and John, who traveled with Him to the Mount of Transfiguration and stayed closest to Him in the Garden of Gethsemane. He had twelve disciples who traveled everywhere with Him, the core leaders of His followers. He had others who were especially close: Mary, his mother, Lazarus, Martha, and Mary, and others as well. Of the thousands who followed Him in His earthly ministry, five hundred were present when He ascended, including His brothers who finally believed. They formed the core of His community, later known as the church, who gathered for prayer, sought the outpouring of the Holy Spirit, and were determined to carry His mission and message throughout the earth. It is important to recognize Jesus did not pray alone on the final night before His crucifixion. He brought His disciples, keeping Peter, James, and John close to Him as He prayed. I am sure they felt bad they fell asleep when Jesus needed their support the most. Since Jesus had a community and close social circle, it is probably

---
[1050] 1 Corinthians 15:33
[1051] John 13:23

essential that every one of us have one. Being alone is dangerous. In nature, herd animals find safety together. Predators separate one from the herd and then attack. The enemy uses a similar tactic. We need friends when we go to our Gardens of Gethsemane, facing our trials and tribulations, so we are not alone.

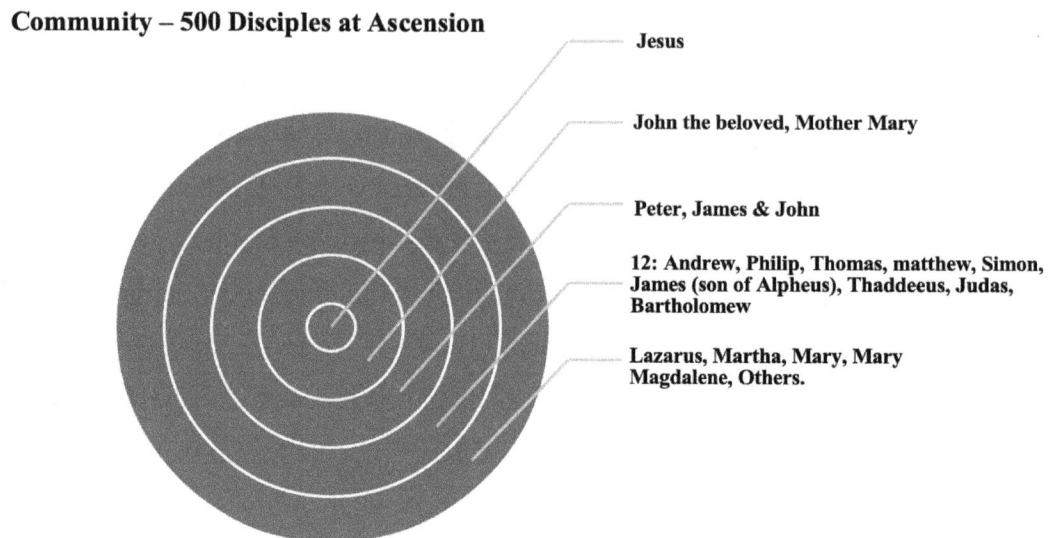

**Figure 7c.
Jesus' Social Network**

What does your community look like? Draw it in a series of concentric relational circles like the one above. What do you need to do to make your social support system stronger?

Throughout my life, I have been blessed with godly people who invested in me: Sunday school teachers like Don, JoAnn, and Freda, church members who showed encouragement and kindness like Johnny, Wayne, and Elmer, mentors like Paul, Frank, Scott, Randy, and Walt, and friends like Mark, Randy, and Bill. These individuals, along with many others, provided support and encouragement in the difficulties I faced. I experienced some of the best of the Christian community as a child and young man. Members regularly encouraged me in my faith and spoke positive words over my future. During times of difficulty, such as the loss of our house to fire, members gave generously to help our family get back on our feet. Their interest and encouragement helped me through many of the normal struggles young people face. As a church leader, I always had mentors who provided encouragement and counsel when I faced important decisions. I shared some of those stories. Friends, built through years of mutual friendship and support, significantly helped me in my hard times. My life has been filled with ups and downs, seasons of blessing, and seasons of loss. I'm sure you have experienced the same. People don't always know what you're going through and how deeply it is affecting you. This is one of the reasons why taking time to build connections with others is so important. I am not the outgoing, life-of-the-party type of person. I prefer to keep personal information private. If you're like me, it takes effort to build close relationships. I am very thankful that I made the effort to let people into my life. God used them to be a powerful support system through the many difficulties I faced, including some serious tragedies. You may not always want to make friends, but you need them. In David's life, in my life, the encouragement and support of others provided incredible power.

How to Build Connection with Others
Live by the "One Another" Commands

Relationships require healthy interactions. You can strengthen the quality of your relationships by following the "one another" commands of Scripture. Numerous commands reveal how to treat others with respect and value (aka love). They are called the "one another" commands because they contain the phrase "one another" in the body of the passage. These character qualities are essential for building and maintaining strong healthy relationships. The first is the "be" list of commands, how to "be toward one another."

Be Humble	Be Compassionate	Be Loving
Be Patient	Be Forgiving	

An attitude of care and concern for the feelings of others is essential for building strong relationships. Like most things in life, attitude is the largest part. Scripture advises you to have the same attitude as Jesus, who, although He was divine, did not try to force people to acknowledge His divinity. He humbled Himself and served humanity.[1052] He demonstrated the value of each person by laying down His life. On the cross, He continued to evidence this attitude by forgiving those who crucified Him. In all these things, He showed His love and concern for people. Jesus is the best example of a loving attitude.

The second list of "one another" commands is the "do" list, behaviors and practices that show others they are important, valued, and loved.

Live in Peace toward	Greet	Comfort
Honor	Serve	Encourage
Live in Harmony with	Carry the Burdens of	Spur on
Build Up	Submit to	Confess Your Sins to
Accept	Prefer	Practice Hospitality toward

These actions clarify how to love one another. Love is selfless; it is other-focused. If you temper your interactions with selflessness and humility, you will strengthen your relationships and create fertile ground for a mutually loving respectful relationship. Love never fails.[1053] What a profound statement.

1052 Philippians 2:5–11
1053 1 Corinthians 13:8

Perhaps more significant is the statement that follows. "Now these three remain: faith, hope and love. But the greatest of these is love."[1054] Love is the most powerful force in the universe. Love is eternal. When everything else has passed away, its power and influence will continue. Loving deposits you make in others will last forever. Love covers a multitude of sins.

Love is far more than a feeling; it is a set of selfless behaviors that enrich others' lives. It communicates that you value the other person, will do your part to keep the relationship safe, and are committed to the other person's well-being. In unhealthy relationships, a person may abuse another person but then state, "I love you. I'm sorry you made me hurt you." The abuser may emotionally feel an attachment they call love, but their behaviors are not love. Perfect love does no harm.[1055] As imperfect people, we struggle to love perfectly. But abuse is below the measure of imperfect love. It is common to hear today, "Love just isn't enough." This statement directly opposes Scripture. Love, as a feeling, will always be incomplete as it is self-focused. However, scriptural love is a commitment to the right thing (in God's eyes) towards another person, to value them in your actions. When your actions follow this definition of love, it is always enough.

Love strengthens both persons in the relationship. It fights for the win-wins, for mutual benefits. Loving relationships start with honoring one another, treating people with respect and dignity, preferring another person's needs in the way you prefer your own, accepting each other, and submitting to one another. Loving relationships are not a form of power politics. They are safe, characterized by peace, harmony, and forgiveness. Loving relationships are supportive, encouraging, building each other up and spurring one another on in hopes and dreams. And finally, people in loving relationships help one another; they serve, practice hospitality, carry each other's burdens, and comfort one another. Relationships are mutual loving bonds of give and take that respect personal boundaries.

The final list of "one another" commands is the "don't do" list, behaviors and practices forbidden in relationships with others.

Do Not Judge	Do Not Take Revenge on	Do Not Grumble against
Do Not Lie to	Do Not Slander	

Allowing these behaviors to dominate your relationships is to allow selfishness to control. Selfishness is inherently destructive to relationships. Some of these behaviors make your wants more important than God, such as taking revenge and judging. The other behaviors are patently disrespectful. They push others down so you can get ahead. Picture holding someone underwater. That's the essence of selfishness. Scripture condemns it as wickedness. Wickedness forces someone to suffer loss so you can get what you want. If you let God handle matters of justice, He will defend and advocate for you. Selfish

---
[1054] 1 Corinthians 13:15
[1055] 1 Corinthians 13:4–8

vengeance not only harms your spirit of love and mercy, it prevents God from working for you in the situation. You don't need to manipulate to get what you want in a relationship. Trust God to provide. He knows what you need. You do not need to make others feel worse so you can feel better. Let the Word of God renew your mind and refresh your spirit. God lifts those who humble themselves. The arrogant and the wicked who reject Christ will ultimately be made low. Pray for them. If you truly knew how bad God's justice (hell) really is, you would not wish it on your worst enemies.

Smile at Others Often

Use smiles to strengthen yourself and your relationships. Because your smile makes people think of you as more courteous, likable, and attractive, it facilitates the building of relationships. Smiling also helps you feel better, releasing feel-good chemicals like dopamine, endorphins, and serotonin that also serve as natural pain relievers.[1056] Smiling can make life more pleasant for those around you, even predicting the level of fulfillment in your marriage. One British researcher found evidence that smiling creates more pleasure in the brain than eating chocolate.[1057] As a recovering chocoholic, I find that hard to believe, but researchers claim that even a forced smile can boost your mood. Sometimes people will not smile back; this should not detract from the practice. Make it a point to smile at everyone you meet. Consider it a means of serving others. A smile sends a warm, friendly message indicating concern and approval. You never know what struggles a person is facing. You can make encouraging others a mission by smiling often, making yourself feel better, and lifting others in the process.

Strengthen Your Family Relationships

Your family is your first layer of community, the primary communication of God's love, and the impartation of generational legacy. Family is such an important social relationship; it is considered a separate dimension of resilience. The family unit is where people learn, model, and teach love, mercy, communication, and other key values and behaviors. In your family unit, you learn both leadership and followership. Healthy family units are critical to the production of healthy individuals. While no family unit is perfect, it should be loving. Perhaps your family was unsafe and destructive. Your challenge is to promote health, love, and sharing in your family as an adult. As most family benefits are caught, not just verbally taught, your example is the key means of reinforcement. Your marriage relationship and relationships with your children or blended family are as critical for you as for them. Your family is a supportive platform for your own well-being as well as every member's. Many people report that family

---

[1056] Ronald E. Riggio, *"There's Magic In Your Smile: How Smiling Affects Your Brain,"* accessed February 26, 2023, Https://www.psychologytoday.com/us/blog/cutting-edge-leadership/201206/there-s-magic-in-your-smile.
[1057] Meg Selig, *"The 9 Superpowers of Your Smile,"* accessed March 27, 2023, https://www.psychologytoday.com/us/blog/changepower/201605/the-9-superpowers-your-smile.

relationships are a major contributor to their present struggles. Family investment is always a good and healthy objective. I once heard a professor restate Jesus' words from Mark 8:36, "What does it profit a man to gain the whole world and lose his [family]?" In over thirty years of ministry, I have never heard anyone near the end of life wish they had worked more. I have heard many express regrets they had not spent more time with their family.

David loved his family, provided for them, and cared deeply about their well-being. His love is evident in Scripture. David followed his wife's counsel on several occasions. After he became king, his sons were royal advisors. While we examined David's close circle of friends at the time of the raid on Ziklag, we also see the fruit of David's investment in his family later in his life. However, David also failed his family on several occasions. One of the refreshing characteristics of the Bible is its portrayal of the victories and failures of great heroes of the faith. The Bible isn't propaganda providing a deceptive characterization for public promotion. Only God is perfect and faultless. David failed to understand some of the relational dynamics among his children on several occasions, failed to address his sons' sinful behaviors resulting in murder and civil war, committed adultery, and acted in selfish pride. Yet David continued to be identified as a man after God's own heart due to his humility, repentance, and sincere devotion. You can learn from David and many others who have gone before. Consider some of the following practices to invest in your family relationships.

The Three Most Important "Three-Minutes" of Every Day

Communication is the key to relationships. You have probably heard the old axiom, "Timing is everything." Put those two thoughts together, and you can identify the importance of having positive interactions during three key moments every day. The three most important moments for members of your family are the first three minutes after they wake up, the three minutes when you reunite after work or school, and the last three minutes before they go to bed. Take advantage of these three moments every day to build loving interactions with your family members. Start the day with encouragement. When everyone comes back together after school or work, talk about what happened during the day. Use active listening to demonstrate your interest. Bedtime is a great time to communicate your love, their importance, and to share anything that wasn't discussed earlier. I encourage you *not* to use these three moments to confront or correct. These moments are reserved to communicate, love, value, and other positive talk. Make them as positive and encouraging as possible.

Active Listening

One of the important disciplines of relationships is to practice being present with the ones you love while spending time together. A common mistake is to be on your phone when someone needs your quality time. The dinner table, restaurant and family outings should be "no phone" zones. Your face in your phone could be sending messages you do not mean to communicate. Even without your phone, it's possible to be thinking about something else when someone you love is trying to share something important with you. You can do extensive damage to your relationships by not valuing the moment. Active listening is the practice of staying engaged in the conversation by verbally acknowledging the importance of what you have heard and non-verbally engaging with your body language and posture. Many times, people say nothing or very little when a loved one is sharing something very important. This sends the message that what was shared (or who is sharing) is unimportant. That is often unintentional, but over time, your loved ones will stop sharing important information with you because they feel you do not care. I confess that I have seen this dynamic play out in my family. It was grievous to realize I was pushing my family away by my inattentiveness. For several years, I have placed greater effort into listening and succeeded in making gains in restoring trust. Active listening involves asking questions to expand on what was shared and provides an emotional response to demonstrate that you are engaged, interested, and concerned. Strengthen your relationships by listening to understand, engaging your full attention, emotionally responding to the information shared, and by asking questions to demonstrate concern and interest.[1058]

Say "I Love You" Often

Your family members need to know that they are important to you. Saying "I love you" is an important way to communicate you care. Three simple words, communicate value, commitment, and affirmation. Every person brings insecurities to their relationships. In truth, even adults require childlike affirmation of their value. Make the people you care about feel more secure, confident, and important to you. People should not have to wonder. They should feel a measure of predictability in your love toward them and in the way you communicate. Some people undermine their family relationships by having inconsistent and explosive reactions, using harsh, demeaning language, and relying on physical intimidation. They diminish relational intimacy and destroy self-worth and confidence. They may treat people at church with boundless patience and kindness only to go home and vent their frustrations on their family members. It is meaningless to say "I love you" to compensate for bad behaviors. Ensure you demonstrate those three powerful words in actions first. Then, use "I love you" often to promote health

---

[1058] CSU Global, *"What is Active Listening? 4 Tips for Improving Communication Skills,"* accessed February 25, 2023, Https://csuglobal.edu/blog/what-active-listening-4-tips-improving-communication-skills.

in the people you love and strengthen your relationships. Look for opportunities to say it multiple times per day.

Be Generous with Hugs

Physical touch is another powerful tool to communicate love and value to your family. Physical touch can communicate when you do not have the right words. Experts have found that physical touch is essential for the emotional and physical health of infants. Studies show that infants denied nurturing physical touch experienced devastating consequences in their development.[1059] Humans never grow out of the need for loving touch. It is the primary means some people know they are loved. The love languages described by Gary Chapman are needs for all people but are especially important for those who hold physical touch as their primary or secondary way of hearing they are loved.[1060] Hug your family members often! They need to feel you love them.

Strengthen Your Marriage Relationship
Have Fun Together, Respect Each Other Always

God intended your marriage to be a safe place of mutual connectedness, a safe and secure foundation from which you can launch into the world with confidence and security. Keep your marriage a source of strength by regularly investing in your relationship. Relationships need time and attention to thrive. Your efforts to strengthen connection can make your marriage a source of great strength in times of trouble. On the other hand, a bad marriage can add significant stress and burdens to your already difficult circumstances. Healthy marriages grow through small daily investments. A spiritual mentor of mine—an older, respected man—shared two keys to success in his marriage. "My wife and I never go to bed angry, and we always try to have fun together." The first key is right out of Scripture.[1061] It directly relates to our "Three most important three-minutes of the day" relationship-builder exercise described above. If you go to bed angry, you will wake up having stewed over the offense all night long, affecting the start of your next day. Two of your most important three minutes of the day may be affected. When you start the day in anger, you have proverbially "gotten up on the wrong side of the bed." Your disposition has been fouled from the start, and you now face an uphill climb to turn your attitude in a positive, constructive direction. Your disposition can potentially affect your interactions all day long.

The second key—having fun together—is essentially engaging the power of laughter in your relationship. Relationships are about sharing life together, the give and take of meeting the needs of your

---

1059 Ann E. Bigelow, and Lela Rankin Williams, "*To Have and to Hold: Effects of Physical Contact on Infants and Their Caregivers*," accessed February 25, 2023, Https://www.ncbi.nlm.nih.gov/pmc/articles/PMC7502223/#__ffn_sectitle.
1060 Gary D. Chapman, *The Five Love Languages* (Chicago: Northfield Publishing, 2010), 14–16,18.
1061 Ephesians 4:26

spouse and vice versa. The more you give, the more deposits you make in the emotional bank account of your relationship. Having fun together is a great way to make deposits and remind your spouse of the value you place on them and the relationship. A sizable relational balance means you can make withdrawals as you need when you have struggles. Problems typically arise when couples selfishly focus on making their needs the primary goal. In this mindset, little emphasis is placed on making deposits. If you constantly make withdrawals, your relational account will end up in the negative. Like banks, people will only extend so much credit in your relationship before they cut you off. Your relationship will sour, and your spouse will become distant. Commit to making deposits in your marriage every day. Having fun together with lots of laughter is a great way to increase the balance in your relational account.

Treating your spouse with respect is another great way to make deposits in your relationship. Disrespect can make huge withdrawals. From my experience, most married couples do more damage to their relationship by disrespect than any other issue. The key is to evaluate your daily interactions with your spouse. Assess your attitude. Are you glad and thankful for your spouse? Do you think of your spouse as irritating and frustrating? Your attitude will set the tone for your speech and color your interactions. Make a point to selflessly love your spouse the way God loves you.[1062] Feeling loved is especially important to women in a marriage as they receive their sense of value, worth, and affirmation through the feelings of love and nurture. In my experience, women tend to describe their marital problems as a lack of felt love. Are you listening to show true concern? Are you attempting to communicate value in your interactions? Is your speech demeaning or degrading? Do you celebrate the victories of your spouse? Do you share sympathy when your spouse is sad? Do you show respect in the way you relate and speak to one another? Men are especially sensitized to disrespectful speech because their primary need in a marriage is honor and respect. Men tend to describe their marital problems as some form of disrespect. It's interesting that men are often tempted to sin against their wives by dominating rather than nurturing them. In the same way, women are tempted to manipulate and control their husbands rather than respect them and support their leadership. These types of sins in marriage make significant withdrawals. You can disagree, solve problems, and resolve conflict with mutual respect. Commit yourself to the discipline of respecting your spouse in every circumstance.

A wise approach to strengthening your marriage is to consider what your spouse needs to remain in love. Become aware of your spouse's most intimate needs and learn to meet them.[1063] Generally speaking (not exclusively), a wife cannot do without affection, intimate conversation, honesty and openness, financial support, and family commitment. A husband cannot do without sexual fulfillment, recreational companionship, an attractive spouse, domestic support, and admiration.[1064] The challenge for most couples is they rarely share the same list. Therefore, each partner must commit to provide for the other's

---

1062 Ephesians 5:21–33
1063 Willard F. Harley, Jr., *His Needs Her Needs: Building an Affair-Proof Marriage* (Grand Rapids, MI: Fleming H. Revell, 2002), 17.
1064 Harley, *His Needs Her Needs*, 18–19.

intimate needs. We discussed general needs from Scripture that address a wife's need for affection (felt love) and a husband's need for admiration (respect). The point here is that a deeper dive into the intimate needs of you and your spouse is the best way to live out your marriage commitment with feelings of love. The challenge for most couples is creating the space for a safe and honest conversation about how these needs can be met more fully. A great action step is to have an annual check-up conversation. Surveys that help you understand your level of need satisfaction are available to assist.

You need your spouse. God gave you a life partner to bless your life. He who finds a wife (or husband) finds a good thing.[1065] Married people live longer and have a greater quality of life. Make your marriage a partnership of love and respect.[1066] Focus on serving one another and stay connected by regular loving communication. You make powerful investments by relating with respect (don't go to bed angry) and by laughing and having fun together. These keys will help you build a great marriage. Continually re-commit to your spouse and determine to make your marriage relationship the very best. Except in extreme cases of abuse or gross sin, you will find more blessing in restoring your marriage than replacing your spouse. Divorce and remarriage can easily become just another selfish attempt to get what you think you need or want. People move from partner to partner, trying to find a person who can perfectly meet their expectations, never dealing with their own issues. God uses marriage to shape character. You cannot make marriage or remarriage work with a selfish focus. Marriage is inherently selfless and redemptive (character-shaping). Your life will be significantly improved by investing in it.

Your strength during hard times is dependent upon solid relationships: first with God, second with your family, and finally with others. Never try to face difficulties alone. A strategy of the enemy is to isolate you from God and others. Include others in your life and be vulnerable enough to include them in your struggles. Some people may disappoint but refuse to become jaded. Continually investing in healthy relationships will bring important returns, providing you added strength during hard times that enables you to overcome.

1065 Proverbs 18:22
1066 Ephesians 5:33

Chapter 8

Set Goals and Make Plans

Commit to the LORD whatever you do, and your plans will succeed.[1067]

Planning and goal-setting are ways of expanding control of your situation. God has given you a significant measure of control over your life through the power of choice. But difficulties have a way of making you feel helpless, hopeless, and, ultimately, powerless. You can take back control by intentionally engaging in a planning and decision-making process. These strategies do not have to push God out of the process. It is an error to exclude God and the counsel of His Word from your choices. You can submit your plans to the teachings of Scripture and the leading of the Spirit. God cautions those who make plans without any consideration of His will.[1068] Some experiences are outside your control—hurricanes, pandemics, and the actions of others, to name a few. But many circumstances can be improved by your choices. Don't surrender your right to make a difference. Don't give in to the hopelessness that can follow a season of difficulty. Start with small, positive steps and build toward life changes that can improve your situation. Some argue that planning is a waste of time, as plans rarely work out the way we intend. General Eisenhower, Supreme Commander of Allied Forces in World War II, stated, "Plans are worthless, but planning is everything."[1069] Even if your plans do not work out as intended, your investment in planning will help you discern God's will and act wisely. Your plans may prove imperfect, but God's plans never fail. God had a plan for the redemption of mankind. Jesus had a plan for the church, preparing His disciples to spread the good news. And God has a plan for your life.[1070] Your best plans are those nested in God's plans and will for your life. But God can use your mistakes and difficulties to release growth, positive life change, and discover new direction for the future. Planning can help you shape these outcomes.

David faced a dark situation at Ziklag. He could easily have succumbed to despair. Instead, he refused to allow his emotional reactions to dominate his response. Rejecting self-pity, he conceived a plan. He decided to pursue the Amalekites and rescue the captives. David's goal: the restoration of every warrior's family and goods. The plan: to find the invaders, attack them, defeat them in battle, and retrieve their families. David's faith placed God at the forefront of his planning. He sought the Lord to determine

---
1067 Proverbs 16:3
1068 James 4:15
1069 Dwight D. Eisenhower, "*Public Papers of the President of the United States, Dwight D. Eisenhower, Containing the Public Messages, Speeches, and Statements of the President, Remarks at the National Defense Executive Reserve Conference,*" November 14, 1957. (Washington D.C.: Federal Register Division, National Archives and Records Service, 1957), 817–818.
1070 Jeremiah 29:11–13

if He would bless his efforts. He committed his plan to the Lord. I believe David would have rejected his own plan if God had forbidden it. After seeking the counsel of God and receiving the green light, he did not hesitate. Even though it seemed like a long shot (the Amalekites had several days' head start), David and his men set out through the desert to find them. With God's providential help, they located an Egyptian slave in the desert. With the help of the Egyptian, they located their camp and prepared a plan of attack using the element of surprise. They courageously attacked the much larger Amalekite force and decisively defeated them, recovering every family member alive with their goods and vast additional amounts of plunder as well. David laid his goals and plan before the Lord, and God honored his efforts.

Goal-Setting

When you face difficulties, it may be hard to know exactly what to do and where to start. Like David, start with seeking God. Do not let the gravity of your situation overwhelm you. Faith does not shrink back in fear.[1071] Faith trusts God for supernatural help. Tell God what you need (identify and share your goal). Ask Him to help you find a way to work through it. Seek the counsel of mature, godly people. As you seek Him and submit your plans to Him, God will providentially make a way even when there seems to be no way.[1072] Involving God is a process that takes patience, allowing time for you to get a sense of God's leading and to recognize decision points along the way as events unfold. For David, the finding of the Egyptian slave provided key information and assurance of God's blessing on their quest. Look for similar direction in your circumstances. Working through the goal-setting process can help you bring clarity to your situation. How do you envision your life when all your difficulties are resolved? How will your life be better? Your vision of the future you desire is called an end state. Goal-setting begins with identifying your preferred end state. What goals do you need to accomplish to make it a reality? Start with the most important goal and work to the lowest priority. Identify the steps to realize your most important goal. Stated another way, how will you get from your present circumstances to your desired ones? I find it helpful to use a backward planning process. Begin with the goal and work your way backward, identifying the required actions and timeline required to accomplish it. For example, if you need to get a new job that provides higher income, use the goal of completing a new job certification program within two years:

Backward Planning Timeline

Present Date + twenty-four months: Complete goal to graduate from a job certification program;

Present Date + thirteen months: Begin studies in the job certification program;

1071 Hebrews 10:38
1072 Isaiah 43:16–19

Present Date + twelve months: Complete all preparations to attend;

Present Date + nine months: Secure financing to pay for the program;

Present Date + six months: Receive final acceptance to a certification program;

Present Date + three months: Complete the application process for all potential certification programs, starting with your top choice;

Present Day: Identify possible certification programs, schools, costs, and prerequisites; rank the most desirable from top to bottom.

I used a similar planning process when I explored the possibility of pursuing an advanced degree. Some goals seem too large to achieve. Breaking the big tasks into smaller, more manageable (bite size) steps will increase your motivation, confidence, and help you focus your efforts. Goal-setting is a powerful planning tool to help you take big steps forward. Ask God to inspire your thoughts and open doors as you execute the plan. In the same way God led David to an Egyptian slave in the desert, God will guide you.

Problem-Solve for Success

In a time of adversity, your most important goal may be to overcome a problem or challenge. The problem-solving process is the more appropriate tool to help you identify causes and solutions. It can help you overcome complex problems by understanding the challenges, developing effective solutions, and implementing a plan to overcome.[1073] Adversity can make you feel hopelessly stuck. Take baby steps through the process as you trust God.

Step 1: Define the Problem

Problem-solving begins with identifying the problem. What is your initial perception of the problem? You may be uncertain what the real problem is. Organize your thoughts on paper to describe your situation. Discussing the problem openly with a trusted friend is another way to help clarify the problem. Many people use a problem statement to identify the real problem they face. One way to write a problem

---

1073 University of Arkansas, *"The Six Step Problem Solving Model,"* accessed February 27, 2023, Https://www.uapb.edu/sites/www/uploads/assessment/webinar/session%203/Newfolder/6%20Step%20Problem%20Solving%20Process.pdf.

statement is to briefly state where you are (starting point) and where you want to go (end state). What is the real problem?

Step 2: Identify the Cause(s)

After you clarify the problem, you are ready for Step 2—identify the cause. Do not assume you know the true cause. Sometimes people are treating symptoms instead of addressing the real issues. Brainstorming is one way of generating multiple possibilities. This list will guide your investigation to determine the real cause of the problem. Part of this phase is to confront your own biases and blind spots to consider information you may dismiss out of hand. Other perspectives can help in the fact-finding phase. Have you missed anything? You are now ready to determine the primary cause of the problem. From your investigation, list the evidence that supports each potential cause. What really caused the problem? Throughout the first two problem-solving steps, you move from general perceptions and theories to specific conclusions based on facts and evidence. Have you distinguished between your facts and assumptions? Facts are information verified by evidence or data, while assumptions reflect what you believe to be true without objective evidence. Your conclusions should be anchored in facts. What is the primary cause of the problem? The diagram below shows how you narrow down your initial perceptions to identify the specific problem and cause.

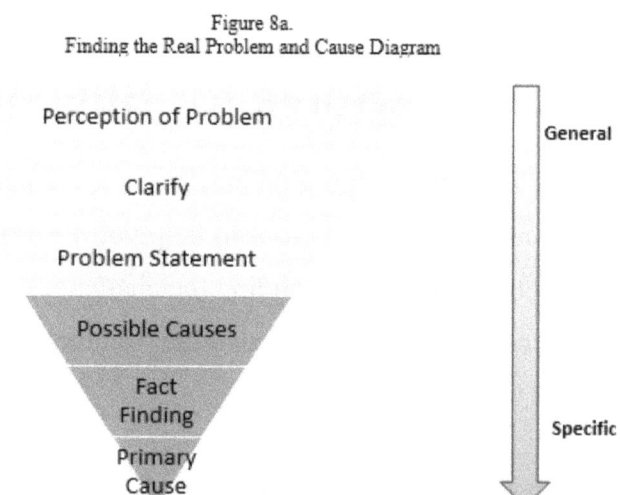

Figure 8a.
Finding the Real Problem and Cause Diagram

Step 3: Generate Possible Solutions

Once you have identified the problems and causes, you are ready for Step 3—generating possible solutions. How can you solve the problem? Brainstorming is one way to develop a list of solutions to address the primary cause of the problem. In this step, you also want to identify the criteria that determine the best solutions or courses of action (COA). Why would you choose one solution over another? Some reasons might be its probability of success (suitability), cost or available resources (feasibility), length of time required, its moral acceptability, or a similar consideration.

Step 4: Evaluate Courses of Action

In Step Four you are ready to begin analysis of courses of action to determine the best solution. You can use a point system or assign a positive/negative to evaluate how each solution fits your criteria. If one solution is too costly, assign it a zero or a negative sign; if it is cheap, assign it a one or a positive sign. If it is in the middle, assign it a value of one half or neutral-neither positive nor negative. If you create a chart that evaluates each solution by your criteria, you can determine which course of action has the highest score and is the best.

Figure 8b.
Solution/COA Evaluation

Criteria	Solution/COA 1	Solution/COA 2	Solution/COA 3
Cost - less	1 / +	0 / -	1 / +
Time - quick	1 / +	1 / +	0 / -
Suitable(success)	1 / +	1 / +	½ /
Acceptable(moral)	1 / +	1 / +	1 / +
Total	4 / 4	3 / 2	2 ½ / 1

If one criterion is more important than the others, you can easily assign it weight by multiplying according to its relative importance to the others. If cost is twice as important as the other criteria, assign it a score of two when present. This gives COA 3 a higher score than COA 2 compared to the previous evaluation without weight. It does not change the best choice in this scenario, but it easily could influence the outcome based on the importance of a given criteria in your circumstances.

Figure 8c.
Weighted Solution/COA Evaluation

Criteria	Solution/COA 1	Solution/COA 2	Solution/COA 3
Cost – less (x 2)	2 / ++	0 / -	2 / ++
Time - quick	1 / +	1 / +	0 / -
Suitable	1 / +	1 / +	½ /
Acceptable	1 / +	1 / +	1 / +
Total	5 / 5	3 / 2	3 ½ / 2

Some separate evaluating possible solutions from selecting the best one. I combine them in this five–step process. The evaluation of each solution may seem intimidating and take a little longer than simply deciding in your mind, but as you see in the tables above, it produces a clear and easily understood choice. What happens if your solutions have a tie score? Weighting the criteria is one way to discriminate or just choose the course of action you like the best. Prayer and God's leading should always be the critical part of your decision-making. The best course in this evaluation process may lead you to God's will. As happens many times in Scripture, you may feel God leading to choose a solution that is not logical or the best in your evaluation. This analysis still has value to understand the trust you are placing in the Lord and counting the cost of the risk you assume in your decisions.[1074] Trusting God means putting your faith in Him to take care of your needs, vulnerabilities, and associated risks.

Step 5: Execute the Plan

Once you have determined the best course of action, you are ready for Step 5: execute your COA. Carrying out your plan takes courage and determination. Many people consider what should be done, but much fewer sacrifice the time, effort, and resources to see it through. That is one reason people remain stuck. They know they need to lose the weight or stop smoking, but it is easier to do nothing. They know they should go to church, but it is so much easier to sleep in. People who refuse to take action to change their circumstances are less resilient. They not only fail to demonstrate the necessary fortitude to overcome, they prevent the development of inner strength that comes from taking positive control. They hinder the growth process that comes from exercising self-discipline. Recognize how important your mind, will, and emotions (soul) are to your actions. This is why spiritually resilient thinking precedes spiritually resilient action. You must be fully committed inside to follow through with actions that decisively change your outer world. Ask God for the strength to follow through.

Step 6: Monitor Progress

The final step (Step 6) is to seek feedback, monitor progress, and make mid-course corrections. Few things in life continue to flourish without attention. Problem solving takes energy and attention. Identify milestones so you can chart your progress. Plans rarely unfold as expected, so be ready to adjust your course of action to changes in your situation. Expect to tweak a few things along the way to improve success. If something radically changes, don't be afraid to start the problem-solving process over with the new information, developing new courses of action. Joseph had to start at the bottom twice due to unforeseen and unjust circumstances. He continued to be the best version of himself as he waited for God's dream to come to pass. Through all the disappointments, he recognized the sovereign purposes of God. God was with him and working for him.

The diagram below illustrates the problem-solving process. Note that monitoring your progress in

1074 Luke 14:28–29

the final step may cause you to start over again if the circumstances dictate.

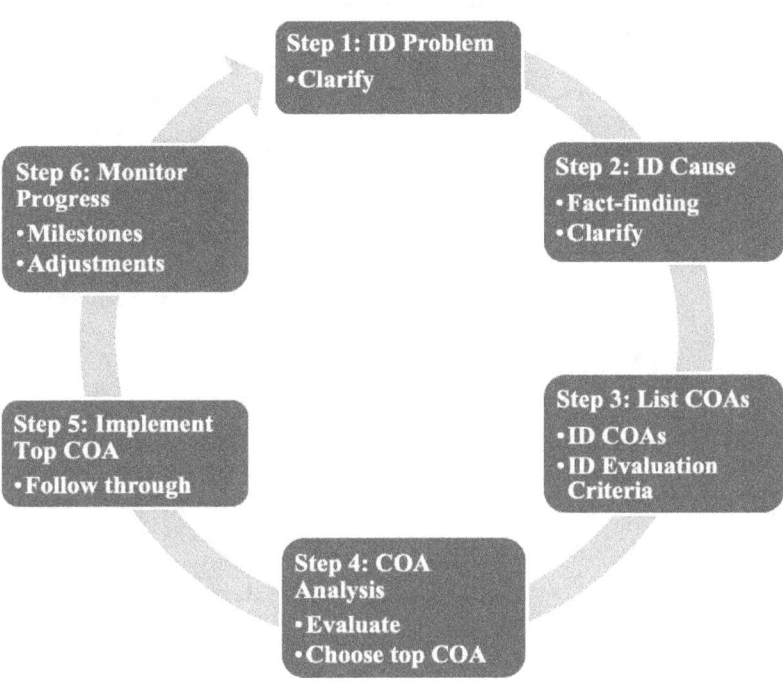

**Figure 8d.
Problem-Solving Process**

Let's consider David's situation at Ziklag. He and his men found themselves in a difficult and complex situation.

Figure 8e.
David's Problem-Solving Process at Ziklag

Problem-Solving Process Step	Analysis at Ziklag	Discussion
ID Problem	Their families & possessions were gone.	You might list David's men ready to revolt as a problem, but it is actually a symptom of the real problem.
ID Cause	Amalekite raiders – David's men could have second guessed David leading them off to battle but the real cause was not David's leadership.	People may assign false guilt, blame, and shame in dark times, but you must steer clear to see the true cause.
Generate Solutions/COAs	David developed a plan to recover their families and sought God whether he should go after the Amalekites	David intuitively developed a course of action and submitted it to God for evaluation. He could have weighed other options such as seeking help from allies in Judah. Scripture doesn't say.
COA Analysis	David sought God's confirmation in his primary COA.	God's will is the best COA. This process helps you get there. The weightiest criterion may be a sense of God's peace or leading in a COA apart from specific direction.
Implement Your Top COA	David immediately set out after the Amalekites after God confirmed his plan. He attacked them and rescued all family members and possessions.	David could have rested his men first, tried to convince them they were wrong about blaming him and/or sought other help against the Amalekites. Instead, he courageously set out with a much smaller force to track down and rescue their families.
Monitor Progress	While carrying out his plan, God helped David by providing an Egyptian slave left behind by the Amalekite army. He used the slave to guide them straight to their location.	David could have killed the Egyptian, left him behind or ignored his need. Instead, David's kindness paid off in a key blessing. Look for opportunities as well as threats in this step.

Problem-solving can be used to plan for victory during adversity. You are welcome to abbreviate steps if time is of the essence. The process is not as relevant for small, simple, or routine problems that require less analysis. Writing your analysis out on paper and discussing it with others can have great value to externalize the problem and simplify it in your thought processes.

Setting goals and making plans are important action steps during adversity that help you take control of your life when circumstances and the work of the enemy have left you hopeless and helpless. You have the power of the Spirit living inside you. You are not adrift on a sea of chaos, you have the wisdom, power, and authority of Christ with you as a child of God. Don't give up your ability to choose the direction of your next step. The enemy views your passiveness and inaction as total surrender. Resist him with everything you have. Face your situation with determination and forcefulness. David didn't give in to self-pity or the loss of confidence in his leadership by his warriors at Ziklag, and neither should you. Planning is a tool to help you move forward as David did.

Chapter 9

Resolve Conflicts Quickly

Blessed are the peacemakers for they shall be called sons of God.[1075]

Be slow to take offense and quick to forgive. Forgiveness is freeing and a catalyst to healing. Seeking peace through reconciliation and forgiveness is true scriptural wisdom releasing inner peace and setting your life on a healthy course.[1076] It demonstrates value and respect for others, mercy, submission, and purity compared to the envy, selfishness, and disorder of unspiritual earthly wisdom. Unresolved anger and unforgiveness lead to bitterness, contaminating your mind and emotions. One author calls it the bait of Satan.[1077] Picture a mouse trap with bait. When you grab that bait, the trap springs. Unforgiveness traps you, now you're stuck. You don't need the additional baggage when you are facing struggles. Unforgiveness undermines your mental-emotional strength and lessens your ability to bounce back from difficulties. The negative mental preoccupation causes numerous problems, including sleeplessness, lack of motivation, feelings of helplessness, and health issues.[1078] Some people think holding a grudge against someone else is a means of revenge. On the contrary, one author provided the framework for this contemporary quote, "Unforgiveness is like drinking poison and waiting for the other person to die."[1079] The point should be obvious—unforgiveness harms the user more than your enemy. In many cases, the other party doesn't even know you are holding a grudge. You have heard the expression, "nursing a grudge." Some people treat their grudge like a baby, feeding it, playing with it, and attending to its every need. All the while, the grudge is sucking the life out of them—the peace, the joy, and love slowly draining away. Decades ago, I heard a person compare the emotional enmeshment that accompanies refusing to forgive to running a three-legged race with them. You think you are pushing the other person away when, in fact, your legs are tied together. You have pulled them closer in an unhealthy mental-emotional soul tie. Forgive the other person and set yourself free.

David had good reasons to live offended. His father assigned him to work in the fields while his older brothers feasted. His oldest brother maligned his place in the family and questioned his motives. Despite faithfully serving the throne, David had to flee for his life from King Saul and unjust accusations of treason. Later, as king, his own son betrayed him to seize the throne. A thorough reading of David's life

---
[1075] Matthew 5:9
[1076] James 3:15–18
[1077] John Bevere, The Bait of Satan: Living Free From the Deadly Trap of Offense (Lake Mary, FL: Charisma House, 2011), 1.
[1078] Amanda Rowett, "The Prison of Unforgiveness: A Christian Counselor's Perspective on Forgiveness," accessed February 27, 2023, Https://bellevuechristiancounseling.com/articles/the-prison-of-unforgiveness.
[1079] Bert Ghezzi, The Angry Christian (Ann Arbor, MI: Servant, 1980), 99.

will show these are only just a few of the offenses that could have ensnared David in the unforgiveness trap. Instead of succumbing to self-pity, resentment, or bitterness, David continued to seek God and lay his burdens before Him. Do not think David just ignored these offenses. Numerous Psalms record the anguished cries of David's heart over these struggles.[1080] However, rather than remain stuck in the offenses, David continually petitioned God to be his help and advocate. David's honesty is a great model for both openly sharing your hurts with the Lord and for trusting Him to help. Reading the Psalms can help you process the pain of your suffering and find encouragement to trust God through offenses. The Psalms help many people find solace in identifying with their sufferings.

Scripture teaches that forgiveness is not optional. If you refuse to forgive, you limit God's grace and blessings in your own life. Jesus taught the Parable of the Unmerciful Servant to show that God will not forgive the one who refuses to forgive others.[1081] Forgiveness is a choice you make to obey God and extend the mercy God showed you to someone else. While technically a legal declaration you make to release someone of the debt owed you, it may also involve a process to get to the point where you are ready to trust God enough to obey. Forgiveness doesn't mean you agree with the person's actions, that you deny the hurt or damage you experienced, or that the person will go free in God's court of justice. The offending person must still account for their wrongdoing, just as we all do. Forgiveness means you release the debt owed you, renounce any right to take revenge, and trust God to dispense justice according to His will.

It is a terrible thing to fall into the judgment of the Almighty God.[1082] The Scripture states God is an All-Consuming Fire.[1083] Every person on earth already stands condemned for their rebellion and rejection of God. In His great love, He gave His most precious gift, Jesus, to enable everyone to escape judgment through believing in His name.[1084] If we truly understood the nature of judgment and hell, we would not wish it on our worst enemies. It is a place God created for Satan and fallen angels.[1085] Hell, also known as the Lake of Fire, is a place where God has fenced off any sense of His presence—a place of physical, mental, and emotional torment where people relive their worst fears, guilt, shame, doubts, and insecurities every moment.[1086] Presently, every human on this Earth, in some manner, enjoys God's sustaining presence. God makes the rain fall on believers and non-believers alike.[1087] Imagine a place devoid of all sustenance, comfort, or rest. To act as judge in sentencing someone to this torture is, in fact, to sentence yourself to the same fate. Jesus said, "The measure [of mercy] you use [in your dealings

---

1080 Psalm 51:1–4, Psalm 1:1–2, Psalm 15:1–5, Psalm 17:3–4, Psalm 18:20–27, Psalm 19:13–14, Psalm 27:12–14, Psalm 32:1–7, Psalm 37:1–17, Psalm 39:1–9, Psalm 40:13–17, Psalm 41:5–13, Psalm 42:9–11
1081 Matthew 18:21–35
1082 Hebrews 10:31
1083 Hebrews 12:29
1084 John 3:18
1085 Matthew 25:41
1086 Revelation 20:14–15
1087 Matthew 5:45

with others] will be measured [by God] to you."[1088] Pray for those that hurt and offend you. Be quick to forgive. You not only release God's grace in your life, but you also walk in the spirit of mercy that God uses in dealing with humanity.[1089] God will bless your obedience and release His healing power in your life. God's mercy will begin the cleansing process in your mind and emotions and, over time (sometimes immediately), will remove all the negativity that accompanied the original offense.

Sin, a Snake Bite

Wrongdoing has many cruel effects, including the multiple ways in which it wounds you. Someone's sin causes you harm. The initial wound, like that of a venomous snake, is where the fangs enter the flesh. It causes pain (sometimes intense and severe pain). But then, the fangs inject venom. This happens when offense and resentment keep you reliving the initial wound, rehearsing what you should have done, blaming the other person, and sometimes blaming yourself for allowing it to happen. The resulting state of unresolved anger eventually becomes bitterness, expressing itself in all kinds of destructive second, third, and fourth order effects. The enemy is actively involved in this dynamic, tempting you to fixate on the offense and formulate plans for revenge. The strategy of the enemy is to maximize the damage of the wrongs against you. If the enemy could destroy us whenever he wanted to, he would have wiped us out a long time ago.[1090] Instead, he must use others, in their sin, to kill, steal, and destroy. Sometimes he uses us to harm ourselves in self-destructive behaviors like unforgiveness. Don't fall for his trap. However, God has given wise instructions to help you process the wrongdoing committed against you and expunge the many accompanying feelings. Reconciliation is a way of lancing the wound, draining the infection, and allowing healing to begin.

A Process for Reconciliation

Jesus described a practical process to release offenses and to restore a right relationship with someone who hurt you.[1091] Reconciliation is a grace-filled conversation and process of restoration through vulnerable confrontation. According to Jesus, conflict resolution begins (Step 1) with a one-on-one meeting.[1092] Resist bringing others into your offense by gossip, slander, or trying to build an army of people who take your side in the dispute. If the initial one-on-one meeting to resolve the conflict fails, then Jesus instructs you to find a wise, impartial, and godly peace-making person to serve as a witness and potential mediator to jumpstart the process (Step 2).[1093] If the second attempt fails, the matter is to be

---
1088 Matthew 7:2
1089 Matthew 5:43–45
1090 Bevere, *Bait of Satan*, 22.
1091 Matthew 18:15–18
1092 Matthew 18:15
1093 Matthew 18:16

brought before church leaders (Step 3) to determine a constructive, godly way to resolve the conflict.[1094]

God's commands against wrongdoing (sin) are meant to protect all humanity from the consequences of evil and to allow people to live their best possible lives in relationship with God and others. They are ideally preventative and protective. However, all people regularly disobey, requiring commands that prescribe a remedy when wounded by sin. It is important to remember that wrongdoing wounds both the victim and the offender. The offender incurs the penalty of judgment from God, broken relationships, vulnerability to Satan, and the guilt and shame of their actions. While it sometimes seems that people commit serious wrongs without consequences, the Bible is clear that, sooner or later, justice will catch them.[1095] Governments are supposed to punish wrongdoing, hence the scriptural observation, "When the righteous are in authority, the people rejoice; but when the wicked rule, the people mourn."[1096] However, vengeful behaviors are not justice. Reconciliation includes trusting God to deal with the offender and to help you work through a process of healing and restoration. Your obedience to God's counsel will light the pathway of forgiveness.

Jesus taught conflict resolution starts one on one. Yet, face-to-face discussions are difficult, and many people shy away from confrontation. Fear is one reason people find it so hard to follow Jesus' teachings. You might be anxious or afraid as well. Reconciliation requires people to leave the fortified positions they have built to protect themselves. Sometimes, these fortresses are feelings of arrogance, superiority, and general insensitivity to the needs/feelings of others. Sometimes, they are feelings of anger, resentment, bitterness, desire for revenge, and the like. Conflict resolution requires vulnerability to figuratively leave your fortified position to move down into the valley of reconciliation. Consider the illustration in the figure below.

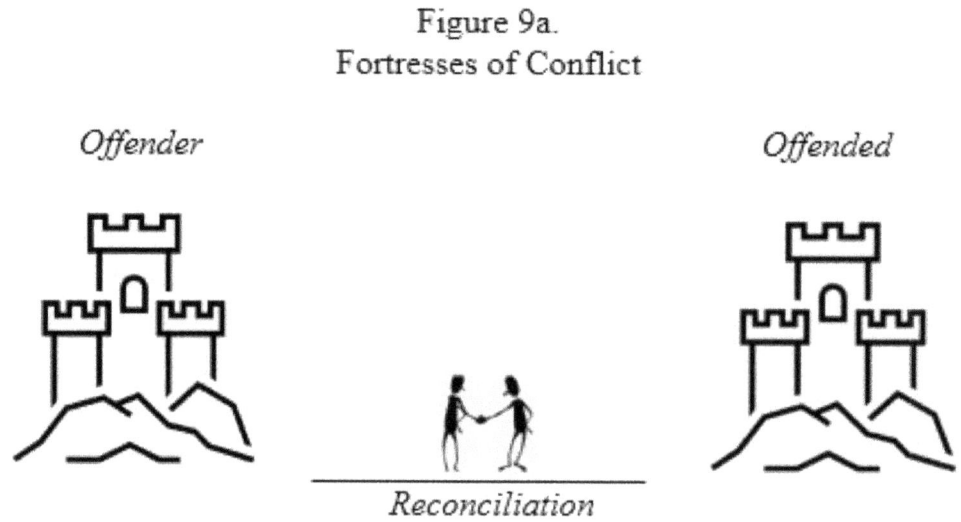

Figure 9a.
Fortresses of Conflict

1094 Matthew 18:17
1095 1 Timothy 5:24
1096 Proverbs 29:2 (KJV)

In conflict, both the offended and the offender normally seek positions of safety. Picture these positions as fortresses on opposing hilltops. The offender may strengthen his position with justifications or excuses for sin, denial, to maintain their innocence, etc. The offended may strengthen his position with resentment, bitterness, vengeance, attempting to bring others onto their side with gossip, slander, etc. Each seeks to build a fortified position against the other. Block by block, they build bigger fortresses in the conflict. In addition to strengthening their defenses, one or both sides may go on the offensive: they verbally attack each other, bring others to their side, use passive-aggressive tactics, or take other actions to harm the other. In our analogy, this is like firing cannons to weaken the other's position.

Conflict resolution requires one or both individuals to come out of the hilltop tower into the valley. Each person must humble themselves enough to seek first, a position that honors God and follows the example of Christ, and second, demonstrates love and value of the other person in the conflict. Selfishness places you in the tower, building your fortifications. Obedience to God, true spiritual maturity, allows you to leave your safety and security for the valley of reconciliation, where conflict resolution and forgiveness can take place. Many people today describe safe space as if it were the end state. Safety is not their end state; that is the selfish fortress. Love and reconciliation are the end state. In truth, your tower is not safe at all. It only feels safe to your flesh. Your tower is a prison that keeps you from enjoying the full blessings of God. It is counterintuitive, but there is more spiritual safety in the valley with God at your side. Your flesh doesn't see it that way through natural sight. Reconciliation requires vulnerability, but it is not weakness. In fact, it takes more strength and courage to leave the fortress. Scripture states, "One who is slow to anger is better than a warrior; one who is self-controlled better than the one who captures a city."[1097] Some people have suffered such mental-emotional, even physical brokenness by the gravity of the sin against them, they are not in the place to leave the fortress for healthy confrontation. In these extreme cases, face to face confrontation and appeals for reconciliation may not be healthy. You don't need to meet face to face to forgive someone. Everyone should seek to forgive and ask for forgiveness where necessary by whatever means to honor God and love/value those involved.

Conflict Resolution Process

It takes preparation to make resolving conflict a regular practice. The good news is, Scripture provides additional wisdom to help you live as a peacemaker. What follows is a simple, practical process to prepare you for face to face confrontation and assist you in following through with scriptural forgiveness. Peacemaking can be a powerful tool in your relational toolbox. It not only allows you to clear the mental, emotional, and spiritual blockages caused by unforgiveness in your own relationships, it can equip you to serve others as a mediator. A process for conflict resolution is illustrated and described below.

[1097] Proverbs 16:32

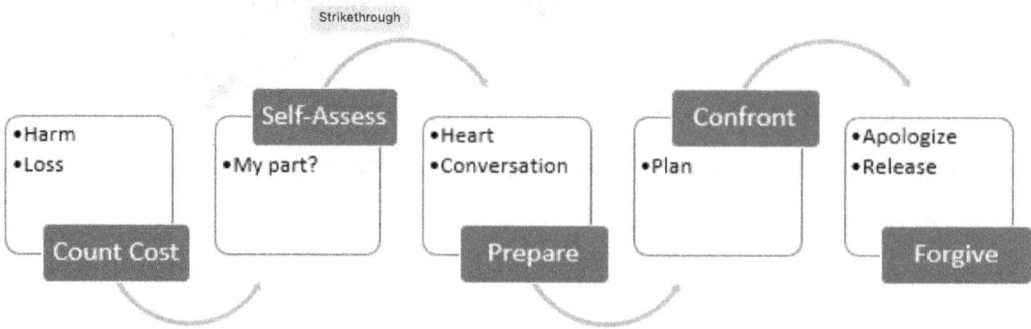

Figure 9b.
Healthy Conflict Resolution

Step 1: Count the Cost of the Offense

The first step in reconciliation is to count the cost of the offense. What happened? How did it cause you harm? Why did the wound hurt so much? This may seem like an obvious and unnecessary step, but forgiveness is difficult if you don't know what you are forgiving. Some people try to sincerely forgive but take the offense up again after they consider anew how the offense affected them. Jesus told a Parable of the King who counted his soldiers and the strength of his enemy as he considered war.[1098] He counted the costs and risks of battle to determine whether he should wage war or sue for peace. Similarly, consider the costs and benefits before you go to war with someone else. You have heard the benefits of seeking peace and the hidden costs of conflict and unforgiveness. An additional calculation is to soberly reflect on how you were affected, acknowledging the thoughts, emotions, and other harm that accompanied the offense. You now have a more complete understanding of how you were wronged, so you can permanently turn the hurts over to God.

Step 2: Honestly Examine Your Own Thoughts, Actions, and Motives

The second step is to honestly examine your own heart and contribution.[1099] Did you, by action or omission of action, contribute to the situation in any way? Have you honored God with your thoughts, emotions, and attitudes throughout the difficult interactions? Humbly judge your own motives and actions, and you will avoid much of the suffering that comes from self-focused, destructive behaviors.[1100] In most cases, your self-examination will reveal areas in which you should assume personal responsi-

---

[1098] Luke 14:31–32
[1099] 2 Corinthians 13:5
[1100] 1 Corinthians 11:31

bility. Your humility in this step will set you up to maximize the potential for true reconciliation, life change, and restoration of relationship. God gives grace to the humble but opposes the proud.[1101] When you assume the role of a peacemaker, your humility welcomes God's grace and blessing. It is a sign of strength, not weakness, to take responsibility for the part you played in causing or exacerbating conflict.

I said in most cases, you should own your contribution to the conflict. Circumstances exist where you have suffered great harm or abuse and have been relatively innocent of provocation or contribution. In such cases, you may feel guilty or responsible for the harm done to you. This is false guilt and condemnation. These feelings are not from the Holy Spirit and are often used by the enemy to further harm those who have been wounded the most.[1102] Confrontation in such cases often remains the best course of action. In cases where the harm has been physical or sexual abuse, some means other than a direct face to face meeting may be required to prevent further harm. While it may not be popular in our contemporary culture to say it, forgiveness is not an option. Forgiveness remains the most profitable path to health and well-being, even in the worst cases of offense. Why would God use forgiveness as a catharsis to help people expunge negative experiences and feelings and then not include those who need it the most? When you forgive someone, you set yourself free. Forgiveness is a gift God gives to reconcile humans to Himself in spiritual freedom. It is also a gift He gives you to release unhealthy soul ties created by wounds and offenses. You are not saying the offense or harm you suffered does not matter. You simply turn the debt the offender owes you over to God. You give God your desire for vengeance and allow Him, in His wisdom, grace, and justice, to do what is right and best. Forgiveness enables you to love as God loves and releases you to experience renewed peace, joy, and right relationship with God and others. Remember, God's judgment is a consuming fire. No one gets away with wickedness. It is a terrible thing to fall into the hands (judgment) of the Living God.[1103] Hopefully, the offender will truly repent and find mercy.

Step 3: Get Prepared

The third step is to prepare your heart and mind for the face-to-face meeting. Humbly examine the events that caused the offense, inventory its effects on your life, and acknowledge any contributions you might have made. Like the spirit of the Beatitudes, embrace a spirit of humility and a desire for reconciliation and blessing for both of you.[1104] If so, it is time to plan your conversation. Consider how to make the conversation a win for both parties. What is the end state God desires for this meeting? Use the *golden rule*.[1105] How would you want someone else to approach you if you had caused the offense?

1101 James 4:6, 1 Peter 5:5–6
1102 Romans 8:1
1103 Hebrews 10:31
1104 Matthew 5:3–9
1105 Matthew 7:12

Consider how you can communicate love and respect to the other person as you confront their behavior. Honestly confront the offense without using accusations or emotionally charged words. Ask God to use you as a catalyst for change and growth. Use these questions to craft a plan and script for what you feel God wants you to say. What will you say if the meeting goes well? How will you respond if the person does not respond well? Develop an exit plan to wrap up the meeting if the conversation breaks down. Be ready with gracious words to end the meeting regardless of the outcome. As you focus on the goal of reconciliation, restoration of relationship, and honoring God in the process, you can temper your attitude and emotions to communicate love and value even as you confront. The nature of conflict resolution can be tense and stressful. The more you pray and think through these issues, the more you reduce your stress and fear of meeting, allowing the Spirit to work through you.

Step 4: Meet and Lovingly Confront

The next step is to meet face to face and lovingly confront the other person. Jesus taught people to leave their gifts at the altar, go, and be reconciled if they have an offense against another.[1106] It takes courage, humility, and self-control to obey God's commands, especially this one. In the last step, you created a plan for the meeting and aligned yourself with the heart and mind of God. Now is the time to execute. Right before you meet, review the important issues that will help you maximize your potential for a positive meeting. What could prevent reconciliation from happening? A closed heart/spirit? Anger? Harsh words? What could you do to de-escalate further conflict if the other person does not receive your message? What could you do if you find yourself losing control? Prepare yourself to identify warning signs and have a backup plan to reorient the conversation to a constructive God-honoring end. Conclude the meeting in prayer, forgiveness, and reconciliation, or if it starts to go the wrong way, gracefully end and seek assistance from others to mediate. You have shaped conditions to promote peace, reconciliation, and restoration. Now, it is time to let go.

Step 5: Forgive and Let Go

The fifth step is to forgive and let go. The goal of the face-to-face meeting is to culminate with forgiveness and reconciliation. At some point in the conversation, the other person may apologize. A great way to make this easy is to be the "bigger," more mature person and be the first to apologize for those areas of responsibility you identified that you contributed to the conflict. Your "I'm sorry for … (specific actions)" can help the other person make their apology. Remember, "Blessed are the peacemakers."[1107] I encourage you to follow their "I'm sorry" with the statement, "I forgive you and release you from any

---

1106 Matthew 5:24
1107 Matthew 5:9

debt you owe me." These powerful words will not only begin the healing process in your life, but they will also help the other person resist ongoing attempts by the enemy to afflict them with guilt and shame. They are a win-win statement. With the declaration and legal pronouncement of forgiveness, you are on the road to healing and, ultimately, letting go of the experience.

The commitment you make in forgiveness is to choose, like God, not to remember the offense—to choose not to hold that offense against the person any longer.[1108] Making the promise does not mean you will never remember it or ever again feel the pain of the event. You will likely have moments where you remember the offense and have intense emotions. Your promise means you pray, "Lord, I gave this offense to you. I refuse to take it back. I put it in your hands and pray for your blessing on _____ (the offender) and for your total healing in my life." You may never totally forget, but you will find the power of the event fade from your consciousness. It will lose its hold over your thoughts and emotions as you live out your promise.

What if the other person receives your apology but never reciprocates with their own? That sounds awkward, but it is a possibility. You are not responsible for the other person's choices and behaviors.[1109] You only answer to God for your own. You can carry out the meeting perfectly, say all the right things, and have your heart and mind in the right place but still walk away without an apology. I know people who have refused to apologize or acknowledge the hurt caused by their sin up to their death. You may never get an apology, but your act and declaration of forgiveness will still bring you healing and freedom as you obey God. Your obedience is your path to peace. God lifts the humble with special grace and blessing.[1110]

What does it mean if the other person refuses to apologize? Restoration of relationship requires mutual reconciliation. Both parties must apologize and forgive. If one party refuses to acknowledge their part, the relationship can never be fully restored. Picture conflict as the creation of two walls between two people. Each person has a wall in front of them. Forgiveness gives each person a sledgehammer, with the invitation to demolish the walls of separation. However, each person can only use the hammer to demolish their wall. You cannot demolish the other person's wall of offense. You only have the authority to tear down the wall of your offense. You may apologize, forgive, and tear your wall down, but if the other person refuses to humble themselves and destroy their wall, you still have a wall of separation remaining between the two of you. You can only get as close to people as they allow. This is one reason Scripture encourages peace, and slowness to take offense.[1111] Numerous Proverbs warn of the danger posed by walls of offense.[1112] Your obedience makes you ready to be fully reconciled and restored to the other person when they are ready to be reconciled and restored to you. It may take a while for God

---
1108 Psalm 103:12
1109 Romans 14:1,4,12
1110 Psalm 147:6, James 4:6
1111 Ephesians 4:3, James 1:19–20
1112 Proverbs 17:14,19, 18:19, 29:11

to soften their heart to bring about restoration. Therefore, do not rebuild that wall of offense while you are waiting on the other person to reciprocate. Remember, forgiveness is not optional, but restoration of relationship is a process God is trying to effect in each person's heart. Stay innocent of evil and guard your heart against all walls. Your heart is the wellspring of life.[1113] Walls people build to keep others out also keep the Lord distant and limit His blessing and favor in their lives.

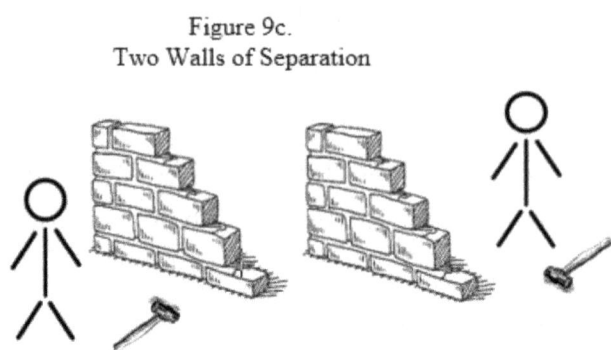

Figure 9c.
Two Walls of Separation

Forgiveness is a healing force in the life of every party involved in a conflict, but it is especially helpful to you when offended. Several principles are essential in forgiving and letting go. While you have read some earlier in the chapter, they bear repeating. Wounds are easier to create than to heal. Be slow to wound others; it takes a lot of time and effort to nurse them back to health. Forgiveness is not an option. It can be as quick as "I'm sorry," but it's often a process that takes time. Forgiveness sets you free. It replaces you on the "Judge's bench" with God, right where He belongs. Forgiveness follows and reveals the Father's heart of grace and mercy. It takes you off the prosecution team and puts you on the side of Jesus, our Advocate (Our Defense Attorney). Forgiveness doesn't let people off the hook; it gives them to God, the Righteous Judge. It is an act of mercy, releasing the same level of God's mercies in your life.[1114]

Follow Through with Your Commitment to Forgive
Release the Debt

You must make reconciliation endure. Do not take up the offense a second time. Follow through with your commitment promises. You have given the offense to God. Now fight to live your forgiveness out toward the other person. Forgiveness is a legal declaration composed of several commitments. Promise 1: "I release the debt you owe me and refuse to punish you for this offense."[1115] When others

---
1113 Proverbs 4:23
1114 Luke 6:38
1115 Matthew 6:12

sin against you (or you sin against others), they (you) incur a spiritual debt. In the Old Testament Law, people not only had to offer sacrifices to God for the sin they committed against others, but they also had to compensate the other person for the damage they caused.[1116] In some cases wrongdoing involved a financial cost as well as a spiritual cost. In the same way, under God's laws and under the nation's Civil Laws, the harm you cause others requires compensation. Today under Civil Law, many of these costs are covered by insurance. The principle is the same, sin against others causes harm that incurs a debt. Forgiveness, then, releases that debt in God's courtroom. Scripture provides an example of the heavenly courtroom with Satan as the accuser.[1117] The same accuser that accuses you before God, the Righteous Judge, accuses the person who has wronged you in the heavenly courtroom. Don't switch sides to the accuser-prosecutor (spiritually, Satan means *adversary* and is called "the accuser"). Stay seated on the side of the advocate-defender (Jesus) who seeks mercy for sinners and desires all to turn to repentance and be saved. Anger, unforgiveness, and bitterness are burdens you don't have to drag along in life.

Keep Forgetting the Offense

Promise 2: "I refuse to continue to hold this offense against you." God forgives you and separates your sin as far as the east is from the west.[1118] This is another way to say your sin is moved infinitely distant from you. He covers your wrongdoing in the deepest seas.[1119] Some call this the Sea of Forgetfulness. God forgets. God is omniscient; He sees everything and knows everything. He does not really forget in the normal sense of the word. Yet He chooses not to remember your sin. In the same way, you must continue to let go of the sins of others. Love keeps no record of wrongs.[1120] The hardest part of reconciliation is living out your promises in the first days and weeks after you forgive. The enemy works overtime to tempt you to take back the offense. He will try to reignite the powerful emotions of hurt and anger. He will try to remind you of the negative thoughts you had toward the other person and the grievousness of their wrong. He will tempt you to continue to live in a spirit of contention with the other person. A simple strategy for battling these temptations is to pray and proclaim blessing over the other person every time you are tempted in one of these ways. Bless them with a prayer or declaration but do it out loud so you can clearly hear it. Speak it out so anyone can hear it. The enemy is listening, and so is God. If you speak out a blessing over the other person, you will strengthen your positive emotions toward the other person and blunt the enemy's attack against you. If you bless every time the enemy attacks, he will soon try some other strategy. The last thing he wants is your obedience to Christ to bless those who have hurt you.[1121] You will walk out the forgiveness for the rest of your life. Your love, faith-

---
1116 Exodus 22:1, 33–34, 35–36 are some examples
1117 Zechariah 3:1–2
1118 Psalm 103:12
1119 Micah 7:19, Romans 4:7
1120 1 Corinthians 13:5
1121 Matthew 5:43–44

fulness, and self-control will speed up your healing, help you put your pain in the rear-view mirror, and help you grow stronger to face the next challenge. Your obedience will make you more resilient with greater strength to stand amidst life's difficulties.

You forgave the person in one permanent legal decree, continually reaffirm your commitment not to think about it, ruminate on it, or allow the negative feelings back into your heart. One day, a person in church screamed at me, making several unfair accusations. I ruminated on the pain of that encounter, rehearsing all the things I should have said and done. Whenever I saw the person, I relived the pain of that first encounter. I tried to avoid him, which was difficult because he worked at the neighborhood grocery store. Finally, after countless hours of reliving the pain, I came to a biblical understanding of forgiveness. I forgave him, gave up my right to be angry, and committed him to God. In obedience to Scripture, I prayed blessings over him every day. I blessed him whenever I saw him, shook his hand, smiled, and took a few minutes to talk. Eventually, I stopped remembering the offense. The pain faded, and I could talk comfortably with him. He never took responsibility for his behavior. He never asked my forgiveness, but I was free. I don't know if he ever was. None of the situation was easy, but it was liberating. You don't have to right every wrong committed against you in life. What you must do is steward the garden of your heart, so the weeds don't choke out your spiritual life, your love, joy, and peace. Let God take care of justice. He is the only one wise enough to do so. While forgiving others is a one-time legal declaration, continuing to actively let go through prayer, blessings, and kindness will cement the victory and release your healing.

Refuse to Repeat the Offense

Promise 3: "I refuse to repeat the offense to others." Repeating the offense keeps you from fulfilling Promise 2. Scripture says repeating an offense separates close friends.[1122] You have not forgotten if you keep bringing it back up. Recognize that it is harder for your family and friends to forgive someone who has wronged you than it is for you. You have the context and grace from God to forgive. When you repeat your offense other than to assist with reconciliation from an impartial, mature, and wise person, you impregnate that person with an offense that is very difficult for them to pardon. They have taken on your offense and, as such, do not have the context, God's grace, nor the spiritual standing in God's courtroom to bring the offense for reconciliation. They must bring their sin of bitterness toward that person to God. You are the one owed the debt, and you have the grace to forgive. I have witnessed people forgive and reconcile with others only to fail to convince their unwilling friends and family to do the same after they had gossiped about the situation. At best, you have a general dislike of the other person by those who love you. At worst, you have a continuing grudge that is very difficult to heal until your supporters

---
1122 Proverbs 17:9

confess their own sin of taking an offense that was not theirs to take. Spiritual maturity means you are careful what you say in your anger and vigilant when you counsel those you love who have been hurt and wronged by others.[1123]

Keep the Door Open for Restoration of the Relationship

Promise 4: "I refuse to allow this offense to keep us from restoring our relationship." Some people find it easier to forgive and move on than others. Grace, mercy, and faith are required. If you are the type of person that tends to hold a grudge, this faith action is especially important for you. Complete reconciliation is the restoration of a healthy relationship. Your relationship with the other person can be stronger than ever through this process. However, it is not automatic. You must remember the goal of reconciliation is restoration. God is in the restoring business. Love is stronger than offense. If you make God's goal for the unity of His people your goal, you will not only keep the door open but pursue deeper relationships with those who hurt you.[1124] Unbelievers are good to those who are good to them.[1125] How is it remarkable if believers act the same? Forgiveness, reconciliation, loving those who have mistreated you—these are the true marks of God's presence and power in your life.[1126] The world will see the extravagant love of God where they see the selfless love of God's people poured out in unity, forgiveness, and the bonds of peace.

If you are the offender and the type of person who finds it hard to forgive yourself, to truly restore the relationship, you must release yourself when you have sought the forgiveness of others.[1127] So much of the guilt and shame people carry around is because they cannot forgive themselves. Forgive yourself and set your mind and emotions free. Forgive yourself and allow yourself to emotionally heal. The enemy will tempt you to act in selfish ways that harm others. Then, he will turn right around and point the accusing finger at you, like you did it all on your own. There's an old English proverb that says, "If you get me once, shame on you, if you get me twice, shame on me." The devil tries to get multiple returns on his schemes. He will try to convince you how great the sin is, how it will give you everything you need and want. Once you do it, he will pour on the accusations, guilt, and shame. "Look at the pain you've caused. Look how you've disappointed everyone. Look at what a mess you've made of your life." Once you are open to regret, he will pour on the condemnation. "You're not worthy of God's forgiveness. You have exceeded the limit of God's mercy. You don't deserve it." In truth, you don't deserve God's mercy. No one does. Grace, by definition, is a gift. He gives it freely to you. "The wages of sin is death."[1128]

1123 Ephesians 4:26
1124 John 17:20–23
1125 Luke 6:33–35
1126 Romans 12:17–21
1127 Proverbs 6:2–5
1128 Romans 6:23a

Everyone suffers the consequences of their wrongdoing because they earned it. "But the gift of God's forgiveness is eternal life through Jesus Christ."[1129] It is an unmerited gift God gives everyone who asks. Scripture is clear, "If you confess your sin (repent), God is faithful and just to forgive your sin and to cleanse you from all unrighteousness."[1130] God offers His forgiveness to clear the spiritual air, to restore the sense of your relationship with Him. Forgiveness is also an emotional catharsis to deal with the feelings of guilt, shame, and condemnation that come from sin. Left unchecked, these emotions will offer the enemy continued manipulative power over you.

The Scripture is clear—God forgives when we ask. If God forgives you, why do you refuse to forgive yourself? Scripture asks a similar question,

> Who will bring any charge against those whom God has chosen? It is God who justifies. Who then is the one who condemns? No one. Christ Jesus who died—more than that, who was raised to life—is at the right hand of God and is also interceding for us.[1131]

God forgives and justifies. What person is greater than God that they have the right to condemn? Jesus Christ intercedes for you in God's court. Is the enemy greater than Jesus or God's righteous decree of forgiveness? We know no one, no person, angel, not even the enemy himself is greater than God or able to override His decree. Nothing can separate you from his love.[1132] Are you greater than the enemy? Can you go against what God has decreed? Can you refuse forgiveness where God has forgiven? Neither then, can you refuse to forgive yourself when God has forgiven. You cannot continue to bring a charge against yourself when God has justified. Therefore, forgive yourself and declare that God has removed your guilt and shame. Eventually, the sharp edge of those feelings will be blunted.

The story of Joseph is a great illustration of total forgiveness. He suffered years of separation from his family, slavery, and imprisonment due to his brothers' jealousy. After his father died, the last barrier to revenge was removed. He had the power and good reason to execute them, and they knew it. When they met him after the funeral, they were understandably afraid. Joseph's response was remarkable.

> But Joseph said to them, "Don't be afraid. Am I in the place of God? You intended to harm me, but God intended it for good to accomplish what is now being done, the saving of many lives. So then, don't be afraid. I will provide for you and your children." And he reassured them and spoke kindly to them.[1133]

1129 Romans 6:23b
1130 1 John 1:9
1131 Romans 8:33–34
1132 Romans 8:38–39
1133 Genesis 50:19–20

Joseph modeled several important principles discussed in this chapter. He kept the issue private, refusing to involve others in their personal matter. He did not allow them to fear him or be intimidated. Fear may seem to work for you, but there is no love in fear. He wanted them to forgive themselves and release their guilt. Reconciliation is all about freedom to move into a better future. He let them save face. Joseph shared the bigger picture of how God used their offense for good. It was not a justification but an explanation of God's faithfulness despite their behaviors. He protected them from having to publicly confess to their father and family members what they had done. In doing this, he protected their reputation. Finally, he made a lifetime commitment to seek their good. Joseph's actions reveal what one author calls, total forgiveness, the complete release of offenses committed against you.[1134] This example can give you inspiration to walk out forgiveness and reconciliation in your life and release their power to strengthen you as you face similar struggles.

Unforgiveness can be a spiritual barrier to your progress and a stronghold the enemy uses to limit your potential. It can bind you in an emotional straight jacket, affect your physical health, and negatively impact your other relationships. Regardless of how deeply you have been wounded, refuse to let the enemy lead you into bitterness, compounding your loss. God's way is the best way. Forgive and take the first step in your own path to freedom.

[1134] R.T. Kendall, *Total Forgiveness* (Sisters, OR: The 1687 Foundation, 2007), 172–177.

Chapter 10

Do the Right Thing—Moral Decision Making

Do not be deceived, whatever a person sows, that he will also reap.[1135]

Do the right thing! It will sustain your inner strength and protect you from a host of negative second, third, and fourth order consequences. While some in our society ridicule morality, especially the values presented in Scripture, others recognize the importance of moral decision-making in organizational leadership and effective organizations.[1136] Scripture repeatedly affirms the value of integrity and strong morals.[1137] Living a high standard of integrity and morality protects you spiritually, inoculating you against numerous physical consequences of self-destructive behaviors such as addiction.[1138] It also fortifies your mind and emotions as you walk in the right relationship with God, with others, and live consistent with your own character and values. Scripture shows that obedience to its principles brings numerous holistic benefits.[1139]

Living in relationship with God means elevating your morality, striving to honor Him with your life, and refusing to follow the crowd in self-indulgent pursuits. The struggle is complicated by the fact that while your spirit is fully committed to God, your mind and body are often drawn to the pleasures of sin, creating inner conflicts. Sin is like a constant gravitational force on your natural appetites (flesh). These desires are not evil in and of themselves, but when they determine the direction of your life, they replace God. Your natural desires create a current that continually draw you back toward a preoccupation with sinful pursuits.

Sin a Destructive Current

When I was a boy, our family went to the beach. My brother and I took rafts and went out to play in the waves. After a while I heard my parents urgently yelling for us to come back to shore. They shouted, "Come in now, there's a riptide!" A riptide is a powerful current that quickly moves water away from the shore out to deeper water, and we were caught in it. I was closer to shore, so I was able to swim back. I turned around and saw my younger brother being pulled farther away from shore. I threw my raft onto

---
1135 Galatians 6:7
1136 Southeastern Oklahoma State University, "Why Ethics are Still Essential in Management," accessed February 27, 2023, https://online.se.edu/articles/mba/why-ethics-are-still-essential-in-management.aspx.
1137 Psalm 1:1–4
1138 Ephesians 6:12–14
1139 Romans 2:13, John 9:31

the beach and swam out to him. By the time I reached his raft, I didn't have much strength left to swim us both back to shore. I tried but the current was strong, and I ended up having to hold on to the raft to take a rest. We were being carried away from my parents parallel to the shore. My parents ran along the beach with us. Unfortunately, nearby the beach ended and a mountainous pile of concrete barriers had been dumped to keep the bank from eroding. When we got in front of them, the riptide released us, and the waves started pushing us back to shore. The concrete had been worn by the waves exposing sharp shells and stones used to make them. A new danger became evident. The waves were going to smash us onto the barriers. My brother and I shifted to the back side of the raft to slow our approach. Our parents carefully made their way down the barriers to catch us as the waves crashed onto shore. A passerby saw the danger and immediately rushed to help. The waves kept pushing us toward the barriers and I wondered how we would avoid being smashed on them. As we made our final approach, a giant wave lifted us up, so my brother and I miraculously made a soft landing on our feet on one of the barriers. The adults grabbed us and pulled us up higher away from the waves. The man who came to help lost his balance and was smashed into the barriers by the wave. He ended up with a broken arm and over one hundred stitches. My brother and I escaped with a few cuts on our feet. The current was deadly but our experience could have been far worse. Sin functions like that riptide. It powerfully pulls you out into deeper water. It is never content with just a one-time moment of weakness; it wants to master you. God warned Cain of this fact, but he refused to listen.[1140] You know how that ended. Cain became an outcast. The consequences of sin are rarely benign. You don't just get to float along out there in the deep water enjoying your day. Its consequences are destructive in your life and often devastating to others. The enemy uses wrongdoing to smash your relationships, health, and well-being on the rocks. It's not just addictive behaviors that present dangers, just one bad decision can change your life forever. God gave you His Word to help you know Him better, but also to protect you from the consequences of sin.

David repeatedly proclaimed the value of God-centered decisions in his life. He compared God to a Shepherd who "led him along the path of right decision making."[1141] Doing the right thing helped him navigate the difficult seasons of life—figuratively, the mountain passes and rocky crags. He described Scripture as "a lamp unto his feet and a light unto his path."[1142] David overcame the struggles of Ziklag with inner confidence, following God's commands and direction. He repeatedly subordinated his needs and desires to be king to his spiritual conviction that honoring God meant honoring his king, even though Saul sought to take his life. This humble, selfless belief system was part of the godly character that earned David the description as a man after God's heart.[1143] Navigating dark patches in life is complicated, but Scripture helped light David's path through times of stress, confusion, and anguish. David

---

1140 Genesis 4:7
1141 Psalm 23:3
1142 Psalm 119::105
1143 1 Samuel 13:14

lamented he could have avoided shame and many troubles by always doing the right thing.[1144] All people would be wise to remember this thought. Consistent moral decision making will keep you from the kinds of troubles that plagued David later in his life.

What is the right thing? That is the subject of much debate in contemporary culture. In previous decades, the popular debate centered around the thought, "You can't legislate morality." In truth, every law and policy are a statement of values and morality. The modern discussion recognizes this is true, carrying ethical considerations into nearly every area of life, from investing to shopping. For many young people today, ethical investing means investing in only socially and environmentally responsible companies. Some political activists today preach a more polemic sermon advocating their positions than you hear from the pulpit against sin on a Sunday morning. While most agree, in principle, with the idea of supporting those companies and organizations that align with one's personal ethical code, the real divide centers around the question, "What is the code?"

Scripture provides a clear framework for moral decision-making that includes summaries in both the Old and New Testaments. In the Old Testament, the Ten Commandments provide a simple, timeless code for relating with God and others. The first four commands promote spiritual health: honor God and worship Him only, don't make images to worship, don't use God's name in vain, and rest on the Sabbath day. The final six dictate how people relate to others: honor your parents, do not commit adultery, kill, steal, lie, or covet.[1145] With respect to relating to others, this code simply covers the major issues that continue to morally shipwreck people today. After thousands of years, they are still relevant, evidence of the divine wisdom behind them.

In the New Testament, Jesus' Sermon on the Mount provided a wide-ranging moral address expounding on the Old Testament Law.[1146] The shocking truth for people of His day was the assertion that wrongdoing was not merely about outward actions, it originated in the heart. True morality considers attitude, motives, and intentions along with behaviors, a much stricter standard. In a later address, Jesus summed up every command from the Old Testament in these simple words, "Love the Lord with all your heart and love your neighbor as yourself."[1147] Love is the key. The counsel of both the Old and New Testaments is in complete harmony. Simply put, love God and love others. A simple test for the law of loving your neighbor is the *golden rule*, "Treat others the way you want to be treated."[1148] The Gospels illustrate Jesus' perfect example of love for God the Father and for others. He was divine, but He did not lord His status over others.[1149] Jesus clearly stated His mission, "For the Son of man did not come to be served, but to serve."[1150]

1144 Psalm 119:5–6
1145 Exodus 20:1–17
1146 Matthew 5–7
1147 Matthew 22:36–40
1148 Matthew 7:12
1149 Philippians 2:5–10
1150 Matthew 20:28

All the commandments and counsel of Scripture guide you in how to truly love God and others. Serving is loving. Sincerity, the honest desire to live for the good of others, not self, is the true test. Sometimes well-intended actions do not produce the desired outcomes in this fallen world, but your heart is always the key. In the Sermon on the Mount, Jesus prioritized the heart over superficial actions.[1151] Doing the right thing is simply loving God and others with sincere action.

Jesus taught that living your life in obedience to God's Word is like building your house on an immovable foundation. Simply, doing the right thing anchors your life on unshakeable bedrock versus the unstable sands of immorality.[1152] Many interpret Christ's teaching here to mean that if you commit your life to Jesus, you build on a solid foundation. While that may be true, that is not the essence of Christ's teaching in this parable. The teaching point is the importance and benefits of obedience to His commands. Unfortunately, many people who profess Christ as Savior do not live in obedience to His clear teachings for loving God and others. Their disregard results in unnecessary hurt to others and themselves. Do not follow the example of those who say one thing and do another. Obedience to Christ's teachings anchors your life on an unshakeable foundation. When the storms of life inevitably come, you will overcome. This parable is Christ's illustration of resilience. You can withstand anything in life if you follow His teachings. Disobedience will cause you to lose your footing. The discussion that follows examines the benefits of doing the right thing and the dangers of wrongdoing, with special emphasis on their effects in hard times. Moral decisions truly stabilize your life.

Doing the right thing comes with its own rewards. The Bible teaches God blesses obedience and curses disobedience.[1153] Practically, this involves several principles. First, God's way is wise, bearing fruit from natural laws. In other words, living your life in obedience to God's Word profits you regardless of whether you believe in God or intentionally try to please Him with your actions. For example, honesty and integrity have their own rewards. They will protect you from many of the troubles in life that come from lying, cheating, and stealing. Consider how the relationships of people you know have been damaged by these behaviors. Similarly, following the moral code found in the Ten Commandments and Sermon on the Mount will yield fruit even if you do not believe they are God's absolute law for mankind.

Second, God actively blesses people as they do the right thing. Obedience activates a supernatural force of divine favor in your life. God is on the lookout for those who do the right thing to strengthen them.[1154] Does this mean God is watching for people to curse their disobedience? If cursing means to bring harm, I do not believe God is in the business of causing harm. The Bible says every good and perfect gift comes from above from the Father of the heavenly lights.[1155] Moses' warning that God curs-

---
1151 Matthew 5–7
1152 Matthew 7:24–26
1153 Deuteronomy 28:13
1154 2 Chronicles 16:9
1155 James 1:17

es disobedience means God will allow the negative consequences of your sins to affect your life.[1156] Sin carries its own punishments. When they were younger, I warned my kids countless times not to do something that would get them hurt, only to see them later do that very thing. I bandaged lots of skinned knees and bruised arms. Did I as their father cause their pain? Absolutely not, but I used the moment to reinforce the principle that if they listen to my instructions, it will help keep them safe. I do that because I love them. If I didn't care, I would let them do whatever they want, regardless of the dangers, even go play in traffic on the highway. God allows consequences as discipline in the natural order of cause and effect that accompanies the God-given right to make our own choices. The purpose of discipline is to draw you back to God, not harm. Discipline serves as a continuing reminder that sin is harmful and living for God is the one true way to find wholeness, health, and blessing. God works through every situation to effect good in your life. He is good, and part of your faith walk is to grow in the appreciation that He is a rewarder of those who seek Him.[1157] Do not fall into the enemy's trap of questioning this truth. Your obedience and faith will always yield rewards in God's timing.

Third, doing the right thing bring many positive consequences, but it also has a protective component. Moral decisions protect you from the many second, third, and fourth order consequences of wrongdoing. Violating your core values fosters spiritual struggles such as feeling abandoned by God, doubting one's beliefs, questioning one's purpose, and feeling conflicted about acting contrary to your beliefs. You can avoid these spiritual consequences and numerous related negative thoughts and feelings simply by doing the right thing. Additionally, you can avoid the complications that almost always accompany doing the wrong thing with the added stress and additional energy required. Sometimes it may seem like the expedient wrong thing worked in your favor, but as Scripture notes, the consequences come back to you, sooner or later.[1158]

Adam and Eve enjoyed the perfection of Eden. Today, Eden is synonymous with utopia and paradise, perfect peace and prosperity. It is the dream of nearly every human. Adam and Eve had it. God had to provide them the option not to love Him, a command they could choose not to follow. Forced love isn't love at all. They were not robots. If they obeyed God's one requirement, they enjoyed paradise. They had only one command to follow, one simple thing to do—to remain in perfect harmony with God and creation. If only it could be that easy today. What if you could avoid all the sin and suffering of the world by following one simple command not to eat fruit from one tree? Adam and Eve could eat fruit from thousands of trees and plants in Eden, even the fruit that sustained their immortality, the Tree of Life. Sadly, they took it all for granted, trading it for a bold-faced lie. Prioritizing your relationship with God above everything else will bless your life and protect you from much pain, suffering, and sorrow. It will not insulate you from everything since we no longer live in Eden. This world has been contam-

---
1156 Deuteronomy 28:15
1157 Hebrew 11:6
1158 1 Timothy 5:24

inated by sin. It works through humanity and creation in many forms of destructive power. However, you can enjoy your best possible life in this fallen world by making your relationship with God your first and foremost priority. Adam and Eve assumed the blessings of God would be permanent regardless of their choices. Do not make the same mistake. Do not take your gifts for granted, and do not put your many blessings at risk by immoral decisions. Like Adam and Eve, doing the wrong thing impacts your relationships. It has many unexpected consequences for the well-being of yourself and others. Left unchecked, it will lead to permanent death. This is the importance of the sacrifice of Christ. By faith in Christ, the sting of sin is removed, and the curse is broken. Through His Spirit living inside you, you can overcome every temptation and make wise, constructive, and godly choices.

Obedience protects your relationship with God. Disobedience makes you feel distant and allows the enemy opportunities to exploit your weaknesses. When Adam and Eve sinned in the Garden, the first thing they did was to hide from God, revealing its effects on their relationship with Him.[1159] God came into the Garden to talk with them, but they were ashamed to meet Him. In the same way, your sin will degrade your relationship with Him. You will likely feel distant, disconnected, guilty, condemned, and outside of God's favor and esteem. You may feel you have to work hard (good works) to cover your sins. Adam and Eve tried to cover their guilt with fig leaves. No one can ever do enough good to pay back for all their wrongdoing. Adam and Eve expended a lot of energy in stress, worry, and fear to cover their guilt, but it was no good. God had to cover them with skins to show them that the result of sin is always death.[1160] There is no cheap atonement, Jesus paid the ultimate price. When you sin, death works in your life, something gets lost, figuratively, something dies. It may be a relationship, trust, peace, joy, etc. That is the meaning of the old sacrificial system. All those sacrifices didn't save anyone. They just reminded everyone that sin caused death.[1161] At Calvary, Jesus back paid all sacrifices all the way back to Adam. Can you imagine working in the Jewish Temple as a priest, watching all the death and blood every day—people bringing their live animals and then killing them at the altar to atone for their sins, draining the blood, sprinkling it, and arranging the carcasses in the fire? I grew up on a farm and had to help butcher animals for meat. I cannot imagine doing it all day long every day. After a while, you get the message: every time I sin, some animal in my household must die. Thank God for Jesus! However, in the Garden of Eden, God was forced to kill innocent animals He created, taking their hides and fashioning garments to cover Adam and Eve's nakedness.[1162] Bloodshed and death entered Creation for the first time in this act. In Christ, your sins, past, present, and future are forgiven. You are not separated from God in the way Adam and Eve were, but sin exposes you to many consequences that affect the totality of your being and relationships. Reconciliation can repair these rifts with the potential to make the bonds stronger,

---

1159 Genesis 3:8–9
1160 Genesis 3:7,21
1161 Hebrews 10:1–14
1162 Genesis 3:17, Romans 8:20–21

but it normally requires a painful process. Adam and Eve would never again enjoy the perfect childlike innocence in their relationship with God in Eden. They were naked in every sense of that word, and they knew it. Sin is a wrecking ball that affects your communion with God and the intimacy you feel. Make your relationship with God and obedience to His Word your priority, and you will continue to grow in Christ-like character and more fully walk out his will for your life.

Obedience protects others, love protects. By its very nature—doing the wrong thing (sin) harms others. Wrongdoing is bad because it results in death; to you, your relationships, and sometimes to those who are innocent. God showed Adam and Eve that their sin brought death, just as He warned.[1163] In the next chapter of Genesis, the full extent of the damage to human relationships is revealed in Cain's murder of Abel. His words to God are chilling, "Am I my brother's keeper?"[1164] You can almost hear the anguish in God's voice as He cries out, "What have you done?" That cry continues to ring through the ages as humans pillage others in their selfish pursuits. You cannot truly love others without obedience to God's Word. You may not believe in Jesus, but the only way to truly love is selflessly.[1165] Love for one another, that which is truly love, is proof of God's love. There can be no love for others without God. It is interesting that even today, people ravage other people in the name of love and justice. Cain felt justified in murdering Abel. It doesn't matter who; apart from God's love, people will only wreak havoc on others in the name of their cause. Consider how much pain and suffering throughout the ages could have been avoided over one simple choice in the Garden. How much human suffering could be avoided if everyone simply followed the *golden rule*? Obedience to God's Word is the only way to ensure your interactions are beneficial and uplifting to others.

Obedience protects all of creation. Adam and Eve along with every creature (animals, birds, and other creatures) were originally vegetarian.[1166] No bloodshed or death had marred God's perfect creation before the fall. Some people look at all the pain in the world and ask, "How could God call this world 'good' after He created it? How can God allow all this suffering?" The answer is, He never called the world as we know it, with all its sin and suffering, "good." He called the original world and everything He created before the fall "good."[1167] The current frustration in creation with the "eat or be eaten, survival of the fittest" principles did not exist until after Adam and Eve sinned.[1168] Today, every creature on Earth gets eaten by something. Creatures protect themselves, eat, sleep, and procreate. Everything they do falls in one of these categories. Animals never just take a vacation; they are never completely at rest. Storms, hurricanes, tornadoes, earthquakes, along with every danger associated with nature, are a result of the fall, of sin. Today, the ills of this world continue to be problems associated with original sin

---

1163 Genesis 3:3
1164 Genesis 4:9
1165 1 Corinthians 13:4–8
1166 Genesis 1:29
1167 Genesis 1:30
1168 Genesis 3:17, Romans 8:20–21

or the continuing sin of humanity in its selfish, must have more, arrogant fallen nature. In truth, today's concerns with the environment are less a result of carbon emissions, pollution, overuse, etc., and more a product of contamination from sin in this world, people's choices to place self-interest, power, greed, and indulgence over love for others and stewardship of God's creation. Sin destroys everything it touches but love and obedience can change the world.

Obedience protects life. In obedience to God, Adam and Eve would have lived forever, having access to immortality through the fruit from the Tree of Life. Their decision to disobey God meant physical death. God exiled them from the Garden with its nourishment and protection.[1169] Physical death illustrated the true nature of sin's work in humanity. The "death" principle works in your life every time you do the wrong thing, releasing a destructive force into your life that causes pain, suffering, and devastation. Frankly, I believe sin is the zombie apocalypse. I heard someone call COVID-19 the zombie apocalypse without the zombies, but sin actually has zombies. The TV show *The Walking Dead* nailed it—sin has turned people into the undead who lurch along believing they are alive. They imitate life, almost always on the move. Sin is the ultimate virus, depleting every good quality of a human while reducing them to ravenous monsters that seek only to fill their own appetites. Have you noticed zombies are always trying to spread the virus? Sin is never content to live and let live. It always tries to expand its control of people and spread its destructive influence to others. There are no truces in the sin-caused zombie apocalypse world. If they can't spread the virus, zombies want to eat you. Zombie movies are pretty gross, but the effects of sin are worse, especially because they are real. People do the unthinkable to one another in the sin-caused zombie apocalypse. And if you don't join them in sin, zombies want to take you out. The sin-virus-controlled zombie Pharisees wanted to kill Jesus, and it's no different today. All over the world, sin-virus-controlled zombies are killing believers in Jesus solely because they accepted Christ. They get so mad at followers of Jesus who take a stand on Scripture, they literally would kill them if they could. The zombies form mobs in the sin-created zombie apocalypse. They cluster on whatever forum they can, using their power to squash anyone who hasn't accepted the sin virus. It was a mob that shouted "Crucify him" to order Jesus' death. But obedience to God protects life; this is not a kill or be killed world. There is a trace of life in the zombies of the sin-caused apocalypse. The anti-virus is the Holy Spirit who delivers the love and mercy of Christ through the message of reconciliation. Do not be overcome by evil; overcome evil with good. Love is the key. You cannot fight the sin virus cursing people out on blogs and social media. Humbly and lovingly share the message of life through Christ in your example. You don't have to become a sin-controlled zombie. You can overcome the sin virus and become a source of healing for others.

While Jesus' sacrifice ultimately destroyed the power of sin and death in eternity, it does not release you from every consequence of your sin in the here and now. You can be sure that God will forgive your

---
1169 Genesis 3:19,23

sin (He has forgiven it) and remove your guilt as you ask in faith.[1170] However, you may continue to wrestle with the consequences of your wrongdoing as well as associated negative feelings. This does not mean you are not forgiven. The enemy will try to heap the guilt and shame onto your thoughts. Stand in faith on the scriptural promise of forgiveness.[1171] You must fight the battle in your mind, as we discussed extensively in Section II. When you are dealing with difficulties in life, do not compound your problems by doing the wrong thing. Exercise wisdom and self-control to protect yourself from dealing with additional bad feelings or having to rectify the consequences of your sinful mistakes. Doing the right thing helps you feel more secure in your relationship with God and helps you maintain a stronger spiritual footing to cope with your present struggles.

A fourth positive consequence of doing the right thing is living in right relationship. Scripture is full of wisdom for improving your relationships. Obedience to God's Word brings harmony with others. Treating others with dignity and respect in the fruit of the Spirit, love, patience, kindness, goodness, gentleness, faithfulness, and self-control builds strong, trusting relationships. Doing the wrong thing degrades them, making you feel distant, disconnected, and insecure. It may make you question your "relationship status." Sin makes you want to distance yourself from the wronged person(s) in the same way Adam and Eve hid from God. The enemy tempts you to use unhealthy means like manipulation (remember Adam's fig leaves?) to compensate for what you did, causing additional stress and producing additional negative consequences. You may lie to cover up the offense or make excuses to justify yourself. As a counselor, I often thought, "How much suffering could have been avoided if this person had admitted their wrong and simply asked for forgiveness?" A lot of contemporary movies build their plot around the machinations people go through to avoid admitting their wrongs. While these often are a source of comedy in movies, they are tragic in real life. Doing the right thing strengthens your relationships and helps you feel more secure and trusting.

A final positive consequence of doing the right thing is the benefit to your inner life. Doing the right thing with a clear conscience gives you courage, strength, and fortitude. Samuel gave Israel his farewell speech with these words, "Whom have I oppressed? If I have wronged anyone, I will make it right."[1172] He proclaimed his feelings of peace toward everyone and offered recompense if anyone felt he had wronged them. In his heart, he carried a clear conscience. Feelings of guilt and shame drain you. They sap your will and cause your morale to deteriorate. You need to preserve your energy and motivation to persevere. Doing the right thing is always a positive step in overcoming difficulties. In the short term, it may seem more difficult, but beware of the expedient solution. Following the counsel of Scripture reinforces good character and produces good consequences. Wrongdoing is not constructive and even less so in times of adversity. In addition to sin's effects on your thoughts and feelings, it produces second

---

1170 1 John 1:9
1171 1 John 1:9
1172 1 Samuel 12:3–5

and third-order effects that worsen your situation. However, obedience does exactly the opposite. Doing the right thing releases healthy, positive second, third, and fourth order effects that continue to work for your good. Love and goodness go places nothing else can go. The Spirit can multiply little efforts and use them to make a large impact. Remember the lesson of the five loaves and two fish. That lunch fed five thousand men and their families.[1173] Over time, doing the right thing produces exponential returns in your life.

We addressed the spiritual and relational effects of wrongdoing, but what about other consequences that come from sinful decisions and choices? God promised Abraham a son to his wife, Sarah, in their old age. However, in their impatience, the couple turned to Sarah's younger handmaiden to fulfill their desire for a child. This faithless act was contrary to God's promise and intent. The child, Ishmael, and his mother, Hagar, became a source of frustration and regret to Sarah, who eventually asked Abraham to send them away—so much for their "easy fix."[1174] Your faithless actions will often spawn new unforeseen problems. David created numerous problems for himself later in life by his disobedience. We are quick to point out his sin with Bathsheba, but we forget the failures to discipline his sons and the hubris behind counting the fighting men of Israel. Both events caused serious trouble for David. His son, Absalom, began a revolution and nearly killed David before he could escape.[1175] His pride caused a plague on the land.[1176] When you are struggling already, you don't need additional problems of your own making to add to the mix. Some choose to cope by numbing their pain with alcohol, drugs, or some other addictive behavior. In the short term, these acts may alleviate your pain, but they have many destructive side effects. Wrongdoing feels good in the moment but always complicates your situation, requiring additional energy and resources to resolve.

I am convinced people need the Lordship of Christ almost as much as Jesus the Savior. Salvation is critical. It begins your new life in Christ as a friend of God and provides the certainty of eternity with God in heaven. However, salvation is the entry point to your new life. It is just the beginning of your relationship with God. Many people camp right on the doorstep never moving deeper. Like marriage, the ceremony (salvation) is just the beginning. You have your whole life ahead of you. Your marriage covenant is lived out in a commitment to your spouse in the same way you live out your commitment to Christ after salvation. Lordship is where you give God control of your life. He is on the throne; he is the captain of your ship. Most people today are firmly planted on the throne of their lives with no thought of ceding authority to anyone else. They are the judge, and they call all the shots. The world needs the Righteous Judge whose decisions are healthy, constructive, and helpful for all mankind. We have enough human opinions being pushed everywhere on the media all the time. Some have no desire for

---
1173 Matthew 14:13–21
1174 Genesis 16
1175 2 Samuel 16:20–19:8
1176 2 Samuel 24:15–17

understanding, they just want to air their opinions.[1177] Today, we call this foolishness finding your voice. The world needs a lot less voices and far more listening. You will be far better served by elevating the basic values of Scripture in pursuit of answers to your problems.

On the other side of the spectrum, many people feel they must follow countless rules to be accepted. The Lordship of Christ is different. We are accepted because God loves us and gave us the unearnable gift of salvation through Jesus' sacrifice. We let Christ lead because we sincerely love him and want to serve and because we trust him even when things get difficult. Scripture states, "The Kingdom of God (the rulership of God) is righteousness, peace, and joy in the Holy Spirit."[1178] God's rule helps us do the right thing and produces peace and joy in our hearts. When you follow Jesus, it is a benefit to your life. He doesn't bring harm. This verse specifically contradicts the notion that God's rule is about following all kinds of rules—dietary and other laws (it is not about eating and drinking). If you're stuck in the drudgery of following rules, you are missing out on the law of love. Follow Jesus because you love Him, and it is the best course for your life. Do not follow rules; follow Christ. You need Jesus to be in charge to live your best life. It only happens when you follow the leading of the Holy Spirit, live the law of love, and seek to obey God's Word. You do not earn your salvation or forgiveness by obedience; those are a gift. You develop wisdom, spiritual maturity, and productive service to Christ through obedience. You reap the benefits of doing the right thing, you learn to trust God's righteous judgment, and you rely on His direction as He leads you. These benefits will serve you well as you face adversity and will protect you from making a bad situation worse.

1177 Proverbs 18:2
1178 Romans 14:17

Chapter 11

Get Back to the Basics—Love Others

Knowledge puffs up, but love builds up.[1179]

Look for opportunities to show love to others. Love is communicating esteem, value, and commitment to others through your actions. It is the most powerful force in the universe, apart from God.[1180] Love can penetrate the hardness of people's hearts and break down relational walls like nothing else. In that sense, it can affect outcomes in miraculous ways. In the previous chapter, we discussed the scriptural priority of loving God and loving others. Spiritual resilience is all about leveraging the power of the spiritual life, with its principles and practices, to overcome challenges. In this chapter, you will learn to harness the power of loving action. These commands are key to reaping numerous benefits that support strength and well-being.

First, love shifts your focus. You can get so focused on your problems; you descend into feelings of self-pity and powerlessness. Adversity tends to make you withdraw. You might find it comforting to dwell on the misery associated with your situation. However, preoccupation with your problems is a prescription for getting stuck. You can help prevent this cycle by looking for opportunities to love others. This shifts your focus away from your difficulties. Second, it helps you connect with other people in their point of need, strengthening your relationships and widening your circle of support. Tough times present an opportunity to deepen current relationships and build new ones. For instance, by joining a small group, you can meet new people and look for opportunities to serve. Third, you will feel better by helping others. The uplifting feelings you experience from helping others are counterintuitive. You may expect giving to others would leave you with less energy. "I'm just too stressed or spent to help anyone else." However, you do not end up with less when you serve; you feel encouraged and strengthened. It is an amazing spiritual dynamic that you can lift yourself by uplifting others. In one sense, all selfless expressions of love are serving and giving. In another sense, you may never connect certain selfless acts that way, such as forgiving someone, encouraging others, or just spending time with a lonely person. Scripture highlights the principle—when you show love and mercy to others, the benefits will be multiplied back to you.[1181] Look for opportunities to share the love of God, and you will uplift yourself.

1179 1 Corinthians 8:1
1180 1 Corinthians 13:13
1181 Luke 6:38, Proverbs 11:25

Love is the basis of the scriptural ethic, yet it means different things to so many different people. It is hard to know what Scripture really means. Some people say they love coffee, surfing, a pro sports team, an artist, an author, a friend, or chocolate. Are those all the same kinds of love? Scripture uses different Greek works for love that reflect its different aspects: *eros*, what we know as the feelings and pleasure of love (such as romantic love—this is the love we idolize in our culture); *philos*, what we know as the mutual sharing of friendship love (like the close friendship of David and Jonathon); *storge* (used in its root form), describing what we understand as the appropriate expressions of love (answering, what is the appropriate way to socially express love for someone, for instance, a spouse, vs. a friend); and finally, *agape*, what we know as the selfless, sacrificial expression of love (it is God's love for humanity). God's agape love is the focus of this chapter. Agape is not a feeling; it is a sacrificial action, even though later it may produce good feelings. Your motivation for showing agape love is not that you feel good or get pleasure in doing it, but rather that you desire to obey God and help others. Scripture states, "For God so loved (agape) the world that he gave his only son."[1182] Jesus did not experience pleasure on the cross. He endured the most painful torture imaginable, yet He loved humanity by offering His life in payment for the debts owed by others. Jesus' love was not the pleasurable felt love of eros. It was fully selfless. You reveal the selflessness of agape love when you uplift others with the sole desire to serve and bless them. You demonstrate the sacrificial aspect of agape love when your loving acts cost you, but you do them anyway. Your sincere acts of agape love will always communicate value, esteem, and God's love for the other person.

Look for opportunities to uplift others regardless of who they are. You can show God's love to a person with whom you do not agree, lack a strong emotional tie, or may even consider an enemy. You do not have to get along with the person to agape love them. In fact, Scripture states, "Love your enemies and do good to those who mistreat you."[1183] Anyone can love someone who is good to them, but God's love serves the person who is working against you.[1184] You radically change your circumstances by releasing the power of love in how you act or respond. You can improve relationships, even those that are strained, and improve your own well-being through living a life of agape love. Consider several additional benefits of living out acts of love during your adversity.

First, love drives out fear.[1185] Fear saps your strength, making it harder to overcome adversity. When you show love to others, you remind yourself how much God loves you. You may know in your mind God loves you, but it can be hard to feel God loves you in difficulties. Scripture is clear: God's love for you is so great that normal descriptions such as height, length, and width cannot define it.[1186] While it may be hard to hear in times of trouble, there is some indescribable dynamic from helping others in

---
1182 John 3:16
1183 Matthew 5:44
1184 Romans 5:8
1185 1 John 4:18
1186 Ephesians 3:18

their difficulties that helps you to receive the value and love God has for you. The more you feel God's love in the depths of your heart, the less you will feel fear. Love drives out fear in another way. Strained relationships with others often cause people to fear being around them. However, when you serve such a person in love, the awkwardness and tension of being around them will begin to dissipate. The more positive interactions you have, the less you will feel stress and anxiety being near them. Acts of love help shape the relational dynamics to effect reconciliation and to help you live in peace.

Second, love has the potential to radically improve your relationships.[1187] Love breaks down walls. As described above, loving acts will help prepare the atmosphere for reconciliation. They will also help transform your heart, making it softer and more open to the person you serve. Several years ago, *The Love Dare* became a bestseller. It shares how you can change your marriage in as little as forty days by sacrificially serving your spouse in love. This principle is based upon the powerful dynamics of God's sacrificial agape love. When you selflessly serve others, you can change how you feel about them and create a powerful opportunity to soften their hearts toward you as well. This will work for anyone. If you are struggling with a person in your life, commit to do at least two things each week for the next six weeks that will communicate you value them. Do not let them know what you are doing; don't throw it back in their face if you get in an argument. This is purely your gift to them in the form of acts of kindness that will bless them. Write down how you feel about them at the beginning and end of the six weeks. It's amazing how your perception of the relationship can change through selfless acts of love.

Love will help you be quick to forgive. Scripture states, "Love covers offenses."[1188] It covers a multitude of sins.[1189] Not only will loving acts change your heart, but they will also soften the hearts of the people you serve. Love makes people more merciful and stretches their capacity to show grace. Love is truly the best way to shape the situation for a win-win scenario. Stronger relationships are a source of strength through adversity.

Third, love will purify your motives. For acts of love to be impactful, they must have the proper motive.[1190] They must derive from a desire to help, encourage, and bless. When you get your attitude and motives right, almost everything else will tend to fall into place. Purity in your inner life serves as a compass to help you make wise and constructive decisions. The healthier your actions, the better your outcomes will tend to be. In times of struggle, orienting your inner compass toward love will help protect you from the damaging effects of guilt and shame.

Fourth, love will draw you closer to God.[1191] The more you serve others in loving acts, the stronger your relationship with God will become. The vertical relationship you have with God is based on His unconditional love expressed in the sacrifice of Christ for your wrongdoing. An important part of

---
1187 1 Corinthians 13:4–8
1188 Proverbs 10:12
1189 1 Peter 4:8
1190 1 Corinthians 13:1–3
1191 1 John 4:16

showing your love and appreciation to God for His love is to love others—all other people from every background and nation for whom Jesus also sacrificed His life. Scripture asks, "How can you love God who is unseen if you cannot love others who you can see?"[1192] Jesus made an interesting observation in the Parable of the Talents, "He who has will be given more."[1193] The more you show love, the more you will get. Many people live life like it's a zero-sum game of limited resources—if you give it away, you lose it. The spiritual principles of Scripture transform the law of limited resources. The more you give away, the more you will get. Spiritual giving is multiplication, not subtraction. As you share love, you will get even more. In fact, Scripture is clear that love is only made complete when it is given away in loving acts.[1194] The circle of God's love, by design, is meant to flow from God to you to others. You can only become spiritually rich by being spiritually generous.

Finally, your acts of love will draw other people to God.[1195] People see the reality of God in the extravagant love of people who love Him. This is true as you uplift others and is especially visible in loving people who are unlovable. Anyone will treat someone well who is good to them. That's normal. But people see a special witness of God's love and presence through the acts of those who love the outcasts or love people when they are not good to them. Can you love the person who mistreats you? Be like Jesus, who even forgave those who crucified Him.[1196] That is the high call of love that will bear witness to the hard-hearted. Scripture describes the power of blessings that follow the one who gives generously.[1197] Adversity can provide special opportunities to walk out your life purpose of revealing God to the world. Demonstrating God's love means living your purpose and adds meaning and hope to your outlook.

People voice their frustration with the problems they see in the world, primarily with the way people treat each other. Everyone should be treated with dignity and respect regardless of the differences or level of agreement. Unfortunately, many people are waiting for the world around them to change before they get involved. They reject the notion that they can make a difference, abdicating their God-given power of choice and responsibility to make the world a better place because they don't feel heard or empowered. Do not resign yourself to this attitude. Love is powerful, it can change your circumstances and the world. After Jesus' death, His followers carried His message to the ends of the earth. They were arrested, beaten, stoned, in many cases, executed for their simple message of God's love and salvation through Jesus Christ. They had no power, no platform, no public way to be heard; the system was stacked against them, no fairness or justice. But that did not stop them. One by one, from city to city, they continued to share the good news with love and good deeds. Their extravagant care for social outcasts: the poor, orphans, widows, prisoners, etc., was remarkable. Eventually, their love changed the

---
1192 1 John 4:20
1193 Matthew 25:29
1194 1 John 4:12
1195 John 13:34–35
1196 Luke 23:34
1197 2 Corinthians 9:12–14

known world. Love can break down walls nothing else can.

Difficulties can cause you to re-examine your life. They present an opportunity to get back to the basics. Love is the essence of human life, *to love and be loved*. Accept God loves you beyond any possible human description.[1198] Get back to the basics, loving God and loving other people more than you ever have before. Loving acts will improve your quality of life and the lives of others on multiple levels. Love is the ultimate win-win strategy for this life and the next.

1198 Ephesians 3:17–19

Chapter 12

Navigate Change—Live in Victory

In all these things we are more than conquerors through him who loved us.[1199]

To overcome adversity, you must be able to navigate change. People generally struggle with the many changes that come with trials and difficulties. They become so overwhelmed by the shock of it all, they fall into the victimization trap. You are meant to overcome all difficulties through faith and the vitality of your spiritual life. One of my favorite things to do on the playground as a kid was to play on the monkey bars. To get to the next bar, you must reach with one hand to grab it. Then, you must let go with the other hand and swing to the new bar. This is an example of faith in times of change. Risk is involved. You must completely leave the bar you are on to get to the next bar. I have watched friends get paralyzed by fear, refusing to let go of the original bar. They end up hanging in between until they drop. Sadly, this happens in life when people fail to navigate change. You choose to overcome in victory or to give up and assume the identity of a victim. Your choices determine your future outcomes more than your experiences. In Christ, you can always be victorious, even when your circumstances are slow to turn around.[1200] David spent years in exile unjustly pursued by King Saul and his soldiers. He had faithfully served the king and even refused to harm Saul when he had opportunities to take his life. He dealt with a lot of change, constantly moving from place to place, from the castle and privilege to ostracism in the wilderness. If anyone could claim the title of victim, it was David. Have you lived outside, in the hills and caves, separated from your family, and wrongly accused as a traitor? David did, yet he repeatedly turned his eyes toward heaven instead of his misery, "The Lord is my rock, fortress, deliverer, my strength in whom I will trust."[1201] He went on to declare his victory, "He delivered me from my strong enemy. Those who hated me were too strong for me, but the Lord was my support. He brought me out into a broad place."[1202] David was able to look back and see the faithfulness of God through it all. He overcame the trials and potential bitterness and eventually replaced Saul on Israel's throne.

If anyone had to deal with unjust circumstances, it was Joseph. Scripture records how his own brothers sold him as a slave. When in Potiphar's house, he was falsely accused by his master's wife and sent to prison. When he helped Pharoah's wine taster in prison, his good deed was forgotten for two years.[1203]

1199 Romans 8:37
1200 1 Corinthians 15:57
1201 Psalm 18:2–3
1202 Psalm 18:17–19
1203 Genesis 37–50

Nearly thirteen years of Joseph's life were lost in slavery and prison, yet he continued to thrive in the worst of circumstances. He opted to believe, to keep trusting God. Eventually he was vindicated, assigned a position second only to Pharoah as ruler of Egypt. He refused to assume the identity of a victim. He rejected self-pity, striving with faith to be the best version of himself. He always pressed forward toward the fulfillment of his dream. He navigated the change from life in his father's house to slave in Potiphar's house, to prisoner in Egypt, to the palace, with resilience and hope. He refused to allow bitterness or self-pity to corrupt his heart.

Scripture records the many trials faced by Paul as he followed God's purpose for his life.[1204] He described the personal effects of these struggles in detail, yet in every case, he refused to allow negativity and self-pity to lead him into a victim mentality. When discouraged, he refused to embrace despair. When persecuted, he refused to believe the lie that God had abandoned him. When things got tough, he refused to quit.[1205] Paul traveled extensively, was rejected in many cities, mistreated, beaten, shipwrecked, and imprisoned. He endured constant change in his life, along with David and Joseph. In their distress, they had the choice to succumb to a victim mentality or, with God's help, to fight to overcome their injustices. In your difficulties, you must choose a positive, victorious mindset that strives to overcome. If you don't fight, the enemy will tempt you to embrace a prison of bitterness and despair.

Change is tough for most, especially when caused by difficulties. Studies show that only a small percentage of people enjoy change. Two and a half percent are the innovators, another thirteen and a half percent are the early adopters. A large group (thirty-four percent) will eventually accept change, while an equally sized group will reluctantly accept change when forced. The laggards (sixteen percent) comprise the group that will ultimately tag along when everyone else has accepted it, and, of course, the small group that will never accept the change, no matter how good it is or how many people follow. This model, following several studies by Rogers, shows how challenging change can be even when it is good.[1206] Combined with the stressors of hardship, it can be challenging to navigate in a healthy manner.

Not all change is good; most change is a mixture of advantages and disadvantages. You may be the type of person who will embrace change for the sake of change, or you may wish to determine how much control you really have over it as you seek to cope. In my lifetime, I have watched technology go from forty-five records and eight-track tapes to cassettes to CDs to the digital age. The same transformation has occurred with computers, from those that used to fill a room to the phone that fits in your hand. A computer-phone with access to the World Wide Web is a great tool for banking, purchasing, entertainment, communicating with family, and many other advantageous tasks that make life easier. On the other hand, it has perpetuated a self-indulged incivility that caters to the worst of human nature. Would society be better without the web and phones? Your response may be based more on your place in the change acceptance curve and generation than you realize.

1204 2 Corinthians 11:23–27
1205 2 Corinthians 4:7–12
1206 Rogers, Everett M. *Diffusion of Innovations*. 3rd ed. (New York: The Free Press, 1983), 22.

Changes derived from adversity are difficult and uncomfortable for most, yet they provide opportunities, including introspection, growth, and potential for improvement. Throughout the years, he was hunted by King Saul, David took advantage of the opportunities. He might have given up, but he had a promise from God that he eventually would be king. He held fast to that belief, trusting God, persevering through many trials, learning patience, and developing wisdom and godly character. At the same time, an inner work was happening in his life, significant events occurred to prepare him for future rule. First, he developed a loyal band of warriors who walked through the trials with him, received several confirmations that God's plan would prevail, began a family, acquired wealth, and gained influence with tribal leaders who would eventually provide the key support to help him ascend the throne. It was probably difficult for David to see a palace when he was hiding in a cave. We know at least once; his best friend Jonathan helped him through discouragement. Yet David persevered through it all. He overcame every adversity and received God's promise and blessing in his life.

You may be tempted to look at your difficulties and lose hope. You may look back and long for better days. For those who are older, the changes in the world may cause you sadness and regret. Scripture advises against asking, "Why were the old days better than these?"[1207] It is not wise. As we shared at the beginning of this book, our hero from *The Lord of the Rings*, Frodo Baggins, lamented to Gandalf the Wizard, wishing he did not have to face the days of darkness in the rising power of Mordor. You may wish you did not have to face your troubles in a world full of trouble. Scripture is clear that God not only assigns you the place you live, but also your time in history.[1208] God will work through your challenges to make you a better, stronger person and to use your testimony and example to impact others. I used to watch the "Six Million Dollar Man" on TV when I was a kid. Astronaut Steve Austin was in a tragic crash that nearly took his life. But doctors rebuilt him with the bionic power of robotic arms and legs. He could run faster, see and hear better, and lift more than ever before.[1209] He became a force for good in the world. In one sense, you are bionic as well. God is rebuilding you through your tragedies to make you a force for good in your world. Do not lose your light because of trials.

Unfortunately, many people get stuck in the struggle. They cannot get past the loss, the pain, or other negative consequences. You cannot overcome life's problems if you assume the identity of a victim. A victim mentality is a dysfunctional thought process that assumes life is out of your control, will always end up with a negative outcome, and out to get you. The victim mindset makes you feel helpless and hopeless, but it has some convenient benefits. You can avoid taking responsibility, you can receive pity and attention from others who will be less likely to criticize or upset you, you can manipulate others, getting what you want more often, and for those who enjoy the drama, you can spice up your life with

---
1207 Ecclesiastes 7:10
1208 Acts 17:24–28
1209 Martin Caidin and Dick Moder, Directors, *Six Million Dollar Man,* March 7, 1973–March 6, 1978.

the unhealthy self-focus.[1210] Unfortunately, it is self-destructive, significantly limiting your ability to cope and hindering other sources of strength, such as relationships.

Jesus encountered the father of a boy with severe convulsions. Jesus asked the boy's father,

> "How long has he been like this?" "From childhood," he answered. "It has often thrown him into fire or water to kill him. But if you can do anything, take pity on us and help us." "'If you can?'" said Jesus. "Everything is possible for one who believes." Immediately the boy's father exclaimed, "I do believe; help me overcome my unbelief!"[1211]

The father was obviously worn out from his lengthy struggle with the boy's condition. He came to Jesus with the best argument he had—an appeal to pity for the remote possibility Jesus could help. We can hear the self-pity, the lack of hope in his request. However, the man did one thing right: he asked Jesus for help. Many people lost in victimhood will not ask for help because they are hopeless. They have become so accustomed to living as a victim, they refuse to abandon the perspective. Why take responsibility when you can blame everyone else? If you can identify with some of the signs below, you may have fallen into the victim trap.

> You're constantly blaming other people or situations for feeling miserable;
> You possess a "life is against me" philosophy;
> You're cynical or pessimistic;
> You see all your problems as catastrophes;
> You think others are purposely trying to hurt you;
> You believe you're the only one being targeted for mistreatment;
> You keep reliving past painful memories that made you feel like a victim;
> You find something to complain about even when things go right;
> You refuse to consider other perspectives when talking about your problems;
> You feel powerless and unable to cope effectively with a problem or life in general;
> You feel attacked when you're given constructive criticism;
> You believe others are responsible for the bad things that happen in your life;
> You believe that everyone is "better off" than you;
> You enjoy feeling sorry for yourself;
> You attract people like you (who complain, blame, and feel victimized by life);

1210 Aletheia Luna, "*23 Signs You're Suffering from a Victim Mentality*," accessed May 28, 2022, https://lonerwolf.com/victim-mentality.
1211 Mark 9:21–23

You believe that the world is a scary, mostly bad place;

You enjoy sharing your tragic stories with other people;

You have a habit of blaming, attacking, and accusing others for how you feel;

You feel powerless to change your circumstances;

You expect sympathy from others, and when you don't get it, you feel upset;

You refuse to analyze yourself or improve your life;

You tend to "one-up" people when it comes to sharing traumatic experiences;

You're constantly putting yourself down.[1212]

Do not deceive yourself. The signs above lock you into a negative downward cycle. You will never prosper if you are bound up in the chains of victimization. You are not a victim. Get rid of the dysfunctional mindset and pursue a constructive way forward. Sculptors see an image of a masterpiece in the marble you and I see as simply a block of stone. They chip away the stone in big chips at first to reveal the general shape. Later, they use smaller refined sculpting to remove the small pieces that remain. They finish the process with sanding and polishing to reveal the fine details of their work. Your life is like that block of marble. The real you, the you God sees, your best life in relationship with Him, is the you that must be freed from all the excess trappings of your life. Your past, the long list of possible reactions to your past like the list above, along with anything else that does not line up with God's Word are not you. Like the marble, they must be chipped away to reveal the true masterpiece of the divine artist.

Everyone experiences troubles. In truth, you have no idea what people around you are going through. The enemy would like to make you feel you are all alone, that you are the only one facing struggles, and that everyone else is doing well. Even people of great faith, like Elijah, faced moments where it felt like they were alone in their struggles.[1213] These thoughts are a lie and feed the victim mentality. Most people have struggles, and as Scripture notes, they are common to all of us.[1214] When facing problems, you can get so focused on your situation, you fail to see the signs of struggle in others' lives. One day while my neighbor and I were talking, he began to talk about how bad his son's life had been. He was in and out of jail, struggled with drug use, and had recently gone through a divorce. I was aware of his son's situation as I was walking through some of these things with him in counseling and prayer. At one point, he observed, "Some people just don't have to go through the struggles others have." At that moment, from his tone and body language, I felt the comment was directed right at me. I did not react to what sounded like a put-down (as if I always had it easy). Instead, I casually observed that all people experience secret struggles. At the time, I was dealing with my own troubles: a disabled son, struggles in my marriage, and significant stressors in my job. My life may have looked good from the outside, but

---
1212 Luna, "23 Signs."
1213 1 Kings 19:10,13–15,18
1214 1 Corinthians 10:13

it was far from problem-free. If you blame everyone else for your troubles, you give up control of your life. You do not have to blame or shame yourself, but you must own your thoughts and actions to move forward on a constructive path.

If you compare the new work God wants to do in your life to a swimming pool, consider the three possible approaches. First, like the early adopters of change, you can put on your bathing suit and jump right in enjoying the new thing the Spirit is doing in your life. Second, like the accepters of change, you can put on your bathing suit and then stick your toe in the water. If it feels good, you're all in. Finally, like the resisters of spiritual change, you can sit on the patio in your formal clothes (dresses and three-piece suits), talk about how good God is, and watch everyone splashing in the pool from afar. Some of those resisters refuse to even approach the patio. People approach change very differently, you may see yourself in one of these groups.

Adversity may compel change. It may help you by removing doubts about whether you should change. I call necessity the great motivator. You know you must get in the swimming pool, the question now is, "Am I going to walk around it a few times, do a cannon ball, or am I diving in?" How is God leading you? Where does He want to take you? Change should normally begin with the end in mind. The swimming pool represents something new God wants to do in your life. Catch His vision for your future and seek Him for how you will get there. God will not leave you hanging, but sometimes you must take a step of faith to get clearer direction. David and his men set out after the Amalekites with a vision of restoration for their families. It wasn't until they found an Egyptian slave that the means to accomplish it became clear. God promised David the throne of Israel. He had a vision of his future as king, but he did not find himself positioned to take his rightful place until after he defeated the Amalekites. The death of Saul and the vast wealth he accumulated in the battle, provided the opportunity. In both cases, when David had God's consent, he jumped right in the pool. You may not have to follow God's leading with David's level of uncertainty, but like him, you must always step out in faith.

Navigating change is not a linear process. The steps below can help you build your plan. You may have to patiently revisit steps out of order to realize your desired outcomes.

Figure 12–1
Build a Change Management Plan

1. Begin and end seeking God—pray for wisdom and discernment.
2. Identify the change, list its negative aspects (Threats to your well-being).
3. What possible advantages does it present? (Opportunities—be thorough and generous)
4. What is your desired end state? How do you want things to turn out?

5. Ask friends for counsel and input.
6. What can you do to change the circumstances if they are within your control? If not, how can you pray for God's help to bring change or to accept it?
7. How can you minimize the negative impacts? (Constructive action, coping behavior)
8. How can you take advantage of the opportunities? (Consider your strengths and weaknesses—what can God use to alter your outcomes?)
9. What has been exposed in your character for change and growth?
10. How can you maintain your motivation?
    a. Visualize your desired end state, create a mental image of what it looks like. Summarize it with a picture. Find an object you can use to remind you of your dream/what you are asking God to do. (If you need a car, get a matchbox car).
    b. Use slogans to energize your action. (God's got this!)
    c. Inspire your faith and/or mock the trouble. (God will soon crush the enemy under my feet.)
    d. Create a faith-filled statement. (How can God use this situation for my good?)
    e. Find a Scripture to encourage you through this difficulty. (i.e., "God can restore what was lost." Psalm 23, Psalm 42)
11. Do your thoughts, attitude, and speech line up with your goals? Are you double-minded or self-destructive in your thoughts and speech?
12. Are your behaviors healthy and constructive?
13. Constantly seek feedback and make adjustments as needed.
14. End asking God for strength and intervention.

Life's problems do not have to control your life. You can emerge victorious if you navigate the changes in a healthy manner. Several important principles can help you avoid getting stuck. The diagram below depicts how your honest evaluation of the situation, your attitudes, thoughts, speech, and behaviors interact to help you process the changes. Change management is an ongoing effort to adapt to life's circumstances with faith and constructive action. Expect to adjust your approach as you continuously evaluate the effectiveness of your response (productive, healthy, and faith-filled) in accomplishing your intended goals. Monitor the situation to adjust to new information you may receive. Seek feedback to determine the effectiveness of your change strategy.

SPIRITUAL RESILIENCY

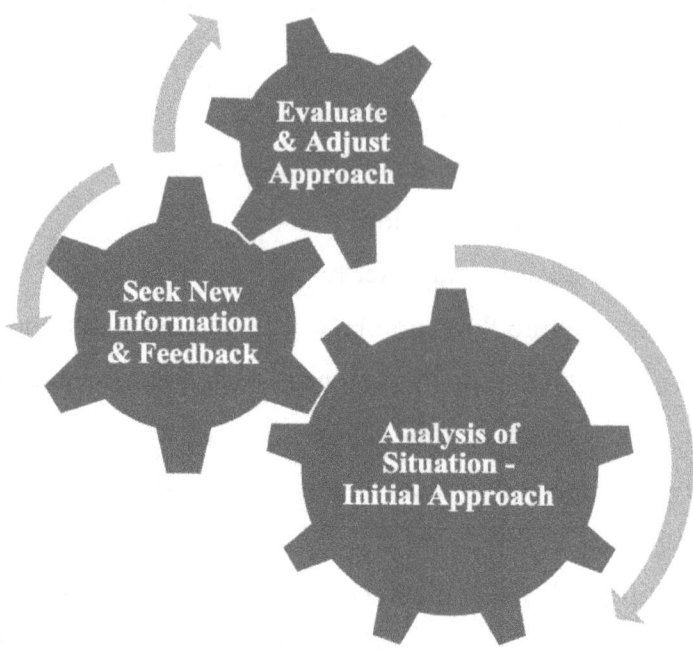

Figure 12a.
Navigating Change

Navigating change can be an uncomfortable and drawn-out process. You can succumb to the temptation to play the victim and remain stuck in superficial and manipulative coping mechanisms, or you can choose to be victorious, accepting no excuses for less than total victory. The enemy's goal through adversity is to drive a wedge between you and God, get you stuck in self-pity or bitterness, and bind you up in self-destructive behaviors. Jesus came to set the captives free.[1215] He has already won the war on your behalf. He, as the God of Peace, will soon crush Satan underneath your feet.[1216] Your strategy for victory in every spiritual battle you will ever face is to draw near to God, resist the enemy, and continue to fight—that means getting back up when you are inevitably knocked down. You can successfully navigate the changes in life that come from adversity. You can become stronger through them as God refines your character and brings you more fully into your life's purpose and mission. Accept no less for yourself than the potential blessings produced through your difficulties. God is the ultimate recycler. He will use everything, including what the enemy meant for evil, to bring good into your life. Together, you can thrive!

1215 Isaiah 61
1216 Romans 16:20

Conclusion

Resilience is the ability to overcome adversity in a healthy and constructive manner. The spiritual dimension is not only the foundation of life, but it also supports every other dimension: social, physical, mental-emotional, family, and any other dimension you identify. Fitness in the spiritual life, then, is the key to your holistic health and to overcoming difficulties. It informs and elevates every other dimension while protecting them from a catastrophic crash. As this work has shown, spiritual disciplines deepen your spiritual life, transforming your thoughts and emotions, which, in turn, enable you to speak and act in more healthy and constructive ways. Spiritual disciplines are the key to developing spiritual fitness and a close relationship with God. The closer you grow to God, the more you can trust Him with the struggles of your life. Your spiritual growth will turn the inner world of your thoughts and feelings into a place of peace and a sound mind. As you renew your mind with positive and faith-filled thoughts, you will transform your behaviors. The words you speak will become more positive and faith-filled, empowering you to act. As you think and speak with greater trust in God, your decision-making process and behaviors will become healthier and more constructive. A healthy relationship with God (built upon healthy spiritual disciplines) will produce a healthier thought life (which, in turn, will produce healthier emotional responses), producing greater health in your speech and healthier decisions and behaviors. A deep relationship with God enables a spiritually resilient thought life, empowering spiritually resilient speech and actions.

While spiritual resilience is presented in a simple model and formula, it by no means implies that developing resilience or overcoming problems is easy. People are complicated and adversity often brings out the worst side of human nature. Your difficulties may make you feel like you're in a cage fight against a much bigger, stronger opponent. The best advice I can give to encourage you is that small things matter. Get started with some small changes that produce quick wins. Open your Bible and hear what God has to say as you read the stories and counsel of others (inspired by the Spirit) who faced their own list of troubles. They were real people who had their own seasons of struggle through the "in between" of trouble and triumph. The encouraging thought is, despite their weaknesses and failures, God always showed up for them. Strive to make God a close friend. Trust Him to see you through. Using the Word and your faith, speak to your mountains and command them to move. Find some mature godly people to help you in your journey, knowing that perseverance is a key to victory. Standing is overcoming. Don't get so focused on your own problems you forget to help others along the way. Your service and giving will come back to you.

SPIRITUAL RESILIENCY

The chapters of this book are written so they can stand alone. You can go to a chapter and find scriptural wisdom and direction to help you focus efforts in that area. Know that you are not alone. No matter how dark the skies appear to get, God is with you and for you. If you have committed your life to Christ, He lives in your spirit. He is always with you. He goes where you go, wherever it is. In Christ, you have angels watching over you. You also have a great cloud of witnesses who have gone before and are cheering for you. And you have a spiritual family who belong to you to help you walk through this life. Some are like that crazy uncle or aunt who may cause more problems, but some are like Johnny K. Johnny was a short, older man with a strong grip who was a longtime member of my home church. When I was young, his looks were a little intimidating, but he always had a smile. Week after week, he greeted me with a huge smile, a firm handshake, and, regularly, a word of encouragement. As I look back on my life, he stands out as one of God's special people. They don't always look like much, but their hearts are one hundred percent for you. They will walk with you to the best of their abilities. The family of God is full of people who love God and others. You are never alone.

If you have never committed your life to Christ, there is no better time than now. Just pray with me…

Dear Jesus,

I confess today that You are Lord. I believe in my heart that You are my Savior, that You laid down your life for my wrongdoing, foremost my rejection of God.

I believe that Your death and resurrection have washed my sins away and set me on a course home to spend eternity with You.

I commit my life to You, to getting to know You better, and to making You Lord of my life.

Come live in my heart as my Savior, Lord, and Friend.

Thank You for loving me!

Amen.

Congratulations! If you prayed this prayer, Heaven is celebrating with you. You have set yourself on a course with destiny. You will never be the same. May God richly bless you as you undertake your new journey of faith and as you take faith-filled steps to overcome your adversity!

Epilogue

Persecution

Persecution is a special category of adversity. God allows His people, both individually and corporately, to experience periods of persecution to reveal the distinction between the character of God and His people and the wickedness of the world. At times, God allows the enemy to have a level of control over the afflictions of His people. Jesus warned that no servant is better than his master—His followers will suffer persecution the same way He suffered.[1217] The early church endured periods of intense persecution. Of the original twelve disciples, only John escaped martyrdom. He spent his final years in prison. Today, the persecution of believers solely for their belief in Christ continues throughout the world. Every day, believers in Africa, Southeast Asia, and many other places are imprisoned, tortured, have their homes destroyed, and even die for their faith. The faith and love some of these display in the face of intense persecution make many of the struggles I face seem minuscule. Like Paul and Silas singing in prison, their example is extraordinary, an inspiration to believers everywhere.[1218] The Book of Revelation describes a future time when, for a season, the enemy is given the power to wage war against and conquer God's holy people.[1219] In the end, Christ and His followers will triumph. History will return to where it started, humanity living in perfect communion with God.

If you are enduring persecution, may God's grace and power be with you. Know that brothers and sisters in Christ all over the world are standing with you in love and prayer. God bless you as you fight the good fight of faith. You are not alone. You are not forgotten.

Rejoice that God has allowed you to represent Him in this way. God provides special grace for those who suffer for His name. Jesus called them blessed.[1220] He encouraged people to rejoice and be glad for the opportunity to identify with Him; for great is their reward in heaven.[1221] The original disciples of Jesus rejoiced to be counted worthy of suffering for His name. Your faithfulness through persecution will provide a powerful witness to those around you. God uses the suffering of His people to shine a bright light into the hearts of those who do not know Him. May you reach many with the brightness of God's love shining through you!

1217 John 15:20
1218 Acts 16:22–25
1219 Revelation 13:7
1220 Matthew 5:11
1221 Matthew 5:12

APPENDICES

APPENDIX I: SCRIPTURE REFERENCES— TWELVE KEY SPIRITUAL DISCIPLINES

Introduction to the Spiritual Disciplines

2 Chronicles 16:9 (NIV)

For the eyes of the LORD range throughout the earth to strengthen those whose hearts are fully committed to him.

Psalm 33:18 (NIV)

But the eyes of the LORD are on those who fear him, on those whose hope is in his unfailing love.

Proverbs 3:3–10 (NIV)

Trust in the LORD with all your heart and lean not on your own understanding; in all your ways acknowledge him, and he will make your paths straight. Honor the LORD with your wealth, with the firstfruits of all your crops; then your barns will be filled to overflowing, and your vats will brim over with new wine.

Jeremiah 29:11–13 (NIV)

For I know the plans I have for you," declares the LORD, "plans to prosper you and not to harm you, plans to give you hope and a future. Then you will call upon me and come and pray to me, and I will listen to you. You will seek me and find me when you seek me with all your heart.

Malachi 3:10 (NIV)

Bring the whole tithe into the storehouse…Test me in this," says the LORD Almighty, "and see if I will not throw open the floodgates of heaven and pour out so much blessing that you will not have room enough for it.

Matthew 6:26–27, 30–33 (NIV)

So do not worry, saying, 'What shall we eat?' or 'What shall we drink?' or 'What shall we wear?' For the pagans run after all these things, and your heavenly Father knows that you need them. But seek first his kingdom and his righteousness, and all these things will be given to you as well.

John 10:10 (NIV)

The thief comes only to steal and kill and destroy; I have come that they may have life, and have it to the full.

Romans 8:28 (NIV)

And we know that in all things God works for the good of those who love him, who have been called according to his purpose.

Romans 8:31 (NIV)

If God is for us, who can be against us?

2 Corinthians 1:20 (NIV)

For no matter how many promises God has made, they are "Yes" in Christ. And so through him the "Amen" is spoken by us to the glory of God.

Ephesians 1:3 (NIV)

Praise be to the God and Father of our Lord Jesus Christ, who has blessed us in the heavenly realms with every spiritual blessing in Christ.

Ephesians 3:20 (NIV)

[God] is able to do immeasurably more than all we ask or imagine, according to his power that is at work within us.

Philippians 4:19 (NIV)

And my God will meet all your needs according to his glorious riches in Christ Jesus.

Hebrews 11:6 (NIV)

And without faith it is impossible to please God, because anyone who comes to him must believe that he exists and that he rewards those who earnestly seek him.

James 1:17 (MSG)

So, my very dear friends, don't get thrown off course. Every desirable and beneficial gift comes out of heaven. The gifts are rivers of light cascading down from the Father of Light. There is nothing deceitful in God, nothing two-faced, nothing fickle.

Spiritual Discipline 1: Read Scripture Every Day

Psalm 119:105 (NIV)

Your word is a lamp to my feet and a light for my path.

Matthew 4:4 (NIV)

Jesus answered, "It is written: 'Man does not live on bread alone, but on every word that comes from the mouth of God.'"

Matthew 24:35 (NIV)

"Heaven and earth will pass away, but my words will never pass away."

Mark 12:24 (NIV)

Jesus replied, "Are you not in error because you do not know the Scriptures or the power of God?

Romans 15:4 (NIV)

For everything that was written in the past was written to teach us, so that through endurance and the encouragement of the Scriptures we might have hope.

Ephesians 6:11–17 (NIV)

Therefore, put on the full armor of God, so that when the day of evil comes, you may be able to stand your ground, and after you have done everything, to stand. Stand firm then…Take the helmet of salvation and the sword of the Spirit, which is the word of God.

2 Timothy 3:16–17 (NIV)

All Scripture is God-breathed and is useful for teaching, rebuking, correcting, and training in righteousness, so that the man of God may be thoroughly equipped for every good work.

Hebrews 4:12 (NIV)

For the word of God is living and active. Sharper than any double-edged sword, it penetrates even to dividing soul and spirit, joints and marrow; it judges the thoughts and attitudes of the heart.

Spiritual Discipline 2: Prayer Fasting & Worship

Psalm 55:22 (NIV)

Cast your cares on the LORD and he will sustain you; he will never let the righteous fall.

Psalm 145:18 (NIV)

The LORD is near to all who call on him, to all who call on him in truth.

Matthew 6:9–13 (NIV)

"This, then, is how you should pray: "'Our Father in heaven, hallowed be your name, your kingdom come, your will be done on earth as it is in heaven. Give us today our daily bread. Forgive us our debts, as we also have forgiven our debtors. And lead us not into temptation, but deliver us from the evil one."

Matthew 7:7–8 (NIV)

"Ask, and it will be given to you; seek, and you will find; knock, and it will be opened to you. For everyone who asks receives, and the one who seeks finds, and to the one who knocks it will be opened."

Luke 18:1 (ESV)

And he told them a parable to the effect that they ought always to pray and not lose heart.

Philippians 4:6–7 (NIV)

Do not be anxious about anything, but in everything by prayer and supplication with thanksgiving let your requests be made known to God. And the peace of God, which surpasses all understanding, will guard your hearts and your minds in Christ Jesus.

James 4:2–3 (NIV)

You do not have, because you do not ask God.

James 5:13–16 (NIV)

Is any one of you in trouble? He should pray. Is anyone happy? Let him sing songs of praise. Is any one of you sick? He should call the elders of the church to pray over him and anoint him with oil in the name of the Lord. And the prayer offered in faith will make the sick person well; the Lord will raise him up. If he has sinned, he will be forgiven. Therefore confess your sins to each other and pray for each other so that you may be healed. The prayer of a righteous man is powerful and effective.

Fasting

Ezra 8:21–23 (NIV)

There, by the Ahava Canal, I proclaimed a fast, so that we might humble ourselves before our God and ask him for a safe journey for us and our children, with all our possessions. I was ashamed to ask the king for soldiers and horsemen to protect us from enemies on the road, because we had told the king, "The gracious hand of our God is on everyone who looks to him, but his great anger is against all who forsake him." So, we fasted and petitioned our God about this, and he answered our prayer.

Nehemiah 1:4–6 (NIV)

When I heard these things, I sat down and wept. For some days I mourned and fasted and prayed before the God of heaven. Then I said: "O LORD, God of heaven, the great and awesome God, who keeps his covenant of love with those who love him and obey his commands, let your ear be attentive and your eyes open to hear the prayer your servant is praying before you day and night for your servants, the people of Israel.

Isaiah 58:5–8 (NIV)

Is this the kind of fast I have chosen, only a day for a man to humble himself? Is it only for bowing one's head like a reed and for lying on sackcloth and ashes? Is that what you call a fast, a day acceptable to the LORD? "Is not this the kind of fasting I have chosen: to loose the chains of injustice and untie the cords of the yoke, to set the oppressed free and break every yoke? Is it not to share your food with the hungry and to provide the poor wanderer with shelter—when you see the naked, to clothe him, and not to turn away from your own flesh and blood? Then your light will break forth like the dawn, and your healing will quickly appear; then your righteousness will go before you, and the glory of the LORD will be your rear guard.

Joel 2:12–13 (NIV)

'Even now,' declares the LORD, 'return to me with all your heart, with fasting and weeping and mourning.' Rend your heart and not your garments. Return to the LORD your God, for he is gracious and compassionate, slow to anger and abounding in love, and he relents from sending calamity.

Matthew 4:1–2 (NIV)

Then Jesus was led by the Spirit into the desert to be tempted by the devil. After fasting forty days and forty nights, he was hungry.

Matthew 6:16–18 (NIV)

When you fast, do not look somber as the hypocrites do, for they disfigure their faces to show men they are fasting. I tell you the truth, they have received their reward in full. But when you fast, put oil on your head and wash your face, so that it will not be obvious to men that you are fasting, but only to your Father, who is unseen; and your Father, who sees what is done in secret, will reward you.

Acts 13:2–3 (NIV)

While they were worshiping the Lord and fasting, the Holy Spirit said, "Set apart for me Barnabas and Saul for the work to which I have called them." So, after they had fasted and prayed, they placed their hands on them and sent them off.

Worship

Psalm 29:2 (ESV)

Ascribe to the Lord the glory due his name; worship the Lord in the splendor of holiness.

Psalm 95:6 (ESV)

Oh come, let us worship and bow down; let us kneel before the Lord, our Maker!

Psalm 103:1–5 (NIV)

Praise the LORD, O my soul; all my inmost being, praise his holy name. Praise the LORD, O my soul, and forget not all his benefits—who forgives all your sins and heals all your diseases, who redeems your life from the pit and crowns you with love and compassion, who satisfies your desires with good things so that your youth is renewed like the eagle's.

Psalm 150:1–6 (ESV)

Praise the Lord! Praise God in his sanctuary; praise him in his mighty heavens! Praise him for his mighty deeds; praise him according to his excellent greatness! Praise him with trumpet sound; praise him with lute and harp! Praise him with tambourine and dance; praise him with strings and pipe! Praise him with sounding cymbals; praise him with loud clashing cymbals!

Habakkuk 3:17–18 (NIV)

Though the fig tree does not bud and there are no grapes on the vines, though the olive crop fails and the fields produce no food, though there are no sheep in the pen and no cattle in the stalls, yet I will rejoice in the LORD, I will be joyful in God my Savior.

Luke 4:8 (NIV)

Jesus answered, "It is written: 'Worship the Lord your God and serve him only.'"

John 4:23–24 (NIV)

"Yet a time is coming and has now come when the true worshipers will worship the Father in spirit and truth, for they are the kind of worshipers the Father seeks. God is spirit, and his worshipers must worship in spirit and in truth."

Hebrews 12:28–29 (NIV)

Therefore, since we are receiving a kingdom that cannot be shaken, let us be thankful, and so worship God acceptably with reverence and awe, for our "God is a consuming fire."

Hebrews 13:15 (NIV)

Through Jesus, therefore, let us continually offer to God a sacrifice of praise—the fruit of lips that confess his name.

1 Peter 2:9 (NIV)

But you are a chosen people, a royal priesthood, a holy nation, a people belonging to God, that you may declare the praises of him who called you out of darkness into his wonderful light.

Spiritual Discipline 3: Trust God!

Psalm 20:7 (NIV)

Some trust in chariots and some in horses, but we trust in the name of the LORD our God.

Psalm 56:3–4 (NIV)

When I am afraid, I will trust in you. In God, whose word I praise, in God I trust; I will not be afraid.

What can mortal man do to me?

Psalm 62:8 (NIV)

Trust in him at all times, O people; pour out your hearts to him, for God is our refuge. Selah.

Psalm 91:1–5 (NIV)

He who dwells in the shelter of the Most High will rest in the shadow of the Almighty. I will say of the LORD, "He is my refuge and my fortress, my God, in whom I trust." Surely he will save you from the fowler's snare and from the deadly pestilence. He will cover you with his feathers, and under his wings you will find refuge; his faithfulness will be your shield and rampart. You will not fear the terror of night, nor the arrow that flies by day.

Psalm 118:8 (NIV)

It is better to take refuge in the LORD than to trust in man.

Proverbs 3:5–6 (NIV)

Trust in the LORD with all your heart and lean not on your own understanding; in all your ways acknowledge him, and he will make your paths straight.

Proverbs 29:25 (NIV)

Fear of man will prove to be a snare, but whoever trusts in the LORD is kept safe.

Isaiah 26:3–4 (NIV)

You will keep in perfect peace him whose mind is steadfast, because he trusts in you. Trust in the LORD forever, for the LORD, the LORD, is the Rock eternal.

Isaiah 40:31 (NIV)

but those who hope in the LORD will renew their strength. They will soar on wings like eagles; they will run and not grow weary, they will walk and not be faint.

Jeremiah 17:7–8 (NIV)

"But blessed is the man who trusts in the LORD, whose confidence is in him. He will be like a tree planted by the water that sends out its roots by the stream. It does not fear when heat comes; its leaves are always green. It has no worries in a year of drought and never fails to bear fruit."

APPENDIX I: SCRIPTURE REFERENCES—TWELVE KEY SPIRITUAL DISCIPLINES

Matthew 6:25 (NIV)

"Therefore I tell you, do not worry about your life, what you will eat or drink; or about your body, what you will wear. Is not life more important than food, and the body more important than clothes?

Mark 11:24 (NIV)

Therefore I tell you, whatever you ask for in prayer, believe that you have received it, and it will be yours.

John 14:1 (NIV)

"Do not let your hearts be troubled. Trust in God; trust also in me.

John 14:27 (NIV)

Peace I leave with you; my peace I give you. I do not give to you as the world gives. Do not let your hearts be troubled and do not be afraid.

Hebrews 13:5–6 (NIV)

God has said, "Never will I leave you; never will I forsake you." So we say with confidence, "The Lord is my helper; I will not be afraid. What can man do to me?"

Spiritual Discipline 4: Express Gratitude

Psalm 100:4–5 (NIV)

Enter his gates with thanksgiving and his courts with praise; give thanks to him and praise his name. For the Lord is good and his love endures forever; his faithfulness continues through all generations.

Psalm 118:1 (NIV)

Give thanks to the Lord, for he is good; his love endures forever.

Ephesians 5:20 (NIV)

Sing and make music from your heart to the Lord, always giving thanks to God the Father for everything, in the name of our Lord Jesus Christ.

Philippians 4:6–7 (NIV)

Do not be anxious about anything, but in every situation, by prayer and petition, with thanksgiving, present your requests to God. And the peace of God, which transcends all understanding, will guard your hearts and your minds in Christ Jesus.

Colossians 2:6–7 (NIV)

So then…continue to live your lives in him, rooted and built up in him, strengthened in the faith as you were taught, and overflowing with thankfulness.

Colossians 3:15–17 (NIV)

Let the peace of Christ rule in your hearts, since…you were called to peace. And be thankful. Let the message of Christ dwell among you richly as you teach and admonish one another with all wisdom through psalms, hymns, and songs from the Spirit, singing to God with gratitude in your hearts. And whatever you do, whether in word or deed, do it all in the name of the Lord Jesus, giving thanks to God the Father through him.

Colossians 4:2 (NIV)

Devote yourselves to prayer, being watchful and thankful.

1 Thessalonians 5:16–18 (NIV)

Rejoice always, pray continually, give thanks in all circumstances; for this is God's will for you in Christ Jesus.

Hebrews 12:28–29 (NIV)

Therefore, since we are receiving a kingdom that cannot be shaken, let us be thankful."

Spiritual Discipline 5: Give Generously

Malachi 3:10 (NIV)

Bring the whole tithe into the storehouse, that there may be food in my house. Test me in this," says the LORD Almighty, "and see if I will not throw open the floodgates of heaven and pour out so much blessing that you will not have room enough for it.

APPENDIX I: SCRIPTURE REFERENCES—TWELVE KEY SPIRITUAL DISCIPLINES

Psalm 112:5–7 (NIV)

Good will come to him who is generous and lends freely

Proverbs 11:25 (NIV)

A generous person will prosper; whoever refreshes others will be refreshed.

Luke 6:38 (NIV)

Give, and it will be given to you. A good measure, pressed down, shaken together and running over, will be poured into your lap. For with the measure you use, it will be measured to you."

2 Corinthians 9:6–8 (NIV)

Remember this: Whoever sows sparingly will also reap sparingly, and whoever sows generously will also reap generously. Each man should give what he has decided in his heart to give, not reluctantly or under compulsion, for God loves a cheerful giver. And God is able to make all grace abound to you, so that in all things at all times, having all that you need, you will abound in every good work.

2 Corinthians 9:10–13 (NIV)

Now he who supplies seed to the sower and bread for food will also supply and increase your store of seed and will enlarge the harvest of your righteousness. You will be made rich in every way so that you can be generous on every occasion, and through us your generosity will result in thanksgiving to God. This service that you perform is not only supplying the needs of God's people but is also overflowing in many expressions of thanks to God. Because of the service by which you have proved yourselves, men will praise God for the obedience that accompanies your confession of the gospel of Christ, and for your generosity in sharing with them and with everyone else.

Spiritual Discipline 6: Serve Others

Isaiah 58:10 (NIV)

And if you spend yourselves in behalf of the hungry and satisfy the needs of the oppressed, then your light will rise in the darkness, and your night will become like the noonday

Matthew 20:28 (NIV)

Just as the Son of Man did not come to be served, but to serve, and to give his life as a ransom for many.

Matthew 23:11 (NIV)

The greatest among you will be your servant.

Mark 9:35 (NIV)

Sitting down, Jesus called the Twelve and said, "If anyone wants to be first, he must be the very last, and the servant of all."

Romans 12:6–7 (NIV)

We have different gifts, according to the grace given us. If a man's gift is prophesying, let him use it in proportion to his faith. If it is serving, let him serve;

1 Corinthians 12:4–6 (NIV)

There are different kinds of gifts, but the same Spirit. There are different kinds of service, but the same Lord. There are different kinds of working, but the same God works all of them in all men.

Galatians 5:13–14 (NIV)

You, my brothers and sisters, were called to be free. But do not use your freedom to indulge the flesh; rather, serve one another humbly in love. For the entire law is fulfilled in keeping this one command: "Love your neighbor as yourself."

Ephesians 2:10 (NIV)

For we are God's handiwork, created in Christ Jesus to do good works, which God prepared in advance for us to do.

Colossians 3:23–24 (NIV)

Whatever you do, work at it with all your heart, as working for the Lord, not for men, since you know that you will receive an inheritance from the Lord as a reward. It is the Lord Christ you are serving.

1 Peter 4:10 (NIV)

Each of you should use whatever gift you have received to serve others, as faithful stewards of God's grace in its various forms.

APPENDIX I: SCRIPTURE REFERENCES—TWELVE KEY SPIRITUAL DISCIPLINES

Spiritual Discipline 7: Express Humility and Self-Awareness

Deuteronomy 8:2–3 (NIV)

Remember how the LORD your God led you all the way in the desert these forty years, to humble you and to test you in order to know what was in your heart, whether or not you would keep his commands. He humbled you, causing you to hunger and then feeding you with manna, which neither you nor your fathers had known, to teach you that man does not live on bread alone but on every word that comes from the mouth of the LORD.

2 Chronicles 7:14 (NIV)

If my people who are called by my name humble themselves, and pray and seek my face and turn from their wicked ways, then I will hear from heaven and will forgive their sin and heal their land.

Proverbs 8:1–5 (NIV)

Does not wisdom call out? Does not understanding raise her voice? …she cries aloud: "To you, O men, I call out; You who are simple, gain prudence; you who are foolish, gain understanding."

Proverbs 8:13 (NIV)

To fear the LORD is to hate evil; I hate pride and arrogance, evil behavior and perverse speech.

Matthew 23:2–12 (NIV)

"The teachers of the law and the Pharisees…love the place of honor at banquets and the most important seats in the synagogues; they love to be greeted in the marketplaces and to have men call them 'Rabbi.' "But you are not to be called 'Rabbi,' for you have only one Master and you are all brothers. And do not call anyone on earth 'father,' for you have one Father, and he is in heaven. Nor are you to be called 'teacher,' for you have one Teacher, the Christ. The greatest among you will be your servant. For whoever exalts himself will be humbled, and whoever humbles himself will be exalted.

Philippians 2:3–8 (NIV)

Do nothing out of selfish ambition or vain conceit. Rather, in humility value others above yourselves, not looking to your own interests but each of you to the interests of the others. In your relationships with one another, have the same mindset as Christ Jesus: Who, being in very nature God, did not consider equality with God something to be used to his own advantage; rather, he made himself nothing by taking the very nature of a servant, being made in human likeness. And being found in appearance as a man, he humbled himself by becoming obedient to death—even death on a cross!

Colossians 3:12–13 (NIV)

Therefore, as God's chosen people, holy and dearly loved, clothe yourselves with compassion, kindness, humility, gentleness and patience.

James 4:6–10 (NIV)

But he gives us more grace. That is why Scripture says: "God opposes the proud but gives grace to the humble." Submit yourselves, then, to God. Resist the devil, and he will flee from you. Come near to God and he will come near to you. Wash your hands, you sinners, and purify your hearts, you double-minded. Grieve, mourn and wail. Change your laughter to mourning and your joy to gloom. Humble yourselves before the Lord, and he will lift you up.

1 Peter 5:5–6 (NIV)

All of you, clothe yourselves with humility toward one another, because, "God opposes the proud but gives grace to the humble." Humble yourselves, therefore, under God's mighty hand, that he may lift you up in due time.

Spiritual Discipline 8: Renew Energy and Stay Motivated

Isaiah 40:29–31 (NIV)

He gives strength to the weary and increases the power of the weak. Even youths grow tired and weary, and young men stumble and fall; but those who hope in the LORD will renew their strength. They will soar on wings like eagles; they will run and not grow weary, they will walk and not be faint.

Romans 12:11–12 (NIV)

Never be lacking in zeal, but keep your spiritual fervor, serving the Lord. Be joyful in hope, patient in affliction, faithful in prayer.

1 Corinthians 15:58 (NIV)

Therefore, my dear brothers, stand firm. Let nothing move you. Always give yourselves fully to the work of the Lord, because you know that your labor in the Lord is not in vain.

2 Corinthians 4:16–18 (NIV)

Therefore we do not lose heart. Though outwardly we are wasting away, yet inwardly we are being renewed day by day. For our light and momentary troubles are achieving for us an eternal glory that far outweighs them all. So we fix our eyes not on what is seen, but on what is unseen. For what is seen is temporary, but what is unseen is eternal.

2 Corinthians 12:9–10 (NIV)

But he said to me, "My grace is sufficient for you, for my power is made perfect in weakness." Therefore I will boast all the more gladly about my weaknesses, so that Christ's power may rest on me. That is why, for Christ's sake, I delight in weaknesses, in insults, in hardships, in persecutions, in difficulties. For when I am weak, then I am strong.

Galatians 1:10 (NIV)

Am I now trying to win the approval of men, or of God? If I were still trying to please men, I would not be a servant of Christ.

Galatians 6:7–9 (NIV)

Do not be deceived: God cannot be mocked. A man reaps what he sows. The one who sows to please his sinful nature, from that nature will reap destruction; the one who sows to please the Spirit, from the Spirit will reap eternal life. Let us not become weary in doing good, for at the proper time we will reap a harvest if we do not give up.

Philippians 4:13 (NIV)

I can do everything through him who gives me strength.

Colossians 3:23–25 (NIV)

Whatever you do, work at it with all your heart, as working for the Lord, not for men, since you know that you will receive an inheritance from the Lord as a reward. It is the Lord Christ you are serving.

Hebrews 10:24–25 (NIV)

And let us consider how we may spur one another on toward love and good deeds. Let us not give up meeting together, as some are in the habit of doing, but let us encourage one another—and all the more as you see the Day approaching.

Hebrews 12:1–2 (NIV)

Therefore, since we are surrounded by such a great cloud of witnesses, let us throw off everything that hinders and the sin that so easily entangles, and let us run with perseverance the race marked out for us. Let us fix our eyes on Jesus, the author and perfecter of our faith, who for the joy set before him endured the cross, scorning its shame, and sat down at the right hand of the throne of God.

Spiritual Discipline 9: Develop Interpersonal Skills-Strengthen Relationships

Proverbs 17:17 (NIV)

A friend loves at all times, and a brother is born for adversity.

Proverbs 18:24 (NIV)

A man of many companions may come to ruin, but there is a friend who sticks closer than a brother.

Proverbs 20:6 (NIV)

Many a man claims to have unfailing love, but a faithful man who can find?

Proverbs 22:24–25 (NIV)

Do not make friends with a hot-tempered man, do not associate with one easily angered, or you may learn his ways and get yourself ensnared.

Proverbs 27:6 (NIV)

Wounds from a friend can be trusted, but an enemy multiplies kisses.

Proverbs 27:9–10 (NIV)

Perfume and incense bring joy to the heart, and the pleasantness of one's friend springs from his earnest counsel. Do not forsake your friend and the friend of your father.

Ecclesiastes 4:9–12 (NIV)

Two are better than one, because they have a good return for their work: If one falls down, his friend can help him up. But pity the man who falls and has no one to help him up! Also, if two lie down together, they will keep warm. But how can one keep warm alone? Though one may be overpowered, two can defend themselves. A cord of three strands is not quickly broken.

John 15:13–14 (NIV)

Greater love has no one than this, that he lay down his life for his friends. You are my friends if you do what I command.

Romans 12:10 (NIV)

Be devoted to one another in brotherly love. Honor one another above yourselves.

Philippians 2:3–4 (NIV)

Do nothing out of selfish ambition or vain conceit, but in humility consider others better than yourselves. Each of you should look not only to your own interests, but also to the interests of others.

1 Thessalonians 5:11 (NIV)

Therefore encourage one another and build each other up, just as in fact you are doing.

1 John 4:7 (NIV)

Dear friends, let us love one another, for love comes from God. Everyone who loves has been born of God and knows God.

Spiritual Discipline 10: Strengthen Self-Control

Proverbs 16:32 (NIV)

Better a patient person than a warrior, one with self-control than one who takes a city.

Proverbs 25:28 (NIV)

Like a city whose walls are broken through is a person who lacks self-control.

Ecclesiastes 10:4 (NIV) If a ruler's anger rises against you, do not leave your post; calmness can lay great errors to rest.

Romans 7:22–25 (NIV)

For in my inner being I delight in God's law; but I see another law at work in me, waging war against the law of my mind and making me a prisoner of the law of sin at work within me. What a wretched man I am! Who will rescue me from this body that is subject to death? Thanks be to God, who delivers me through Jesus Christ our Lord! So then, I myself in my mind am a slave to God's law, but in my sinful nature a slave to the law of sin.

Galatians 5:22–23 (NIV)

But the fruit of the Spirit is love, joy, peace, forbearance, kindness, goodness, faithfulness, gentleness, and self-control. Against such things there is no law.

Titus 2:11–12 (NIV)

For the grace of God has appeared that offers salvation to all people. It teaches us to say "No" to ungodliness and worldly passions, and to live self-controlled, upright and godly lives in this present age.

2 Peter 1:5–6 (NIV)

For this very reason, make every effort to add to your faith goodness; and to goodness, knowledge; and to knowledge, self-control; and to self-control, perseverance; and to perseverance, godliness;

Spiritual Discipline 11: Tame Your Tongue

Psalm 141:3 (NIV)

"Set a guard, O Lord, over my mouth; keep watch over the door of my lips!"

Proverbs 12:13–14 (NIV)

"Evildoers are trapped by their sinful talk, and so the innocent escape trouble. From the fruit of their lips people are filled with good things, and the work of their hands brings them reward."

Proverbs 12:18 (NIV)

The words of the reckless pierce like swords, but the tongue of the wise brings healing.

Proverbs 13:3 (NIV)

Those who guard their lips preserve their lives, but those who speak rashly will come to ruin.

Proverbs 15:1 (NIV)

A gentle answer turns away wrath, but a harsh word stirs up anger.

Proverbs 15:4 (NIV)

The soothing tongue is a tree of life, but a perverse tongue crushes the spirit.

Proverbs 16:24 (NIV)

Gracious words are a honeycomb, sweet to the soul and healing to the bones.

Proverbs 18:4 (NIV)

The words of the mouth are deep waters, but the fountain of wisdom is a rushing stream.

Proverbs 21:23 (NIV)

Those who guard their mouths and their tongues keep themselves from calamity.

Proverbs 25:18 (NIV)

Like a club or a sword or a sharp arrow is one who gives false testimony against a neighbor.

Matthew 12:36 (NIV)

But I tell you that everyone will have to give account on the day of judgment for every empty word they have spoken.

Matthew 15:18 (NIV)

But the things that come out of a person's mouth come from the heart, and these defile them.

Ephesians 4:29 (NIV)

Do not let any unwholesome talk come out of your mouths, but only what is helpful for building others up according to their needs, that it may benefit those who listen.

James 1:26 (NIV)

Those who consider themselves religious and yet do not keep a tight rein on their tongues deceive themselves, and their religion is worthless.

James 3:5–6 (NIV):

Likewise, the tongue is a small part of the body, but it makes great boasts. Consider what a great forest is set on fire by a small spark. The tongue also is a fire, a world of evil among the parts of the body. It corrupts the whole body, sets the whole course of one's life on fire, and is itself set on fire by hell.

James 3:8 (NIV)

But no human being can tame the tongue. It is a restless evil, full of deadly poison.

1 Peter 3:10 (NIV)

Whoever would love life and see good days must keep their tongue from evil and their lips from deceitful speech.

Spiritual Discipline 12: Continually Learn and Grow

1 Samuel 2:26 (NIV)

And the boy Samuel continued to grow in stature and in favor with the LORD and with men.

Job 17:9 (NIV)

Nevertheless, the righteous will hold to their ways, and those with clean hands will grow stronger.

Psalm 94:12–14 (NIV)

Blessed is the man you discipline, O LORD, the man you teach from your law; you grant him relief from days of trouble, till a pit is dug for the wicked. For the LORD will not reject his people; he will never forsake his inheritance.

Proverbs 24:16 (NIV)

For though the righteous fall seven times, they rise again, but the wicked stumble when calamity strikes.

Matthew 23:23 (NIV)

"Woe to you, teachers of the law and Pharisees, you hypocrites! You give a tenth of your spices—mint, dill and cumin. But you have neglected the more important matters of the law—justice, mercy and faithfulness. You should have practiced the latter, without neglecting the former."

Matthew 23:25 (NIV)

"Woe to you, teachers of the law and Pharisees, you hypocrites! You clean the outside of the cup and dish, but inside they are full of greed and self-indulgence."

Luke 2:52 (NIV)

And Jesus grew in wisdom and stature, and in favor with God and men.

APPENDIX I: SCRIPTURE REFERENCES–TWELVE KEY SPIRITUAL DISCIPLINES

John 15:2 (NIV)

"He cuts off every branch in me that bears no fruit, while every branch that does bear fruit he prunes so that it will be even more fruitful."

John 15:4–5 (NIV)

Remain in me, as I also remain in you. No branch can bear fruit by itself; it must remain in the vine. Neither can you bear fruit unless you remain in me. "I am the vine; you are the branches. If you remain in me and I in you, you will bear much fruit; apart from me you can do nothing."

Romans 5:3–5 (NIV)

Not only so, but we also glory in our sufferings, because we know that suffering produces perseverance; perseverance, character; and character, hope. And hope does not put us to shame, because God's love has been poured out into our hearts through the Holy Spirit, who has been given to us.

1 Corinthians 3:1–3 (NIV)

"Brothers and sisters, I could not address you as people who live by the Spirit but as people who are still worldly–mere infants in Christ. I gave you milk, not solid food, for you were not yet ready for it. Indeed, you are still not ready. You are still worldly. For since there is jealousy and quarreling among you, are you not worldly? Are you not acting like mere humans?"

1 Corinthians 13:11 (NIV)

"When I was a child, I talked like a child, I thought like a child, I reasoned like a child. When I became a man, I put the ways of childhood behind me."

2 Corinthians 5:17 (NIV)

"Therefore, if anyone is in Christ, the new creation has come: The old has gone, the new is here!"

Ephesians 4:13–16 (NIV)

Until we all reach unity in the faith and in the knowledge of the Son of God and become mature, attaining to the whole measure of the fullness of Christ. Then we will no longer be infants, tossed back and forth by the waves, and blown here and there by every wind of teaching and by the cunning and craftiness of men in their deceitful scheming. Instead, speaking the truth in love, we will in all things grow up into him who is the Head, that is, Christ. From him the whole body, joined and held together by every supporting ligament, grows and builds itself up in love, as each part does its work.

Ephesians 4:20–24 (NIV)

You, however, did not come to know Christ that way. Surely you heard of him and were taught in him in accordance with the truth that is in Jesus. You were taught, with regard to your former way of life, to put off your old self, which is being corrupted by its deceitful desires; to be made new in the attitude of your minds; and to put on the new self, created to be like God in true righteousness and holiness.

Philippians 1:6 (NIV)

Being confident of this, that he who began a good work in you will carry it on to completion until the day of Christ Jesus.

Philippians 2:13 (NIV)

For it is God who works in you to will and to act in order to fulfill his good purpose.

Colossians 1:9–10 (NIV)

For this reason, since the day we heard about you, we have not stopped praying for you and asking God to fill you with the knowledge of his will through all spiritual wisdom and understanding. And we pray this in order that you may live a life worthy of the Lord and may please him in every way: bearing fruit in every good work, growing in the knowledge of God.

Colossians 2:6–7 (NIV)

So then, just as you received Christ Jesus as Lord, continue to live in him, rooted and built up in him, strengthened in the faith as you were taught, and overflowing with thankfulness.

Hebrews 5:12–14 (NIV)

In fact, though by this time you ought to be teachers, you need someone to teach you the elementary truths of God's word all over again. You need milk, not solid food! Anyone who lives on milk, being still an infant, is not acquainted with the teaching about righteousness. But solid food is for the mature, who by constant use have trained themselves to distinguish good from evil.

Hebrews 6:1 (NIV)

Therefore let us leave the elementary teachings about Christ and go on to maturity, not laying again the foundation of repentance from acts that lead to death, and of faith in God,

APPENDIX I: SCRIPTURE REFERENCES—TWELVE KEY SPIRITUAL DISCIPLINES

Hebrews 12:1–2 (NIV)

"Therefore, since we are surrounded by such a great cloud of witnesses, let us throw off everything that hinders and the sin that so easily entangles. And let us run with perseverance the race marked out for us, fixing our eyes on Jesus, the pioneer and perfecter of faith."

Hebrews 12:5–7 (NIV)

And have you completely forgotten this word of encouragement that addresses you as a father addresses his son? It says, "My son, do not make light of the Lord's discipline, and do not lose heart when he rebukes you, because the Lord disciplines the one he loves, and he chastens everyone he accepts as his son." Endure hardship as discipline; God is treating you as his children. For what children are not disciplined by their father?

James 1:2–4 (NIV)

Consider it pure joy, my brothers and sisters, whenever you face trials of many kinds, because you know that the testing of your faith produces perseverance. Let perseverance finish its work so that you may be mature and complete, not lacking anything.

2 Peter 1:5–9 (NIV)

For this very reason, make every effort to add to your faith goodness; and to goodness, knowledge; and to knowledge, self-control; and to self-control, perseverance; and to perseverance, godliness; and to godliness, brotherly kindness; and to brotherly kindness, love. For if you possess these qualities in increasing measure, they will keep you from being ineffective and unproductive in your knowledge of our Lord Jesus Christ. But if anyone does not have them, he is nearsighted and blind, and has forgotten that he has been cleansed from his past sins.

1 Peter 2:1–3 (NIV)

Therefore, rid yourselves of all malice and all deceit, hypocrisy, envy, and slander of every kind. Like newborn babies, crave pure spiritual milk, so that by it you may grow up in your salvation, now that you have tasted that the Lord is good.

2 Peter 3:18 (NIV)

But grow in the grace and knowledge of our Lord and Savior Jesus Christ. To him be glory both now and forever! Amen.

APPENDIX II:

ADDITIONAL SCRIPTURAL REFERENCES

Fear

Isaiah 41:10 (NIV)

"So do not fear, for I am with you; do not be dismayed, for I am your God. I will strengthen you and help you; I will uphold you with my righteous right hand."

Psalm 56:3 (NIV)

"When I am afraid, I put my trust in you."

Philippians 4:6–7 (NIV)

"<u>Do not be anxious about anything</u>, but in every situation, by prayer and petition, with thanksgiving, present your requests to God. And the peace of God, which transcends all understanding, will guard your hearts and your minds in Christ Jesus."

John 14:27 (NIV)

"Peace is what I leave with you; it is my own peace that I give you. I do not give it as the world does. Do not be worried and upset; do not be afraid."

2 Timothy 1:7 (NIV)

"For God has not given us a spirit of fear, but of power and of love and of a sound mind."

1 John 4:18 (NIV)

"There is no fear in love. But perfect love drives out fear, because fear has to do with punishment. The one who fears is not made perfect in love."

Psalm 94:19 (NIV)

"When anxiety was great within me, your consolation brought joy to my soul."

Isaiah 43:1 (NIV)

"But now, this is what the Lord says…Fear not, for I have redeemed you; I have summoned you by name; you are mine."

Proverbs 12:25 (NIV)

"An anxious heart weighs a man down, but a kind word cheers him up."

Psalm 23:4 (NIV)

"Even though I walk through the valley of the shadow of death, I will fear no evil, for you are with me; your rod and your staff, they comfort me."

Joshua 1:9 (NIV)

"Have I not commanded you? Be strong and courageous. Do not be terrified; do not be discouraged, for the Lord your God will be with you wherever you go."

Matthew 6:34 (NIV)

"Therefore do not worry about tomorrow, for tomorrow will worry about itself. Each day has enough trouble of its own."

1 Peter 5:6–7 (NIV)

"Humble yourselves, then, under God's mighty hand, so that he will lift you up in his own good time. Leave all your worries with him, because he cares for you."

Isaiah 35:4 (NIV)

"Tell everyone who is discouraged, Be strong and don't be afraid! God is coming to your rescue…"

Luke 12:22–26 (NIV)

"Do not worry about your life, what you will eat; or about your body, what you will wear. Life is more than food, and the body more than clothes. Consider the ravens: They do not sow or reap, they have no storeroom or barn; yet God feeds them. And how much more valuable you are than birds! Who of you by worrying can add a single hour to his life? Since you cannot do this very little thing, why do you worry about the rest?"

ADDITIONAL SCRIPTURAL REFERENCES

Psalm 27:1 (NIV)

"The Lord is my light and my salvation—whom shall I fear? The Lord is the stronghold of my life—of whom shall I be afraid?"

Psalm 55:22 (NIV)

"Cast your cares on the Lord and he will sustain you; he will never let the righteous fall."

Mark 6:50 (NIV)

"Immediately he spoke to them and said, 'Take courage! It is I. Don't be afraid.'"

Deuteronomy 31:6 (NIV)

"Be strong and courageous. Do not be afraid or terrified because of them, for the Lord your God goes with you; he will never leave you nor forsake you."

Isaiah 41:13–14 (NIV)

"'For I am the Lord, your God, who takes hold of your right hand and says to you, Do not fear; I will help you. Do not be afraid, for I myself will help you,' declares the Lord, your Redeemer, the Holy One of Israel."

Psalm 46:1 (NIV)

"God is our refuge and strength, an ever-present help in trouble." ~

Psalm 118:6–7 (NIV)

"The Lord is with me; I will not be afraid. What can man do to me? The Lord is with me; he is my helper."

Proverbs 29:25 (NIV)

"Fear of man will prove to be a snare, but whoever trusts in the Lord is kept safe."

Mark 4:39–40 (NIV)

"He got up, rebuked the wind and said to the waves, "Quiet! Be still!" Then the wind died down and it was completely calm. He said to his disciples, "Why are you so afraid? Do you still have no faith?"

Psalm 34:7 (NIV)

"The angel of the Lord encamps around those who fear him, and he delivers them."

1 Peter 3:14 (NIV)

"But even if you suffer for doing what is right, God will reward you for it. So don't worry or be afraid of their threats."

Psalm 34:4 (NIV)

"I prayed to the Lord, and he answered me. He freed me from all my fears."

Deuteronomy 3:22 (NIV)

"Do not be afraid of them; the Lord your God himself will fight for you."

Revelation 1:17 (NIV)

"Then he placed his right hand on me and said: 'Do not be afraid. I am the First and the Last.'"

Mark 5:36 (NIV)

"Jesus told him, 'Don't be afraid; just believe.'"

Romans 8:38–39 (NIV)

"And I am convinced that nothing can ever separate us from God's love. Neither death nor life, neither angels nor demons, neither our fears for today nor our worries about tomorrow—not even the powers of hell can separate us from God's love."

Zephaniah 3:17 (NIV)

"The Lord your God is in your midst, A victorious warrior. He will exult over you with joy, He will be quiet in His love, He will rejoice over you with shouts of joy."

Psalm 91:1–16 (NIV)

"He who dwells in the shelter of the Most High will rest in the shadow of the Almighty. I will say of the Lord, "He is my refuge and my fortress, my God, in whom I trust."…He will cover you with his feathers, and under his wings you will find refuge; his faithfulness will be your shield and rampart. You will not fear the terror of night, nor the arrow that flies by day, nor the pestilence that stalks in the darkness, nor the plague that destroys at midday. A thousand may fall at your side, ten thousand at your right hand, but it will not come near you…For he will command his angels concerning you, to guard you in all your ways…"Because he loves me," says the Lord, "I will rescue him; I will protect him, for he acknowledges my name. He will call upon me, and I will answer him; I will be with him in trouble, I will deliver him and honor him…"

Joy

Psalm 16:11 (NIV)

"You make known to me the path of life; you will fill me with joy in your presence, with eternal pleasures at your right hand."

Nehemiah 8:10 (NIV)

Do not grieve, for the joy of the LORD is your strength.

Isaiah 55:12 (NIV)

"You will go out in joy and be led forth in peace; the mountains and hills will burst into song before you, and all the trees of the field will clap their hands."

Psalm 30:5 (NIV)

"For his anger lasts only a moment, but his favor lasts a lifetime; weeping may stay for the night, but rejoicing comes in the morning."

Psalm 126:5–6 (NIV)

"Those who sow with tears will reap with songs of joy. Those who go out weeping, carrying seed to sow, will return with songs of joy, carrying sheaves with them."

Zephaniah 3:17 (NIV)

"The LORD your God is with you, the Mighty Warrior who saves. He will take great delight in you; in his love he will no longer rebuke you, but will rejoice over you with singing."

Proverbs 10:28 (NIV)

"The prospect of the righteous is joy, but the hopes of the wicked come to nothing."

Psalm 71:23 (NIV)

"My lips will shout for joy when I sing praise to you— I whom you have delivered."

Habakkuk 3:17–19 (NIV)

"Though the fig tree does not bud and there are no grapes on the vines, though the olive crop fails and the fields produce no food, though there are no sheep in the pen and no cattle in the stalls, yet I will rejoice in the LORD, I will be joyful in God my Savior. The Sovereign LORD is my strength; he makes my feet like the feet of a deer, he enables me to tread on the heights."

John 15:11 (NIV)

"I have told you this so that my joy may be in you and that your joy may be complete."

Romans 15:13 (NIV)

"May the God of hope fill you with all joy and peace as you trust in him, so that you may overflow with hope by the power of the Holy Spirit."

James 1:2 (NIV)

"Consider it pure joy, my brothers and sisters, whenever you face trials of many kinds."

Galatians 5:22 (NIV)

"But the fruit of the Spirit is love, joy, peace, forbearance, kindness, goodness, faithfulness."

Acts 2:28 (NIV)

"You have made known to me the paths of life; you will fill me with joy in your presence."

Romans 12:12 (NIV)

"Be joyful in hope, patient in affliction, faithful in prayer."

John 16:24 (NIV)

"Until now you have not asked for anything in my name. Ask and you will receive, and your joy will be complete."

Romans 14:17 (NIV)

"For the kingdom of God is not a matter of eating and drinking, but of righteousness, peace and joy in the Holy Spirit."

Psalm 5:11 (NIV)

"But let all who take refuge in you be glad; let them ever sing for joy. Spread your protection over them, that those who love your name may rejoice in you."

Philippians 4:4 (NIV)

"Rejoice in the Lord always. I will say it again: Rejoice!"

Romans 12:15 (NIV)

"Rejoice with those who rejoice; mourn with those who mourn."

1 Peter 1:8–9 (NIV)

"Though you have not seen him, you love him. Though you do not now see him, you believe in him and rejoice with joy that is inexpressible and filled with glory, obtaining the outcome of your faith, the salvation of your souls."

1 Thessalonians 5:16–18 (NIV)

"Rejoice always, pray continually, give thanks in all circumstances; for this is God's will for you in Christ Jesus."

1 Peter 4:12–13 (NIV)

"Dear friends, do not be surprised at the fiery ordeal that has come on you to test you, as though something strange were happening to you. But rejoice inasmuch as you participate in the sufferings of Christ, so that you may be overjoyed when his glory is revealed."

Psalm 32:11 (NIV)

"Rejoice in the LORD and be glad, you righteous; sing, all you who are upright in heart!"

2 Corinthians 6:10 (NIV)

"...sorrowful, yet always rejoicing; poor, yet making many rich; having nothing, and yet possessing everything."

Psalm 70:4 (NIV)

"But may all who seek you rejoice and be glad in you; may those who long for your saving help always say, 'The LORD is great!'"

Resolve Conflicts Quickly

Proverbs 6:2–5 (NIV)

…if you have been trapped by what you said, ensnared by the words of your mouth, then do this, my son, to free yourself, since you have fallen into your neighbor's hands: Go and humble yourself; press your plea with your neighbor! Allow no sleep to your eyes, no slumber to your eyelids. Free yourself, like a gazelle from the hand of the hunter, like a bird from the snare of the fowler.

Proverbs 14:29 (NIV)

Those who control their anger have great understanding; those with a hasty temper will make mistakes.

Proverbs 17:14 (NIV)

Beginning a quarrel is like opening a floodgate, so drop the matter before a dispute breaks out.

Ecclesiastes 7:8–9 (NIV)

Finishing is better than starting. Patience is better than pride. Don't be quick-tempered, for anger is the friend of fools.

Matthew 18:15–18 (NIV)

If your brother sins against you, go and show him his fault, just between the two of you. If he listens to you, you have won your brother over. But if he will not listen, take one or two others along, so that 'every matter may be established by the testimony of two or three witnesses.' If he refuses to listen to them, tell it to the church; and if he refuses to listen even to the church, treat him as you would a pagan or a tax collector. "I tell you the truth, whatever you bind on earth will be bound in heaven, and whatever you loose on earth will be loosed in heaven.

Romans 12:17–21 (NIV)

Do not repay anyone evil for evil. Be careful to do what is right in the eyes of everybody. If it is possible, as far as it depends on you, live at peace with everyone. Do not take revenge, my friends, but leave room for God's wrath, for it is written: "It is mine to avenge; I will repay," says the Lord. On the contrary: "If your enemy is hungry, feed him; if he is thirsty, give him something to drink. In doing this, you will heap burning coals on his head." Do not be overcome by evil but overcome evil with good.

ADDITIONAL SCRIPTURAL REFERENCES

Colossians 3:19 (NIV)

And you husbands must love your wives and never treat them harshly.

Ephesians 4:26 (NIV)

And "don't sin by letting anger gain control over you." Don't let the sun go down while you are still angry.

1 Thessalonians 5:11 (NIV)

So encourage each other and build each other up, just as you are already doing.

Bibliography

Adaptiv. "Navigating Around Icebergs." Accessed October 4, 2021. www.adaptivlearning.com/blog/bid/103406/Resilience-In-Recerssion-Tip-5–Navigating-Around-Your-Icebergs.

Alexander the Great. As quoted in *The British Battle Fleet: Its Inception and Growth Throughout the Centuries to the Present Day.* 1915. Frederick Thomas Jane. Accessed April 16, 2021. Lions - Wikiquote.

Allen, Summer. "The Science of Gratitude." May 2018. Accessed November 13, 2022. https://Ggsc.berkeley.edu/images/uploads/GGSC-JTF_White_Paper-Gratitude-FINAL.pdf.

Army Resilience Directorate. "Five Dimensions of Personal Readiness." Accessed March 12, 2021. ARD: Five Dimensions of Personal Readiness (army.mil).

Baker, John. Life's Healing Choices: Freedom from Your Hurts, Hang-Ups, and Habits. New York: Howard Books, 2007.

Beliefnet. "Serenity Prayer." Accessed October 12, 2021. www.beliefnet.com/prayers/protestant/addiction/serenity-prayer.aspx.

Bevere, John. The Bait of Satan: Living Free from the Deadly Trap of Offense. Lake Mary, FL: Charisma House, 2011.

Bigelow, Ann E., and Lela Rankin Williams. "To Have and to Hold: Effects of Physical Contact on Infants and Their Caregivers." Accessed February 25, 2023. Https://www.ncbi.nlm.nih.gov/pmc/articles/PMC7502223/#__ffn_sectitle.

Boater Exam. "Boat Hull Types & Designs." Accessed October 2, 2021. https://www.boaterexam.com/boating-resources/boat-hull-types-designs/.

Brillstein, Bernie, Frank Peppiatt and John Aylesworth. *Gloom, Despair and Agony on Me*. Recorded by Buck Owens and Roy Clark. Red Boot Records, 1969.

Buettner, Dan. Live to 100: Secrets of the Blue Zones, An Unexpected Discovery, S1, E2, Netflix, 2023.

Burrows, James. Director. *Cheers*. Season 1, Episode 1. "Give Me a Ring Sometime." Aired September 30, 1982. NBC.

Caidin, Martin and Dick Moder, Directors. *Six Million Dollar Man*. March 7, 1973–March 6, 1978.

Chapman, Gary D. *The Five Love Languages*. Chicago: Northfield Publishing, 2010.

Clausewitz, Carl von. *On War*. Translated by J.J. Graham. Ware, England: Wordsworth Classics of World Literature, Wordsworth Editions. 1997.

Cohen, Marisa T. "Resilience and Relationships." *Psychology Today*. January 30, 2020. Accessed December 10, 2022. https://www.psychologytoday.com/us/blog/finding-the-love-the-scientific-take/202001/resilience-and-relationships?amp.

CSU Global. "What is Active Listening? 4 Tips for Improving Communication Skills." Accessed February 25, 2023.
Https://csuglobal.edu/blog/what-active-listening-4–tips-improving-communication-skills.

Degges-White, Suzanne. "How many Friends Do You Need in Adulthood?" Accessed October 13, 2021. https://www.psychologytoday.com/us/blog/lifetime-connections/201908/how-many-friends-do-you-really-need-in-adulthood.

Eisenhower, Dwight D. "Eisenhower Spurs G.O.P. Vote Drive to Win Congress by William S. White." *New York Times*. January 31, 1958. ProQuest.

Eisenhower, Dwight D. "Public Papers of the President of the United States, Dwight D. Eisenhower, Containing the Public Messages, Speeches, and Statements of the President, Remarks at the National Defense Executive Reserve Conference." November 14, 1957. Washington D.C.: Federal Register Division, National Archives and Records Service, 1957.

Ghezzi, Bert. *The Angry Christian*. Ann Arbor, MI: Servant, 1980.

Bibliography

Global Day of Unplugging. Accessed April 19, 2021. National Day of Unplugging.

Glynn, Patrick. *God the Evidence: The Reconciliation of Faith and Reason in a Postsecular World.* Rocklin, CA: Prima Publishing, 1997.

Goewey, Don Joseph. "85% of What We Worry About Never Happens." Accessed April 19, 2021. https://www.huffpost.com/entry/85–of-what-we-worry-about_b_8028368.

Gorrell, Angela William. The Gravity of Joy: A Story of Being Lost and Found. Grand Rapids, MI: Wm B Eerdmans, 2021.

Hackney, Charles, and Glenn Sanders. "Religiosity and Mental Health: A Meta-Analysis of Recent Studies." *Journal for the Scientific Study of Religion.* Vol. 42, No.1, March 2003.

Harley, Willard F., Jr. His Needs Her Needs: Building an Affair-Proof Marriage. Grand Rapids, MI: Fleming H. Revell, 2002.

Harvard Health. "When to Worry About Worrying." Accessed October 12, 2021. www.health.harvard.edu/mind-and-mood/when-to-worry-about-worrying.

Herold, J. Christopher. "The Mind of Napoleon." New York: Columbia University, 1961. Indicates it's from a "Conversation with Fontanes." Cited in Martel, III, 7" Tancred Martel, Napoleon Bonaparte:Oeuvres Littéraries. 1888.

Higher Education Research Institute. "The Spiritual Life of College Students: A National Study of College Students' Search for Meaning and Purpose.*" Accessed May 22, 2019.* https://spirituality.ucla.edu/docs/reports/Spiritual_Life_College_Students_ Exec Summary.pdf.

Hoyle, Fred. *The Origin of the Universe and the Origin of Religion.* Wakefield, RI: Moyer Bell, 1993.

Jackson, Peter, dir. *Lord of the Rings: Fellowship of the Ring.* USA: New Line Cinema / WingNut Films, 2001. DVD.

Kendall, R.T. Total Forgiveness. Sisters, OR: The 1687 Foundation, 2007.

Kennedy, Rory. *The Volcano: Rescue from Whakaari*. Netflix. 2022.

Khalaf, O, S. Resch, L. Dixsaut, V. Gorden, L. Glauser, and J. Graff. "Reactivation of Recall-induced Neurons Contributes to Remote Fear Memory Attenuation." *Science*. 360(6394): 2018.

Killion, Julie. "What are Cognitive Distortions?" Accessed October 4, 2021. www.mindpathcare.com/blog/what-are-cognitive-distortions/.

Koenig, Harold G., Michael E. McCollough, and David B. Larson. Handbook of Religion and Health. New York: Oxford University Press, 2001.

Lasseter, John. *Toy Story*. Burbank, CA: Walt Disney Pictures/Pixar, 2005.

Leaver, Kate. "How Many Friends Do We Need to Be Happy." Accessed October 13, 2021. www.google.com/amp/amp.abc.net.au/article/everday/12589694. Based on Research by Dr. Robin Dunbar, Oxford.

Lord Kelvin, as quoted in A.W. Smith and J.N. Cooper. *Elements of Physics*, 8th edition. New York: McGraw-Hill Publishing, 1972.

Lucado, Max. Anxious for Nothing: Finding Calm in a Chaotic World. Nashville, TN: Thomas Nelson, 2017.

Luna, Aletheia. "23 Signs You're Suffering from a Victim Mentality." Accessed May 28, 2022. https://lonerwolf.com/victim-mentality.

Marshall, George C. *Speech at Trinity College*. John Hopkins University, 1941. Accessed April 16, 2021. 2–484 Speech at Trinity College, June 15, 1941 - Library (marshallfoundation.org.

Marshall, Paul, and Timothy Shah. "Why People Need Religious Institutions and Why Religious Institutions Need Freedom." Religious Freedom Institute, 2021.

Bibliography

Marx, Karl. *Introduction: A Contribution to the Critique of Hegel's Philosophy of Right.* Translated by A. Jolin and J. O'Malley. Edited by J. O'Malley. Cambridge: Cambridge University Press, 1970.

Mayo Clinic. "Resilience: Build Skills to Endure Hardship." Accessed March 12, 2021, Resilience: Build skills to endure hardship - Mayo Clinic.

Meadows, Sarah O., Megan K. Beckett, Kirby Bowling, Daniela Golinelli, et al. *Family Resilience in the Military: Definitions, Models and Policies.* Santa Monica, CA: Rand Corporation, 2015.

Mental Help. "Resilience: Optimism." Accessed October 3, 2021, https://www.mentalhelp.net/emotional-resilience/optimism/.

Merrill, Ray, Jeffrey Folsom, and Susan Christopherson. "The Influence of Family Religiosity on Adolescent Substance Use According to Religious Preference." *Social Behavior and Personality.* Vol. 33, No.8, 2005.

Merton, R. K. "The Self-Fulfilling Prophecy." *The Antioch Review. 8*(2).

Miller, Emily McFarlan. Christian Persecution Higher than Ever as Open Doors' World Watch List Marks 30 Years, (Bethesda, MD: Religion News Service, January 17, 2023.

Miller, Lisa. *The Awakened Brain: The New Science of Spirituality and Our Quest for an Inspired Life.* New York: Random House, 2021.

Miller, Lisa. *The Spiritual Child: The New Science on Parenting for Health and Lifelong Thriving.* New York: Picador, 2015.

Miriam Webster. "Definition of Resiliency." Accessed March 12, 2021. Resiliency | Definition of Resiliency by Merriam-Webster (merriam-webster.com).

Moberg, David. "Research in Spirituality, Religion, and Aging." *Journal of Gerontological Social Work.* Vol. 45, No.1, 2005.

Nair, Gautam. "Most Americans Vastly Underestimate How Rich They Are Compared To The Rest Of The World. Does It Matter?" *Washington Post.* August 23, 2018. Accessed December 07, 2022. https://www.washingtonpost.com/news/monkey-cage/wp/2018/08/23/most-americans-vastly-underestimate-how-rich-they-are-compared-with-the-rest-of-the-world-does-it-matter/.

Naoumidis, Alex. "Thinking Traps: 12 Cognitive Distortions That Are Hijacking Your Brain." Accessed October 3, 2021. www.mindsethealth.com/matter/thinking-traps-cognitive-distortions.

National Archives. "The United States Bill of Rights." Accessed March 12, 2021. The Bill of Rights: A Transcription | National Archives.

Nicholas, Robin. "How Do My Thoughts Impact My Life?" Accessed December 12. 2022. Https://www.chariscounselingcenter.com/blog/how-do-my-thoughts-impact-my-life/.

Pliny. *Natural History, Book IV.* trans, by H. Rackham, 1949.

Riggio, Ronald E. "There's Magic In Your Smile: How Smiling Affects Your Brain." Accessed February 26, 2023. Https://www.psychologytoday.com/us/blog/cutting-edge-leadership/201206/theres-magic-in-your-smile.

Rowett, Amanda. "The Prison of Unforgiveness: A Christian Counselor's Perspective on Forgiveness." Accessed February 27, 2023. Https://bellevuechristiancounseling.com/articles/the-prison-of-unforgiveness.

Scazzero, Peter. Emotionally Healthy Spirituality. Nashville, TN: Thomas Nelson, 2006.

Selig, Meg. "The 9 Superpowers of Your Smile." Accessed March 27, 2023. https://www.psychologytoday.com/us/blog/changepower/201605/the-9–superpowers-your-smile.

Shadyac, Tom. *Bruce Almighty.* United States: Universal Pictures, 2003.

Shaw, Mary, Mitchell, Richard, and Danny Dorling. "Time for a Smoke." Accessed December 7, 2022. https://www.ncbi.nlm.nih.gov/pmc/articles/PMC1117323/.

Bibliography

Sivilli, Teresa I. and Thaddeus W. Pace. "The Human Dimensions of Resilience: A Theory of Contemplative Practices and Resilience." Accessed April 15, 2021. The Human Dimensions of Resilience_9_9_14_14 (garrisoninstitute.org).

Sorge, Bob. Envy: The Enemy Within. Ventura, CA: Regal Books, 2003.

Southeastern Oklahoma State University. "Why Ethics are Still Essential in Management?" Accessed February 27, 2023. https://online.se.edu/articles/mba/why-ethics-are-still-essential-in-management.aspx.

Southwick, Steven M., Sippel Lauren, and Pietrzak, Robb. "Why are Some Individuals More Resilient than Others: The Role of Social Support." *World Psychiatry,* Feb 2016: 15(1) 77–79, accessed February 25, 2023, Https://www.ncbi.nlm.nih.gov/pmc/articles/PMC4780285/.

Stibich, Mark. "How Anxiety Affects Health and Longevity." Accessed May 28, 2022. https://www.verywellmind.com/worry-and-anxiety-impact-longevity-2223983.

Sun Tzu, *The Art of War.* Translated by Samuel B Griffith. Oxford: Oxford University, 1988.

Tams, Lisa. "ABC's of Changing Your Thoughts and Feelings in Order to Change Your Behavior." Accessed October 3, 2021. www.canr.msu.edu/news/abcs_of_changing_your_thoughts_and_feelings_in_order_to_change_your_behavior.

Tay, Joel and Robert Carter. *Do These Skulls Prove Common Ancestry Between Apes and Humans?* www.creation.com/ape-human-transitional-skull.

Thomas, Brian. *Two Excuses for Human Evolution Confusion.* www.icr.org/article/two-excuses-for-human-evolution-confusion.

Tolkien, J.R.R. *The Lord of the Rings: The Fellowship of the Ring.* New York: Ballantine, 1965.

Tolkien, J.R.R. *The Lord of the Rings: The Return of the King.* Boston: Mariner Books, 2004.

University of Arkansas. "The Six Step Problem Solving Model." Accessed February 27, 2023.

Https://www.uapb.edu/sites/www/uploads/assessment/webinar/session%203/Newfolder/6%20Step%20Problem%20Solving%20Process.pdf.

University of Michigan Health. "Stress Management: Breathing Exercises for Relaxation." Accessed 02 January 2022. Www.uoFmhealth.org/health-library/uz2255.

University of Minnesota. "Impact of Fear and Anxiety." Accessed October 11, 2021. www.Takingcharge.csh.umn.edu/impact-fear-and-anxiety.

UN World Food Program. "Causes of Hunger." Accessed December 30, 2022. www.wfpusa.org/drivers-of-hunger/.

U.S. Department of the Army. "*Comprehensive Soldier and Family Fitness (AR 350–3).*" Washington DC: U.S. Department of the Army, 2014.

Van Edwards, Vanessa. "The Benefits of Music: How the Science of Music Can Help You." Accessed November 12, 2022. https://www.scienceofpeople.com/benefits-music/#music-improves-workouts.

Wachholtz, Amy, and Kenneth Pargament. "Is Spirituality a Critical Ingredient of Meditation? Comparing the Effects of Spiritual Meditation, Secular Meditation, and Relaxation on Spiritual, Psychological, Cardiac, and Pain Outcomes." *Journal of Behavioral Medicine.* Vol. 28, No.4, 2005.

Walker, Mort. *Beetle Bailey.* June 3, 2007. King Features Syndicate, NY, 1950.

Wood, Todd. "Life & Design: Humans & Apes," *Beyond is Genesis History, Vol. 2*, DVD, 2018.

Yeung, Douglas, and Margaret Martin. *Spiritual Fitness and Resilience: A Review of Relevant Constructs, Measures, and Links to Well-Being.* Santa Monica, CA: Rand Corporation, 2013.

Your Body Can Heal Itself: Over 87 Foods Everyone Should Eat. Peachtree City, GA: FC&A Medical Publishing, 2008.

Zemeckis, Robert. *Forest Gump.* United States: Paramount Pictures, 1994.

Printed in the USA
CPSIA information can be obtained
at www.ICGtesting.com
LVHW080913160424
777536LV00010B/250